Culture(s) in International Relations

Grażyna Michałowska / Hanna Schreiber (eds.)

Culture(s) in International Relations

PETER LANG
EDITION

Bibliographic Information published by the Deutsche Nationalbibliothek
The Deutsche Nationalbibliothek lists this publication in the Deutsche Nationalbibliografie; detailed bibliographic data is available in the internet at http://dnb.d-nb.de.

Library of Congress Cataloging-in-Publication Data
Names: Schreiber, Hanna, editor. | Michałowska, Grażyna, editor.
Title: Culture(s) in international relations / Hanna Schreiber, Grażyna Michałowska.
Description: Frankfurt am Main ; New York : Peter Lang, 2017.
Identifiers: LCCN 2017017248 | ISBN 9783631679029
Subjects: LCSH: International relations–Social aspects. | International law–Social aspects.
Classification: LCC JZ1251 .C8535 2017 | DDC 327–dc23 LC record available at https://lccn.loc.gov/2017017248

This publication was financially supported by the University of Warsaw.

Principal reviewer: Professor Teresa Łoś-Nowak, University of Wrocław, Poland

Cover image: Courtesy of Maciej Zych http://www.maciej-zych.com

ISBN 978-3-631-67902-9 (Print)
E-ISBN 978-3-631-72588-7 (E-PDF)
E-ISBN 978-3-631-72589-4 (EPUB)
E-ISBN 978-3-631-72590-0 (MOBI)
DOI 10.3726/b11522

Peter Lang Edition is an Imprint of Peter Lang GmbH.

Peter Lang – Frankfurt am Main · Bern · Bruxelles · New York · Oxford · Warszawa · Wien

This publication has been peer reviewed.

www.peterlang.com

Table of Contents

Grażyna Michałowska, Hanna Schreiber

Introduction. Culture(s) in International Relations

> *No matter how much one trains one's attention on the supposedly hard facts of social existence, who owns the means of production, who has the guns, the dossiers, or the newspapers, the supposedly soft facts of that existence, what do people imagine human life to be all about, how do they think one ought to live, what grounds belief, legitimizes punishment, sustains hope, or accounts for loss, crowd in to disturb simple pictures of might, desire, calculation, and interest. [...] Bent on certitude, Olympianism, or codifiable method, or simply anxious to pursue a cause, one can ignore such facts, obscure them, or pronounce them forceless. But they do not thereby go away.* ***Whatever the infirmities of the concept of 'culture' ('cultures', 'cultural forms'...) there is nothing for it but to persist in spite of them. Tone deafness, willed or congenital, and however belligerent, will not do.***
>
> Clifford Geertz[1]

The 'tone-deafness' of international relations researchers with respect to the impact of culture on the contemporary world may be now considered an illness of the past. For over thirty years (or even longer, depending on the history of particular discipline) we have been witnessing a 'cultural turn' in virtually all social sciences and disciplines of the humanities, including international relations[2].

Subsequent surges of interest in the role of culture in international relations, especially from the Western point of view were marked by specific events: the breakdown of the division of the world into two blocks and its consequences, the Balkan conflict, 9/11 attacks, Iraq and Afghanistan interventions, the Arab Spring, activities of ISIS, conflict in Syria, and the migration crisis in EU, among others.

The end of the Cold War in 1989 seems to have been a breakthrough in terms of the return of culture[3] to international relations. The year 1989 brought a wave

1 C. Geertz, *After the Fact: Two Countries, Four Decades, One Anthropologist*, Harvard University Press 1995, p. 43.

2 H. Schreiber, 'Religia jako element "zwrotu kulturowego" w stosunkach międzynarodowych' (*Religion as an Element of a 'Cultural Turn' in International Relations*), in A. Solarz, H. Schreiber (eds.), *Religia w stosunkach międzynarodowych* (*Religion in International Relations)*, Warsaw University Publishing, Warsaw 2012, p. 51.

3 Here, we refer to the 'return' of culture to the study of international relations, where it had an important place in the 1940s, 1950s and 1960s. When writing about the return of culture into international relations, Yosef Lapid refers to it metaphorically as the

of optimism and gave rise to the concepts of the end of history, global governance, and global civil society. An emphasis was put on the human rights and democratic discourse; actions were undertaken for a mine-free world and ending the impunity era, such as the adoption of the Rome Statute of the International Criminal Court in 1998.[4] The post-Cold War period seemed to be a time of blissful transformation, and Samuel Huntington emphasised that the euphoria at the end of the Cold War generated an illusion of harmony.[5] In the meantime, after the thawing of the global dualism, the underlying conflicts of ethnic and identity-related (i.e. cultural) nature were uncovered.[6] Despite this revelation, however, the impact of culture on the post-Cold War international relations has been long underestimated. The fundamental importance of culture, though still standing in the background of international relations, was not visible until the 9/11 attack on the World Trade Center in New York. This date is mentioned by all the researchers engaged in the study of the role of culture in international relations (e.g. Joseph Nye, Samuel Huntington, Zygmunt Bauman, Mary Kaldor) as key to the 'discovery' of the role of culture in this field. Due to the context of these events, culture, and especially religion (as an important element thereof) – together with its influence on the creation of new thought paradigms in terms of security, diplomacy and foreign policy – have been pushed to the foreground of scientific research.

The term 'cultural turn' is understood here as an 'inflated' need for knowledge that concerns human cultural diversity and its impact on relations between individuals, states, cultures and civilisations, as well as the tendency to put a greater emphasis on the cultural factor in international relations research.

Every researcher who has devoted his scientific life to culture will surely admit that it is such a complex issue that it is simply impossible to define, identify

---

return of culture's ship, forced to sail the open sea for decades, to the safe harbor of international relations. See Y. Lapid, 'Culture's Ship: Returns and Departures in International Relations Theory', in Y. Lapid, F. Kratochwil (eds.), *The Return of Culture and Identity in International Relations Theory*, Lynne Riener Publishers, Boulder London 1996, p. 5.

4 Some of these elements are pointed out by Mary Kaldor in *New and Old Wars. Organized Violence in a Global Era*, Polity Press, Cambridge 2006, p. IX.

5 S. Huntington, *The Clash of Civilizations and the Remaking of World Order*, Penguin Books 1997, p. 31.

6 Such conflicts naturally existed throughout the Cold War and were fueled or even initiated both by the U.S. and by the Soviet Union as supporters and funding parties of civil wars taking place in Africa (Angola, Mozambique, South Africa). See M. Mamdani, 'Good Muslim, Bad Muslim. A Political Perspective on Culture and Terrorism', *American Anthropologist. New Series*, vol. 104, no. 3, September 2002, p. 769.

and describe unambiguously and in a way that would satisfy everyone. Different disciplines of science make efforts to grasp it, attempting to adjust it to their own research needs. They select or highlight some dimensions and manifestations of culture, while disregarding others. That is the reason why culture is sometimes labelled as a 'cursed' (Raymond Williams) or 'suspicious' (Yosef Lapid) word[7]. It is however also a 'sacred' one; placed on the pedestal of contemporary social sciences and humanities. Culture is 'a matter of life and death' (Mahmood Mamdani), 'culture is everywhere' (Ulf Hannerz), 'culture makes almost all the difference' (David Landes), culture 'is on everyone's lips' (Marshall Sahlins), 'culture counts' (Samuel Huntington), 'culture matters' (Lawrence Harrison)[8]. As a result, the proliferation of the meanings associated with this notion has gone so far that researchers now seem all but helpless and give up on any attempts to order the terminological chaos and organise the utter freedom of employing the concept of 'culture'. If we look at scientific literature on the subject, the use of the snowball metaphor seems more than justified. Zygmunt Bauman goes even further than that, claiming that culture is just an ideology created by intellectuals; a 'conspiracy' aimed at creating a specific type of discourse independent of policy-makers and power structures.[9] It has become an all-encompassing and totalising concept; impossible to define. Therefore, the 1950s – the time in which Clyde Kluckhohn's and Alfred Louis Kroeber's book *Culture. A Critical Review of Concepts and Definitions* was published, with (merely) 164 scientific definitions of culture – might be thought of as 'blissful'.[10]

The aim of this publication is to present a critical reflection on how the presence of culture in international relations is perceived nowadays or for what reasons it is ignored. Is culture a theoretical tool which we know how to use in order to make the analysis of international relations more relevant? What are the problems that we face while attempting to operationalise the notion of 'culture' for the needs of research in the field of international relations? How do we use it? The

---

7 Y. Lapid, 'Culture's Ship..., p. 6.

8 See M. Mamdani, 'Good Muslim..., p. 767; U. Hannerz, *Transnational Connections: Culture, People, Places*, Psychology Press 1996, p. 30; M. Sahlins, *Culture in Practice: Selected Essays*, Zone Books 2000, p. 474; S. P. Huntington, L. E. Harrison (eds.), *Culture Matters: How Values Shape Human Progress,* Basic Books 2000, p. xiii – S. Huntington, p. xvii – L. Harrison, p. 1 – David Landes.

9 See Z. Bauman, '*Legislators and Interpreters. Culture as the Ideology of Intellectuals*', in *idem*, *Intimations of Postmodernity*, Routledge 1992.

10 A. L. Kroeber, C. Kluckhohn, *Culture. A Critical Review of Concepts and Definitions*, Vintage Books, New York 1952.

achievements of which sciences do we draw on when trying to tame it? What 'stories' in international relations (histories of international relations) does culture allow us to tell? Whose voices it allows us to hear?

The results of analyses presented in this book are meant to contribute to solving at least some of the existing confusion, to identify the research fields where culture either appears or should appear, as well as to present the outcome of analyses of the diverse forms in which culture manifests itself in international relations: both in theory and in practice.

From the very beginning, therefore, we have faced the key questions: how culturally dependent are the studies in the fields traditional to our discipline, such as international political, economic or military relations (and their results), and should international relations treat culture as simply one of its determinants (the other, equally important factors being politics, military, law, etc.)? So, what is the nature of the presence of 'culture' and 'cultures' in international relations? Even the very fact that the cultural perspective was rarely used in the studies of international relations in the past could be actually a product of IR scientific culture as well. Therefore, is it only a short-lived 'fashion for culture' or does it comprehensively change our understanding of this discipline?

This book shows diverse approaches to culture in theory and practice of international relations. It analyses their influence on the development of international law and law enforcement, as well as various types of interactions in contemporary international relations.

The authors present their assessments of the impact of internationalisation of the social life on the preservation of cultural identity and cultural differences. They describe various aspects of international relations and different ways of searching for answers as well as opinions and views, sometimes controversial, on the role of culture; also with regard to the fundamental issue of using precise definitions of concepts built around culture as the main point of reference: strategic culture, political culture, security culture on the one hand, and on the other hand, cultural relativism, cultural imperialism, gender, etc.

The authors employ various methodologies of research and definitions of culture, sometimes they present their own operational understanding of culture useful for the analyses that they conduct. In some cases they do not explain their choice of definition at all, assuming that the reader will intuitively adopt the most appropriate definition. By doing this they make a very similar assumption to that of Herbert Blumer, namely that abandoning definitive concepts and definitions for 'sensitising concepts' is a justified academic procedure. The difference is that 'whereas definitive concepts provide prescriptions of what to see, sensitising concepts merely suggest directions along which to look'.[11] Although sensitising concepts are not formal definitions, this does not mean that they cannot be articulated – only instead of precise reference and identifying signs we have a general sense of what is significant, and instead of a definition we have a description.[12]

Consequently, one should not be surprised by the multitude of approaches, divisions and means of understanding the ambiguous concept of culture. This was already observed by the 18th-century philosopher Johann Gottfried Herder, who noted that 'nothing is more indeterminate than this word, and nothing is more deceptive than its application to all nations and periods'.[13] This is also how more than 200 years later, in 1996, the Commission of the European Communities diagnosed the possibility of defining culture, stating that 'the concept of Culture is a nebulous one which can vary from one school of thought to another, from one society to another and from one era to another'.[14] Even by now, there has been no single, normative and legally binding definition of culture developed in international relations (and perhaps this is for the better).

Hence, if we were to invoke Kroeber's and Kluckhohn's classification, the definitions adopted by the authors of the articles included in this book belong in the group of normative definitions, which emphasise the subordination of human behaviour to the norms, models and values dominant in the given social group. But they also exhibit aspects of the psychological approach, taking into account the motives of behaviour, forms of expression, dictates and prohibitions, opinions and judgements. Nowadays, such definitions are classified as the broadest, anthropological definitions, which treat culture as a relatively integrated whole which covers human behaviours following certain models, common for the given social community, developed and acquired during interactions, and which comprises the products of such behaviours.[15]

---

11 H. Blumer, *Symbolic Interactionism: Perspective and Method*, Berkley and Los Angeles, CA: University of California Press 1986, p. 148.

12 *Ibid.*

13 After: J. Lyons, *Language and Linguistics*, Cambridge: Cambridge University Press 1982, p. 301; see also: J. G. Herder, 'Przedmowa' (Foreword), in J. G. Herder, *Myśli o filozofii dziejów* (*Ideas for the Philosophy of the History of Humanity*), transl. J. Gałecki, Warszawa 1962, vol. 1, p. 4.

14 Commission of the European Communities, *1st Report on the Consideration of Cultural Action in European Community Action*, COM(96) 160 Final, Brussels, 17 April 1996.

15 A. Kłoskowska, *Kultura masowa. Krytyka i obrona* (*Mass Culture. Critical Remarks and Defence*), Warszawa 1983, p. 40.

Culture has always played a very important role in the process of identification and integration of social groups, including nations. As Polish philosopher Leszek Kołakowski wrote, it is 'a form of the current lasting of the nation'.[16] However, even if one considers the process of enculturation to be a natural, intergenerational, conscious and unconscious acquisition of the cultural competences typical of a certain group by an individual, there has never been agreement in science as to whether cultures constitute these groups or are in fact reflections thereof.

In the studies of intergroup relations, culture has been examined also from the perspective of the changes taking place in it, the consequences of endogenous development, and of the inevitable process of diffusion and its determinants (usefulness, compliance with the existing culture, the prestige of those who pass it on, the prestige of the intermediaries). As a result, in this form, it was for a long time the subject of interest mainly for sociologists of culture.

On the other hand, researchers – particularly cultural and social anthropologists – have focused on cultural relativism, the possibility of comparing various cultures, the disputes whether they can be objectively studied and evaluated. Cultural relativism has precluded the existence of absolute, universal criteria that could be the basis for evaluating cultures. It has been a philosophical concept and an almost universally applied foundation in the methodology of research in cultural anthropology (especially in the USA). It has rejected extreme forms of ethnocentrism, believing them to be a tendency to treat one's own culture as higher than other cultures and, consequently, to judge other cultures according to one's own standards.

Scholars usually agree that the pioneer of cultural relativism was Franz Boas, who formulated this idea already in the late 19th century. According to relativists, every culture is a unique creation and as such should be studied comprehensively, taking into account the social and historical context of its emergence and continued existence, and it should be judged according to its own standards. This approach was further developed by Boas's students, including Ruth Benedict, Margaret Mead, Edward Sapir and Melville Herskovits.

This seemingly strong and established position, according to which all cultures deserve full protection and equal treatment, has been slowly eroding and has been contested with the spreading of universal human rights standards. Transplanted to institutionalised international relations, this problem has become conditional.

16 L. Kołakowski, *Czy diabeł może być zbawiony i 27 innych kazań* (*Can the Devil Be Redeemed and 27 Other Sermons*), Warszawa 1983, p. 303.

A question appeared whether the sense of good and evil can really be the same in every culture and if it is not subject to evolution and changes in time as well.

There are questions about the acceptability of cultural phenomena such as violence in the name of honour, physical punishment in penitential systems, child marriage, and inequality between the genders or races. A broad discussion of gender inequality resulting from cultural determinants can be found in the article by **Grażyna Michałowska** – *Legal, Political and Cultural Determinants of Gender Policy*. Discussing the dignity of every human being, the author says: '[...] the question whether dignity is an objective value remains open, since the interpretation of dignity is strongly culture-dependent. Sometimes, women's dignity is at variance with the dignity of men or a group and the government's compensating actions hit an insurmountable barrier or fall on a completely barren ground. It is so deeply rooted in the local tradition that even the threat of sanctions cannot change it, while any more radical actions involve the risk of causing a disintegration of social groups. The permanence of cultural differences remains so fundamental that, most probably, international standards will remain just an idea – as valuable as it is – for a long time to come' (p. 295).

But can cultural traditions be considered sufficient justification for infringing upon fundamental human rights? This problem is discussed by **Agnieszka Bieńczyk-Missala** (*Cultural Determinants of the Development and Observance of Universal Human Rights*) and **Patrycja Grzebyk** (*Culture and Prosecution of International Crimes*). Bieńczyk-Missala notes that: 'Culturally motivated infringements on human rights will surely persist, as a consequence of the power of traditions, religious laws, beliefs, prejudice, and often also their structural nature, which is difficult to overcome' (p. 271).[17] Answering the question how – taking into account the cultural factor – not only 'ordinary' infringements, but also international crimes are to be prosecuted, Patrycja Grzebyk concludes that: 'The judges need to be culturally sensitive in order to properly assess the severity of the deeds and the guilt of the culprits, in order to establish contact with the witnesses and properly read their testimonies. However, the judges should not use culture to justify their surrender in the struggle for uncovering the truth and to defend the culprits' actions' (p. 366).

The issue of protection of cultural rights is discussed also by **Janusz Symonides.** He focuses on the protection of minorities and indigenous peoples. While the degree of cultural differences of national minorities is an issue quite frequently

17 See e.g.: M. Koenig, P. Guchteneire, *Democracy and Human Rights in Multicultural Societies*, Ashgate 2006.

discussed in academic literature, indigenous peoples and their rights have been drawing the attention of researchers only since very recently and to a relatively limited extent. The source of this disproportionate interest stems from the difficulties encountered during attempts to define indigenous groups and their specific cultural interests and needs, so different from those of national minorities. Countries are not particularly interested in a clear regulation of the rights of indigenous peoples which would eliminate the ambiguities, because they fear that giving them autonomy (even cultural) could finally lead to their secession, constituting a serious threat to these countries' territorial integrity and independence. Therefore, the author qualifies these groups as particularly at risk. He mentions the already existing relevant international instruments, including Convention No. 107 of the International Labour Organisation of 1957 noting, however, that the historical definition of indigenous populations was the subject of many controversies and has never been universally accepted. Thus, Convention No. 169 of 1989, concerning indigenous and tribal peoples in independent countries, has extended the previous definition. It is supposed to guarantee respect for the specific values and practice of these groups and their protection. What is important, it ensures the possibility of applying their own procedures in events of offences committed by their members and the right to recognise the ownership of the lands that they have traditionally occupied. In the author's opinion, however, this convention does not seem to fully satisfy any of its addressees either. Only the Declaration on the Rights of Indigenous Peoples, drawn up by the Human Rights Council and adopted in 2007 by the UN General Assembly seems to open a new stage with regard to these special ethnic groups and provide an impetus to ensuring stronger guarantees of their rights in international law.

The problems with taking account of cultural differences in international law, including the very principles underlying it, have also been noticed by **Bogusław Lackoroński** (*Culture in the Making of Public International Law – Custom and General Principles of Law Recognised by Civilised Nations*): 'However, attempts to infuse rules of international law with cultural content, which is supposed to be a part of universal law, can also divide the international community. Such situations occur, for example, during discussions on human rights, which give rise to doubts as to whether the values subject to protection under these rights are indeed universal. Culture can therefore be an 'obstacle' in the creation of universal international law, if the rules of this law are created in a way that takes into account the cultural background of one civilisation, leaving out the others'. (p. 249)

At the borderline of these two research fields are the problems of multicultural societies. This concerns not only multiculturalism resulting from historical multiethnicity, as is the case, inter alia, in Belgium, Spain, Canada[18] or many Asian and African countries, but also multiculturalism 'acquired' fairly recently through migrations.

The problem is particularly interesting in the context of the European societies which are becoming increasingly ethnically diverse. Immigration carries the risk of introduction of traditions and customs in certain segments of life, that are at variance with international law and legal norms of the host countries, who then need to face the serious dilemma how to reconcile political correctness, tolerance and the policy of multiculturalism with the fundamental principle of equality vis-à-vis legal regulations. In many situations, they simply seem helpless.

Cultural differences imply social judgements. In the wealthiest European countries, more and more questions appear about the limits of solidarity, especially during the economic crisis bound with migration crisis, when culturally foreign immigrants reject the possibility of integration and, at the same time, adopt demanding attitudes towards the host countries, sometimes even attempting to enforce their demands by publically demonstrating their displeasure.[19]

As a result, in the host societies, there are examples of indifference or unspoken consent to radical – although in many cases legally dubious or even illegal – actions of authorities aimed at reinstating the allegedly necessary sanitary order, and a disapproval of behaviours that include culturally justified intrusive begging, reluctance to engage in regular work and the unwillingness to educate children.[20]

Sometimes people protest against the establishment of immigrant ghettos, enclaves of monoculturalism, 'islamisation' of the social life, domination of certain districts in cities by certain religious or ethnic groups, increasing numbers of state-funded mosques, etc. With individual groups isolating themselves from each other, the overtone of the political debate is changing. Multiculturalism is viewed with growing scepticism and the dominant populations are less and less

---

18 In the opinion of Wojciech J. Burszta, multiculturalism is considered to have originated in four countries: the USA, Canada, Australia, and New Zealand (W. J. Burszta, *Antropologia kultury. Tematy, teorie, interpretacje* [*Cultural Anthropology. Topics, Theories, Interpretations*], Poznań 1998, p. 151).

19 In 2005, the announcement of the French government that it would cease to provide assistance and social privileges to young unemployed immigrants from North Africa caused a wave of protests and riots, during which property worth EUR 200 million was destroyed.

20 The so called 'Zigeuner Protokol' of 1992 in Germany, the expulsion of the Romanian Roma from France in 2010.

responsive to arguments about improving demographic indexes or the need to maintain dialogue and tolerance.[21]

The problems of a multicultural state were analysed by **Jakub Zajączkowski** in his text about India. The multiplicity of languages and religions and the particularisms of ethnic groups are major challenges for India. The author analyses the challenges of multiculturalism in this country and notes that because of this linguistic and religious variety, it is hard to even talk about an Indian nation in the meaning ascribed to that term in other countries. The foundation of India's cohesion is the Indian civilisation, expressed in the social system, in the philosophical systems and concepts of the world, and in the sense of uniqueness. On the macro level, this foundation is provided by the secularity of the state guaranteed by the constitution and the democratic governance system, tolerance and the belief stemming from the ancient times that development is achieved through dialogue and debate. Regardless of the many internal differences, the priorities of Indian strategy are integrity, development, attracting foreign investment, overcoming social problems, inter alia through stability, compromise and prevention of the aggravation of conflicts that could be used by other countries to undermine the position of India. Thus, in 2000, taking into account the local interests, three more constituent states were created and four new languages were recognised as official. This does not change the fact that despite experiencing dynamic development, India still consists of two parallel worlds: in the first one people benefit from economic and social reforms and in the second they are left on their own. Nevertheless, Indian society is characterised by an opposition to revolution and extremist views. Although violence does appear from time to time, it is not systemic. The state is a major factor in integrating citizens, and most Indians believe that their country is a major power. Traditional Indian philosophy, however, imposes a peaceful way of change, hence the country's military potential grows relatively slowly in relation to the growing economic opportunities.

Apart from the aforementioned practical problems, the cultural perspective is clearly spreading to other dimensions of international relations as well. In 1991, Joseph Nye introduced the term 'soft power' into the theory of international relations (he used it for the first time in 1980). He adopted the thesis that next to the military and economic potential (hard power), there are other factors that influence the position of the state: the attractiveness of its culture, foreign policy

21 K. Malik, 'The Failure of Multiculturalism. Community versus Society in Europe', *Foreign Affairs*, March-April 2015.

and political values.[22] He assumed that only combined, hard and soft power form the 'smart power': a wise and effective force with the potential to attract allies.[23] 'Culture is an important component of this power of attraction; it has the ability to set the preferences of other participants in international relations. In international politics, the sources of soft power are, inter alia, the values which are manifested in the cultures of states or organisations', writes **Anna Wojciuk** in the article on *Culture in the Theories of International Relations* (p. 36). The author also broadly describes the constructivist approach in the study of the influence of culture on international relations.

The highly popular concept of soft power (as Anna Wojciuk notes, it is equally popular as Huntington's 10-year-younger concept of 'the clash of civilisations') is discussed in other aspects also by **Justyna Nakonieczna**. She focuses on how the soft power of a state, based on its culture, influences its image and reputation (*Culture and Nation-State's Reputation*), and wonders: 'Should all countries look after their reputation? On the one hand, it is obvious that first of all those countries that do not have any particular distinguishing features should consciously manage their images. Since they usually do not have particularly developed 'hard' resources, their own culture is their best support. It is through culture that they can become recognised by other people. On the other hand, the standards of promotion are set by the largest and most active entities of international relations and it is they who decide what is desirable and acceptable' (p. 192).

The problem of studies on culture in international relations is also discussed by **Edward Haliżak**. The author wonders whether culture can be helpful in the analysis of international relations. Since the 1990s, the explanatory potential of the approach takes into account the cultural factor has been increasingly appreciated, which can be considered a 'cultural turn' in the study of international relations. As the basis of his article, the author takes two political and intellectual debates that involve cultural explanations. The first one regards the attempts to identify the sources of the economic success of East Asian countries. The second one refers to the cultural and civilisational criteria of conflict analysis in the post-Cold War world. Culture appears at every stage of the cognitive process. However, the author warns that it is easy to fall into dogmatism when trying to explain almost all the modern challenges with cultural diversity.

---

22 J.S. Nye, *Soft Power: The Means To Success In World Politics*, New York: Public Affairs, 2004; Polish edition: *Soft Power. Jak osiągnąć sukces w polityce światowej*, transl. J. Zaborowski, Warszawa 2007.

23 *Ibid.*, p. 34.

The political and economic changes that took place in the world in the last decade of the 20th century have modified the configuration of cooperation and rivalry of various participants in international relations. The end of the Cold War and the emergence of new economic powers have also brought previously little known dilemmas and challenges to the international community which it is yet to face. How states handle these today is largely determined by the already well-established political culture, which – as **Franciszek Gołembski** points out in the article *Political Culture in Contemporary International Relations* – is a consequence of the civilisational context: 'Against this background, there appears a broader issue, concerning the determinants of political culture related to civilisation. Political culture is not merely a function of the axiological principles underlying the system of values characteristic of a nation state, but of much broader conditions [...]. In connection to this, there appears the fundamental problem of the importance of civilisation-related determinants of the emergence and influence of political culture in the general dimension, in other words in international relations' (p. 61).

The sphere of diplomacy and diplomatic negotiations has for years been the area where different dimensions of cultural influence on international relations have appeared particularly evident; focusing on it made it obvious that knowing the culture of the other party that sits at the negotiations table is crucial. **Stanisław Bieleń** points out (*Culture in International Negotiations*) that nowadays 'the very nature of international negotiations is being redefined. Although they are treated as an important legal and diplomatic instrument, it is exactly for cultural reasons that they are becoming the key to understanding the complexity of the globalised world and especially to legitimising the changes which take place in it' (p. 133).

The processes of globalisation and the growing interdependence of states have highlighted the importance of cultural differences for civilisational development. In a sense, they have also contributed to a renaissance of identity-oriented attitudes. The regress of local cultures and disappearance of the identities of ethnic groups – especially of small indigenous peoples who have no significant instruments to protect it – once considered a natural process of adjustment, now is treated as a threat to mutual cultural inspirations, something that adversely affects mankind and hampers sustainable development.

The problems of culture are now transplanted to entirely new areas, including the functioning of the economy in both the internal and external aspect. **Aleksandra Jarczewska** (*Culture and the Economy – How Culture Influences the Economy*) writes that 'while on the one hand, culture is among the key factors of economic development (which can either considerably increase it or dramatically limit it), on the other hand, economic development is conducive to changes which can contribute to cultural transformations in societies. We are, therefore, dealing with a complex interrelation – culture influences economic processes and these processes change culture' (p. 128).

What is analysed is not only the influence of culture on the dynamics of development and image of the state, but also on the effectiveness of actions of transnational corporations in culturally foreign environments, both when there is need for people from different cultures to cooperate and when, for example, the board comes from a different country than the regular employees. In the evaluation of relations, the issues taken into account are the organisational culture, the systems of values that stimulate the employees, the requirements concerning conduct(sometimes contrary to established customs), the styles of management, and the criteria for establishing the authority of leaders. These problems are discussed in the article by **Dorota Heidrich** (*Culture in International Organisations*): 'Conflicting cultural factors may prove constructive if tackled properly by an organisation's institutional capabilities, determined by the organisational culture. At the same time, contradictions between cultural values may lead IOs to deadlocks that hurt their credibility and ability to act. Overcoming such damaging circumstances hugely depends on the type of organisation as well as its subjective and objective competences. At the same time, external political, ideological or economic determinants might influence the overall performance of IOs.' (p. 154).

Culture is also perceived differently today in the context of contemporary armed conflicts. In the past, even during World War II, one of the instruments for destroying the enemies was plundering and destroying their cultural heritage[24] and dismantling their culture-forming groups (the elites, the intelligentsia). In contemporary wars, which are much different, culture is perceived – as a whole – as something that can influence the effectiveness of military actions when people from different civilisations clash. This subject is analysed broadly by **Wiesław Lizak** (*Cultural Determinants of Conflicts*): 'cultural determinants are among many factors influencing the emergence and evolution of conflicts in the contemporary world. However, this influence is very special, due to their consciousness-based nature. Specifically, it is a function of the existing social values, attitudes, religious beliefs, as well as ideological convictions and outlooks on life. As a result, they refer to the fundamental determinants that shape the identity of nations, social groups and individuals, and, consequently, they become very hard to 'negotiate'

24 This is why one of the first conventions of the UNESCO was the Convention for the Protection of Cultural Property in the Event of Armed Conflict adopted in 1954. Earlier, this problem was partly addressed in the IV and IX Hague Convention of 1988/1907.

at the stage when contradictions and different interests arising in the processes of social interaction are revealed' (p. 195).

In contemporary wars it is no longer that regular armies – bound by rules established under international law –face each other, but instead it is the insurgents and rebel groups or formations with different strategies, tactics and degrees of organisation. Their culturally determined actions are less predictable and create the risk of a military stalemate and – without learning the opponent's culture – may make it impossible to end the conflict. The way strategic studies have become interested in the influence of culture on the effectiveness of actions undertaken in these areas is discussed by **Bolesław Balcerowicz** (*Culture in Military Science – from Strategic Culture to the Cultural Turn*). Elaborating on the genesis of the interest in culture in contemporary armies, the author notes that: 'The cultural approach as a path to understanding the nature of armed conflicts and wars has finally found its place – and a central one at that – with the cultural turn in the sphere of military science. This significant change – a cultural turn, or a turn to culture – was determined by the pressing need to discover the fundamental reasons for continuously repeating failures of military operations, stabilisation missions and expeditionary actions undertaken by the United States (and their allies) against foes weaker by several levels of magnitude. The turn was also a (forced) reaction to the dramatic question voiced by the American society: 'Why they hate us?' (p. 73).

This essential shift from the sphere of material to non-material culture does not exclude cases of following the old, well-established practices of destroying the enemy's cultural sacrum in order to eliminate their fundamental points of reference and their national pride.[25] When these actions are systematic and on a massive scale, they can also lead to what is referred to as 'culturecide' (cultural genocide), a phenomenon discussed by **Hanna Schreiber**: 'we cannot ignore the dramatic cases of struggling with culturecidal practices or their consequences, which last at least a lifetime of the people who experienced them. The right to live in one's own culture is the extension of the fundamental right to life, as even the physical survival of a group does not guarantee its existence if its members cannot develop through and in their own culture' (p. 335).

In his comment on the term 'cultural turn', Yosef Lapid writes: "There is, in short, little to gain and much to lose by mistaking the return for a 'revolutionary

---

25 In July 2012, during the conflict in Mali, radical Muslims started destroying monuments in Timbuktu, considered the jewel of the desert, including mausoleums of Sufi saints and libraries containing manuscripts dating as far as the 12th century.

move' in IR scholarship."[26] The concept of return thus makes us ponder those issues which already had their place in the IR discourse, which have been 'waiting by the shore' for a long time, even when the 'Culture's ship' was in exile.[27] The abandoned ideas deserve to be re-included and reevaluated, but they are nothing new or unfamiliar to the field of international relations (which is supported both by the existing theories and by the abundant literature on the subject). Naturally, these ideas cannot return to the reality they had left upon their 'expulsion'. Their potential and timeliness can be expressed precisely by the word 'turn', but, following the sailing metaphor used by Lapid, the ship is not to head in a new direction, but instead return to the lands it has already explored.

Coming back to the observed 'cultural turn' in international relations: why should we be interested in it at all? Firstly, because it is a clear evidence for the inclusion of a cultural perspective and the processual and dynamic concept of culture into the analysis of international relations, that goes in line with the changes observed in scrutinised reality. Secondly, because it underlines the need for expansion of international relations as an interdisciplinary field by adding other disciplines, including cultural anthropology – to the spectrum. Thirdly, because it points to the erosion of the earlier predominant perception of international relations, and offers a fresh and an attractive perspective instead. It must be emphasised, however, that this perspective is an effect, not the cause of the changes encountered in the modern world, including the achievements of world political science.

Contemporary international relations undergo violent changes, which call for caution in predicting change directions and analysing the reality at hand. Awareness of the role of culture may prove very useful, but will not provide us with an ultimate solution. The talk of 'cultural turn' cannot erase other cognitive approaches or dethrone the hitherto prevailing methods of interpretation applied to the reality we want to study. However, taking a closer look at the role of culture in international relations is indispensable, if we are looking for a more adequate research tools, that would be adjusted to contemporary world events, allow for a more accurate understanding and evaluation of these events and equip us with predictive power. We must adapt the tools to the problem and not the problem

---

26 Y. Lapid, 'Culture's Ship…, p. 6. Note that Y. Lapid makes use of the term 'revolutionary move' and not 'turn'. Nonetheless, he seems to be assigning the same meaning to it, which is confirmed by the title of one of the sections of his introduction: *On the Move: 'Turns' and 'Returns' in IR Theorizing*, in *ibid.*, p. 5.

27 We use Yosef Lapid's metaphor adapted from R. L. Jepperson and A. Swidler, 'What Properties of Culture Should We Measure?' *Poetics*, no. 22, 1994, pp. 359–371.

to the tools we use. The absence, or scarce representation, of culture in the modern political science tools leads to tailoring modern problems into inadequate although well-known research methods.

Although the field of culture should not be viewed as the ultimate source of answers and solutions to the problems raised by international relations, we believe that adopting a cultural approach in the course of their analysis may be equivalent to acknowledging the following facts:

1. International relations are conditioned not only by the existing balance of (economic, military, political) power, but also by the different representations of the world, values and behavioral patterns accumulated in the course of history, passed on and culturally transformed, expressed and used by the participants of international relations in various types of global interaction.
2. The place occupied by a given IR participant within the international community is largely dependent on the cultural potential (as an important soft power component) which supplements and influences hard power, as well as on the ability to create a credible narrative concerning one's place and role in shaping the modern world.
3. Cultural diversity gives rise to a variety of perceptions concerning IR. Awareness of cultural differences (cross-cultural awareness) and principles governing one's own culture (cultural awareness) are necessary components of an in-depth analysis of modern international relations.
4. Culture is a dynamic, processual and polymorphic concept that can be studied within a variety of distinct semantic fields as a xenogamous category[28].

After opening this introduction with the quotation from Clifford Geertz, we would also like to end with his words, sheding the light on the current situation in IR embedded in culturally complex reality:

> *'We seem to be in need of a new variety of politics, a politics which does not regard ethnic, religious, racial, linguistic, or regional assertiveness as so much irrationality, archaic and ingenerate, to be suppressed or transcended, a madness decried or a darkness ignored, but, like any other social problem – inequality say, or the abuse of power – sees it as a reality to be faced, somehow dealt with, modulated, brought to terms. The development of such a politics, which will vary from place to place as much as the situations it faces do, depends on a number of things. It depends on finding out the springs of identity-based differentiation and discord in this case or that. It depends on developing a less simplistically demonizing, blankly negative attitude toward it as a relic of savagery or some earlier stage of human existence. It depends on adapting the principles of liberalism and social democracy, still our best guides*

28 H. Schreiber, 'Religia jako element…', pp. 62–63.

for law, government, and public deportment, to matters with respect to which they have been too often dismissive, reactive, or incomprehending; philosophically blind. ***But perhaps most important, it depends on our constructing a clearer, more circumstantial, less mechanical, stereotypic and cliché-ridden conception of what it consists in, what it is. That is, it depends on our gaining a better understanding of what culture, the frames of meaning within which people live and form their convictions, their selves, and their solidarities, comes to as an ordering force in human affairs.*** *(...)*

We do not know, really, how to handle this, how to deal with a world that is neither divided at the joints into ingredient sections nor a transcendent unity – economic, say, or psychological – obscured by surface contrasts, thin and concocted, and best set aside as inessential distractions. A scramble of differences in a field of connections presents us with a situation in which the frames of pride and those of hatred, culture fairs and ethnic cleansing, survivance and killing fields, sit side by side and pass with frightening ease from the one to the other. Political theories that both admit to this condition and have the will to confront it, to expose and interrogate the order of difference, rather than perfecting classroom visions of Hobbesian war or Kantian concord, only barely exist. Much depends upon their growth and development: ***you can't guide what you can't understand.***[29]

The publication *Culture(s) in International Relations* has been compiled under statutory research funded by the Ministry of Science and Higher Education of the Republic of Poland, with additional financial assistance from the University of Warsaw. Handing this book to the readers, we are aware that the subject has not been exhausted and merits further discussion. Bearing in mind the heated discussions during seminars and conferences among the authors of the articles on the main subject of this book, we would finally like to thank everyone for their involvement and openness to critical and substantive debate.

Grażyna Michałowska and Hanna Schreiber

29 C. Geertz, *Available Light. Anthropological Reflections on Philosophical Topics*, Princeton University Press 2000, pp. 245–246 and 250.

Part I. Culture in International Relations Scholarship

Anna Wojciuk

Culture in the Theories of International Relations

Key words: international relations theory, culture, constructivism, clash of civilizations, realism, strategic culture

Abstract: The article analyses how culture was incorporated into international relations theories. Starting from the considerations for strategic culture during the Cold War, it discusses culture from the realist perspective of Samuel Huntington and finally seeks to explain the cultural sources of whole social reality under constructivism.

The 1990s were a time of the most intensive debate on the relations between culture and international relations[1]. The reason for this was, on the one hand, the 'shock' of the end of the Cold War, and on the other hand, the 'thawing' of nationalisms and ethnicity-based conflicts. It is then that the international relations scholarship saw the most noteworthy works published with the word 'culture' in the title, and numerous conferences and seminars were dedicated to discussing a new direction of development of international relations, taking culture into account.[2] Peter Katzenstein notes that the end of the Cold War was as important for the development of international relations discipline as the sinking of the *Titanic* for naval engineers.[3] At that time, people also used to say that the theory

---

1 I would like to thank Professor Jacek Czaputowicz for his valuable feedback that greatly contributed to this article.

2 In Polish academic literature, issues related to culture and civilisation were discussed by, among others: G. Michałowska, 'Porządek międzynarodowy w perspektywie paradygmatu cywilizacyjnego' (International Order in the Perspective of Civilisational Paradigm'), in R. Kuźniar (ed.), *Porządek międzynarodowy u progu XXI wieku* (*International Order at the Verge of 21st Century*), Warszawa 2005; M. F. Gawrycki, 'Kultura a stosunki międzynarodowe' (Culture and International Relations), in M. F. Gawrycki, *Uwikłane obrazy. Hollywoodzki film a stosunki międzynarodowe* (*Entangled Images. Hollywood Film and International Relations*), Warszawa 2011; H. Schreiber, 'Religia jako element «zwrotu kulturowego» w stosunkach międzynarodowych' (Religion as an Element of a 'Cultural Turn' in International Relations), in A. M. Solarz, H. Schreiber (eds.), *Religia w stosunkach międzynarodowych* (*Religion in International Relations*), Warszawa 2012.

3 See: P. Katzenstein (ed.), *The Culture of National Security. Norms and Identity in World Politics*, New York 1996, p. xi.

of international relations 'slept' through the political revolution. This is why in these times so much effort was put into questioning realism, neorealism and neoliberalism, and into the search for new narrations to describe and explain the contemporary phenomena in international relations. This text will primarily refer to the publications from this period. While refraining from adopting any form of cultural determinism, in the 1990s theoreticians of international relations began to wonder how to successfully correct their theories by including variables connected with cultural identity.

In the first decade of the 21st century, the temperature of this debate considerably decreased. There were many reasons for this. On the one hand, the cognitive dissonance was greatly reduced through the development of the constructivist paradigm, which takes into account the cultural component in studying the social reality, including the international reality. On the other hand, important events and processes taking place in the empirical sphere of international relations have drawn the scholars' attention away from this debate. The early years of the 21st century saw growing interest in the study of the War on Terror, height of the United States' power, growing power of China, and a possible beginning of a transformation of the international order. The theories in the field of international relations partially followed these research problems, focusing less on culture.[4]

Culture according to (neo)realists and neoliberals

After the Cold War ended, the theory of international relations was dominated by a discussion between neorealists and neoliberals who argued which approach was better for explaining international phenomena. At that time, realists were largely under the influence of the structural theory of Kenneth Waltz, according to which the domestic characteristics of states (including the cultural ones) were unimportant from the perspective of the analysis of international politics. Neoliberals, however, were much more willing to study the level of states and societies but usually also neglected the cultural characteristics. Constructing their theories since the 1970s, both neorealists and neoliberals were inspired by economics and adopted important principles of neoclassical economy including the rationality of individuals (and other actors in international relations) and the interests pursued

4 This article does not address the place of 'culture' in postmodern approaches to international relations, as doing this would require a separate, in-depth and comprehensive research effort that does not fit within the framework of the present undertaking. This is a subject which could yield interesting research results and is surely worth taking up in the future.

by them. Both neorealism and neoliberalism assumed that the agents behave rationally and maximise their utility functions, which – as understood by theoreticians at that time – were similar for different actors. It was also assumed that all political entities have similar interests and that these interests do not change considerably in time and in space, but while neorealists defined them in terms of relative power and security, neoliberals perceived them as absolute political and economic gains. When the fundamental interests of all actors of international relations are similar, any possible cultural differences between them, while certainly interesting, are unimportant from the point of view of international relations. In both approaches, entities (individuals, anthropomorphised states, and less frequently other anthropomorphised participants) and their interests were treated as known variables and scholars focused on searching for the results of interactions between these entities in different situations.

During the Cold War, in the theory of international relations, references to culture as a factor which could influence international relations were rare and very limited. At this point, we should mention the studies on strategic culture carried out under the broadly understood realist approach.[5] In 1977, an American think-tank RAND published an analysis entitled *The Soviet Strategic Culture: Implications for Limited Nuclear Options* by Jack Snyder. While it was not a theoretical text, it addressed important topics of this nature. Maintaining the general assumptions of realism, the author argued that neither Soviet nor American strategists were game theorists free from cultural influences and various preconceptions, and that their strategic doctrines had developed in different organisational, historical and political contexts in response to different situational and technological constraints. Therefore, it would be wrong to assume that the opponent will automatically accommodate to the American model of a rational actor applied in simulated nuclear confrontations based on the game theory. Already back then, Snyder wrote that 'a set of general beliefs, attitudes, and behavioural patterns with regard to nuclear strategy has achieved a state of semipermanence that places them on the level of "culture" rather than mere "policy"'.[6] It is interesting from a theoretical point of view that culture was included in these analyses of nuclear

5 At this point, the notion of studies of strategic culture will be described only generally, as it is elaborated in detail further in this book, in the article by Bolesław Balcerowicz titled *Culture in Military Science – from Strategic Culture to the Cultural Turn.*

6 J. L. Snyder, *The Soviet Strategic Culture: Implications for Limited Nuclear Options*, Santa Monica, CA 1977, p. v.

strategies[7]; they were of the greatest practical use at these times, and if badly conducted, they could have lead to disastrous consequences such as confrontation threatening survival of the whole humanity.

However, this movement should not be overestimated. Two years after Snyder's publication, another well-known work appeared. It was written by Kenneth Waltz and it was a compendium of neorealism which completely ignored cultural differences between countries. Entitled *Theory of International Politics*, it had a profound impact on the development of the theory of international relations in the final period of the Cold War.[8] In the approach presented by Waltz and his followers, and in the name of elegance of a system theory, structural neorealism took the assumptions of realism to the extreme by assuming that states were functionally undifferentiated entities that strived to maximise their utilities. Utility was defined as power and security. States were meant to work towards achieving necessary capabilities and assets, constrained only by ahistorical and acultural variables such as geography, capabilities of other actors, threats and the tendency to avoid behaviours which could directly threaten their continued survival.[9] In a sense, the assumption of rational behaviour was limited, e.g. in the works by Robert Jervis at that time, researchers tended to use the categories of misperception and imperfect information, disregarding the deep historical and cultural differences able to determine the choices made by individual participants in international relations.[10] Other researchers, such as Graham Allison, who also adhered to the general framework set out by realism, introduced nuances to its principles by pointing to the organisational determinants of the decision-making process.[11] The application of the neorealist framework to the analysis of the foreign policies of states led to the conclusion that regardless of the perception and organisational determinants, being in the same place, time and role, people from different cultures and shaped by different historical narrations would make the same choices.[12] Moreover, the theory of international relations, which developed most dynamically in the United States, was heavily influenced by American ethnocentrism,

---

7 For more on the notion of strategic culture see: J. Czaputowicz, *Bezpieczeństwo międzynarodowe. Współczesne koncepcje* (*International Security. Modern Conceptions*), Warszawa 2012, pp. 172–174.

8 K. Waltz, *Theory of International Politics*, New York 1979.

9 B. Bueno de Mesquita, *The War Trap*, New Haven, CT 1981, pp. 29–30, 64.

10 R. Jervis, *Perception and Misperception in International Politics*, Princeton 1976.

11 G. Allison, *Essence of Decision*, Boston 1971.

12 A. I. Johnston, *Cultural Realism, Strategic Culture and Grand Strategy in Chinese History*, Princeton 1996, pp. 2–3.

implicitly bringing a lot of hidden assumptions embedded in this particular tradition. Researchers, however, became aware of this only at the end of the Cold War.[13] Interestingly, unlike in international relations scholarship, in the public debate the cultural and civilisational boundaries were drawn and maintained by the discourses about East and West on both sides of the iron curtain. The way those concepts were used implied that there was a deep cultural underpinning of both blocks, decisive for the division[14].

'Return' of culture to the theory of international relations

In 1996, while writing about the specifics of the Chinese strategic approach, Alastair Iain Johnston treated culture as a variable which could not be ignored and pondered on the issues related to various states using force to further their political goals. Johnston went a step further than Snyder had done almost two decades earlier and wrote that 'ahistorical or "objective" variables such as technology, skills, levels of threat, and organisational structures are all of secondary importance: it is the interpretative lens of strategic culture that gives meaning to these variables'. Johnston thus believed that the notion of strategic culture can be analytically linked to the model of bounded rationality. The participants in international relations indeed make rational calculations but in his opinion, they 'employ culture-based heuristics to simplify reality'.[15] This means that the simplified rules of drawing conclusions that people use instinctively to shorten their thought processes have a cultural background and are not uniform for everyone. They differ between human groups. This is the reason why the application of the game theory to analyse the strategies of individual actors sometimes stumbles upon barriers in the form of culturally different heuristics. Hence, including strategic culture does not imply an automatic rejection of rationality, but instead it opposes the ahistorical and acultural method of analysing international relations in the spirit of realism. In reaction to the changes that took place in political reality, the changes that the realist theory could not convincingly explain, theoreticians included variables concerning the internal context of the state in their analyses.

---

13 J. S. Nye, S. Lynn-Jones, 'International security studies: A Report on a Conference on the State of the Field', *International Security*, vol. 12, no. 4, 1988, pp. 5–27.

14 P. T. Jackson, *Civilising the Enemy: German Reconstruction and the Invention of the West,* 2006, Ann Arbor: University of Michigan Press and P.T.Jackson, 'Civilizations as Actors: A Transactional Account', in M. Hall and P. T. Jackson (eds.) *Civilizational Identity,* New York: Palgrave, pp. 33–49.

15 A. I. Johnston, *Cultural Realism…*, p. 1.

While analysing various areas from the viewpoint of culture, scholars first of all noted the phenomena of nationalism and the ethnic factor, and recently also the religious factor.[16] This was a clear departure from Waltzian systemic theory and, to a certain extent, it fits in the mainstream of neoclassical realism.[17]

In realism itself, corrections have been taking place rather slowly and did not stop the tide of criticism against it that surged in the 1990s. Looking for the sources of this criticism, scholars usually point to empirical phenomena, especially the end of the Cold War, which allowed many ethnic conflicts and nationalisms to surface, thus forcing the discipline to rethink its assumptions formed during the Cold War. In the times of confrontation between the two superpowers, the state was in the centre of attention, but after the end of the Cold War it turned out that the dominant state-centric theories were unable to predict and could not explain the events that took place after 1989.[18] Another factor conducive to the absence of culture in international relations was the long-standing domination of positivism and preference for approaches firmly set in the empirical methodology, especially the quantitative one, which had so far found it difficult to study cultural phenomena. The criticism of positivism, the postpositivist movement and a renewed interest in normativism facilitated the emergence of a discussion on principles of good life and values in international relations, and those are inherently a part of culture.[19] The last two decades have been therefore a time of widespread criticising and undermining of the hegemonic realist tradition, especially in the Waltzian version of structural neorealism. Because it is neorealism that is the furthest from recognising the importance of culture in international relations, the crumbling of its hegemony creates favourable conditions for a renewed interest in culture in the theory of international relations.

---

16 J. Snyder (ed.), *Religion and International Relations Theory*, New York 2011. This work concerns not only realism but also other theoretical approaches in international relations, such as neoliberalism and constructivism.

17 A. Wojciuk, *Dylemat potęgi. Praktyczna teoria stosunków międzynarodowych* (*Power Dilemma. Practical Theory of International Relations*), Warszawa 2010, pp. 68–77.

18 Y. H. Ferguson, R. W. Mansbach, 'The Past as Prelude to the Future? Identities and Loyalties in Global Politics', in Y. Lapid, F. Kratochwil (eds.), *The Return of Culture and Identity in IR Theory*, Boulder, CO 1996, p. 21.

19 Cf.: A. Wojciuk, 'Nauka o stosunkach międzynarodowych. Między namysłem filozoficznym a metodologią empiryczną' (Science of International Relations. Between Philosophical Reflection and Empirical Methodology), in A. Gałganek, E. Haliżak, M. Pietraś (eds.), *Wielo- i interdyscyplinarność nauki o stosunkach międzynarodowych* (*Multi- and Interdisciplinarity of the Study of International Relations*), Warszawa 2012.

In the 1990s, reference to cultures and civilisations in theories concerning the international reality was probably the most pronounced in Samuel Huntington's concept of the clash of civilisations. The famous article 'The Clash of Civilizations?' published in *Foreign Affairs* in 1993 and the book from 1996 which elaborated on it, roused great interest among public intellectuals and more generally in the public domain, while they engaged a relatively small number of scholars who tried to empirically test the hypothesis. Huntington's claim provoked considerable controversy among theoreticians of international relations and even more among the general public.[20] Huntington argued that the post-Cold War conflicts are most often caused by culture rather than ideology and instead of confronting the capitalist world with the socialist world, as it was before, they are rather a manifestation of a clash between different civilisations. Moreover, civilisations will clash with each other due to their different values and political contradictions that are impossible to reconcile. Although Huntington used the terms culture and civilisation, adapted from the works of Arnold Toynbee and Oswald Spengler, the framework of his theory was essentially very close to realism. The concept of 'state' was replaced with 'civilisation' as the new primary object of observations in international relations.

However, we should ask to what extent Huntington's civilisations have indeed introduced a new quality to the studies of international relations. On the one hand, under this approach it is the cultural affiliation and not class or ideology that determines the objects of observation, but on the other hand it quickly turns out that they strive exactly after the same values that states seeked in the theories of realists, that is survival, obtaining influence and when it is possible, domination. Their choices are governed by motivations identical to those of states in the Cold War period. Civilisations are deceptively similar to the poles of power described by realists and the international reality is governed by familiar mechanisms. The main principles of international relations – according to Huntington – have not at all been modified by the end of the Cold War. Critics of Huntington's views point out that his innovation bears the hallmarks of an attempt to describe Galileo's observations made using a telescope by means of the tools provided by Aristotelian physics.[21]

---

20 Cf.: S. P. Huntington, 'The Clash of Civilizations', *Foreign Affairs*, vol. 72, no. 3, 1993, pp. 22–49; and S. P. Huntington, *The Clash of Civilizations and the Remaking of World Order*, Simon & Schuster, New York 2011.

21 R. E. Rubenstein, J. Crocker, 'Challenging Samuel Huntington', *Foreign Policy*, no. 96, p. 115, 1994.

This is why Huntington is sometimes referred to as the last realist[22], which can be safely called an exaggeration.

Challenging Huntington's approach, Peter Katzenstein offered a concept of plural and pluralist civilisations, conceived as configurations, constellations and complexes. Unlike Huntingtonian unitary entities, here civilisations are culturally loosely integrated, they generate debate and contestation. Encompassing disparate modes of thought and different senses of past, present, and future, they evolve gradually responding to internal pluralism and external encounters[23]. Violent clashes happen rather within civilisations than between them. Inter-civilisational relations for most part consist of encounters, engagements, and borrowing. Katzenstein opposes essentialist view of civilizational entities, admitting that they can sometimes become political reifications[24].

An important strand of research inspired by cultural and civilisational factors are the studies that relativise the dominant importance of state in international relations and show that the state-centric character of the international reality is a historical and not an absolute phenomenon and that often the foundation underlying state-centrism is a more or less overt Europocentrism. What is more, classical realism has always had a tendency to disregard the fact that the modern state as we know it has entered the international arena gradually, mainly in Europe and only from the 16th or 17th century onwards; on the other hand, its future has not been sealed yet. Moreover, realism theorised international relations as if they had started 350 years ago with the Treaty of Westphalia of 1648.

Barry Buzan and Richard Little, in turn, point out that the first fully developed international system emerged in 3500 BC in the area between the Tigris and the Euphrates.[25] In their theoretical deliberations, the two authors have tried to include various cultural formations which created pre-international and international systems, such as tribes, chiefdoms, city-states, empires, nomadic tribes, and

22 J. Czaputowicz, *Teorie stosunków międzynarodowych. Krytyka i systematyzacja* (*Theories of International Relations. Critical Remarks and Systematisation*), Warszawa 2007, p. 206.

23 P. J. Katzenstein (ed.), *Civilisations in World Politics. Plural and Pluralist Perspectives,* New York: Routledge, 2010, pp. 3–5.

24 P. J. Katzenstein (ed.), *Anglo-America and Its Discontents. Civilizational Identities beyond East and West,* New York: Routledge, 2012 and P. J. Katzenstein (ed.), *Sinicization and the Rise of China. Civilizational Processes beyond East and West,* New York: Routledge, 2012.

25 B. Buzan, R. Little, *International Systems in World History: Remaking the Study of International Relations*, Oxford: Oxford University Press, 2000, p. 1.

finally modern states.[26] As a matter of fact, for the entire period of its existence, the English school has conducted comparative studies of international systems in various historical periods and in various areas.[27] The scholars active in this current mainly called upon the historical and civilisational perspective, inspired by the works of Arnold Toynbee, and were not using the term 'culture' *expressis verbis* in their theories of international relations, however, they included those aspects that the proponents of post-Cold War cultural approaches have been calling for.[28] In the past, we were dealing with highly diverse forms of political communities. States did not exist always and everywhere. People tied their political behaviours and loyalties to various identities and accomplished them in various types of communities, such as tribes, families and clans, cities, empires, and nations. The model alternative to the state-centric one shows the complex reality of overlapping, multilevel and interrelated political communities.[29] Among the communities closest to us in terms of time, the functioning of which is important in contemporary international relations, a very interesting example is the nation, which turns out to be rather weakly represented in the theories of international relations.[30] Within the frameworks of these theories, scholars have rarely pondered over the nature of the nation and its aspects such as the 'here feeling', which is closely related to the joint inhabitation of a given territory and an identification with it; and the 'we feeling' connected to the feeling of solidarity and the identification with common attributes such as language, religion, history, and institutions.[31]

Apart from relativising the state as the focal point for the development of the identity of individuals in the international context, attention is also paid to the fact that individuals have many different political loyalties and identifications simultaneously, and as a result, they participate in different networks and are subjected to different forms of authority. Each network has the ability to mobilise them in relation to issues that concern its interests and those that give rise to similar emotions among its participants. As a consequence, boundaries become blurred and it would be wrong to continue claiming that it is still solely or primarily the

---

26 See also: Y. Lapid, F. Kratochwil, 'Revisiting the "National": Toward an Identity Agenda in Neorealism?', in Y. Lapid, F. Kratochwil (eds.), *The Return of Culture...*, p. 123.

27 J. Czaputowicz, *Teorie stosunków międzynarodowych...*, p. 257.

28 A. Nuri Yurdusev, 'Civilisations and International Systems. Toynbee, Wight and Bull', British International Studies Association, 27th Annual Conference, LSE, 16–18 December, 2002.

29 Y. H. Ferguson, R. W. Mansbach, 'The past as prelude...', p. 35.

30 Y. Lapid, F. Kratochwil, 'Revisiting the "National"...', p. 130.

31 Y. H. Ferguson, R. W. Mansbach, 'The past as prelude...', p. 35.

state – or civilisation, as understood by Huntington – that is the fundamental and the only political community which individuals identify themselves with. These different identities and the resulting loyalties coexist and become activated in specific situations.

In the theory of international relations, the 1990s saw a lively discussion on Huntington's theory, the relativisation of the meaning of state, and a reflection on the complex identity of the participants in international relations. In the first decade of the 21st century, Joseph Nye formulated a concept which proved to be no less a success in the public debate than the idea of 'the clash of civilisations' had been two decades before. It was the concept of 'soft power', presented in the fullest version in 2004 in a book with the same title. While Nye's popular term is not in itself an independent theoretical approach – rather an element of the liberal approach to international relations – it is still quite important as its author gives culture a prominent place in the development of soft power in international relations. At this point, we should also emphasise that Nye's liberalism does not radically contradict realism and does not exclude realist analyses of international relations but rather introduces essential corrections to this approach. The most important ones include firstly, relaxing the assumption that states are the only actors of international relations and secondly, calling into question the assumption that international relations are always and only a zero-sum game. And although Nye believes that striving after power seems the goal of all states and some non-state actors as well, he also notices and appreciates that next to the traditional force, there is also another, less forceful aspect of state power, which he consequently refers to as 'soft power'. Culture is an important component of this power of attraction, as it has the ability to set the preferences of other participants in international relations. In international politics, the sources of soft power are, inter alia, the values which are manifested in the cultures of states or organisations. Nye understands culture as a collection of values and practices which are important for the society. Thus, culture itself has the best chance to produce a soft power of state when its values are universal. The author compares universal values, attractive for the rest of the world, with parochial values, unfit to be adapted and transplanted to other places – this concerns both the so-called high culture and popular culture.[32] However, while appreciating the role of culture in international relations, and especially in the development of international power of different actors, in his core theoretical assumptions Joseph Nye remains closer to realists

32 J. S. Nye, 'Soft Power: The Means to Success in World Politics', *Public Affairs*, New York 2004, p. 11.

and Huntington than to constructivists, for whom culture is the very foundation, not a mere addition to power and rationality.

Constructivism – internalised culture

Alexander Wendt notes that identity of states themselves was not sufficiently taken into account in the theories of international relations of the Cold War period; he believes it to be the decisive factor driving the behaviour of these actors. Wendt argues that the international system is not inherently anarchic, as Waltz and other neorealists had claimed, but anarchy itself functions as long as the identity of states is based on the conviction that they operate in the anarchic environment. Anarchy is what states make of it, to cite perhaps the most famous quote from Wendt.[33]

Moreover, Alexander Wendt points out the fact that culture is one of the factors that determine the identity of states. Identity, in turn, does not determine the political choices made by actors in the international arena but instead provides them with a 'menu' of selections and with references for valuing the different variants. By claiming that ideas and identities matter, constructivism is a form of idealism or, rather, as Wendt would have it, idea-ism.[34] Consequently, another eminent father of the constructivist paradigm, John Gerard Ruggie, observes that even if the so-called neo-utilitarianism,[35] adopted by neorealism and neoliberalism, analyses the ideational factors, it treats them as nothing more than instruments useful or useless for individuals maximising their own and always striving after the realisation of their materialist interests.[36] Wendt, Ruggie and other constructivists thus call for taking into account the immanently intersubjective[37] nature of the social reality which differentiates it from the natural reality. It is the intersubjective, ideational, and consequently cultural dimension of international relations

---

33 A. Wendt, 'Anarchy Is What States Make of It: The Social Construction of Power Politics', *International Organization*, vol. 46, 1992, pp. 391–425.

34 A. Wendt, 'Identity and structural change in international politics', in Y. Lapid, F. Kratochwil (eds.), *The Return of Culture...*, p. 48.

35 J. G. Ruggie writes about constructivism in opposition to neo-utilitarianism; other scholars, e.g. Jacek Czaputowicz, position constructivism at the opposite pole to rationalism. In both cases, the approaches analyse the participants in social interactions in categories similar to the rational choice theory and game theory. Cf.: J. Czaputowicz, *Teorie stosunków międzynarodowych...*, pp. 295–301.

36 J. G. Ruggie, 'What Makes the World Hang Together? Neo-Utilitarianism and the Social Constructivist Challenge', *International Organization*, vol. 52, no. 4, 1998, p. 855.

37 For more on the notion of intersubjectivity see: A. Wojciuk, *Dylemat potęgi...*, pp. 202–203.

that makes them irreducible to the language used by the natural sciences. While in the natural sciences materialism is ontologically and epistemologically much more justified, in social studies it not only exhibits excessive and unacceptable reductionism (so far, science has always been immanently reductionist) but, as constructivists argue, we can observe on the level of research practice that it also leads scholars intellectually astray.

The consequence of the cultural aspect of human activity is that in the social world there appears an entire category of facts which have no raison d'être in the world of material objects. The existence of these facts depends on people agreeing that they do exist and usually requires the presence of suitable institutions established by people. The facts falling under this category are, for example, money, property rights, sovereignty, marriage, football, and Christmas. They have a clearly different nature from rivers, mountains and gravity, which exist regardless of whether people agree on it or not. Therefore, while studying the international reality, constructivism tries to take into account human awareness and its role in international life.[38]

Constructivist criticism goes much deeper than the slight 'pro-cultural' corrections proposed by realists or liberals, as it affects the very foundations of the ontological and epistemological scientific paradigms. This does not mean, of course, that material factors are of no significance to constructivists. The intersubjective social reality, including the international one, contains both ideational and material elements. The ideational ones are more important as the participants in international relations act on the basis of meanings they ascribe to material factors they possess or that other actors in the system own. International norms, rules, customs, institutions, conventions, ideologies, and laws are, according to constructivists, cultural formations.[39]

A well-known example, very often analysed by constructivists, is the issue of nuclear weapons. Possessing them is a material fact, however this fact itself is of no significance unless it is ascribed by the participants in the system. In international relations an entity that possesses nuclear weapons is always understood in category of friend or foe, among others. It thus turns out that purely materialist objects such as weapons cannot exist in politics without the cultural component. For the United States, the fact that the United Kingdom owns these kinds of weapons has an entirely different meaning than Russia owning them.

38 J. G. Ruggie, 'What Makes the World Hang…', p. 856.

39 A. Wendt, *Social Theory of International Politics*, Cambridge: Cambridge University Press, 1999.

While neorealists and neoliberals emphasise the importance of material factors and assume that they explain the entirety of the international life, constructivists believe that ideational factors are the most important, as it is only through ideas that we understand the material world. Consequently, in their opinion, all notions described in the international relations scholarship with the use of the materialist language, such as, for example, balance of power or the Cold War, have a cultural background; however, it must be remembered that they cannot be reduced to ideational factors.[40] It should also be noted that both the conflictual and the cooperative elements of international relations have a cultural aspect which is manifested in certain norms, rules, customs, and institutions.

The cooperation of several participants of international relations can bear the hallmarks of a collective action as understood by Mancur Olson, and as such, it can be narrowed down to the question of how to induce actors that have diverging interests to engage in cooperation.[41] However, if we include the notion of identity in the analysis, we can observe that actors can have common goals that are deeply set in their common identity and in the common understanding of problems and aims of their interaction.[42] Admittedly, neoliberals acknowledge that institutions change the behaviours of actors, but they locate the source of this change on a purely behavioural level; for constructivists, in turn, the behavioural changes stem not only from the institutional factors that have been identified by neoliberals, but from deeper identity transformations. Dependence and interdependence can have both a material and a behavioural dimension, e.g. through institutions, but they can also take place on a deeper ideational level. In this case we speak of changes taking place on the intersubjective level.[43] In accordance with the rational choice theory and the game theory, the principles of which are adopted by neorealism and neoliberalism, interests are exogenous in relation to the game. In international relations we could say that the interests and preferences of participants are known and independent from the situation; in other words, they are in a sense externally defined in relation to the analysed situation. This approach is useful for permanent interests, but constructivists believe that identities – and along with them also interests and preferences – sometimes change during the game and then

40 A. Wendt, 'Identity and Structural Change...', p. 49.

41 M. Olson, *The Logic of Collective Action: Public Goods and the Theory of Groups*, Cambridge 1965.

42 A. Wendt, 'Identity and Structural Change...', p. 52.

43 *Ibid.*, p. 55.

they become endogenous.[44] Taking Axelord's experiment further one can say that players that initially do not cooperate with each other can learn to cooperate and not only correct their choices on the behavioural level but also develop a common identity as a group in which certain norms exist. In this context, Wendt notes that repeated interaction can change the interdependence of the results of the game (an exogenous change on the behavioural and materialist level) to interdependence of the players' utility function (endogenous change on the intersubjective level).[45]

Therefore, it is not international anarchy as understood by Waltz but historical sequence of movements that explains most regularities of friendly and hostile behaviours between the participants in international relations. History provides us with knowledge and understanding as to why participants in international relations are as they are and explains their choices. Following the logic of the game theory, strategy is the choice of a specific action based on particular interest and preferences, but the approaches taking into account intersubjectivity and identity focus on the actions that change the preferences of the participants and their perception of their own interests.[46]

The ceaseless bilateral interaction between structure and agency[47] which is the foundation of the constructivist approach to social reality on the one hand inherently includes culture as an important part of the structure, and on the other hand the individual and her agency, which actively produces culture and is able to alter its character. In his most important work, *Social Theory of International Politics*, Alexander Wendt wrote that this social structure was first of all people's shared knowledge, otherwise known as culture.[48] Thus, for Wendt and the other constructivists, 'culture' is the intersubjective knowledge shared by a group of people. Structure thus has a cultural dimension when the participants in international relations share the understanding of certain concepts, e.g. friend and enemy, war and peace.[49] According to Wendt, culture is a 'self-fulfilling prophecy'; people forced to interact in given situations first need to define these situations and only

---

44 For more on this see e.g.: J. Czaputowicz, *Teorie stosunków międzynarodowych...*, p. 296.

45 A. Wendt, 'Identity and Structural Change...', p. 57.

46 Y. Lapid, F. Kratochwil, 'Is the Ship of Culture at Sea or Returning?', in Y. Lapid, F. Kratochwil (eds.), *The Return of Culture...*, p. 212.

47 For more on structure and agency, notions essential for the understanding of constructivism, see: J. Czaputowicz, *Teorie stosunków międzynarodowych...*, pp. 312–314; and A. Wojciuk, *Dylemat potęgi...*, pp. 203–204.

48 A. Wendt, *Social Theory...*, p. 141.

49 *Ibid.*, p. 158.

then they adopt a certain strategy of behaviour that suits the circumstances. These definitions usually take into account, on the one hand, the identities and interests that reflect the understanding of who the participant is in a given situation, and on the other hand, the understanding of what the behaviour of the other party will be, which reflect the beliefs concerning the identities and interests of the other participants in the given situation. If these various understandings are not shared, then there is no cultural definition of the situation and as a result, there can be a greater chance that the participants will be surprised by each other's actions and that the effects of the actions will cause an uncertainty regarding their previous understanding of themselves and of others. It is as if someone drove a car not knowing what red light and green light meant and assumed that they had meanings opposite to the ones they actually have, writes Wendt. It is the shared understanding of what red light and green light mean as well as what the analogous rules in international relations are, that is what exactly constitutes the cultural part of the structure.[50]

In their studies concerning the agent, i.e. the human being, constructivists arrive at the conclusion that the understanding (defined in the non-essentialist way) of 'human nature' should depart from the perception in terms of *homo oeconomicus* that has been dominant so far (especially in neorealism and neoliberalism) and which, in their opinion, was simplified and reductionist. In the opinion of certain constructivists, humans have not only a rational nature (according to the proponents of the rational choice theory in international relations, one resulting from fear and ruthless struggle for own safety) and a greedy nature (resulting from the desire to maximise profits) but also a normative one, which makes them care for honour and spiritual matters. Thus, realism overestimates rationality and its underpinning fear, and liberalism assigns too much importance to greed.

Richard Ned Lebow, who works within the framework of the broadly understood constructivist approach, argues in his *Cultural Theory of International Relations* of 2008 that modern times and the theories of international relations of the 20th century that followed forgot about the meaning of spirit and honour which have always been present in the social life and in international relations.[51] Realising his very ambitious idea of constructing a theory of international relations based on the understanding of human nature defined as a common set of psychological characteristics, the author returns to ancient Greece and its philosophical thought. In antiquity, scholars believed that there are three types of motivations

50 *Ibid.*, pp. 186–187.

51 R. N. Lebow, *A Cultural Theory of International Relations*, Cambridge 2008, pp. 26–28.

of human actions: they are the result of actions of the spirit, appetite and reason. According to Lebow, the theories presented so far have not appreciated the spirit and have overestimated reason (especially realism) instead, thus absolutising the motivation of human actions and arguing that all actions result from fear. Liberalism, in turn, overrates the role of appetite, emphasising people's desire to accumulate wealth and putting their greed as the fundamental motive behind all actions. Modernity, he argues, has forgotten about the meaning of spirit and honour which were and are present in international relations. Interestingly, prestige – which according to Lebow belongs to the domain of spirit and honour – has always been taken into account by realists, but in a purely instrumental way. In Lebow's theory prestige/honour is itself a separate and important goal of man's actions in politics.[52] The author argues that although we will find these three motivations – appetite, reason and honour – in all human actions, one of them will always prove to be dominant.

The proportions of these three motivations are governed by culture. Thus, culture can make human actions more subtle or more brutal; it introduces values to motivation and allows men to rise above the vicious circle of the struggle for survival and overcome greed.[53] Lebow is therefore the most open to culture among the constructivists whose views are discussed here. In his work he identifies it not as an additional variable or a mere part of the structure that can be identified only empirically and cannot be judged as positive or negative, but as a positively identifiable part of the structure, as far as cultural norms mitigate aggression in human behaviour. According to Lebow, culture is not only an inseparable background of social processes but first of all, an element of the structure that limits motivations fuelled by fear and greed and allows people – at least in some situations – to be guided by spirit, honour and values.

This is not to say, however, that honour and spirit always lead people to repress their aggressive behaviours. On the contrary, warrior communities were usually based on honour as the primary motivation. Moreover, in the light of the case studies described by the author, striving after prestige is a frequent case for wars. However, under Lebow's theory, all self-limiting norms of behaviour that reduce the level of aggression between people are a matter of spirit and honour, and these are shaped by culture to a much greater extent than appetite or reason/fear. Consequently, under Lebow's theory, we can risk claiming that culture not only gives a normative dimension to social life, but it is itself also subject to judgement in

52 *Ibid.*, p. 557.
53 *Ibid.*, pp. 26, 72.

terms of values. As shown by the numerous and exhaustive case studies presented by the author, in various ages and in various places, cultures can be more or less advanced in the role that they ascribe to certain norms in social life.

Within the framework of constructivism, Lebow attempts to link human behaviours with identities.[54] Identity is developed on the basis of feedback that accompanies human behaviours and on the analysis of the consequences of these behaviours. Furthermore, people also reflect on the motives behind behaviours. Lebow assumes that culture produces identity and that it does so in two ways. First, it highlights and promotes certain motivations for actions and decreases the significance of others. Second, it regulates the manner of realising and expressing the approved motives. In the case of spirit itself, it is the culture that specifies what behaviours bring respect and recognition and what mechanisms make it possible to win and celebrate respect. It is also culture that creates social hierarchies, which are a prerequisite for social diversification. Motivations are thus an important factor that co-constitutes human identity; identity is important because it determines people's interests and they in turn underlie behaviours. Hence identity, interests and behaviours are social constructs, although the participants – just as it was in the theories of other constructivists – are not slaves to the processes of socialisation.[55]

The relation between honour and identity fits with the notion of ontological security within the framework of the theory discussed here. Following Giddens, Lebow argues that people need to limit their anxiety by developing the belief that they understand the physical and the social world. The largely routine form of social relations helps people structure their identity and increase the ability to act effectively, and consequently, gives them a sense of security. The upsetting of these routine beliefs and actions by new and critical situations is the source of anxiety.[56] The concept of ontological security has been previously applied in the theory of international relations, among others, by Hedley Bull.[57] Routine actions undertaken as a part of a foreign policy support identity; this particularly concerns referring to a permanent narration regarding the history and specific characteristics of the given state. A public person that would like to justify foreign policy on the basis of other aspects of state history and values different from those usually

---

54 *Ibid.*, p. 562.

55 *Ibid.*, p. 563.

56 A. Giddens, *The Constitution of Society: Outline of the Theory of Structuration*, Cambridge: Polity Press, 1984.

57 H. Bull, *Anarchical Society: A Study of Order in World Politics*, Basingstoke 2002, pp. 7–8.

emphasised will meet with strong resistance.[58] Not only declarations of friendship but also strategic alliances are made bearing in mind the preservation of identity, the desire to be among friends and on the historically right side. The concept of ontological security assumes that identities are structured around various narrations and values which, once established, provide leaders with strong motivations to adhere to them. The respect for oneself is the key component of identity and is maintained by caring for one's own honour and position. Ontological security involves the subjective sense of who one is; it is the prerequisite of subjectivity, separate identity and self-awareness. It involves the sense of purpose and the belief that one is a part of the society.[59] Jennifer Mitzen argues that ontological security concerns not only individual human beings but also states. To survive, states need a cementing narration which creates identity, a narration including history, the genesis of the state and its vision of the future.[60]

Conclusion

Readers who make the effort to study the extensive and ambitious work by Richard Ned Lebow can be surprised at how rarely the word 'culture' can appear in a book which has this word in the title. Even in the key fragments, where the author presents his theory, it is used only a few times. One could get the impression that the author went to great pains to avoid this particular word wherever possible, using terms such as 'identity', 'norms' and 'values' instead. Only a single short fragment of the ending to this over seven hundred pages long book includes a laconic reference to culture. But the author never explicitly explains why he decided to name his theory of international relations 'cultural'.

What is interesting, this situation seems to be typical for the entire theory of international relations because even when it tries to take cultural issues into account, it almost always does so under a different label, for example disguised as ideas, norms, identities, values, and less frequently civilisations. Therefore, while summing up the review of culture-related concepts in the theories of international relations, one cannot help but to get the impression that the return of culture to the theory of international relations that was announced in the 1990s happened to a large extent fragmentarily, by taking into account essential notions of cultural

---

58 J. Huysmans, 'Security! What Do You Mean?', *European Journal of International Relations*, vol. 4, no. 2, 1998, pp. 226–255.

59 J. Czaputowicz, *Teorie stosunków międzynarodowych…*, p. 179.

60 J. Mitzen, 'Ontological security in world politics: State identity and the security dilemma', *European Journal of Foreign Relations*, vol. 12, no. 3, 2006, p. 345.

nature. To be precise, we should actually say that it is the ideas, norms, values, and identity that returned to the theory of international relations as their relevance was obvious for most scholars in 1920s and 1930s. Even those contemporary authors who, just as Richard Ned Lebow, consider culture as an important factor in the description of international phenomena, in practice look for other terms to operationalise their theories. The analysis of the works discussed in this text shows that these terms are narrower, more precise and easier to define. While writing this article I searched in theories of international relations for all major concepts that can be qualified as cultural, even if the authors did not label them as such. As a result, even if constructivists do not explicitly state in the cited works that culture is a part of the structure, I understand, interpret and present their theory as such. However, it should be noted that in this article the word 'culture' often appears in contexts in which the authors of the theories concerned apply some other, narrower and more precise terms. A significant exception to this is the milestone work of Alexander Wendt, *Social Theory of International Politics*.

It seems that the 1990s were a time of great enthusiasm regarding the possibility of including culture in the theory of international relations. However, it turns out that in the later years the number of works with titles or keywords combining the words 'culture' and 'theory of international relations' decreased, and even Lebow's work, which is a perfect example of such a title, presents different conclusions than what enthusiasts of a return of culture to the theory of international relations in the 1990s might have expected. Already in 1996, Friedrich Kratochwil, the editor of the joint publication *The Return of Culture and Identity in IR Theory*, frequently referred to in the present article, cautioned against the temptation of a simple inclusion of culture in the theory of international relations. While recognising the significance of culture, he wrote that it could not be considered an answer to all the questions that the theory of international relations was struggling with at that time. It is easy to say that all the phenomena that are inexplicable can be somehow explained by cultural differences. If something explains everything, then it explains nothing, wrote Kratochwil.[61]

However, Kratochwil also pointed out that notions that have very broad meanings and can be ambiguous and imprecise are sometimes inevitable in studying the social reality. In his opinion, this is the case with culture and its numerous definitions.[62] The history of international relations scholarship after the Cold War has shown that taking into account cultural factors has become an important element

61 Y. Lapid, F. Kratochwil, 'Is the Ship of Culture...', p. 205.
62 *Ibid.*, p. 206.

of the dynamics of this discipline's development, but authors exhibit a puzzling restraint in using the word 'culture'. With the development of constructivism, we can observe a process of departing from treating the society as the sum of individuals and studying individuals as separate entities in favour of taking into account their embededness in historical and cultural roots. These changes are important for the theory of international relations and for the international relations scholarship as a whole, as well as for the methodologies applied in this discipline.[63]

The original version of this text was published in the academic journal "Społeczeństwo i Polityka", no. 4, 2012.

63 *Ibid.*, p. 210.

Franciszek Gołembski

Political Culture in Contemporary International Relations

Key words: political culture, axiology, foreign policy, Europe, civilisation

Abstract: The article analyses why and how issues related to cultural factor play an important role in the study of political relations including their international dimension. One cannot in fact analyse a political process without taking into account the importance of the cultural factor mirroring the values characteristic of each political system.

The importance of the cultural factor in social studies and the concept of political culture

The term 'culture' is particularly difficult to describe precisely and as such, it has many, often contradictory definitions. The concept of culture involves many ambiguities as a consequence of the complex process of development, in which its denotational content has been changing considerably. Initially, it referred primarily to human activity in the natural environment; to working the land. With time, however, it acquired new meanings, connected with human activity in the spiritual sphere, and thus became linked to the axiological dimension. This, in turn, led to the perception of the products of human activity as important from the point of view of social and individual values. Considering the scientific context, culture exhibits a far-reaching diversity, which results from differences in research methods and subjective scopes of research. Hence, there is a multitude of theories regarding culture.

For the purpose of this article, we shall refer to the approach of the German philosopher of culture Ralf Konersmann. In his attempt to describe the meaning of the term 'culture', he distinguishes four primary meanings.

The first one is descriptive. Konersmann states that culture describes the world created by people, the forms of their production and reproduction within the framework of perceptible customs and traditions, mental habits and symbolic orders. This notion of culture coincides with the equally ambiguous concept of civilisation.[1] It is indeed a broad definition, which coversthe reference to the

1 R. Konersmann, *Kulturphilosophie zur Einführung*, Hamburg: Junius, 2003, Polish edition: *Filozofia kultury. Wprowadzenie*, trans. by K. Krzemieniowa, Warszawa 2009, p. 13.

complex process of social development based on human creations, both material and spiritual. This also concerns the sphere of structures regulating human relationships, manifested in the symbolic dimension. In this sense, Konersmann identifies culture with civilisation, which is characteristic of the German reflection in the study of this subject.

The second meaning refers to the dynamic sphere. Konersmann notes that apart from the material sphere, there exists a sphere of reflection, and with it, the practice of constantly describing oneself. Within this framework, the conventions, main ideas and fundamental principles of coexistence are recognised and reproduced but also tested.[2] According to the German author it is the sphere of reflection that forms the basis for the development of axiological dimensionssuch as the conventions and rules of social intercourse, and thus leads to the creation of structures of social relations.

The third meaning refers to what Konersmann calls 'the archaeological concept'. It defines the conditions, contexts of messages and traditions that we presuppose when arranging our lives. They belong to the unconscious sphere, an area of deeply rooted beliefs and sentiments that are describable from a distance.[3] This applies to this 'deep' dimension that underlies attitudes and behaviours, which has roots in the individual and collective past.

Finally, argues Konersmann, the fourth meaning is normative and differentiating because it proceeds from reconstructing to determining differences which are reflected in hierarchical orders. In this approach, culture becomes the key word in this universal game of mimesis and moreover, departs from the model which originates at least in the times of global expansion in the period of European modernity: in the conflict between the need to identify *here*, and the 'almost identical' *there* with its equally passionate expression of the 'narcissism of small differences'. This area of conflict is also on the spectrum of the concept of culture, therefore it seems that culture has long ago allocated the positions of friend and foe.[4] It is a dimension that includes the desire to perpetuate cultural autonomy in the interaction with other systems of values, the striving to acknowledge one's own cultural 'I'. Today, this problem is present in the conditions of extensive intercultural relations.

The concept of culture as presented by Konersmann allows for a wider interpretation of culture in diverse systems of social life. He links it to the concept of

2 *Ibid.*
3 *Ibid.*, p. 14.
4 *Ibid.*

civilisation, which is sometimes merged with the concept of culture, but he also clearly underlines the concept of culture itself.

Philosophical ideas as well as research in the field of social sciences also often refer to the notion of 'civilisation'. Many theories with philosophical considerations perceive social processes from the point of view of the conceptual category of civilisation. Such approaches attempt to present the general principles underlying the development of social processes, and the civilisational dimension becomes the supreme form of this development.[5] Theories of civilisation include the attempt to build a coherent approach with the possibility of general explanation of the very essence of civilisational development as well as its stages. They also seek to reveal the conditions of the emergence, development and extinction of each civilisation in the course of its historical development and to emphasise mutual relations between civilisations.

The issues related to the cultural and civilisational factors play an important role in the study of political relations, including their international dimension. One cannot in fact analyse a political process without taking into account the importance of the cultural and civilisational factor. This aspect is directly related to the system of values characteristic of each political system. Analysing a political process without considering the cultural factor makes it impossible to find adequate answers to questions about the course of this process and the forms it takes. For the analysis to be relatively complete, it has to include an exhaustive presentation of the individual components of the political process, also those relating to the axiological sphere. The very term 'political process' refers directly to the temporal dimension, and therefore contains historical elements. If these elements are taken into account in the analysis of this process, there should also be a reference to the formation of cultural factors.

Each axiological system existing in the social dimension has a historical background. The values that manifest themselves in a political system are often derived from a particularly complex historical process. Therefore, no political process can be considered without its axiological and historical elements. Hence, with respect to this process, the axiological factor of cultural dimension is an obvious

---

5 For example, we can quote all those theories of civilisation that are based on the model of historical and social studies and that aspire to discover the main rules of development underlying individual civilisations. In the 20th century, the best known authors attempting to build their own theories of civilisation were, among others: Oswald Spengler, Arnold Toynbee, Samuel Huntington. Among the Polish authors, let us name Feliks Koneczny and Oskar Halecki.

methodological requirement underlying modern social sciences, including political science, and in particular, international relations.

In the mid-twentieth century, research initiatives emerged in social sciences, especially in political science, aimed at using the term 'political culture'. The introduction of this term was not purely nominal, it was also connected with the search for new research objectives, and the focus on political processes. The term 'political culture' itself was used before but has never had a clearly established conceptual content.[6] Subsequently, the issues of political culture became associated with problems related to political and military strategies, giving rise to additional terms: 'strategic culture' and 'political-strategic culture'.[7] In the analyses of the role of culture in international relations, there also appeared issues connected with the concept of political culture.[8] Thus, it can be observed that the concept of 'political culture' has also been extensively used in the study of international relations. Many contemporary topics concerning the various aspects of these relations include a reference to political culture. This concerns the analyses that focus on research regarding the foreign policies of individual states as well as the system of international relations as a whole.

Political culture is directly related to the normative dimension. It refers to the spheres of social relations, which are conditioned by axiological factors. In the

6 The contemporary definition of the term 'political culture' was introduced to the academic language in the 1960s as a result of the work of two American scholars, Gabriel Almond and Sidney Verba, who were conducting comparative studies of various political systems of individual countries, in particular concerning the axiological sphere in decision making and in the attitudes of politicians. Cf.: G. A. Almond, S. Verba, *The Civic Culture: Political Attitudes and Democracy in Five Nations*, Princeton, NJ 1963. In Poland, studies of political culture were initiated by Franciszek Ryszka. He took some concrete steps in this respect, including a joint initiative with Professor Gerd Meyer from the University of Tübingen. The fruit of these studies was a monograph edited by the two academics: F. Ryszka, G. Meyer (ed.), *Przemiany wartości a system polityczny* (*Changing Value Patterns and the Political System*), Warszawa 1990.

7 The terms 'strategic culture' and 'political-strategic culture' appear in the works of many authors analysing the changes in political processes after World War II, in particular in the period of the bipolar order international relations. One of the most recent presentations of this issue can be found in the following article: K. Booth, 'Strategic culture: validity and validation', *Oxford Journal on Good Governance*, vol. 2, no. 1, 2005.

8 These issues are now also broadly discussed in academic literature. See e.g.: J. E. Horrocks, D. W. Jackson, *Self and Role: A Theory of Self-process and Role Behavior*, Boston 1972. For Polish works, see e.g.: Z. J. Pietraś, *Pojęcie i klasyfikacja ról międzynarodowych* (*The Concept and Classification of International Roles*), Lublin 1989.

political process, it is a permanent elementthat points to the relevant determinants related to a wide range of values revealed in it. This applies both to the material dimension and to ideas.

The first dimension covers the entirety of material products existing in the social environment which make up material culture and which, in a particular way, influence the processes related to social interaction. The second dimension refers to the realm of ideas, that is to a set of notions and symbols that are relevant for the development of the axiological dimension and that are present in social relations.

Analysing international relations in their axiological aspect

As one of the manifestations of social relations in a broad sense, international relations inherently involve a reference to the axiological sphere, therefore the study of international relations must take into account the axiological factor. Observing the development of international relations from the historical perspective, we can see that in all periods they are marked by the presence of the cultural factor. In the past, it manifested itself in various forms, and often adopted different solutions. This resulted from the variety of political and social structures of the actors involved in international relations. The underlying factor behind the disparate political structures of individual countries or groups of interacting countries was their axiological diversity. Cultural differences took autonomous forms, relating to the various spheres of social life: the demographics, politics, economy, the military, and religion. Each of them became the carrier of its own values. On the other hand, as a result of mutual interaction, some universal values have also emerged.

The elements that were particularly clearly revealed in the sphere of international relations, and that were associated with the differences between political systems have become the basis of the analyses of the principles of their functioning. This was emphasised already by ancient philosophers[9] and gave rise to progress of the knowledge most adequate for each stage of civilisation, especially in the case of the so-called West. This concept contains in itself a reference to the development of the European civilisation, which in various historical phases searched for elements that would allow it to retain autonomy. The question of

9 The fact that many political conceptions are derived from the philosophical theories of Plato or Aristotle clearly shows that their views on the functioning of political structures taking into account the axiological factor were fully developed. Any analysis of the structures, institutional solutions of a state is based on, on the one hand, the knowledge of elements related to the individual sphere, and on the other, the knowledge of collective life.

European identity has become one of the key ones, not only in the historical dimension but also in modern times. This, in turn, leads to another question – regarding Europe's attitude to the surrounding worlds, which again is directly related to international relations in its regional, intercontinental and global dimensions.[10]

The introduction of the term 'political culture' into research in the field of international relations creates the need to seek new methodological solutions. These solutions should focus on the deepening of the research on international relations, which gives the possibility of delimiting its objective scope anew. It should be noted that the concept of 'political culture' should not be mechanically transferred to the sphere of international relations. Instead, it should be understood in a way that is relevant to the specifics of this field. Studies of political culture have been undertaken with the intention of finding a new research tool, in particular in relation to social relations, in the study of political processes and the related internal and external determinants. By contrast, the special character of the study of international relations requires a slightly different approach, which could become the basis for finding the relevant conditions, existing mainly within what concerns the relationality between the various actors involved in these relations. It is in fact the central reference to the study of international relations. Of course, it can be analysed from the perspective of the political process, thus emphasising its importance for the system of relations between the various entities involved in international relations, but this would narrow down the topic of research. International relations should also be seen from the perspective of their overall structure. Therefore, in this case it is necessary to analyse them also in terms of political culture.

Consequently, it is possible to look at the research on political culture in international relations on two basic levels. The first one comprises of the main entities involved in international relations: states, groups of states, international institutions. The second is the structure of international relations, viewed as a specific set of relations between the various actors, which can be analysed from the overall point of view. This kind of conceptual distinction points to the possibility of a diversified approach in using the term 'political culture'. These distinctions include the possibility of defining the object of research, which can concern the relation between the subjective and structural dimension, between the part and the whole.

10 In the 1950s, Arnold Toynbee made an attempt to present briefly the attitudes of various political and cultural systems to the Western world, including that of Russia, the world of Islam, India and the Far East. See: A. Toynbee, *The World and the West*, New York 1953.

Political culture in terms of foreign policy of states

The natural environment for the foreign policy of states is at the international level. The way of conducting foreign policy, especially its effectiveness, depends on many internal and external factors. The political structures of states are in turn associated with systems of values, which manifest themselves in the characteristics of political systems. They implicitly assume the observance of the accepted norms of conduct that define their doctrinal assumptions and the strategic framework aimed at achieving the state's goals.

Foreign policies of states are determined by internal and external factors. In both of those spheres of politics, there are specific links to political culture. These refer to the political system of the state, which contains certain values that are directly reflected in the structure of the state and its public institutions shaped by tradition. This also applies to social attitudes, which result from acting in accordance with the accepted cultural values. They translate into concrete political objectives of the state, also in terms of its approach to foreign policy.

In his analysis of the development of European relations from the sixteenth century to the present, the French author Pierre Béhar points out that each period saw a characteristic shift of the centre of gravity from some political centres to others. This was determined not only by the changing political, military or economic positions of various European actors but also to their different systems of values, translating into political objectives.[11] Hence, those objectives that manifested themselves in actions aimed at obtaining a dominant position were deeply rooted in political culture. European powers such as Spain, France, Great Britain, Russia, Prussia, and the Habsburg Monarchy, competing with each other for primacy in Europe, stemmed from different cultural traditions, which were reflected in the axiological sphere. The unification of Germany in the last quarter of the nineteenth century was also the result of a complex historical process, during which various conceptions, reflected also in the sphere of values, clashed with each other.

Moreover, the alliances forming between European powers were also not free from axiological elements. They were most often established not only for the sake of certain defensive goals acceptable to all concerned states but also due to their common axiological background, as exemplified by the Holy Alliance formed after the defeat of Napoleon (1815) with the aim of safeguarding common interests stemming from axiomatic assumptions (protection against revolutionary trends in Europe), or the North Atlantic Treaty Organisation (1949), which was

11 P. Béhar, *Une géopolitique pour l'Europe. Vers une nouvelle Eurasie?*, Paris 1992.

intended as protection against a possible aggression of the Soviet Union, with principles based on a system of values characteristic of democracy. This does not mean, however, that there were no differences of interests between the countries participating in those alliances.

The idea of a nation state, related to the social transformations in Europe, as well as the formation and development of European nationalisms in the nineteenth century clearly show how the objectives of foreign policy are connected with national interest. Although the determinants of this process varied, the reference to the values characteristic of a given state was always present. These values can be related to political culture, with one substantial difference: the nationalism of Western European countries was based on a system of values characteristic of the emerging economic and social structures of the industrial era; in contrast, that of Eastern European and South-Eastern European countries was based on cultural values. The American theorists Ivo Lederer and Peter Sugar called this type of nationalism 'cultural nationalism'.[12]

The system of values can contribute to the formation of political culture and it is largely associated with tradition. Moreover, it is strongly related to the foreign policy objectives of the state, as shown in the process of shaping foreign policy determined by traditional values. These values do not remain unchanged as they are subject to both internal transformations originating in the social sphere, and to external influences such as foreign practices and changes in the distribution of power in international relations. The fact that nation states strive to maintain their identities is logically connected with the desire to maintain their own system of values, which forms the basis of conducting foreign policy in the spirit of state identity.

For example, the tradition of British foreign policy, consistently implemented during the construction of the imperial position of the United Kingdom, was continued with increasing difficulty in the unfavourable conditions of the twentieth century, especially in the external sphere. Tradition played a significant role in this case, established by the effectiveness of British foreign policy in the past historical periods. It therefore shows the importance of continuity of political thought influencing the scope and nature of the actions of states in the external sphere. These assumptions stemmed from the belief that the decisions taken so far were effective and from the attempt to cope with the complex and changing distribution of power in the world. In addition, the United Kingdom was convinced of the superiority of the British civilisation over the rest of the world, the world that

---

12 P. F. Sugar, I. J. Lederer (eds.), *Nationalism in Eastern Europe*, Seattle 1969.

was seen as primitive or barbaric in many areas. This is best illustrated by the opinion of Harold Macmillan, a well-known British politician, who was sent by Churchill to Washington with the task of seeking support from the United States in the complex situation at the beginning of World War II. Macmillan, who later became British Prime Minister, was aware of the fact that the alliance with the United States would mean a decline of the British position in the world in favour of a new hegemon – the United States. The American author Edward T. Oakes notes that Macmillan tried to seek solace in history, by comparing the situation to the Roman conquest of Greece, after which the country maintained its advantage in the spiritual sphere over the military power of the Roman hegemony. According to Oakes, Macmillan hoped that the British influence would revive the American dominance from within, through British culture, if it could not achieve this through the Anglo-Saxon military strength anymore.[13]

In this particular case, the conviction that British culture is superior to the others translates into political thought in the strict sense, relating to international relations. In the historical perspective, and thus in its dynamic aspect, British political culture can be related to the political system of the United Kingdom, to the functioning of parliamentary democracy in the form of a monarchy, to economic liberalism ensuring access to world markets, and to the imperial structure embedded in the colonial system. All these elements have been affecting the scope and nature of its foreign policy, with the main goal of maintaining the priority of the interests of the United Kingdom in the international system. When the position and hegemonic role of the United Kingdom subsequently collapsed, the country was forced to look for a new model of foreign policy but without giving up entirely the axiomatic foundations reflected in the traditional values of its political culture. The US hegemony in international relations forced the UK to accept the new distribution of power in the world, expressed by the special partnership with the United States, but at the same time the UK made attempts to retain the autonomous elements present in the axiomatic foundations of British political culture. In contrast, Harold Macmillan's hopes to gain influence on the values of the American society proved to have no real basis. The British example clearly shows the importance of political culture for shaping of the canon of foreign policy. This strong foundation in the system of own values allowed the UK to develop a foreign policy that serves the interests of the country and to create the conditions for its security. While the basic axiomatic principles are maintained

---

13 E. T. Oakes, 'Review of "Eccentric Culture: A Theory of Western Civilization" by Rémi Brague', *First Things*, no. 34, 2003, p. 42.

even in adverse conditions, there is, even in the case of the UK, a clearly visible aspect related to changes in the approach to foreign policy. But due to the fact that the British had built on the foundations of political culture, they were able to keep a relatively good position in international relations despite unfavourable external conditions and to seek solutions that would delay and mitigate the effects considered negative in terms of their national interest.

Another example would be the political culture that develops in the conditions of totalitarian or authoritarian political systems.[14] Let us use the example of the Soviet Union. In contrast to the British model, in which tradition played a very important part and had substantial influence on the shaping of foreign policy, the ideological principles of the Soviet system required the state to depart from tradition and build a qualitatively new axiological model. The ideology adopted by the Bolsheviks called for fundamental changes that could be realised only if the existing political system was completely dismantled. Thus, they sought to introduce changes typical of a new model of political system, based on the principles of the communist ideology.[15] The political culture of the Soviet Union had to be built on new principles, completely negating any reference to the old political and social order. Tradition played a less significant role in this respect and therefore was rejected in the official programme of the Bolsheviks. However, there was one element of tradition that was maintained in one aspect during the development of the Soviet state. Although never openly referring to it and instead using other slogans consistent with the emerging political system, the Soviet Union upheld the continuity of imperial interests. Those interests, however, had to be modified in such a way as to ensure that they were no longer directly linked to the past. What allowed the Soviet Union to do this was ideology. The foreign policy of the Soviet state was based on the principle of having a global influence, and ultimately at building a global Soviet republic. However, due to the pragmatic approach, the Soviets intended to pursue this goal gradually.[16] It is important to note that

---

14 Each political system, due to its axiological dimension, is a carrier of a political culture. Totalitarian and authoritarian systems also create a relevant type of political culture.

15 In the process of emergence and development of the new political system, ideology plays an important role, thus becoming one of the main carriers in the axiological dimension.

16 Thus, a doctrine of peaceful cooperation of countries that have different political systems was created at the beginning of the 1920s. Its aim was to avoid a direct clash with the West.This was caused, among various factors, by the defeat in the war with Poland in 1920, which had eliminated the possibility of progressing further into Europe to expand the communist political system. The principle of 'permanent revolution', under

the centre of activities aimed at the achievement of this global goal was Moscow, which means that the future global communist order was seen from the perspective of the main political centre. A victory of communism on a global scale would have been consistent with the imperial ambitions of the Soviet state.[17]

Hence, when the Soviet Union chose to work together with Western countries (in the official ideological interpretation they were usually called capitalist states), the Soviets treated this is as only temporary cooperation. It was perceived pragmatically, as dictated by current needs, especially when there was a threat to security. The most spectacular example of this type of situation was the anti-Nazi coalition during World War II. After the war had ended and a new world order emerged, the contradictions between the partners of the coalition re-surfaced in all their intensity.[18]

In this case, the sphere of political culture clearly reflected how different were the systems of values of the two main adversaries in the international arena – the Soviet Union and the United States. The reconciliation of these fundamentally conflicting systems characteristic of the two superpowers proved to be impossible. The only solution would be an armed conflict or a collapse of one of the two actors in this game; the latter happened in the late 1980s and early 1990s with the dissolution of the USSR. The Russian Federation that emerged from the collapse of *imperium sovieticum* departed from the principles of political culture characteristic of the Soviet model. This required the country to resign from a number of axiomatic elements that had been a direct or indirect consequence of the system referred to as communist, which included the departure from the fundamental characteristics of the former political system, at first based on totalitarian models, and a subsequent development evolving towards the authoritarian model.[19] This translated into the foreign policy of the Russian Federation, which had to be

---

which revolutions were to be incited on a global scale, was thus abandoned as a threat to the further existence of the Soviet state.

17 An analysis of the political culture of the Soviet Union, with its implications for the strategic dimension, can be found, for example, in J. L. Snyder, The *Soviet Strategic Culture: The Implications for Limited Nuclear Options*, Santa Monica, CA 1977.

18 The American theoretician Morton Kaplan calls it a 'tight bipolar system', in which there was an extreme tension in the relations between these two superpowers. See: M. Kaplan, *System and Process in International Relations*, New York–London 1957.

19 There is a separate question whether a complete elimination of an existing political culture and replacing it with a different one is possible when a new political system is formed. It is a complex process, taking place in several stages. The remains of the previous political culture still exist and are gradually replaced by new values.

implemented in the new political configuration and in the search for a new, suitable place for Russia in international relations. What is important now is whether in these new internal and external conditions the Russian Federation will move on towards a new model of foreign relations or whether the deep-rooted imperial tradition will continue to play an important role in the actions of the Russian state, especially in the formulation of its political doctrine. This shows clearly the importance of political culture as well as political-strategic culture, which in the current conditions must seek new forms, but in a way that allows retaining the possibility of maintaining continuity in the realisation of the fundamental objectives reflected in the sphere of foreign policy.

The British and Russian examples point to the importance of political culture in the creation of foreign policy and in the formulation of strategic goals of countries in the changing internal and external conditions. Although the political systems of those countries whose political objectives took the imperialistic form differed substantially (democratic in the UK, authoritarian in Russia), in particular global orders there appeared a need to take into account adaptive measures to adjust to the changing conditions. In both cases it was about choosing the right kind of adaptation measures that would guarantee the realisation of the priorities stemming from the desire to safeguard the fundamental national interests. The main problem therefore became the question of how to adjust the traditional values to the new conditions. The Russian Federation, even at the moment of radical change and departure from the previously functioning political system (the transition from a monarchy to a communist regime, and then to the new model, after the dissolution of the Soviet Union), has retained those values that have been deeply rooted in the imperial tradition.

At this point, we could pose fundamental questions about the relations existing between political cultures and foreign policies of states. To what extent the system of values characteristic of a given political culture affects the process of shaping foreign policy, its directions, methods of decision-making as well as basic principles of the doctrine, and to what extent the internal and external environment of a country determines its system of values characteristic of the political culture? Is this a typical example of the model of interactions that by mutually influencing each other they lead to the emergence of a certain system of values, or is it rather the result of some independent determinants? The answer is not simple due to the fact that political culture is a multi-layered system in which it is impossible to simply identify elements that are permanent and not merely an effect of ad-hoc changes. The axiological sphere is particularly difficult to define unambiguously. Its presence in the foreign policy of states is most often undefinable and cannot be subjected to a fully rational analysis. The irrational factor may in fact occur in the political sphere and can influence the actions of states, and is also present in the doctrinal dimension of foreign policy.

Political culture as an element of international relations

Political culture analysed from the perspective of the foreign policy of a particular country can easily be correlated with the basic axiological factors that determine the external activities of states. A much more difficult task is analysing the factors related to political culture in the structure of international relations. This may concern their multi-layered character because there are various layers of international relations on the global, regional or sub-regional level.

This issue is fairly complex due to the nature of contemporary international relations. The basic problem concerns the question to what extent international relations are an autonomous structure that can be analysed as a whole, and to what extent they are derivatives merely reflecting the relations of individual countries, groups of countries or organisations and institutions in the international dimension. Political culture in the first meaning refers to states, pursuing their foreign policy by entering into various forms of international interactions.[20] It therefore concerns primarily the state level. We can also attempt to define the significance of political culture in relation to international structures.

In this respect, there appears the problem of the relationship between the whole and the part, namely, between international relations seen in the global context and its parts: countries, groups of countries, and international organisations. Mutual relations between these two spheres are complex, subject to certain internal conditions concerning individual countries or groups of countries as well as external conditions, related to regional systems or to the global system.

This issue can also be considered taking into account the dichotomous division into universalism and particularism. Both of these concepts apply to political culture. Political culture may implicitly refer to universal or particularistic elements. This concerns the nation state, whose external activity may show tendencies involving universal axiological elements, and on the other hand, it may also display tendencies resulting from the particularistic approach. A foreign activity

20 The term 'state' is, in this case, used in line with the traditional interpretation, as a political structure of a nation, equipped with the attributes of sovereignty and independence on the territory that it owns. Another most commonly named factor is the legal system characteristic of a given state. In this sense, international relations are understood as interactions between sovereign and independent states.

of the state can combine these two axiological elements depending on the political objective that it seeks to achieve on the international scene. Thus, in this case political culture may be considered to be a carrier of two axiological elements.

The particularistic dimension of political culture is directly reflected in the activities of states, mainly regarding the implementation of their national interests. In foreign activity, it is connected with striving to determine the priorities of foreign policy and its subsequent implementation. The ability of a state to achieve effects consistent with its objectives in the international sphere depends on a number of internal and external factors. Thus, the realisation of particularistic objectives of a state in the international sphere can lead to a clash of interests with other states. This may also reveal contradictions arising from the different patterns of political culture. These contradictions result, on the one hand, from the differences in their objectives in the international sphere, and on the other hand, from the differences reflected in their political cultures. Political culture in this case is related to a whole set of factors that shape the system of values of the given state, consolidated as a result of a complex historical process. It includes the stereotypes functioning in a given society about other countries, nations or ethnic groups. They can refer not only in relation to other countries but also to the international system in its different dimensions (regional, global).

We can also point to the differences that occur as a result of divisions in a given country because of differences in political systems, ideological principles and accepted cultural patterns. Hence, countries can differ substantially in their preferred model of political culture. These differences can also depend on what party or coalition of parties holds power in a given period and what system of values is considered the most important.

The political culture of a nation state also inherently includes the axiological elements that refer to a broadly defined dimension beyond the autonomous model of political culture associated primarily with native values. This means that even at the particularistic level some elements of the universal dimension can be found. The concepts of 'international relations', 'foreign policy', 'world order', etc. contain a reference to the non-particularistic context, pointing to transnational and supranational forms. This makes it necessary to take a particular position in relation to what occurs beyond the particularistic context but what may in a certain way be permanently embedded in the accepted axiological system.

This is a particularly complex issue, especially in the axiological dimension. A system of values that includes universal elements can apply to the international relations as a whole or only to the regional dimension. It has its source in preferences, with an inclination to one vision of the international order over another, derived from the accepted system of values arising from the traditions of the civilisation represented by the given state or states.

Against this background, there appears a broader issue, concerning the determinants of political culture related to civilisation. Political culture is not merely a function of the axiological principles underlying the system of values characteristic of a nation state but of much broader conditions that determine the sphere of values characteristic of a group of countries or regions, taking the form of values applicable on a broader, transnational scale. This means that the political culture of a nation state is to some extent also a function of these general determinants. In connection to this, there appears the fundamental problem of the importance of civilisation-related determinants of the emergence and influence of political culture in the general dimension, in other words in international relations.

Values related to civilisation can be understood as those that determine the attitudes and methods of operation of states belonging to a given civilisation. This means that the factor of civilisation may influence the way of acting in the international sphere through recognised and commonly accepted canons which are in conformity with the principles of the civilisation. Thus, in this case, political culture is understood as the effect of the influence of civilisation and is derived from the basic principles.

This issue is particularly important in the study of contemporary international relations in the context of the present universalist ideas as well as progressing globalisation. Universalist ideas stem from the roots of civilisations and, as such, are always derived from a certain system of values. Thus, universalism has particularistic foundations, which in certain cases aspire to play a global role and therefore, to cross the borders of one's own civilisation.

Terms such as 'global governance', 'world peace' or 'world government' refer to universal values that may be reflected in the global dimension. These terms stem from a particular civilisation. If we can assume that there are multiple civilisations, then these terms must refer to one of them. They cannot cover several civilisations at the same time. This, in turn, leads to the basic question of the relations between various civilisations.

The Western civilisation is defined as a set of values that emerged and developed in the European tradition and were subsequently transplanted – as a result of complex historical processes – into areas outside Europe.[21]

---

21 Geographically, Western civilisation, often called simply the West, covers Europe, the United States, Canada, Australia, and New Zealand. This shows that cultural space does not completely overlap with purely geographical divisions (into continents).

The West is, in this case, perceived as the representative of a particular set of values, which manifest themselves in various forms relating to particular dimensions of social life. In the socio-political dimension, this system is usually defined in the category of the liberal-democratic system, the category that is also considered a basis of Western political culture.

In the past, Western civilisation clearly dominated over the system of global relations. In addition to the political system based on democratic and liberal principles, the main carrier of expansion in global markets was the economic model of free-market economy. Finally, Western science and technology were equally important. The level of development of modern technology is directly related to the Western tradition stemming from European roots. The modern period has initiated a new type of European natural sciences, which in turn became the basis for a dynamic development of technology. Due to this technical and technological potential that the Western civilisation has been able to continuously expand.

The key question concerns the ability of the Western civilisation to use its significant position in the world to promote the liberal-democratic model and the type of political culture characterised by it. Every civilisation contains universal elements that form the basis for its identity. The universalism of Western civilisation has a significant power of influence, of going beyond its own system of values and seeking the opportunities to influence other civilisation systems. We may wonder whether it is actually possible that the Western civilisation and the political culture derived from it will manage to transplant its system of values to the global level. This would essentially mean the striving of Western civilisation to achieve a dominant position on the global scale and the consolidation of the principles of global relations based on the Western axiological model.

This leads to the fundamental question whether any civilisation is able to make its values global and to break the barriers separating civilisations. Is it a realistic process? Many researchers of civilisation are of the opinion that there is no interaction between civilisations which could lead to the replacement of their underlying values because this would violate the foundations of their identities. A civilisation exists only as long as the system of values lying at its core creates the conditions to maintain the civilisation's autonomy and is the foundation of its identity.

Every civilisation implicitly contains its own universal values that give it an autonomous character. The process of surrendering to foreign values must thus lead to the blurring of civilisational identity and to its gradual decline, hence interactions between civilisations cannot infringe on the basic systems of values lying at their core.[22] This does not exclude interaction and assimilation of certain solutions existing in other civilisations, but it means that they cannot violate civilisational identity.[23]

This thesis is reflected in the concept used by Samuel Huntington, the 'clash of civilisations'. According to Huntington, the advancing globalisation, by which he means the changes taking place in the economic, social and technological sphere of the modern world, does not eliminate the differences between civilisations. Although the importance of nation states is indeed declining, interregional or transregional relations are still characterised by civilisational differences.[24] This means that conflicts in the modern world will have mainly a cultural background and that is what the American author called the 'clash of civilisations'.

Taking this thesis as a starting point for the analysis of the importance of political culture in contemporary international relations, we can conclude that it is inherently anchored in the civilisational system. For example, Western civilisation has some homogeneous characteristics translating into its political culture despite the existing cultural differences between its countries. Assuming that the common feature of Western culture is a set of democratic and liberal political values, the political cultures represented by the individual states of this group and their foreign policies will also belong to this category.[25] By contrast, the countries that

---

22 A very characteristic example for this is when a number of substantial reforms was implemented in Japan in the 19th century, called the Meiji reforms, with the aim to adopt the technological achievements of the West in order to modernise the country. However, the process of modernisation was combined with maintaining the fundamental values characteristic of the historically developed Japanese civilisation. Thus, the modernisation covered the technological sphere and the ability to compete with the West but without changing the identity of Japanese culture.

23 Feliks Koneczny believes that there can be no exchange of values between civilisations, while it is possible in the sphere of cultural differences. Cultural values are subject to mutual influence and can lead to the emergence of hybrids. Such a process cannot take place in the conditions of functioning of a civilisation because it would effectively lead to its extinction.

24 S. Huntington, *The Clash of Civilizations and the Remaking of World Order*, Simon & Schuster, New York 2011, p. 20.

25 Francis Fykuyama's 'end of history' thesis was derived from the conviction that the political system based on democratic and liberal principles was universal and has no alternative. This happened after the fall of the Soviet Union and the transformations in the Eastern and Central-Eastern European countries. It is however controversial at least whether this thesis is defendable on the global scale. It would be, for example, contradictory to Huntington's assumptions. See: F. Fukuyama, *Koniec historii*, transl. T. Bieroń, M. Wichrowski, Kraków 2009.

can be qualified as belonging to other civilisations (Chinese, Indian, Japanese, or Islamic) link their political cultures with the axiological basis characteristics of the principles of their own civilisations.

Despite all those contradictions in the axiological dimension in the contemporary world, can we still find some common global elements that would be relevant from the point of view of global political culture? At this moment, there is no clear answer to this question. It depends on the further development of international relations as well as on the possibility of eliminating contradictions among civilisations. It would be difficult to predict at present if there is indeed a possibility that such a global concept will develop. What is more, there is also the equally important issue of the dominance of the Western civilisation in the models of future global solutions. It is also undoubtedly the factor that makes it difficult to develop a common, universal strategy of development and to construct a new type of international relations.

The original version of this text was published in the academic journal "Społeczeństwo i Polityka", no. 4, of 2012.

Bolesław Balcerowicz

Culture in the Military Sphere – From Strategic Culture to the Cultural Turn

Key words: strategic culture, cultural turn, security culture, Revolution in Military Affairs, cultural determinism.

Abstract: The ongoing debate on the presence of culture in strategic studies, in the art of war and in the sphere of military science has been dominated by two notions – strategic culture and the cultural turn. The article analyses these two concepts, that remain in a specific relation with the theories and approaches in the science of international relations.

The ongoing debate on the presence of culture in strategic studies, in the art of war and in the sphere of military science has been dominated by two notions – strategic culture and the cultural turn. The two notions and the two concepts behind them remain in a specific relation with the theories and approaches in the science of international relations.

The cultural turn in the sphere of military science and the art of war has been taking place only for a couple of years. It is perhaps not a coincidence that this has been a time when liberal arts and social sciences have been turning to the cultural paradigm in their lively debate on the anthropologisation of the humanities. Previously, it was the concept of strategic culture, which emerged only a quarter of a century ago, that was widely used in strategic studies. It was the answer to the need – a surprisingly narrow one from today's perspective – for a deeper analysis of the USSR's nuclear strategy.

The concept of strategic culture

The concept of strategic culture was meant to answer the question about 'the sum of ideas, conditioned emotional responses, and patterns of habitual behaviour that members of a national strategic community share with regard to nuclear strategy.' This was the first definition of strategic culture, formulated by Jack L. Snyder.[1] It is clear that with this definition Snyder opposed technological determinism,

1 First time in J. L. Snyder, *The Soviet Strategic Culture: Implications for Limited Nuclear Options*, Santa Monica, CA 1977; see also: http://www.rand.org/content/dam/rand/pubs/reports/2005/R2154.pdf (accessed on 18 April 2013).

which was at that time and for a long time thereafter the dominant notion in the sphere of military science, especially in the United States. As it turned out two decades later, he was not particularly successful because it was the technological determinism that became the foundation for the famous 'Revolution in Military Affairs' (RMA).

Soon, broader definitions of strategic culture emerged, which were not limited to behaviour regarding nuclear threats and strategic preferences of certain national communities. The one considered classic was presented by Alastair I. Johnston, who defined strategic culture as 'an integrated system of symbols (e.g., argumentation structures, languages, analogies, metaphors) which acts to establish pervasive and long-lasting strategic preferences by formulating concepts of the role and efficacy of military force in interstate political affairs, and by clothing these conceptions with such an aura of factuality that the strategic preferences seem uniquely realistic and efficacious.'[2] According to Johnston, the 'system of symbols' refers to two parts of strategic culture – the first one concerns the strategic environment that is the place and role of war in social life, as well as the nature of the enemy and the threats; the second one focuses on the conditions and means of using armed forces, on their abilities and effectiveness.

The scope of research of strategic culture includes:

- issues related to the perception of threats and reactions to them;
- concepts of national security;
- a debate on the role and place of the armed forces in society.

Regardless of the classic definitions of strategic culture and their 'capacity', their 'hard core' was in most cases formed by the perception of threats and the attitude towards the use of force. In its relatively short history, this concept underwent a dynamic development. Academic literature divides it into three periods, or three generations of strategic culture studies.[3]

Three generations of strategic culture studies

The first period roughly covers the 1970s, when scholars focused mainly on military issues, including the analysis of the superpowers' nuclear strategy. In the

---

2 A. I. Johnston, 'Thinking about strategic culture', *International Security*, Spring 1995, pp. 33–64.

3 Cf.: R. Wiśniewski, 'Kultura strategiczna czyli o kulturowych uwarunkowaniach polityki zagranicznej i bezpieczeństwa (Strategic Culture. On Cultural Factors in Foreign and Security Policy), *Przegląd Strategiczny*, no. 1, 2012.

1980s – the second generation of studies on this subject – strategic culture became an issue of interest also outside the scope of strategic studies, especially among the researchers dealing with international relations. From then on, it has been treated as a tool useful for understanding others, ourselves, and how others perceive us.[4] With this, it was becoming one of the research instruments useful in the science of international relations, which could be applied in the analysis of and devising of foreign and security policy. In the 1980s, a new trend emerged in the study of culture. It focused on issues related to the instrumental use of cultural models by political elites in order to shape specific attitudes and maintain legitimacy of policies using force. In this current, culture was treated as an illusion created by the elites (and needed by the elites). Although this approach has many weaknesses, unsolved (unsolvable) dilemmas, and even paradoxes, it still allows for additional interpretations of certain behaviours, which facilitate certain decisions and the development of strategies.

The third research movement appeared in the 1990s. It treats strategic culture as an independent variable explaining specific actions of states in international relations. This trend was characterised by a more disciplined and rigorous approach towards the research procedure and the research subject. The occasional focusing of the scope of research and limiting of the analysis of the sources of strategic culture to late modern history allowed this approach to achieve an increased usefulness of conceptions for empirical studies and case studies. On the one hand, the definitions of strategic culture formulated by this school exhibited a very important quality in terms of practical application – they could be operationalised. In the poststructuralist approach, on the other hand, strategic culture is not a variable that has influence on the decision-making process but only on the context of the processes discussed.[5]

Essentially, the said differences in the research approaches do not change the fact that strategic culture can neither be separated from culture in general nor from the concepts of national culture or political culture. It is hard to argue with Colin Gray, an eminent authority in the field of strategic studies, who stated that strategic culture is derived directly from political culture and that it is a part of it.

Owing to scholars such as Krzysztof Malinowski, 'safety culture' has been added to the set of already existing culture-related concepts needed for analyses in the field of military science. According to Malinowski, safety culture concerns

---

4 C. S. Gray, 'Comparative Strategic Culture', *Parameters*, Winter 1984, p. 26.

5 J. Glenn, 'Realism Versus Strategic Culture: Competition and Collaboration', *International Studies Review*, vol. 11, 2009, pp. 531–541.

the sphere of convictions shared by the society and by the political elites which refer to the security policy, i.e. its place in the international system; and in the narrower sense, to political aspects of the use of military power.[6] It is thus quite clear that this concept involves a definition with a broader objective scope. Its author treats strategic culture as a part of the safety culture, thus leaving it the beliefs and values that focus on the principles of using military power. Another scholar to use the notion of national security culture is Jan Czaja, in the book *Kulturowe czynniki bezpieczeństwa*.[7]

The development of the general concept of strategic culture was also accompanied by a process of its natural decomposition. Thomas G. Mahnken divided it into three levels: the national, the military and the one related to the types of armed forces. According to the author, the national level refers to the norms and values concerning the state in its surroundings and the circumstances of using armed forces. The military level of strategic culture is the national way of waging war. The lowest level is a culture characteristic of the individual types of armed forces.[8] With subsequent transformations, the concept of strategic culture has thus developed a complex network of notions which functions in a hierarchical system – just as it is the case with the above decomposition: From culture in general to the culture of organisation.

Functions of strategic culture

Studies of strategic culture have brought tangible results. As Roman Kuźniar writes, the most important results they have brought is the discovery of national styles of strategy originating from different national cultures – strategic cultures. It was an important achievement that strategic culture as a part of political culture

6 K. Malinowski, 'Kultura bezpieczeństwa narodowego, koncepcje i możliwości zastosowania' (National Security Culture – Concepts and Possible Applications), in K. Malinowski (ed.), *Kultura bezpieczeństwa narodowego w Polsce i Niemczech* (*National Security Culture in Poland and Germany*), Poznań 2003, p. 16.

7 However, Jan Czaja does not see any greater differences between strategic culture and national security culture. He writes that cultural strategy can be most generally referred to as national security culture (J. Czaja, *Kulturowe czynniki bezpieczeństwa* [*Cultural* Factors of Security], Kraków 2008, p. 227).

8 T. G. Mahnken, 'United States Strategic and Organizational Subcultures', in K. M. Kartchner, J. L. Johnson, J. A. Larsen (eds.), *Strategic Culture and Weapon of Mass Destruction*, New York 2009, pp. 70–78; see also: *United States Strategic Culture*, Report for Defense Threat Reduction Agency, http://www.au.af.mil/au/awc/awcgate/dtra/mahnken_strat_culture.pdf (accessed on 18 April 2013).

started to be treated as one of the elements shaping the strategic environment. The achievements of the studies on this issue include the identification of the functions of strategic culture listed by Kuźniar. Thus, cultural strategy:

- provides strategists and the politicians who set particular goals and tasks before strategists with ideas and norms;
- conditions the perception of the strategy's environment (internal policy and the international situation);
- constitutes a 'filter' through which the world and the processes taking place in it are viewed and evaluated;
- is the framework in which the selection of strategic options takes place;
- determines the capability to mobilise national goals for the purpose of goals set by strategy;
- sets the framework of the public debate on national security.[9]

The identification of the abovementioned functions of strategic culture is only one among the many academic achievements related directly to safety strategy and national strategies made by the researchers dealing with this subject. It should be noted, however, that in this case the concept essentially does not go beyond the framework of strategic studies.

Moreover, the concept of strategic culture proved to be an excellent tool for interpreting and understanding the subtleties of strategic documents published by states, especially since the norm of publishing national security strategies and defence strategies has been adopted within the framework of Confidence Building Measures. If we disregard the context of the political/strategic culture of the publishing state and do not apply a suitable 'filter', these documents are so similar that sometimes they do not say much about any specific strategy at all. On the other hand, however, after a careful examination we may notice some characteristic cultural peculiarities of a document's author or group of authors.[10] What is more, the concept related to national cultures can also be applied to international

---

9 R. Kuźniar, *Polityka i siła. Studia strategiczne – zarys problematyki* (*Politics and Force. Strategic Studies – An Outline*), Warszawa 2005, pp. 186–187.

10 They are the easiest to notice when one studies (closely) the strategic concepts of the Russian Federation but also of the United States, France, and the United Kingdom. The concept of strategic culture constitutes one of the key tools for the identification of state strategies during classes with IIR students titled 'Polistrategie wybranych państw' (Polystrategies of Selected States).

organisations, as shown by the attempts made by, among others, Robert Kupiecki to define the strategic culture of NATO.[11]

With its increasingly broader applications, the concept remained primarily 'in the service' of strategic studies and security policy. At the same time, its significance was also growing as a useful, original and attractive method of explainingthe behaviour of actors in the international arena. The concept, as previously stated, has also found its place among the instruments used for the interpretation of international relations. However, it has reached military practitioners with some difficulty. It has, in fact hardly left research centres, as it focused on the topmost level of analysis – the level of grand strategy. What we are lacking thus is a good translation into operational art and tactics. The results of studies of strategic culture were also insufficient to meet the growing needs of theory of war and military theory – the need to understand the nature and character of contemporary wars and armed conflicts. This need became almost dramatic after the Western failures in the wars in Iraq and Afghanistan.

Heralds of the cultural turn

After the Cold War, parallel to the development of the concept of strategic culture, there was also a boom in the theory of the art of war as well as in the studies of wars and armed conflicts. A natural impetus for this was caused by the emerging armed conflicts of a quite new character. Up to then, the first experiences with these conflicts had shown that there was a pressing need to conduct a critical – at least – review of the predominant theory explaining the etiology, anatomy and function of wars; a need to thoroughly review the theory of the art of war. In these circumstances and in response to this need, numerous theories started emerging in the 1990s. The first one among them that merits attention was the concept of civilisation waves by Alvin and Heidi Toffler, applied to warfare and military science.[12] The theory, which won universal renown and well-deserved recognition after the First Gulf War (1991), effectively ignores the cultural aspect of warfare. It defines civilisations in simple terms, through means of production, enrichment and destruction. It was one of the pillars on which the technocratic concept of the 'Revolution in Military Affairs' (RMA) was founded. Under the influence of the experience of the wars in Yugoslavia and the Caucasus the concept of 'new

---

11 R. Kupiecki, *Siła i solidarność. Strategia NATO 1949–1989* (*Force and Solidarity. NATO Strategy 1949–1989*), Warszawa 2009.

12 A. and H. Toffler, *War and Anti-War: Survival at the Dawn of the 21st Century*, Little Brown & Co 1993.

wars'has emerged, which not only notices but also emphasises the importance of cultural factors in contemporary armed conflicts.[13]

On the other hand, the influence of – or rather the fascination with – the American successes in the war with Iraq (1991) and the military operation in Yugoslavia (1999), conducted with no casualties of their own, gave rise to the popular (for a short time) 'theory' of virtual war. The attributes of such a war – a war of the future – were supposedly the invisibility and impunity of the attacker as well as the precision and effectiveness of strikes. The proponents of this theory announced that the time has come when finally wars could be won without the Clausewitzian 'friction' and 'fog of war'. Such a war was supposed to be waged (and always won!) by elite, godlike, virtually immortal and superbly armed professionals. As a result of the absence of any own casualties in the Kosovo War, the model was considered highly promising. For a short time, after 11 September 2001, the idea of virtual war was however put on hold.[14] The theory outrightly ignored the cultural aspect of warfare.

The need to identify and explain the sources and nature of contemporary conflicts and wars has been painfully demonstrated by the US' and its allies' failures in Iraq and Afghanistan. These failures were neither a result of a deficiency of potential, power or materiel supremacy necessary to overcome the foe, nor of a lack of the will to achieve victory. They were (and still are!) the consequence of intellectual and mental helplessness in the face of unexpected and inexplicable attitudes and behaviour of the local people, in the face of the strategy and tactics used by the enemies and their strategic culture. These circumstances caused an emergence of new theories, conceptions and ideas which were supposed to explain the phenomena encountered in contemporary warfare, especially during counterinsurgency wars. The theory that gained a certain measure of popularity was the theory of Fourth-Generation War (4GW), according to which the fourth generation wars were those in which various forms of armed uprisings were dominant – modernised through the modification of goals and the means used. In my opinion, this theory has not sufficiently dealt with the cultural aspect of warfare.

Some of the terms used most frequently in the recent years – and not only in the context of the art of war and strategy – include: 'asymmetry', 'asymmetric threats', 'asymmetric conflicts' or 'asymmetric warfare'. Asymmetry in military strategic studies refers to situations where we are dealing with incompatibility,

---

13 Cf.: M. Kaldor, *New and Old Wars: Organized Violence in the Global Era*, Stanford, CA 1999.

14 It was essentially buried, as Michael Ignatieff put it (M. Ignatieff, *Virtual War: Kosovo and Beyond*, London 2001).

disproportion or dissimilarity of the subjects of comparison.[15] It should be stressed that asymmetry is a notion which concerns both the material sphere, that is the measurable potential of the sides/entities, and the non-material sphere – the cultural dimension. The latter has not always been sufficiently appreciated. In the last decades, Americans and their allies have always been waging wars or conducting armed interventions in the conditions of asymmetry and asymmetric advantage. In these wars, materiel and technological supremacy proved of surprisingly little use. This naturally forced them to look for new solutions, strategies and concepts. In the United States, asymmetric threats and warfare became the focus of expert centres, centres of strategic studies and eminent strategists (e.g.: Lawrence Freedman, Anthony Cordesman) and all branches of the armed forces established specialised staff dealing with these issues. In the West, and in Poland as well, the fascination with asymmetry is virtually universal. Asymmetry and advantage are both omnipresent in the history of warfare. Academic literature on this subject is dominated by the belief that contemporary asymmetric conflicts/wars differ from the ones that preceded them in the scale of the asymmetry – the scale of the divergence of potentials, civilisation advancement (including technology), and cultural differences. Yet history has, indeed, already seen all this. Suffice to mention the conquests of the Americas and the colonial wars. The sense of 'newness' is rather a result of the fact that for several past generations, strategists focused principally on classic wars, wars which were more or less symmetrical.

One of the most recent American attempts to capture the nature or 'grammar' of contemporary warfare, which was to break the deadlock in military thought, is the concept of hybrid warfare and hybrid threats. Its starting point is the observation that, essentially, the common element of the emerging theoretical models of warfare is the dichotomous division into classical wars and irregular wars. The basis of the concept, in turn, is the assumption that contemporary wars are more complex, that they also include (and sometimes are largely composed of) elements which are incompatible, which make up a hybrid medley. The war hybrids described by the proponents of this concept did not pay due attention to cultural factors.

On the basis of his substantial experience, the British General Rupert Smith wrote about the decline of the classical paradigm of warfare. He contrasted the paradigm of industrial warfare with a new paradigm, one that suited the

---

15 Cf.: M. Madej, *Zagrożenia asymetryczne bezpieczeństwa państw obszaru transatlantyckiego* (*Asymmetrical Threats to the Security of Transatlantic States*), Warszawa 2007, p. 33.

contemporary reality, called 'war amongst the people'.[16] Although the elaborate (and promising) name of Smith's concept might lead us to believe that it involves a distinct cultural approach, the new paradigm of war fails to include cultural factors among the six major characteristics of the 'war amongst the people'.[17]

Cultural turn in military science

The cultural approach as a path to understanding the nature of armed conflicts and wars has finally found its place – and a central one at that – with the cultural turn in the sphere of military science. This significant change – a cultural turn, or a turn to culture – was determined by the pressing need to discover the fundamental reasons for continuously repeating failures of military operations, stabilisation missions and expeditionary actions undertaken by the United States (and its allies) against foes weaker by several levels of magnitude. The turn was also a (forced) reaction to the dramatic question voiced by the American society: 'Why they hate us?'[18]

Before we identify and describe the nature of the cultural turn, we should note that the cultural approach was present (and significant) in the studies of war and warfare much earlier, regardless of the trends and turns predominant in the given period. One of the proponents of treating wars as cultural phenomena was the British researcher John Keegan, who contested Clausewitz. Culture, he wrote, is the principal determinant of the nature of war, the way war is waged; culture is what drives wars.[19] Military historians enjoying universal recognition have not been underestimating the cultural factor either. Even the Europocentric *The Cambridge History of Warfare* by Geoffrey Parker starts with the following sentence: 'Every culture develops its own way of war'.[20] An important impetus that stimulated increased interest in the cultural dimension of armed conflicts was, undeniably, Samuel Huntington's concept of the 'clash of civilisations', later

---

16 R. Smith, *The Utility of Force: The Art of War in the Modern World*, New York: Knopf 2007.

17 For more on these and other deficiencies of the concept of General Smith see the review of his book by B. Balcerowicz, *Sprawy Międzynarodowe*, no. 3, 2010, pp. 142–148.

18 This and similar questions could also be seen on the covers of prestigious magazines – *Newsweek* and *Time*.

19 J. Keegan, *Historia wojen* (*A History of Warfare*), trans. from English by G. Woźniak, Warszawa 1998, pp. 35–71, 377–382; English ed.: J. Keegan, *A History of Warfare*, London 1993.

20 G. Parker (ed.), *The Cambridge History of Warfare*, Cambridge University Press, Cambridge 2005, p. 1.

usually reduced to the relation between the East and the West.[21] It should be noted that the attention of renowned authors writing about the cultural dimension of wars focused essentially on the differences between these wars. The Eastern way of waging war is described as more complex, refined, taking advantage of the full spectrum of conflict, including the mental and physical dimensions.[22] We should also remember that the cultural turn was preceded by a strong interest and fascination with the classic work by Sun Tzu.

The event accepted as the one that clearly marks the cultural turn in the art of war is the commencement of work on culture-centric warfare in 2004.[23] The work on this project pushed the concept of network-centric warfare, popular after the operations in Iraq and oriented at the use of technological achievements, to the background. The cultural turn in military science finally became a fact in the United States in 2006, when a field book on counterinsurgency warfare was published. The cultural dimension of actions thus has become one of the key principles of the American military doctrine.

The American version of the cultural turn is strictly pragmatic. Its idea translates into a series of specific actions, planned and coordinated by the staff. The main effort in the actions aimed at implementing the idea of the turn focuses on educating and training personnel. The curricula of American military academies now include a new set of subjects linked by the topic of cultural studies. Officers believe that the ability to understand and appreciate the influence of culture on politics and strategy is one of the critical strategic abilities. Headquarters and staffs implement a new element of the systemic approach to decision-making – The Analytical Cultural Framework for Strategy and Policy (ACFSP). This approach is to ensure that the world is perceived from various angles.[24]

---

21 Note the much telling title (and content) of the book: T. Camous, *Orients/Occidents, 25 siècles de guerres* (*East/West: 25 Centuries of War*), Paris: Presses Universitaires de France 2007.

22 For more see: P. Bracken, *Fire in the East: The Rise of Asian Military Power and the Second Nuclear Age*, New York: Harper Collins 1999. The symbol of Eastern warfare is, according to the author, a bow and arrow; a bow, which is by nature a transitory weapon, and an invisible archer.

23 One of the fathers of this conception was General Robert Scales, who in the 1990s was the head of a team tasked with developing the model of a future fighting force, the Army After Next.

24 For more see: J. Kim (ed.), *Cultural Dimensions of Strategy and Policy*. Report of the Army War College, http://www.strategicstudiesinstitute.army.mil/pdffiles/PUB919.pdf (accessed on 19 April 2013).

Anthropology in the service of the military

The idea of providing anthropological support to the troops has found a pragmatic application. In 2006, the Pentagon established a team including a large number of cultural anthropologists, which was to develop a special intelligence support system – the Human Terrain System (HTS), with the task of obtaining data and knowledge about the cultural environment in given areas. Intelligence services, in turn, implemented the concept of Ethnografic Intelligence (EI). Yet another interesting fact, showing the importance ascribed to the cultural turn in the United States, is that the head of the section of the Department of States which deals with counterterrorism has a PhD in political anthropology.

The turn is taking place in the context of a lively discussion, which is heavily influenced by the opinions of experienced generals. One officer quoted particularly often is general Robert Scales – the initiator of the concept of culture-centric warfare. Another one, whose views bear particular weight due to his experience from Iraq and Afghanistan, is general David Petraeus.[25] The participants of the debate include such well known and renowned researchers, scholars, analysts and writers as: Colin Gray, Jack Snyder, Alastair I. Johnston, or Patrick Porter. Robert Kaplan, a veteran 'chronicler' accompanying American military expeditions and dedicated proponent of the cultural approach also voices his opinions[26]; the experience of the legendary Thomas E. Lawrence in the Arab revolt against the Ottoman Empire is quoted quite often as well. A topic which frequently surfaces in the discussion is also Keegan's paradigm of warfare, antithetical to Clausewitz's argument. It treats war as a cultural phenomenon; as culture expressed by different means or even a continuation of culture.[27] The turn has also bore fruit in the form of several significant monographs. One of the most representative ones is the book by Jeremy Black, a famous warfare historian, titled *War and the Cultural Turn* and published in 2012.[28]

The aid of anthropology and anthropologists is widely used in the development of culture-centric conceptions and for providing background support to military

---

25 His authority is also connected to the well-known 'Petraeus Doctrine' of culture-centric counterinsurgency.

26 He argues that Herodotus's ethnographic tales about alien cultures are a better guide to understanding the nature of wars than Thucydides's attempts to identify the rules governing warfare. See: R.D. Kaplan, 'A historian for our time', *Atlantic Monthly*, January–February 2007, pp. 78–84.

27 J. Keegan, *A History...*

28 J. Black, *War and the Cultural Turn*, Cambridge, UK–Malden, MA 2012.

actions. This evokes diverse reactions in academic circles. Critics of this relationship have been writing about an unacceptable use of this discipline in the service of the Pentagon, about using it to further the goals of the Bush administration and support actions which resemble police operations conducted in colonies. In extreme cases, the researchers working with the military have been even called mercenary anthropologists. These ethical dilemmas of anthropologists are probably well justified; the rising tide of the cultural turn in the sphere of military science gives rise to a new entity in the United States which comprises of at least a few non-state corporations supporting the Pentagon. At this point, however, we should note that the relationship between science and warfare has a long history and scientific achievements have always been used by the armed forces to gain advantage on the battlefield.[29] Therefore, we should treat the problems and dilemmas faced by anthropologists with understanding and recall the quandary that nuclear physicists were in a few decades ago.

The terms 'militarisation of culture' and 'militarisation of anthropology' appearing in the said debate evoke highly diverse associations and emotions. Thus formulated, these expressions do not adequately reflect the nature of the relations taking place at the intersection of culture/anthropology and warfare. A syntactic analysis of these expressions leads to a rather absurd image of militarised culture/ anthropology, while what we are actually dealing with is the opposite, something we could call the 'culturalisation' of military science. Even though the term 'militarisation of culture' has already been adopted by Polish academic literature (*militaryzacja kultury*) it would be wise to avoid it, since it has rather ambiguous connotations. However, in the armed forces we are dealing with something that we should be rather referring to as 'operationalisation of culture',[30] as the evaluation of the cultural factor is becoming one of the elements of the classic, routine, staff-level situation assessment – the evaluation of the circumstances and environment where military operations are conducted.

29 Cf. e.g.: E. Volkman, *Science Goes to War: The Search for the Ultimate Weapon, from Greek Fire to Star Wars*, New York: Wiley 2002; A. and H. Toffler, *War…*

30 For more on 'militarisation of culture' and 'operationalisation of culture' in the concept of intercultural awareness in the armed forces see e.g.: H. Schreiber, *Świadomość międzykulturowa. Od militaryzacji antropologii do antropologizacji wojska* (*Cross-Cultural Awareness. From the Militarisation of Anthropology to the Anthropologisation of the Military*), Warszawa 2013.

Between Sun Tzu and Clausewitz

In the cultural turn, which concerns a broad spectrum of the functioning of armed forces and which endavoursto understand the nature of contemporary armed conflicts, the centre of attention lies in the issues of insurgency and counterinsurgency operations. This comes of no surprise given that in the recent decades, the Westhas only been involved in expeditionary wars in which it has usually faced enemies employing guerrilla tactics and strategies. In the US, in turn, the 'Global War on Terrorism' is being replaced by the global problem of counterinsurgency, or even a 'global counterinsurgency'.[31]

In the pragmatic undertakings of the cultural turn, a lot of attention is paid to developing cultural and intercultural awareness. This awareness plays an important role in stabilisation operations, and even the key role in nation building operations. While the state and its society are being rebuilt, it is not only the troops involved (usually too excessively) that have to exhibit cultural and intercultural awareness. Thus, this problem is not limited to the sphere of military science. What we need first is a cultural turn in politics.

Cultural interpretation of conflicts and wars has a certain weak point. Contrasting the philosophies of Sun Tzu and Clausewitz involves several simplifications. Sun Tzu's concept is less specific than its interpretations as it includes also ideas other than the Eastern ones. Suffice to compare it with, for instance, Machiavelli's pragmatism. Even Clausewitz, the European classic whose thought is considered to be the opposite of the ancient Chinese thinker's vision, indeed wrote about such phenomena in wars as guerrilla warfare in Napoleonic Spain and non-European tactics of the Tatars. In the 'paradigmatic' sphere of the cultural turn we find many simplifications as well. Culture is far too often treated without sufficiently taking into account its diversity and the changes taking place in it; as a monolith, a static entity.[32] It is not difficult to get utterly deceived by myths and simplifications, as noted by Alastair Johnston in his analysis of the Chinese strategic culture.[33]

A turn signifies a radical change, a departure from 'the old' to 'the new'. In science, it signifies a change of paradigm. The cultural turn in the sphere of military science, in the art of war, is a departure from technological determinism. At this

31 For more on 'global counterinsurgency' see: J. D. Kelly et al. (eds.), *Anthropology and Global Counterinsurgency*, Chicago 2010.

32 For more on this issue see: P. Porter, 'Good anthropology, bad history: The cultural turn in studying war', *Parameters*, Summer 2007, pp. 45–58.

33 A. I. Johnston, *Cultural Realism. Strategic Culture and Grand Strategy in Chinese History*, Princeton 1998.

point, we should ask ourselves the question whether a turn involves replacing one determinism with another. Attempts at a thorough redefinition of the classical (Clausewitzian) paradigm of war or even at negating it, which appear on the rising tide of the cultural turn, should be approached with a large amount of caution. For the cultural paradigm is but an added value of sorts here; it is applied in order to fill the gaps (considerable ones) in the interpretations of the phenomenon of war. The cultural approach as an analytical and descriptive approach is a very useful tool in the history of the art of war, but as Jeremy Black stresses, mainly as the context for alternative analytical matrices, such as technology.[34] It is far too often that the paradigm-related debate involves an immature and completely false polarisation into the children of Clausewitz attached to the principle of advantage and decisive battles on the one side of the fence, and on the other the acolytes of Sun Tzu who prefer more elaborate (Eastern!) methods of warfare and indirect actions.

Conclusion

The Revolution in Military Affairs (RMA), oriented at hastening the progress in the field of technology, has not lived up to expectations. Although its legacy includes many valuable ideas which have changed warfare, the RMA itself seems to have been forgotten after the announcement of the cultural turn. The cultural turn clearly signifies a departure from technological determinism, or at least from its dominance, and it involves, as it has already been mentioned, the risk of replacing one determinism with another. A turn in the form of another revolution could easily become a counterrevolution. Every revolution (and counterrevolution) is best approached with cold reserve, but cultural revolutions (and cultural turns) should be approached even more carefully.

The cultural turn in strategic studies, the art of war, military science, is a part (although relatively delayed) of a broader cultural turn in the humanities, where scholars depart from the long-lasting dominance of objectivist approaches modelled after the natural sciences in favour of anthropologisation.

The original version of this text was published in the academic journal "Społeczeństwo i Polityka", no. 4, of 2012.

---

34 J. Black, *War...*

Edward Haliżak

Culture and the Study of International Relations

Key words: Josif Lapid, international society, cultural turn, strategic culture, cultural identity.

Abstract: The aim of this chapter is to investigate the explanatory role of culture in IR studies. It represents an approach called 'cultural turn'. We argue that culture should be treated as an independent variable in explaining the behavior of states and the structure of the international system. Culture is indispensable for better understanding the complex relationships of diverse communities at all levels of analysis of IR.

The aim of this article is to answer the question whether culture can be helpful in explaining the nature of international relations, and if yes, to what extent. This has been one of the most frequently posed research questions in the discipline of international relations for more than two decades now and the significance of the question is sufficient enough for scholars to speak of a 'cultural turn' in the study of international relations. The turn was initiated in the early post-Cold War years, that is the 1990s, and resulted from the belief common at that time, that military power would no longer play such an important role as in the Cold War era and that it was the time to take advantage of the peace dividend. As a result, it was only natural that researchers started to formulate views on the need for new research approaches and for greater attention paid to the role of values, ideas, norms, identities, and culture. The first ones to note this were Judith Goldstein and Robert Keohane, in their work published in 1993.[1]

In a work on the cultural turn published three years later, which was of fundamental importance for the discipline, Yosef Lapid wrote that culture and identity were experiencing a dramatic return to social theories and practice towards the end of the 20th century.[2] In the same year, in a joint publication dedicated to the culture of national security, Peter Katzenstein said: 'security interests are defined

1 J. Goldstein, R. Keohane, *Ideas and Foreign Policy: Beliefs, Institutions and Political Change*, Ithaca: Cornell University Press, 1993.

2 Y. Lapid, 'Culture's Ship: Returns and Departures in International Relations Theory', in Y. Lapid, F. Kratochwil (eds.), *The Return of Culture and Identity in International Relations Theory*, London: Lynne Rienner, 1996, p. 3.

by actors who respond to cultural factors'.[3] Furthermore, one of the most important publications of the 1990s dealing with the role of culture in international relations was a work by Christian Reus-Smith. The author took advantage of the historical-comparative method to answer the question regarding the four historical systems of international relations (Ancient Greece, Italy of the Renaissance, Europe of absolutist monarchies, and the contemporary system of international relations). He asked why is it, that these states that lacked a sense of security and stability due to international anarchy, consequently established completely different international institutions.[4]

The importance ascribed to cultural explications is further proven by two great political and intellectual debates that emerged in the early post-Cold War era. The first one was connected with the discussion on the sources of the economic success of East-Asian countries. It was soon recognised that it was simply impossible to identify its reasons without taking into account the Confucian tradition and the related cultural and civilisational determinants. Taking into account the specific ways of governing this area, the concept of East-Asian capitalism is in general as much of an economic category it is a cultural one.[5] The second of the two fundamental debates, initiated by Samuel Huntington's work on the paradigm of the clash of civilisations,[6] referred to the cultural and civilisational criteria to an even greater extent, making them the primary criterion of identity, dispute and conflict in contemporary international relations. It thus became common, or even trendy to invoke the following statement made by the British researcher Martin Wight: 'We must assume that a state and system will not come into being without a degree of cultural unity among its members.'[7]

3 P. Katzenstein, 'Introduction: Alternative Perspectives on National Security', in P. Katzenstein (ed.), *The Culture of National Security: Norms and Identity in World Politics*, New York: Columbia University Press, 1996, p. 2.

4 Ch. Reus-Smith, *The Moral Purpose of the State. Culture. Social Identity and institutional rationality in international Relations*, Princeton: Princeton University Press, 1999, pp. XI–XII.

5 See e.g.: Ch. Johnson, *MITI and Japanese Miracle: The Growth of Industrial Policy 1925–1975*, Stanford 1982; L. W. Pye, M. W. Pye, *Asian Power and Politics: The Cultural Dimensions of Authority*, Cambridge: Cambridge University Press, 1985; Chen Chung, J. Sheppard, M. Dollinger, 'Max Weber Revisited: Some Lessons from East Asian Capitalistic Development', *Asia–Pacific Journal of Management*, no. 2, 1992, pp. 310–325.

6 S. Huntington, *The Clash of Civilizations and the Remaking of the World Order*, New York: Simon and Schuster, 1997.

7 M. Wight, *System of States*, Leicester: Leicester University Press, 1977, p. 33.

The growing interest in the cultural factor in international relations proves that an increasing number of researchers appreciate its cognitive and explanatory advantages as compared to the material factors, which have traditionally been ascribed the leading role in the analysis of state behaviour and the development and functioning of international structures. Realism – one of the main theories in the discipline of international relations – considers the objectively countable parameters of state power and the international distribution of power to be the most important explanatory criteria. This is especially true of structural realism.[8] As noted by the prominent British researcher Andrew Hurrell, 'material structures matter, but these material structures cannot be understood outside of the shared knowledge and shared understandings held by the actors themselves. Among these shared understandings and inter-subjective knowledge, norms and institutions play a number of fundamental roles.'[9] This approach accentuates the fact that cultural values, aspirations, ideas, convictions or perceptions play an important role in the understanding of the material parameters of power. This kind of approach in the study of international relations focuses on the changes in the behaviour of states in terms of identity and values, and argues that these changes cannot be explained using only material criteria. The father of the constructivist theory of international relations, Alexander Wendt, believes that in this case, we need to consider using the logic of appropriateness in explication.[10]

The fact that the cultural factor is appreciated in the study of international relations does not at all imply that there is a commonly accepted set of rules and research methods that would unambiguously situate its role in the research process of this field of social relations. The essence of the problem is that cultural science researchers usually have little knowledge about the nuances of the functioning of international relations. On the other hand, scholars who consider themselves researchers of international relations generally do not appreciate the significance of the cultural factor because they are too attached to the paradigm of power politics or, at best, treat it as one of many variables andwhat is more, unfortunately they tend not to be well-versed in the nature of cultural phenomena and processes. Generally speaking, we need to consider how to operationalise the notion of culture in the study of international relations in theoretical and methodological terms. Essentially, it is about showing to the extent to which the issues

---

8 K. Waltz, *Theory of International Politics*, New York, Random House, 1979.

9 A. Hurrel, 'Norms and Ethics in International Relations', in W. Carlsness, T. Rise, B. Simmons (eds.), *Handbook of International Relations*, Los Angeles: Sage, 2010, p. 142.

10 A. Wendt, *Społeczna teoria stosunków międzynarodowych* (*Social Theory of International Relations*), Warszawa: Scholar, 2008, pp. 112–114.

of international relations are present in the fields of study of other disciplines and what instruments used by these disciplines can be consequently used in the study of international relations. With regard to the interdisciplinary approach, we must redefine the concepts taken from other disciplines, taking into account the context and specificity of international relations.[11]

Bearing the above in mind, in this chapter the author shall propose the following solution to the above research problem. First, as already mentioned, the general goal is to present the role of culture as a factor (variable) in every phase of the research process, i.e. in description, explication and prediction of international relations. Second, invoking the general principles of the philosophy of science, the author will try to show the significance of culture in the structure of knowledge about international relations, i.e. taking into account the fields of ontology, epistemology and methodology. Third, the author will present the role of culture on various levels of analysis of international relations, which is a commonly applied research procedure in international relations studies. This concerns three fundamental levels of analysis: a) the level of the individual, b) the level of states – the subsystem level, c) the level of the international system (the global and/or regional dimension).

The ontological dimension of culture in international relations

Let us recall that according to Wendt, the issue of ontology refers to how we should analyse that which is happening when actors interact with each other. Considering something *a priori* is necessary in every explication due to the simple fact that nobody can treat everything as a problem at the same time. As a consequence, differences in opinion are inevitable on the ontological level, even when it comes to facts – as all the facts that we gather will be pervaded with ontological assumptions as to what we perceive, which in turn is very difficult to classify.[12]

Different ontologies exist primarily because of a lack of a uniform and commonly accepted conceptual network. With regard to the sphere of international relations, on the levels of systems and subsystems (foreign policy) there is a set of accepted concepts and terms that are agreed upon, although they exhibit a

11 See: E. Haliżak, A. Gałganek, M. Pietraś (eds.), *Wielo- i interdyscyplinarność nauki o stosunkach międzynarodowych* (*Multi- and Interdisciplinarity of the Study of International Relations*), Warszawa: Polish Society of International Studies, Rambler, 2012, p. 12.

12 A. Wendt, *Społeczna teoria…*, pp. 42–43.

considerable degree of generalisations. These are: power, balance of power, security, raison d'État and national interest.

This in turn concerns also the understanding of international relations, which are usually defined as a form of social relations, i.e. the relations between nations, comprised of individuals.[13]

This operational definition of international relations subsequently directs our attention to its cultural and social dimension. The nation, organised in the form of a state institution, is as much of a political concept as it is a cultural phenomenon; the notion of national culture (Polish: *kultura narodowa*), is reffered to by the Polish researcher Antonina Kłosowska as a universe shared by a given community that cannot be learned or understood without taking into account the individual processes of its internal experience by the members of this community, because national culture is an intersubjective phenomenon realising itself subjectively and confronted with objective facts.[14]

The criterion of defining international relations as intercultural international relations is as much justified as international politics, not to mention international economics. There are countless international declarations and agreements calling for the recognition of cultural determinants and differences between states in their relations with others.[15] The common belief that the dominant attribute of international relations is that they are political seems false from the ontological point of view and can be falsified in every space-time situation. The very term 'international relations' confirms the significance of the cultural perspective when we consider their definition as 'relations between nations' – this essentially differentiates it from inter-state relations. Furthermore, these relations exist, above everything else, between nations with national identities shaped by historical processes.[16] Moreover, these identities actually develop noton the basis of endogenous factors but rather on the basis of exogenous ones, because they develop largely during interactions between national communities and the outside world through an acceptance, internalisation or rejection of foreign values. Only on this

---

13 W. Landecker, 'The Scope of Sociology of International Relations', *Social Forces*, no. 2, 1938, p. 175.

14 A. Kłoskowska, *Kultury narodowe u korzeni* (*National Cultures at the Roots*), Warszawa: PWN, p. 79.

15 See e.g. the UN report: *Global Report on Human Development*, New York: UNDP.

16 See: A. Kłoskowska, 'Tożsamość i identyfikacja narodowa w perspektywie historycznej i psychologicznej' (National Identity and Identification in the Historical and Psychological Perspetive), *Kultura i społeczeństwo*, no. 1, 1992.

basis can state institutions be formed.[17] An adequate illustration of this process is the Prague Slavic Congress held in March 1848. In the speech delivered at the event, the representative of the Czech Republic stated that he was a Czech of Slavic heritage and that with all he possessed he dedicated himself entirely to serve his nation and that even though his nation might be small, since time immemorial it has had its own separate character regardless of who was ruling it at a given time.[18]

Furthermore, while we recognise the culture-derived significance of identity as an important criterion for the formation of international relations,[19] we should also mention the three specific aspects of this influence:

a) in the sphere of axiology of international relations, which is derived from culture;
b) on the subsystem level, that is on the level of foreign policy of states;
c) on the system level – international relations.

In the assumptions concerning the relation between culture and international relations on the level of ontology one simply cannot omit the normative sphere. It is a key issue for the identification of the specificity of international relations because the normative analysis involves passing judgement on the behaviour of states, evaluating the state of the relations between them and the international order. A problem closely related to this is the recognition of norms as binding and important as well as their hierarchy in international relations.

There are three important principles originally derived from the sphere of culture and given the attribute of politicality in the next sequence. The first one is the principle of equality, which plays a key role in the catalogue of values determining the functioning of international relations because:

- as an ethical principle, it determines the relations between states;
- as a principle and norm of international law, it affects the rules of state action;
- it opposes the phenomenon of inequality and development-related disproportions in international relations.

The second value, commonly accepted as universal, is justice in international relations, which originates in the philosophy of Thomas Hobbes and – in present times – John Rawls. The two types of justice distinguished are formal justice and

---

17 See: E. Haliżak, I. Popiuk-Rysińska (eds.), *Państwo we współczesnych stosunkach międzynarodowych* (*The State in Contemporary International Relations*), Warszawa: Scholar, 1995.
18 H. Kohn, *Pan-Slavism. Its History and Ideology*, New York: Vintage-Books, 1960.
19 See: M. Castells, *The Power of Identity*, Oxford: Oxford University Press, 1997.

concrete justice.[20] Hedley Bull, one of the fathers of the concept of social justice and the pioneer of the English school of international relations, considered international justice to be the most important value constituting this community and, consequently, distinguished the following varieties: general, particular, substantive, formal, arithmetical, proportionate, commutative, and distributive justice.[21] In the academic literature on the subject, international justice is associated with notions such as human rights,[22] the functioning of international trade – the principle of fair trade[23] as well as the development-related disproportions in world economy.[24]

However, the most frequently declaredand hence the most often analysed international value is peace. It is considered a necessary condition for survival of all participants in international relations. The classic researcher of these issues, Johan Galtung, distinguished negative peace, which he understood as the lack of military, political and cultural threats, and positive peace – actions aiming towards the elimination of all forms of violence, i.e. direct personal violence, structural violence and cultural violence.[25] In the studies of peace, the key notion is the 'culture of peace', understood as the conditions and criteria for ensuring lasting peace and preventing war. Two decades after the end of the Cold War, the thesis of democratic peace, referring to the cultural context, has made a stunning career.[26]

Another set of assumptions concerns the role of culture in the international activity of states, which is usually analysed in terms of actions and influence of nation states treated as political entities. Under this approach, the cultural context

---

20 See: E. Kornaś, *Sprawiedliwość międzynarodowa* (*International Justice*), Kraków: Wydawnictwo UJ, 1983.

21 H. Bull, *The Anarchical Society: A Study of Order in World Politics*, London: Macmillan, 1977, pp. 74–94; H. Bull, 'Order vs. Justice in International Society', *Political Studies*, vol. xix, no. 3, September 1971, pp. 269–283.

22 See e.g.: G. Best, 'Justice. Community and Human Rights', *International Affairs*, no. 4, 1995, pp. 774–799.

23 See e.g.: E. Weisband, *Poverty amidst Plenty. World Political Economy and Distributive Justice*, Boulder: Westriev Press, 1989.

24 See: J. Clark, *Worlds Apart. Civil Society and the Battle for Ethical Globalization*, London: Earthscam, 2003.

25 J. Galtung, 'Violence. Peace and Peace Research', *Journal of Peace Research*, no. 3, 1969, pp. 167–191; *Idem*, 'Cultural Violence', *Journal of Peace Research*, no. 3, 1990, pp. 291–305.

26 See e.g.: Ch. Layne, 'Kant or Cant: The Myth of Democratic Peace', *International Security*, no. 2, 1994, pp. 4–49; S. Rosato, 'The Flawed Logic of Democratic Peace, Theory', *American Political Science Review*, no. 4, 2003, pp. 568–585.

is considered secondary. If we assume that states come down to national cultures, this fundamentally changes the perception of the international activity: foreign cultural policy, cultural diplomacy, public diplomacy, or soft power policy.[27]

The assumption concerning the role of culture on the level of the international system is based on rejecting the concept of 'global culture' as the ontological basis of international relations, which was promoted after the end of the Cold War and treated as the symbol of modern globalisation.[28] Instead, it would be more adequate to use the term 'cultural forces in world politics',[29] which coexists with political or economic forces – to mention only the most important ones. This constitutes a basis for the delimitation of international cultural relations as one of the fields of international relations in terms of actors and scope.[30]

While appreciating the significance of the cultural dimension in international relations, we should reject the thesis of cultural determinism, characteristic of the colonial era of cultural imperialism. John Stuart Mill, an eminent British scholar of the 19th century, wrote that the laws and norms of civilised nations could not be applied in the relations with non-civilised nations.[31] However, the theses of a clash of civilisations formulated by certain American scholars who consider the Western system of values universal sound equally false.[32] The growing popularity of the post-colonial theoretical perspective proves that the fear of Western cultural domination is strong.[33]

Guided by the principle of cognitive holism, we can formulate two theses concerning the ontology of culture on the subsystem and system levels.

First, in their international activity, states are guided by three equally important goals of existential nature which determine their survival and functioning

---

27 See: J. Nye. 'Soft Power: The Means to Success in World Politics', *Public Affairs*, New York, 2004; J. Manheim, *Strategic Public Diplomacy: The Evolution of Influence*, New York: Oxford University Press, 1990.

28 A. Smith, 'Toward a Global Culture?', in M. Featherstone (ed.), *Theory. Culture and Society*, Newbury Park: Sage Publications, 1990, pp. 171–193.

29 See: A. Mazrui, *Cultural Forces in World Politics*, London: Heinemann, 1990.

30 See the two important works on the subject in Polish academic literature: G. Michałowska, *Zmienność i instytucjonalizacja międzynarodowych stosunków kulturalnych* (*The Changeability and Institutionalisation of International Cultural Relations*), Warszawa 1991; A. Ziętek (ed.), *Międzynarodowe stosunki kulturalne* (*International Cultural Relations*), Lublin: Wyd. UMCS, 2011.

31 See. J.S. Mill, *Utylitaryzm, O Wolności* (*Utilitarism. On Liberty*) Warszawa 2005, p. 199.

32 S. Huntington, 'The Clash of Civilizations?', *Foreign Affairs*, vol. 72, 1993, pp. 22–49.

33 P. Darby, A. Paolini, 'Bringing International Relations and Postcolonialism', *Alternatives*, vol. 19, 1994, pp. 371–394.

in international relations: power (politicality), wealth (economy) and the identity (culturality) formulated in the process of contrasting 'us' and 'them'. In different states and in different space-time circumstances, the hierarchy of these goals is different as well, and as a result we speak of 'military powers', 'economic powers' or 'cultural powers'.

The starting point for our discussion is the reflection on the nature of states as subjects of international relations from the cultural perspective. Some scholars that study international relations believe that their sole attribute is politicality. This, however, is an example of dangerous reductionism which leads to a cognitive 'dead-end' and implies a totalitarianism of thought through the suggestion that scientific cognition is based on political valuation.[34] In such a case, determining whether an approach is scientific or not becomes a function of political valuation. Second, in international relations – i.e. on the system level – there is an equality of interactions of a political, economic and cultural nature. This regularity manifests itself through the conditions of contemporary globalisation of international relations and is pointed out by prominent researchers such as Ulrich Beck, who stated the following: 'the ideological core of globalism is that a basic difference of the first modernity is hereby liquidated, that is, the difference between politics and economics. [...] Globalism implies that a complete structure such as Germany – its state, its society, its culture, its foreign policy – can be run in the way that a company is run.'[35] Furthermore, in another essential work on globalisation, its authors invoke the following statement by the German researcher Klaus von Beyme: 'The knowledge that everything is politics leads us astray if it is not supplemented with the insight that everything is also economics or culture.'[36] Also in Poland there are scholars who perceive international relations as a cultural, economic and political reality.[37]

In the ontological aspect, the place of culture in international relations can be imagined as a three-part structure – a regular triangle, the vertices of which represent politics, economy and culture.

34 This method of research is characteristic of post-communist scholars in Poland.

35 U. Beck, 'What is Globalization?', in D. Held, A. McGrew (eds.), *The Global Transformation Reader*, Polity Press, 2000, p. 100–101.

36 After: U. Beck, A. Giddens, S. Lash, *Reflexive Modernisation. Politics, Tradition and Aesthetics in the Modern Social Order*, Stanford: Stanford University Press, 1994, p. 34.

37 R. Zenderowski, *Stosunki międzynarodowe. Vademecum* (*International Relations. A Vademecum*), Wrocław: Altaz, 2006, p. 15.

Figure 1: Graphical representation of the place of culture in the ontology of international relations.

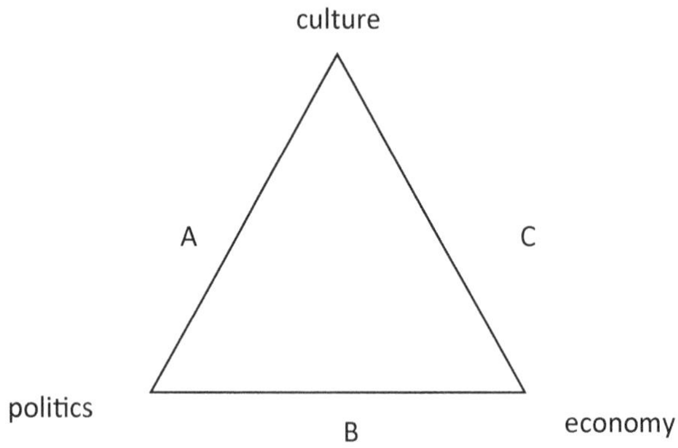

Source: Own compilation

In this model, culture is one of the aspects of international relations, equal to politics and economics and remains in bilateral, mutual interactions which consequently allow for the identification of the problems, phenomena and processes closely connected with the sphere of culture.

The A-type relation draws our attention to the relation between politics and culture on the subsystem and system levels, which is manifested as, for example, the cultural determinants of national and international security, strategic culture, foreign cultural policy, cultural diplomacy as well as the cultural determinants of the decision-making processes.

The B-type relation signifies the convergence of the spheres of politics and economics, which constitutes international political economy (IPE).

The C-type relation concerns the relations between the processes of governance and the sphere of culture. The significance of this issue is reflected in the debate on whether capitalism is an economic phenomenon or a cultural and civilisational one.[38]

From the point of view of our research objectives in this chapter, the most essential relations are those between A and C. Due to their explicitly delimited actors and substantive scope they can be treated as materialist ontology – if we adopt either the positivist or the fundamentalist point of view, that is, if we perceive

38 See e.g.: L. Greenfeld, *The Spirit of Capitalism: Nationalism and Economic Growth*, New York: Harvard University Press, 2001.

reality as independent from us; a reality that we can study by observing and quantifying empirical facts and trying to establish the relations of cause and effect between them – it is in this way that we prove that we have empirical sensitivity.

Epistemology

On the level of ontology, we ask what about the nature of the real world but on the level of epistemology, we ask how we can study it. This involves choosing a specific theoretical model. The problem of studies of international relations is that they offer redundant research instruments in the form of competing theories. The three most important mainstream theories are: realism, liberalism and constructivism. In the mid-1980s, Kalevi J. Holsti described the discipline of international relations as a dividing one.[39] According to Margaret Herman, this makes it more difficult for the community of scholars studying international relations to communicate.[40] On the other hand, there is a considerable group of researchers who argue that the development of competing theories, approaches and pragmatic debates in the discipline of international relations should be interpreted as scientific progress,[41] because the ontology, epistemology, methodology, and their conceptualisation does not exclude, but rather complements each of them.[42]

It is a positive feature of theoretical pluralism that every theory approaches a given problem in its own way and helps establish its meaning in comparison to others. With regard to the problem analysed here, i.e. the perception of the significance of culture in various theoretical approaches within the discipline of international relations, we inevitably have to choose one of them. In this procedure, we will be in fact utilising the cultural criterion of the attitudes and values dominant at a given time.

Jacek Czaputowicz, the author of the first work in the Polish academic literature on this subject, who provides a comprehensive systematisation of the state of studies of international relations, believes that the choice of theory as the instrument

39 K. Holsti, *The Dividing Discipline: Hegemony and Diversity in International Relations Theory*, Boston: Allen and Unwin, 1985.

40 M. Herman, 'Many Perspectives: Building the Foundations for a Dialogue', *International Studies Quarterly*, no. 4, 1998, pp. 605–624.

41 See: A. Lijphart, 'International Relations. Theory: Great Debates and Lesser Debates', *International Social Science Journal*, no. 1, 1974, pp. 11–21; S. Walt, 'International Relations: One World. Many Theories', *Foreign Policy*, vol. 110, 1993, pp. 29–46.

42 See: M. Kornprobst, 'International Relations as a Rhetorical Discipline: Toward (Renewing Horizons)', *International Studies Review*, vol. 11, 2009, pp. 87–108.

of research depends on the values and attitudes dominant in the given historical period. These values and attitudes determine the normative mood of the era, which is manifested in four dimensions. The first dimension is the opposition of free will vs. determinism, which refers to how the course of events can be influenced. When the common belief is that political conditions cannot be changed, the dominant approach is realism, and when it is accepted that these conditions could be reformed, it is liberalism that gains the upper hand. The second dimension, optimism vs. pessimism, concerns the direction of change and specifies whether the conditions are improving or not. Liberalism is dominant where there is optimism, and pessimism implies realism. The third dimension concerns the opposition of rivalry vs. communality. In periods of rivalry for limited resources and of constant comparisons between oneself and the others, when the philosophy of relative gains is dominant, realism prevails, while in periods of cooperation and comparing the current situation to the past, that is when the philosophy of absolute gains is dominant, liberalism prevails. The fourth dimension: elitism vs. egalitarianism, concerns the question whether the global order should be determined only by superpowers and the political-diplomatic establishment as realists would have it, or also smaller countries as well as the national and international public, as advocated by liberals.[43]

The problem of selecting a specific theoretical model on the basis of its usefulness in the study of the connection between culture and international relations also depends on what we want to achieve:

- discovering the motives behind the actions and behaviours of state and non-state participants; or
- revealing regularities in the development and functioning of international relations.

With regard to the first goal, it requires formulating and empirically testing the cause-and-effect hypotheses dealing with how culture (identity) affects the behaviour of entities. This problem is dealt with as part of the studies of foreign policies of states, where the variable of culture and identity is not considered of secondary importance. Already half a century ago, scholars from the US argued that if such culturally determined variables as public opinion and the personality of the decision-maker are not taken into account, it is impossible to properly reconstruct the

43 J. Czaputowicz, *Teoria stosunków międzynarodowych. Krytyka i systematyzacja* (*Theory of International Relations. Critical Analysis and Systematisation*), Warszawa: PWN, 2007, p. 25.

process of decision-making in foreign policy.[44] Since then, culturally determined foreign policy studies have been developing with remarkable speed, as proven by the extensiveness and diversity of the issues covered by this discipline, and it is simply impossible to describe all of them in this chapter.

Two directions or areas of culturally oriented foreign policy studies deserve particular attention.

The first one concerns nationalism and nation-related issues. The key problem is to make a distinction between the state and the nation, which is reflected in the concepts of 'national interest' and 'state interest'.[45] It is a highly interesting fact that increased interest in nationalism, and fully emerged only after the end of the Cold War, and while it lasted, until 1991, researchers did not consider the category of nationalism to have any unusual explanatory value. One of the scholars of that time claimed that while it could be used to study general processes and tendencies, it could not be used to examine specific behaviours of entities.[46]

The second important area of foreign policy studies concerns identity. Contrary to the common belief, the theories on this subject were not brought into the discipline of international relations by constructivists. They were actually introduced much earlier, when the principle of self-determination of nations was formulated, and when the identity-related criteria played an important role. In the age of decolonisation of the 1950 and 1960s, the identity of the newly established states of the Third World and the nations constituting them became the subject of particularly intensive studies.[47]

As an analytical category in the studies of foreign policy of states, identity was first used in the 1990s, when researchers became aware of the fact that in the post-Cold War era cultural criteria needed to be taken into account to an equal degree as material ones. A pioneer work in this regard, already mentioned in this article, was the work written by J. Goldstein and R. Keohane and published in 1993.[48] However, there are also other noteworthy works written in that period

---

44 See: J. Bruner, M. Smith, R. White, *Opinions and Personality*, New York: Wiley, 1956.

45 L.-E. Cederman, 'Nationalism and Ethnicity', in W. Carlsnaes, T. Risse, B. Simmons (eds.), *Handbook of…*, p. 42.

46 A. Waldron, 'Theories of Nationalism and Historical Explanatory', *World Politics*, vol. 37, 1985, pp. 420–441.

47 See e.g.: R. Emerson, 'Self-Determination Revisited in the Era of Decolonization', Center for International Affairs, Paper no. 9, 1964, Harvard University; H. Mammi, *The Colonizer and the Colonized*, Boston: Beacon, 1967.

48 J. Goldstein, R. Keohane (eds.), *Ideas and Foreign Policy: Beliefs, Institutions and Political Change*, Ithaca, Cornell Univesrity Press, 1993.

which elevated identity to the role of the key variable in foreign policy studies.[49] It should be stressed that, in this regard, the main role was played by constructivists, who believe that: 'state behaviour is shaped by elite beliefs, identities, and social norms. Individuals in collectivities forge, shape, and change culture through ideas and practices. State and national interests are the result of the social identities of these actors. Thus, the object of study is norms and practices of individuals and the collectivity [...].'[50] The initial enthusiasm and hopes concerning the explanatory values of identity, however, were soon replaced by realism, once scholars became aware of the extent of the ambiguity and vagueness regarding the concept. Consequently, it is stressed that it is always necessary to adopt specific assumptions in order for constructivism to be able to play an effective role in the study of foreign policies of states.[51]

Within the broad framework of foreign policy studies that take into account the influence of cultural factors, we can distinguish three approaches, each with coherent assumptions, explicitly identifying the subject of the analysis. Owing to these criteria, they can be treated as universal explicatory models. The models in question are as follows:

1) The culturally determined concept of the 'perception' of international reality by state actors. As ambiguous as the term 'perception' is, it is impossible to reconstruct the behaviour of states in international relations with no reference to it.[52] Robert Jarvis made an interesting proposal in this context, namely to take into account the category of beliefs in foreign policy studies, which – he argues – are the basis on which the commitments of international actors are shaped;[53]

---

49 See e.g.: V. Hudson, *Culture and Foreign Policy*, Boulder: Lynne Rienner, 1997; T. Hopf, *Social Construction of International Politics: Identities and Foreign Policies*, Moscow 1995 and 1999, Ithaca: Cornell University Press, 2002.

50 K. Mingst, *Essentials of International Relations*, 2nd edition, New York–London: W.W. Norton & Company, 2003, p. 76.

51 D. Houghton, 'Reinvigorating the Study o Foreign Policy Decision Making: Toward a Constructivist Approach', *Foreign Policy Analysis*, no. 3, 2007, pp. 24–45.

52 R. Jervis, *Perception and Misperception in International Politics*, Princeton: Princeton University Press, 1976; 'Deterrence and Perception', *International Security*, no. 7, 1982/83, pp. 3–30; 'Report. Politics and Intelligence Failures. The Case of Iraq', *Journal of Strategic Studies*, no. 29, 2006, pp. 3–52.

53 R. Jervis, 'Understanding Beliefs', *Political Psychology*, no. 5, 2006, pp. 641–663.

2) The culturally determined concept of international strategy of states in the form of 'strategic culture' initiated by Jack Snyder's fundamental work on Soviet strategic culture of 1977;[54]
3) Peter Katzeinstein's model, which explains, in a particularly interesting manner, the relation between two variables: cultural norms and national security.[55]

The abovementioned theoretical models prove the thesis that there has been a 'cultural turn' in the discipline of international relations. The thesis is even more justified if we take into account the role of the cultural factor in the study of the regularities in the development and functioning of international relations or the international system. The essence of the analysis of international relations on the system level is the search for an answer to the question whether interactions between the participants are shaped only by material determinants of power. Since the very beginning of the discipline of international relations, scholars have been aware that this was not the case and that the characteristics that constitute the identity of international actors need to be taken into account as well. The first ones to raise this issue were the researchers who referred to the concept of the 'international society',[56] which has become the central analytical category of the English school of international relations,[57] and stood in clear opposition to the American international relations studies.

The challenge related to the new approach in the study of the international system was aptly identified by Hurrel, who wrote as follows: 'Central to the "system" is historically created and evolving structure of common understandings, rules, norm, and mutual expectations. The concepts of state, sovereignty, international law or war are not given by the game of Power politics. Rather shared and historically grounded understandings of war or sovereignty define what the nature of the game is and how it is to be played and, very critically, how it might change or evolve.'[58]

Bearing the above in mind, we should ask ourselves whether referring to the broadly understood cultural context has, in fact, contributed to scientific progress,

---

54 J. Snyder, *The Soviet Strategic Culture*, Rand Corporation, 1977; See also: A. Johnson, *Cultural Realism: Strategic Culture and Grand Strategy in Chinese History*, Princeton: Princeton University Press, 1996.

55 P. Katzenstein, *Cultural Norms and National Security: Police and Military in Postwar Japan*, Ithaca: Cornell University Press, 1966.

56 C. Manning, *The Nature of International Society*, New York: John Wiley and Sons, 1962.

57 T. Dunne, *Inventing International Society: A History of English School*, Basingstoke: Macmillan, 1998.

58 A. Hurrel, *Norms and Ethics...*, p. 142.

and to the development of a coherent and commonly accepted theory of international relations. The answer is 'no' but still, it has lead to the emergence of many innovative approaches, models, theoretical generalisations and conceptualisations, with significant explicatory value. While not aspiring to exhaust the whole problem, we should briefly discuss some of these innovative solutions.

The most significant one has been formulated by the British researcher Colin Wight and – as it has been noted previously – it concerns the cultural community, a common system of values that is the foundation of the international system. Two hypotheses have been put forward on this basis and they are subject to a particularly lively discussion. The first one is that culture is the prerequisite of the formation of a community of states and the second one is that a community of states that is not based on cultural community and that expands beyond its own original basis will be unstable.[59]

Another scholar whose works have contributed to the cultural breakthrough in the discipline of international relations was Alexander Wendt. His article published in 1987 on the analysis of the relationship between entity and structure was of particular importance.[60] Wendt's hypotheses are as follows: 1. people and the institutions they create are consciously operating actors that lead to changes in the society they live in; 2. the society is a network of relations which influence the structure of relations between actors; 3. people are interrelated as social entities and structures.

These statements have been incorporated in the discipline of international relations and have become the basis for the social theory of international relations, in which the nature of the anarchic international system was described in terms of 'Hobbesian culture', 'Lockean culture' and 'Kantian culture'.

The most comprehensive and culturally determined theory of international relations was created by Richard Ned Lebow. In this case, we can even speak of a type of cultural determinism because it bases the explaination of the behaviour of international actors and the operational principles of the international order on four variables of cultural nature: wealth, spirit, reason, and concerns, which he considers the fundamental motives of human needs that respectively shape

59 M. Wight, *System of States....*

60 A. Wendt, 'The Agent-Structure Problem in International Relations Theory', *International Organization*, 1987, no. 3, pp. 335–370; See also: D. Dessler, 'What's Stake in the Agent-Structure Debate?', *International Organization*, no. 3, 1989, pp. 441–473; W. Carlsnaes, 'The Agency-Structure Problem in Foreign Policy Analysis', *International Studies Quarterly*, no. 3, 1992, pp. 245–270.

the attitudes to cooperation, conflict and risk.[61] The dominance of one of these cultural values implies a given state of international relations. If in international relations the actors are guided by reason, the natural state is cooperation. Of course, conflicts do exist but they are easy to resolve due to common goals and a shared understanding of justice. A similar type of behaviour prevails when spiritual values such as friendship, common fate and observance of mutual commitments are dominant. In this case, cooperation is routine and the stronger actors support the weaker ones. A very specific situation is when one of the spiritual values, namely honour, is dominant as this often hampers cooperation and gives rise to conflicts. With regard to wealth, for example, itnaturally implies cooperation based on common interests, but conflicts and disputes are not out of the question – with an exception, however, that they do not involve the use of force. When concerns dominate the relations between states, conflicts are inevitable because the remaining norms are too weak to prevent or suppress them. The sense of insecurity grows, which results in arms races, expansions of alliances and cooperation aimed against others.[62]

The studies of cultural determinants of globalisation, on the other hand, are concerned with discovering new relations between culture and its economic dimension. They involve the development of numerous approaches, models and theories of intercultural governance.[63] At their basis lie two assumptions. The first one, formulated by Arjun Appadurai, is the multidimensionality of contemporary globalisation, which manifests itself in five spatially identified dimensions ('scapes'): financescapes, technoscapes, ethnoscapes, mediascapes and ideoscapes.[64] The second assumption refers to a statement by Samuel Huntington on the emergence of eight cultural groups (civilisations) in international relations: Indian, Chinese, Japanese, Muslim, Western, Protestant, Latin-American, and African.[65]

---

61 R. N. Lebow, *A Cultural Theory of International Relations*, Cambridge: Cambridge University Press, 2008.

62 *Ibid.*, pp. 505–557.

63 See: M. Kostera, *Postmodernizm w zarządzaniu* (*Postmodernism in Governance*), Warszawa: PWE, 1996; M. Kostera, M. Śliwa, *Zarządzanie w XXI wieku. Jakość, twórczość, kultura* (*Governance in the 21st Century. Quality, Creativity, Culture*), Warszawa: WAiP, 2010; G. Hofstede, *Culture's Consequences: Comparing Values, Behaviours, Institutions and Organizations Across Nations*, Sage Publications, 2001.

64 See: A. Appadurai, *Modernity at Large: Cultural Dimensions of Globalization*, Minneapolis: University of Minnesota Press, 1996, p. 33.

65 S. Huntington, 'The Clash of Civilizations?'..., p. 25.

Basing on the above assumptions, scholars construct different models of business culture in international relations which aspire to generalise the relations between cultural values and the logic of governance in contemporary globalisation. In one of the major publications on this subject – the result of an international research programme – it has been stated that international relations are dominated by two business cultures: the Western and the Eastern. Within the framework of the former, five specific varieties have been identified: Latin Europe, Nordic Europe, Germanic Europe, Anglo-Saxon states, Latin America, while the following business culture varieties have been identified within the latter: Confucian Asia, Southern Asia, the Middle East, Sub-Saharan Africa, and Eastern Europe.[66]

The methodological aspect

With regard to the methodological aspect of the relations between culture and the study of international relations, we should note that since the very beginning of the development of the theory, cultural values and content have always been a part of it, regardless of whether it was realism or liberalism. The increased interest in this issue that we are currently witnessing proves that there are attempts to reevaluate its role and significance in the research process. In most general terms, the goal is to include the variable of culture in the existing theories of international relations to an even greater extent than currently. One researcher justifies this by the need to better understand their nature. He wrote that including the cultural construct of the notion of civilisation combined with historiography in one's studies allows to overcome the imperfections of nationalist-realist theorising.[67]

The underappreciation of the cultural factors in the studies of international relations was particularly evident in the Cold War era, when they were dominated by material criteria connected with power, the policy of military security and strategic thinking in military terms. It seems that this state of affairs caused the theoreticians of international relations of that time to fail to properly diagnose the possibility of the end of Cold War. In his excellent article dedicated to this issue, John Luis Gaddis admitted outrightly that the lack of inclusion of cultural values attributed to the prognostic failure of the studies conducted at that time. He stated: 'My point [...] is not to suggest that we jettison the scientific approach to the study of international relations; only that we bring it up to date by recognizing that

66 J. R. House (ed.), *Culture. Leadership and Organization. Globe Study of 62 Societies*, Thousand Oaks: Sage Publications, 2004.

67 S. Chakrabatri Pasic, 'Culturing International Relations Theory; A Call for Extension', in Y. Lapid, F. Kratochwil (eds.), *The Return of Culture...*, pp. 102–103.

good scientists, like good novelists and good historians, make use of all the tools at their disposal in trying to anticipate the future. That includes not just theory, observation, and rigorous calculations but also narrative, analogy, paradox, irony, intuition, imagination, and – last but not least – style.'[68]

Culture surely cannot aspire to the status of the central analytical category in the discipline of international relations, as it is the case in anthropology or ethnology, largely because of the lack of a commonly accepted operational definition of culture and concepts related to it. An absolute novelty in this respect, proving that a qualitative methodological change has actually taken place, is the departure from the practice of attempting to develop unambiguous definitions of culture and aspiring to make them universal or comprehensive. Given the cultural polyarchy of contemporary international relations, such a traditional approach to culture would involve more shortcomings than just the lack of contextualisation.[69]

As every other social process and phenomenon, culture is neither permanent nor unchangeable; it is subjected to constant redefinitions, mainly through the actions and influences of social groups and political entities (states) in the political process of foreign relations. As a subject to internal and external changes, culture is created, reproduced and redefined – in other words, it is continually constructed. This methodological solution complies with the assumptions of constructivism, according to which the structures of international relations –more social than material in nature – result from the fact that international politics are, by nature, constructed.[70]

One of the most important elements of the process of construction – perhaps even the key one –is contextualisation. According to philosophy of science, contextualism is a position inwhich knowledge, and more precisely the truth conditions sentences attributing knowledge, depending on the context of the statement (belief) of a given person and/or the person attributing knowledge to this given person.[71] In the discipline of international relations, the cultural context of the

68 I. Gaddis, 'International Relations Theory and the End of Cold War', *International Security*, no. 3, 1992/1993, pp. 57–58.

69 R. L. Jepperson, A. Swindler, 'What Properties of Culture Should We Measure?', *Poetics*, no. 22, 1994, pp. 359–371.

70 A. Wendt, 'Constructing International Politics', *International Security*, no. 1, 1995, pp. 71–81.

71 R. Wieczorek, *Kontekstualizm jako współczesna próba odpowiedzi na problem sceptycyzmu* (*Contextualism as a Possible Contemporary Answer to the Problem of Scepticism*), Warszawa: Wydawnictwa Uniwersytetu Warszawskiego, 2010.

scientific discourse is considered to be a very important issue,[72] as it implies the choice oftheoretical approach.

The methodological problems indicated above concern the operationalisation of the notion of culture in the discipline of international relations. The significance of this problem is proven by research results which bring diverse conclusions regarding the importance of the cultural factor. An adequate example is the history of the discourse on the role of values in East Asia. Let us recall that in the early 20th century, Max Weber claimed that the key element of China's culture – Confucianism – was responsible for the country's backwardness due to excessive attachment to tradition. Toward the end of the same century, scholars formulated entirely different conclusions – that the economic successes of newly industrialised states, and later China, were possible due to the positive influence of the values ofConfucian culture.[73] This problem was subsequently addressed by Peter Gourevitch, a professor at the University of California in San Diego, who wrote that one cannot manipulate culture as a variable alternatively ascribing to it a negative role in the economic development of China, and then a positive role. Furthermore, if culture is to possess explanatory power, it must have a permanent content, otherwise it will be used as a tool for manipulation through a free selection of its constitutive values.[74]

Professor Gourevitch's opinion shows the importance of the problem of 'methodological culture', understood as adequacy, professionalism and objectivism in the application of the methods and procedures of research conduct, which are most efficient in heuristic terms. Thus, the related research challenge essentially comes down to the choice between two methodological options.

The first one is the positivist approach, which consists of research procedures with hypotheses that are then verified during the research. In this case, it is a search for objectivised reality and universal laws. The core of this approach is the reduction of subjective points of view to the absolute minimum, or in other words, explaining and discovering cause and effect. What is more, according to Ernst Hocas, it is a method useful in the study of nationalism.[75]

72 G. Holden, 'Who Contextualizes the Contextualizers?, Disciplinary History and Discourse about IR Discourse', *Review of International Studies*, vol. 28, 2002, pp. 253–270.

73 Ch. Chung, J. Shepard, M. Dollinger, 'Max Weber Revisited: Some Lessons From East Asian Capitalistic Development', *Asia-Pacific Journal of Management*, no. 2, 1992, pp. 310–320.

74 P. Gourevitch, *The Pacific Region. Challenges to Policy and Theory*, San Diego: Sage Publications, 1989, p. 12.

75 E. Hocas, 'What Is Nationalism and Why Should We Study It?', *International Organization*, no. 3, 1986, pp. 707–720.

The second option is the interpretative approach, based on the assumption that the reality that surrounds us is a social construct, therefore it does not objectively exist. It is a striving to understand and interpret the actions of social groups.

These two methodological options allow the researchers of international relations to face the choice between positivism and postpositivism, objectivism and subjectivism, and between explaining and understanding.[76] Dilemmas such as these accompany the studies of the connection between culture and international relations. In contrast to the economic sphere or even the military sphere however, culture surrenders itself to quantification only to a small degree. Thus, the positivist method has a limited explanatory power, especially when it comes to various types of formal models, in which culture is treated as one several variables.[77]

Moreover, the deficiencies of the positivist methodology have inspired the development of an alternative, postpositivist methodology, which should be based – as argued by Yosef Lapid – on rejecting the traditional global ontology of international relations originating in realism and its reinterpretation in such a way as to have it reflect the dynamic pluralism, changeability and complexity of the phenomena and processes of cultural character that take place in international relations. This, in turn, helps deepen the researchers' reflection and improve their sensitivity to cultural issues.[78]

Culture is important not only in international relations, however, but also in the way the research in this field is conducted. We need to consider the identity of the discipline of international relations and the answer to the question whether it has universal value and significance or whether it has its own specificity in every state where such research is conducted. The problem was raised by the American researcher Stanley Hoffmann already in the 1970s.[79] Undeniably, the discipline of international relations was born in the US and as such it initially dominated the research in other countries. The phenomenon of the 'English School' of international relations proves, however, that the American principles of this discipline

76 See: R. Jackson, G. Sørensen, *Wprowadzenie do stosunków międzynarodowych. Teorie i kierunki badawcze* (*Introduction to International Relations. Theories and Approaches*), Kraków: Wydawnictwa UJ, 2003, p. 280.

77 Y. Lapid, 'Cultures Ship: Returns and Departures in International Relations Theory', in Y. Lapid, F. Kratochwil (eds.), *The Return of Culture...*, p. 10.

78 *Ibid.*, pp. 10–11.

79 S. Hoffmann, 'An American Social Science: International Relations', *Daedalus*, vol. 106, 1977, pp. 41–59.

have not been universally accepted,[80] and in time there even emerged views that the domination of American science was one of the manifestations of Western imperialism.[81] The debate on this subject is particularly heated and extensive, and thus impossible to discuss comprehensively in this article.[82] We only mean to draw attention to the fact that cultural references are present in the studies of international relations in various countries. It is especially interesting that Chinese researchers also participate in this debate and that by using references to the achievements of American science, they try to combine them with their own tradition.[83] This is what one of them said about what he believes should be the characteristics of a 'Chinese school of international relations': 'The school seeks to create an IR theoretical system of both Chinese substance and universal significance by discovering China's traditional thought and practice as well as by drawing on Western IR theories. Its purpose is not to displace existing IR theories but to enrich both them and existing human knowledge'.[84]

Conclusion

The attempts to define or determine the role of culture in the discipline of international relations entail three types of risks: of extreme undervaluation and omission, of cultural determinism and of banal statements stating that it is important in the shaping of state behaviour. In order to avoid these traps it is necessary to:

- adopt logical assumptions on the ontological level;
- verify and test the models and theories in which culture is ascribed important explanatory functions, bearing in mind two levels on which this is performed. The first one is the level of the actors, where culture influences the shape and

80 See e.g.: E. Krippendorf, 'The Dominance of American Approaches in International Relations', *Journal of International Studies*, no. 2, 1987, pp. 207–214.

81 J. Hobson, 'Is Critical Theory Always for the White West and for Western Imperialism?, Beyond Westphalian Towards a Post-Racist IR', *Review of International Studies*, no. 33, 2007.

82 See the two major articles on this subject: O. Waever, 'The Sociology of a Not So International Discipline: American and European Developments in International Relations', *International Organization*, no. 4, 1998, pp. 687–727; S. Smith, 'The Discipline of International Relations: Still an American Social Science?', *British Journal of Politics and International Relations*, no. 3, 2000, pp. 374–402.

83 Y. Xuetong, *Ancient Chinese Thought. Modern Chinese Power*, Princeton and Oxford: Princeton University Press, 2011.

84 Z. Feng, 'The Tsinghua Approach and the Inception of Chinese Theories of International Relations', *The Chinese Journal of International Politics*, no. 12, 2012, p. 79.

content of the decision-making processes and behaviours of entities in international relations. The second one is the system level, where the key question seems to be whether in international relations we are dealing with a system of states shaped according to the rules of power and politics or rather with an international community on the global or regional scale shaped by cultural values.

In terms of methodology thus, the important thing is not really to choose between positivism and postpositivism but rather to observe the rules and principles of the research procedure in which contextualisation plays the key role.

To sum up, we can formulate the following conclusion: the presence of culture in the discipline of international relations is indispensable for its existence. The discipline develops on the basis of the fundamental assumption that the internal sphere of states and the international sphere are incomparable. This characteristic is especiallypronounced in the sphere of culture, where on the one hand, we are dealing with culturally homogenous countries and, on the other hand, with culturally pluralist international systems. This justifies the practice of conducting culturally-oriented studies of international relations which are integrally combined with the political and economic spheres.

Part II. Culture in the Practice of International Relations

Aleksandra Jarczewska

Culture and the Economy

Key words: culture, economy, individual, entrepreneurship, corporations, business culture, values, attitudes.

Abstract: The article examines the specific nature of the relation between culture and the economy. It aims to present the influence of culture on economic processes as well as to show the possible approaches to discussing the relations between these two phenomena. The main assumption is that cultural factors indeed have influence on economic processes and this can be referred to as soft influence on the economy.

Although there are many definitions of the phenomenon of culture, it is most often perceived as a set of material and non-material products of a given society, passed from generation to generation.[1] In this article, the focus will be primarily on the non-material sphere of culture, that is the systems of norms, values and behaviours characteristic of a given society. The relations between culture understood in this way and the economy can be approached from various perspectives. First, we can give thought to whether – and if yes, then how – culture influences the economy (taking into account its various elements influencing the economic processes). Second, we can also examine the problem of relations between these phenomena from a reversed perspective and discuss how the economy influences culture – whether economic factors contribute to cultural transformations in a given social group and if they do, then in what way.[2] This article, however, shall focus on the former, that is examining the economy's dependence on culture, which in simple

1 See e.g.: J. Szczepański, *Elementarne pojęcia socjologii* (*Elementary Concepts of Sociology*), p. 26, available at: http://biblioteka.wdinp.uw.edu.pl/zasoby/Teksty/Szczepanski-Elementarne%20poj%C4%99cia%20socjologii.pdf (accessed on 21 April 2013).

2 This problem is examined by researchers dealing with the processes of modernisation, e.g. Daniel Bell (*The Cultural Contradictions of Capitalism*, 20th ed., Basic Books, 1996) or Ronald Inglehart (*Culture Shift in Advanced Industrial Society*, Princeton 1990; *Modernization and Postmodernization: Cultural, Economic and Political Change in Forty-Three Societies*, Princeton 1997; as well as: 'Culture and Democracy', in S. Huntington, L. Harrison (eds.), *Culture Matters: How Values Shape Human Progress*, Basic Books, New York 2001, pp. 80–97).

terms comes down to the problem of the influence of culture on economic growth, or more broadly, on economic development of individual states.[3]

The differences in economic development between individual parts of the world as well as countries or even social groups within a single country (especially multinational states) inspire researchers in various fields to look for the answer to what factors determine the wealth and poverty of countries or societies. These studies most often focus on economic issues (analysis of governance models and the use offactors of production), political issues (consequences of colonialism, dependency, wars, conquests), geographical issues (the influence of geographical location, climate, amount of natural resources), or sociological issues (studying social models or structures and rules governing societies), depending on the specialty of the scholar who conducts them. At the same time, until recently, relatively little attention has been paid to the analysis of the influence of cultural factors on economic issues. In the recent years, this gap in research seems to have become filled with ever more numerous and methodologically advanced studies. The multitude and diversity ofapproaches and interpretations of the analysed problem can however be indicative of chaos in research and methodology. It is for this reason that this article aims to present the mostknown and most frequently commented-on approaches to studying the influence of culture on economic processes as well as to show the possible approaches to discussing the relations between culture and the economy. Such analyses are undeniably important for understanding the issues related to the functioning of states in the international environment. They can contribute to a better understanding of the differences and divisions in the economic map of the world and bring us closer to answering the question why some countries are more and others are less effective in their economic activity.

The main assumption on which this article is based is the thesis that regardless of the sceptical views and discrepancies in studies, cultural factors indeed have influence on economic processes. This can be referred to as soft influence on the economy, which alongside other factors constitutes a complex of determinants of the economic growth or the development of a given country. The key issue in this context is the role of individuals, who are in a way carriers or transmitters of culture. The article is therefore divided into three sections. The first section presents the basic terminology, so that the second section can present the positions of scholars dealing with the issues in question. The third section is dedicated to the relations between culture and the economy from the point of view of individuals and their roles in relation to the cultural context.

---

3 Terminological issues will be explained further in this article.

Culture, the economy and the individual as the cementing element

Culture and the economy can seem to be two very distinct phenomena, without much in common. However, in order to verify this we should look closer into both, and define the fundamental terms and notions necessary for further discussion.

A characteristic feature of culture is the multitude of approaches and possible interpretations. While looking for its definition, we should first of all consult the studies performed by sociologists and anthropologists. In the 1950s, two anthropologists, Alfred Louis Kroeber and Clyde Kluckhohn analysed more than a hundred definitions of culture and divided them into six different types, implying six different approaches to understanding culture.[4] However, regardless of the multitude of definitions and approaches to the phenomenon, culture is usually perceived as a set of non-material and material products of a given society, passed from generation to generation.[5] As I have already noted above, in this chapter the focus shall be primarily on the non-material sphere of culture, that is the systems of norms, beliefs, values, and behaviours characteristic of societies, resulting from a common heritage, tradition, religion, and upbringing. Thus understood, culture determines the activity of individuals by providing them with a pattern or model of conduct, which at the same time also concerns governance processes.

It should also be noted that although culture is ephemeral and difficult to measure, for years researchers have been trying to develop tools which would allow them to gather empirical data concerning attitudes, beliefs and values of as many individuals as possible and subsequently 'translate' them into concrete actions in the political, economic and social sphere. What proved particularly useful in the analysis of the relations between culture and the economy was the research conducted by Geert Hofstede as well as Charles Hampden-Turner and Alfons Trompenaars, who took advantage of many years of observations conducted among employees of corporations (mainly managers) from different countries that aimed at identifying the characteristic features of individual national cultures and determining how this affects issues related to economic development (this

4 A. L. Kroeber, C. Kluckhohn, *Culture. A Critical Review of Concepts and Definitions*, Cambridge, MA 1952.

5 See e.g.: J. Szczepański, *Elementarne pojęcia…*, or A. Giddens, *Sociology*, 5th ed., Cambridge 2006, Polish edition: *Socjologia*, transl. by A. Szulżycka, Warszawa 2007, p. 45; see also the entry for 'Kultura' (Culture) in *Encyklopedia PWN*, available at: http://encyklopedia.pwn.pl/haslo.php?id=3928887 (accessed on 21 April 2013).

concept will be presented in more detail further in the article).[6] However, a much more universal instrument for studying culture is the World Value Survey.[7] It is a large-scale research project that has been carried out since 1981. It is headed by Ronald Inglehart and researchers and enthusiasts from approximately a hundred participant countries. The goal of the cyclical survey studies conducted by this group is to determine the attitudes, values and convictions of people from the entire world.[8] Basing on a factor analysis of the data collected in each country participating in the survey, researchers examine how culture influences various aspects of the life of societies.[9] The fruits of this work include such compilations as a global map of cultures. The map is based on the evaluation of two aspects of cultural diversity: 1) the attitude to power – from traditional to secular-rational; and 2) the dominant values – from favouring survival to self-expression.[10]

The second notion of key importance to this article (analysed mainly by economists but also by researchers working in other fields) is the economy and the phenomena related to it, such as economic development and growth.[11] In the approach presented in this article, by 'the economy' we mean the entirety of economic activity (production of goods and services) conducted in a given area

6 See: G. Hofstede, G. J. Hofstede, M. Minkov, *Cultures and Organizations: Software of the Mind*, 3rd ed., McGraw-Hill, 2010; and Ch. Hampden-Turner, A. Trompenaars, *The Seven Cultures of Capitalism: Value Systems for Creating Wealth in the United States, Japan, Germany, France, Britain, Sweden, and the Netherlands*, 1st ed., Doubleday Business, 1993.

7 The World Value Survey has the most universal scope among the surveys of this type and now covers already approximately a hundred countries. However, it should be noted that there are also noteworthy studies with a lesser scope, e.g. the all-European studies called the Eurobarometer, http://ec.europa.eu/public_opinion/cf/index_en.cfm, as well studies concerning individual societies, such as the German General Social Survey (ALLBUS), http://www.gesis.org/en/home, the American General Social Survey, http://www.norc.org/Pages/default.aspx, or the Polski Generalny Sondaż Społeczny, http://pgss.iss.uw.edu.pl/index.php?v=E.

8 More information and detailed reports of these studies can be found at: http://www.worldvaluessurvey.org (accessed on 21 April 2013).

9 For more see the website of the World Value Survey at: http://www.worldvaluessurvey.org/wvs/articles/folder_published/article_base_56 (accessed on 21 April 2013).

10 Comparative global culture maps are presented in R. Inglehart, Ch. Welzel, *The WVS Cultural Map of the World*, available at: http://www.worldvaluessurvey.org/wvs/articles/folder_published/article_base_54 (accessed on 21 April 2013).

11 The list of economic processes and phenomena which could be presented is, naturally, very long but here shall present only the ones which are of key importance regarding the issues described in this article.

(a country, a region, the world) in certain circumstances (material, institutional, social, and political).[12] We should also draw a terminological distinction between national economy and global economy. In the first case, we refer to the entirety of economic activity in a given country, while the latter means the system of relations between national economies which constitutes the international system of production and exchange. Furthermore, we need to explain the notions of economic growth and economic development as well. By economic growth weunderstand the increase of annual production of goods and services in a country.[13] This process is associated with the generated national income and is represented in statistics as GDP or GNP in a given time. For economic growth, there are two principal variables concerning recorded quantitative changes – production and consumption. The factors that determine economic growth are:

- labour (in quantitative terms – the number of employees; in qualitative terms – the attitudes, values, discipline, level of education, qualifications, motivation for work);
- capital (capital goods or means of production, financial capital);
- technology (science, engineering, entrepreneurship, management);
- natural resources (usually considered invariable and therefore not included in the calculations).[14]

Economic growth should lead to the growth of social prosperity, frequently considered equivalent to economic or social development but it is often not the case. GDP growth itself does not guarantee an improvement of living conditions (e.g. due to unequal distribution and other disrupting factors). Therefore, since the 1970s, scholars have also been applying the category of development. Development is a broader concept than economic growth and apart from quantitative changes, it takes into account the qualitative changes in the economy and, more broadly, in society (e.g. changes of social relations, improvement of the standard of living, civilisational progress).[15] It should be noted, however, that it is hard to

---

12 See e.g.: R. Milewski (ed.), *Elementarne zagadnienia ekonomii* (*Elementary Problems of Economics*), Warszawa 1995, pp. 16–17; D. R. Kamerschen, R. B. McKenzie, C. Nardinelli, *Economics*, 2nd ed., Houghton Mifflin, 1989.

13 Cf.: R. Milewski, *Elementarne zagadnienia...*, pp. 203–222.

14 *Ibid.*, pp. 209–211.

15 *Ibid.*, p. 203; see also: Instytut Globalnej Odpowiedzialności, 'Rozwój to nie wzrost gospodarczy – raport o rozwoju społecznym' (Development is Not Economic Growth – A Report on Social Development), a commentary on the presentation of the report on social development at a meeting held in the Presidential Palace in Warsaw on

clearly determine the boundary between economic development and social development. Due to this fact, in academic literature these two notions are often combined into a single one: socioeconomic development. Among the primary indexes describing the state of socioeconomic development of states we can point out, for example: the social inequality ratio, i.e. the Gini index,[16] the unemployment rate or the percentage of people living below the poverty threshold. Essential information concerning differences in the level of development of societies can also be obtained by comparing the gross domestic product per capita at purchasing power parity – GDP (PPP) per capita in USD.[17] However, an even more popular index (although not without any flaws and limitations) is the Human Development Index (HDI).[18] It was created by the Pakistani economist Mahbub ul Haq in 1990 and is presently calculated using four primary elements:

---

14 December 2011, available at: http://igo.org.pl/aktualnosci/polityka-rozwojowa/219-rozwoj-to-nie-wzrost-gospodarczyraport-o-rozwoju-spoecznym (accessed on 21 April 2013); and R. Szarfenberg, *Rozwój społeczny, czyli detronizacja PKB* (*Social Development – the Deposition of the GDP*), Instytut Polityki Społecznej UW, 8 February 2011, available at: http://rszarf.ips.uw.edu.pl/pdf/KrytykaPKB.pdf (accessed on 21 April 2013).

16 The Gini index is a ratio used for observation of inequalities within a given country (the greater the inequalities, the higher the index). It is often used for determining disparities in income. For example, according to the data of the CIA World Factbook published in 2013, the Gini index for Sweden is 23 (smallest inequalities) and 63.2 for Lesotho (greatest inequalities); for Poland the index is 34.1 (it should be noted, however, that the index values concern different years, which makes it more difficult to compare them). See: CIA World Factbook, *Country Comparison: Distribution of Family Income – Gini Index*, available at: https://www.cia.gov/library/publications/the-world-factbook/rankorder/2172rank.html?countryName=Poland&countryCode=pl&regionCode=eur&rank=89#pl (accessed on 18 January 2013).

17 In accordance with the data of the IMF, *World Economic Outlook 2012*, the first ten places in terms of GDP (PPP) per capita in USD are occupied by: 1. Qatar (102 943 USD); 2. Luxembourg (80 119 USD); 3. Singapore (59 711 USD); 4. Norway (53 471 USD); 5. Brunei (49 384 USD) and Hong Kong (49 137 USD) – included on the list but not considered a country and thus not being assigned a separate number; 6. the US (48 387 USD); 7. the United Arab Emirates (48 158 USD); 8. Switzerland (43 370 USD); 9. the Netherlands (42 183 USD); 10. Austria (41 822 USD).

18 In accordance with the date of the UNDP, the first ten places in terms of HDI are occupied by: 1. Norway (0.943); 2. Australia (0.929); 3. the Netherlands (0.910); 4. the US (0.910); 5. New Zealand (0.908); 6. Canada (0.908); 7. Ireland (0.908); 8. Liechtenstein (0.905); 9. Germany (0.905); 10. Sweden (0.904), while the last ten includes the following: 177. Eritrea (0.349); 178. Guinea (0.344); 179. Central African Republic (0.343); 180. Sierra Leone (0.336); 181. Burkina Faso (0.331); 182. Liberia (0.329); 183.

- life expectancy at birth;
- years of schooling received by citizens aged 25 and older;
- expected years of schooling of children beginning their process of education;
- gross national product per capita in USD, at purchasing power parity.[19]

The deliberations presented above might suggest that an attempt to collate culture with the economy is bound to fail, first of all because of the 'incomparability' of the two. Culture, especially in the non-material aspect, is certainly ephemeral, unquantifiable and hard to define or examine, while the economy is usually discussed in terms of economic sciences and described mainly using models and statistical methods. An additional difficulty in analysing the influence of culture on the economy is selecting proper tools which would allow for conducting objective studies. Furthermore, economics most often uses a formalised set of tools (mathematical analysis, statistics, econometric models), while studies of culture are based on the methodology typical of the humanities and social sciences (e.g. observation of relations, phenomena, processes in a specific timeframe).

However, if we look closer into the matter, we can find many concepts which combine elements of culture and the economy – e.g. organisational culture, business culture, and agricultural culture. Furthermore, also the genesis of the term 'culture' refers directly to the processes of transforming reality – farming or animal husbandry. It comes from Latin, where the word *cultura* meant tilling the soil or spiritual development, and this word in turn comes from *colere*, that is to till, cultivate, nurture, perfect. Moreover, the economies of individual states distinguish between the so-called sector of culture, which – as a special branch of the economy – should be included in the statistical figures concerning contributions to the GDP, generating jobs or value added (i.e. to what extent it facilitates development

Chad (0.328); 184. Mozambique (0.322); 185. Burundi (0.316); 186. Niger (0.295); 187. Democratic Republic of the Congo (0.286). See: UNDP, *Summary – Human Development Report 2011; Sustainability and Equity: A Better Future for All*, UNDP, 2011, available at: http://hdr.undp.org/en/media/HDR_2011_EN_Summary.pdf (accessed on 21 April 2013).

19 For more see: UNDP, *About Human Development*, available at: http://hdr.undp.org/en/humandev/ (accessed on 21 April 2013); UNDP, *Human Development Index (HDI)*, available at: http://hdr.undp.org/en/statistics/hdi/ (accessed on 21 April 2013); and UNDP, *International Human Development Indicators*, available at: http://hdr.undp.org/en/statistics/ (accessed on 21 April 2013).

of cooperation, contributes to the establishment and tightening of social relations as well as to the development of models and attitudes of individuals).[20]

Undoubtedly, however, the main cementing factor of the two spheres (a common denominator) is the human individual, which in collective forms congregates to form societies, creates networks of relations, and in a broader (sociological) perspective is a constituent of social capital.[21] The individual is a 'product' of culture and its carrier but also the creator of the economy – along with its character, effectiveness and the ideas dominant in the given economic system. We should also emphasise that economists have not completely rejected the role of the human factor in economic processes, but they have been exhibiting a rather specific approach to it instead. The representatives and proponents of the classical school of economics believed that humans (*homo oeconomicus*) are rational individuals whose actions are guided by maximisation of profits and working towards their own best interest.[22] Such an approach, however, did not take into account other factors conditioning these actions and economic choices (psychological, e.g. emotions, or cultural, e.g. values, attitudes and traditions), which made it too narrow to allow understanding of the complex processes of economics. For this reason, it has gradually been broadened in terms of perspective, no longer limiting itself to purely economic issues. Charles Hampden-Turner and Alfons Trompenaars stress that 'economics is so concerned with counting and itemising that it has lost sight of the one component, almost unmeasurable, that makes all economic activity possible: human relationships'.[23] Consequently, the relations between culture and the economy should be examined in a much broader perspective, one not restricted solely to the analysis of economic indexes but also taking into account the role of humans.

---

20 Data showing the importance of the sector of culture for the European economy can be found in the study prepared for the European Commission titled *The Economy of Culture in Europe*, KEA European Affairs, August 2006, available at: http://www.keanet.eu/ecoculture/studynew.pdf (accessed on 21 April 2013).

21 F. Fukuyama presents an interesting discussion on the importance and role of social capital in the economic development of states in the chapter 'Social Capital', in S. Huntington, L. Harrison (eds.), *Culture Matters…*, pp. 98–111. D. Landes, in turn, stresses the role of human capital shaped by culture as the source of the Japanese economic success. For more see: D. Landes, 'Culture Makes Almost All the Difference', in *ibid.*, pp. 2–13.

22 The notion of *homo oeconomicus* is broadly discussed in, for example, the publication by I. Bittner *Homo oeconomicus*, Łódź 2009.

23 Ch. Hampden-Turner, A. Trompenaars, *The Seven Cultures…*, p. 5.

The impact of culture on the economy – a review of concepts and interpretations

The problem of the relations between culture and the economy has been approached by many scholars representing various fields of science that often reach very different conclusions. The ones particularly sceptical with regard to the determination of interrelations between culture and economic processes are anthropologists (especially due to cultural relativism[24]) and economists. The latter usually dismiss culture as not being an important element affecting the economic growth of states and instead stress the importance of economic elements, such as the economic models, effective use of the instruments of economic policy, the degrees of economic freedom, resources, etc. In order to find the answer to what factors determine the state of a given economy and explain the source of economic differences between countries, economists develop theories of economic growth and development. Among the theories of economic growth we can distinguish two groups of concepts: 1) neoclassical models (also called exogenous or autonomous, not requiring new input of factors of production), by Robert Solow, Frank Ramsey and Peter Diamond; 2) endogenous models (ones stimulated by investments in fixed assets or improving the quality of human resources through education, etc.) by Robert Lucas, Sergio Rebelo, Peter Howitt; as well as the Mankiw–Romer–Weil model, which combines the previous two (based on Solow's thought and referring to endogenous concepts by taking into account the role of the human capital).[25] The theories of economic development (that emerge where economics and sociology overlap) take into consideration – next to the factors connected with economic growth – also civilisational progress. The best-known concepts are the ones developed by Karl Marx (stages of social development from primitive communism, through slave society, feudalism, capitalism, to communism), Walt Whitman Rostow (five stages of economic development from traditional to mass consumption), Daniel Bell (three stages of social development: pre-industrial,

24 In accordance with this concept culture cannot be judged better or worse, and in this particular case facilitating or hampering economic development.

25 For more see: R. J. Barro, X. Sala-i-Martin, *Economic Growth*, Cambridge–London 2003, available at: http://down.cenet.org.cn/upfile/8/200751171644184.pdf (accessed on 21 Aril 2013); M. Próchniak, *Modele wzrostu gospodarczego, materiały do zajęć* (*Models of Economic Growth. Materials for Class*), Warszawa, available at: http://akson.sgh.waw.pl/~mproch/Z_teoria_wzrostu/modele_wzrostu.pdf (accessed on 21 Aril 2013); as well as P. Aghion, S. N. Durlauf, *Handbook of Economic Growth*, Amsterdam 2005.

industrial and post-industrial) as well as Alan Fisher's and Colin Clark's three-sector hypothesis (development from agriculture, through industry, to a service-based economy).[26] We could also mention the theories that remain outside the main current of economic theories, the dependency theory (according to which the lagging behind of poorly developed/peripheral countries is the result of their exploitation by highly developed/central countries)[27] and the sustainable development theory, to which David W. Pearce, Edward B. Barbier and R. Kerry Turner greatly contributed.[28] In the search for interpretations of economic growth or development of states, the authors of these theories focus primarily on such factors as: resources, investments, state policies, institutions, regulations, technology, or progressing through the various stages of social development connected with the changes in governance methods. It should be noted, however, that almost all concepts and approaches referring to economic growth (excluding the neoclassical models of exogenous growth) and economic development, although different in terms of content and developed in different periods, also take into account the role of the human factor, which can be associated with cultural issues.[29] In this context, we should also note the compelling approach to the study of the relations between culture and the economy proposed by Jim Granato, Ronald Inglehart and David Leblang in the article *The effects of cultural values on economic development*.[30] They

---

26 For more on the models of economic development see: M. P. Todaro, S. C. Smith, *Economic Development*, Upper Saddle River, NJ 2011, available at: http://www.aw-bc.com/info/todaro_smith/Chapter4.pdf (accessed on 9 January 2013); see also: D. R. Kamerschen, R. B. McKenzie, C. Nardinelli, *Economics*....

27 This theory, mainly concerning Latin American countries, was promoted by such scholars as: Hans Singer, Raúl Prebisch and Paul Prebisch, as well as André Gunder Frank or Immanuel Wallerstein.

28 R. K. Turner, D. W. Pearce, 'Sustainable Development: Ethics and Economics', CSERGE Working Paper PA 92–09, available at: http://www.cserge.ac.uk/sites/default/files/pa_1992_09.pdf (accessed on 21 April 2013).

29 At this point, we could also refer to the endogenous growth theory or to the works of the representatives of new institutional economics, e.g. C. D. North. The scholars dealing with this subject include F. Fukuyama ('Culture and economic development: cultural concerns', in *International Encyclopedia of the Social & Behavioral Sciences*, Amsterdam–New York 2001, p. 3132).

30 J. Granato, R. Inglehart, D. Leblang, 'The Effects of Cultural Values on Economic Development: Theory, Hypotheses, and Some Empirical Tests', *American Journal of Political Science*, vol. 40, no. 3, 1996, available at: http://www.class.uh.edu/hcpp/jimgranato/TheEffectOfCulturalValuesOnEconomicDevelopment.pdf (accessed on 15 December 2013).

assume that cultural factors are among the elements discussed under endogenous models of economic growth and can affect economic growth in two ways. The culturally conditioned orientation towards economising and success is the source of economic growth, while post-materialist attitudes[31] have a negative effect on it. In order to verify these hypotheses, the researchers constructed an empirical model which combined economic and cultural variables.[32]

Representatives of the humanities and social sciences (e.g. anthropology, cultural studies, sociology, political science), in turn, are those who much more frequently consider culture to be one of the key determinants of economic development. Scholars with a particularly eminent contribution to the analysis of the relations between culture and the economy include experts such as Max Weber, Samuel Huntington, Lawrence Harrison, or David Landes, and their works deal with the broad perspective (that is studying nations and ethnic groups).[33] These researchers are determined proponents and promoters of the thesis of the essential importance of culture for economic processes. What is more, in their opinion, culture is the foundation of the development of political and economic behaviours of societies.[34]

Among the aforementioned studies, one deserving particular attention is the multiannual project of David Landes, followed by the publication titled *The Wealth and Poverty of Nations*. In his performance of in-depth historical analyses, he shows that in most societies that have achieved economic success culture played a considerable role in this process. Landes' work covers issues related to economic development of states presented in the historical perspective. The author focuses on a multi-factor approach to the reasons why individual states or societies achieved success or suffered a defeat in economic terms, but he pays special attention to culture in this context. However, he assigns primacy to the

31 Post-materialism is a concept developed by Ronald Inglehart, according to which in highly developed societies people abandon the materialist approach and start focusing on post-material values, e.g. self-actualisation, better quality of life and expressing their own opinions. See e.g.: R. F. Inglehart, 'Changing Values among Western Publics from 1970 to 2006', *West European Politics*, vol. 31, no. 1–2, 2008, available at: http://www.worldvaluessurvey.org/wvs/articles/folder_published/publication_559/files/values_1970-2006.pdf (accessed on 21 April 2013).

32 For more see: J. Granato, R. Inglehart, D. Leblang, *The Effects...*

33 See e.g.: M. Weber, *The Protestant Ethic and the Spirit of Capitalism*, transl. by Talcott Parsons, Courier Dover Publications 2003; D. S. Landes, 'The Wealth and Poverty of Nations: Why Some Are So Rich and Some So Poor' W. W. Norton & Company, New York–London 1999; S. Huntington, L. Harrison (eds.), *Culture Matters...*

34 See also: R. Inglehart, *Culture and Democracy...*, p. 80.

achievements of the Western civilisation in this respect, which has repeatedly earned him criticisms and accusations of being Europocentric.[35]

Another interesting approach is the one of Samuel Huntington. His works, including the flagship *The Clash of Civilizations and the Remaking of World Order*, provide the readers with a broad view of the cultural determinants of the development of societies. Huntington claimed that 'culture and cultural identities, which at the broadest level are civilisation identities, are shaping the patterns of cohesion, disintegration, and conflict in the post-Cold War world'.[36] In his opinion culture, understood as values, norms and attitudes characteristic of a given civilisation, influences economic processes and growth because it determines the opportunities of cooperation, sharing and using experience. Thus, the consequence of the fact that 'the roots of economic cooperation are in cultural commonality'[37] is economic development within a given civilisation. However, Huntington's vision is a rather grim one because he assumes that cultures and civilisation become 'closed' to one another, hermetic, which can lead to conflicts (of course, he presented the concept of clash of civilisations more broadly with regard to politics). Although Huntington's conceptions have been repeatedly criticised for venturing into simplifications, using stereotypes and even for ignorance, they are nonetheless an important and influential attempt at presenting the relations between culture and economic and political processes.[38]

On the largest scale, however, Samuel Huntington conducted studies on the influence of culture on the economy together with Lawrence Harrison. One of their especially noteworthy projects is the one to which they invited the most esteemed experts from many various fields. During the famous symposium held at

---

35 Landes's work is criticised by such scholars as William McNeill (review in *New York Review Books* 1998) and André Gunder Frank (*Review of 'The Wealth and Poverty of Nations'*, available at: http://rrojasdatabank.info/agfrank/landes.html [accessed on 22 April 2013]), who also participated in a debate with D. Landes on the concept and vision of the economic development of the world. For more see: http://www.c-spanvideo.org/program/116051-1 (accessed on 22 April 2013).

36 S. Huntington, *The Clash of Civilizations and the Remaking of World Order*, Simon & Schuster, New York 2011, p. 20.

37 *Ibid.*, p. 135.

38 See e.g.: E. Said, 'The Clash of Ignorance', *The Nation*, 4 October 2001, as well as a broader discussion of the subject in P. Marczewski and P. Świeżak (eds.), *Zderzenie cywilizacji:sąd nad teorią Samuela Huntingtona* (*The Clash of Civilisations; An Assessment of Samuel Huntington's Theory*), Portal of Foreign Affairs, Institute of Foreign Affairs, Warszawa 2006, available at: http://psz.pl/images/stories/strefa/psz.pl_zderzenie_cywilizacji.pdf (accessed on 22 April 2013).

Harvard in 1999 and titled 'Cultural Values and Human Progress', they discussed issues concerning the relations between culture and economic, political and social development.[39] This conference bore fruit in the form of the famous publication *Culture Matters: How Values Shape Human Progress.* In this book, Huntington, Harrison and a group of other researchers analysed in detail and using many different perspectives the notion of the influence of culture on economic development, among others. The project was also complemented by the Culture Matters Research Project (CMRP), headed by Harrison and executed in 2002–2005. The result of the project was the book *The Central Liberal Truth*, in which he once again argued for the aptness of the thesis that culture matters.[40]

From a different, narrower perspective, the influence of culture on the economy is discussed by Geert Hofstede (in *Cultures and Organizations...*) as well as Charles Hampden-Turner and Alfons Trompenaars (in *The Seven Cultures of Capitalism*). They focus on analysing business relations and identifying the sets of characteristic features of the functioning of organisations/enterprises, which are particularly important for conducting international business activity.

Apart from the research projects that have already been mentioned, there are other interesting but less well-known studies concerning the subject of this article, and there are also other noteworthy publications of some of the authors mentioned above. One particularly interesting study was conducted by Luigi Guiso, Paola Sapienza and Luigi Zingales – *Does culture affect economic outcomes?* The authors try to show the influence of culture on the economy by using a three-stage procedure combining the methodology characteristic of the humanities with the methodology of economic sciences (they verify how culture 'reduced' to the category of values and attitudes affects economic factors).[41] The regional approach to the issue of the relations between culture and the economy is presented is such

---

39 Cf.: S. P. Huntington, L. E. Harrison (eds.), *Culture Matters...*, p. xxii. It should also be noted that this debate was continued at the symposium 'Samuel P. Huntington Memorial Symposium on Culture, Cultural Change and Economic Development', organised in Moscow in 2010 shortly after S. Huntington passed away. For more information see the website at: http://huntington.hse.ru/en/ (accessed on 22 April 2013).

40 L. E. Harrison, *The Central Liberal Truth: How Politics Can Change a Culture and Save It from Itself*, New York 2006.

41 L. Guiso, P. Sapienza, L. Zingales, *Does Culture Affect Economic Outcomes?*, Working Paper 11999, National Bureau of Economic Research, 2006, available at: http://www.nber.org/papers/w11999.pdf?new_window=1 (accessed on 23 April 2013).

studies as: *Cultural values and economic growth in Asia: An empirical analysis*;[42] *Cultural determinants of economic growth: the case of European countries*;[43] *Culture and economic growth: a general argument with illustrations from the Islamic world*.[44] A narrower (micro-perspective) approach, in turn, was presented for instance by Randall G. Holcombe, in his study titled *Entrepreneurship and economic growth*.[45]

Relations between culture and the economy – the importance and roles of individuals

As it has already been mentioned, human individuals (together with values, beliefs and behaviours representing them) are a 'transmission belt' between culture and the economy. Depending on the 'economic roles'[46] they assume, individuals can influence economic processes in two dimensions – the internal and the external (national and global economy) as well as in the macro and micro perspectives (the level of the economies and the level of enterprises).

The proposed diagram (Fig. 1) shows in a simplified manner how individuals can affect the economic process using these two different approaches.

In the macro perspective, the focus should be on to the extent that the attitudes, values, beliefs, actions and behaviours of individuals, being an emanation of the culture of a given social group, influence economic processes in the internal (national) dimension and the external (global) dimension. In this context, it is surely worth examining the actions of states regarding their cultural policy conducted both internally (i.e. development and support for the cultural sector within the given country) and externally (under the so-called cultural diplomacy).

---

42 M. M. Khan *et al.*, 'Cultural Values and Economic Growth in Asia: An Empirical Analysis', *International Journal of Business and Social Science*, vol. 1, no. 2, 2010.

43 B. Dima, M. Mutaşcu, C. Enache, *Cultural Determinants of Economic Growth: The Case of European Countries*, Munich Personal RePEc, MPRA Paper no. 5688, September 2006, available at: http://mpra.ub.uni-muenchen.de/5688/1/MPRA_paper_5688.pdf (accessed on 23 April 2013).

44 K. Griffin, 'Culture and Economic Growth: A General Argument with Illustrations from the Islamic World', *Journal of Islamic Studies*, vol. 10, no. 2, 1999.

45 R. G. Holcombe, 'Entrepreneurship and Economic Growth', *The Quarterly Journal of Austrian Economics*, vol. 1, no. 2, 1998.

46 By economic role we understand the actions undertaken by an individual aimed at fulfilling a certain goal. It should also be noted that individuals usually have several overlapping 'economic roles' at the same time – e.g. while being an employee – they are also a consumer.

Figure 1 – The individual and the economy.

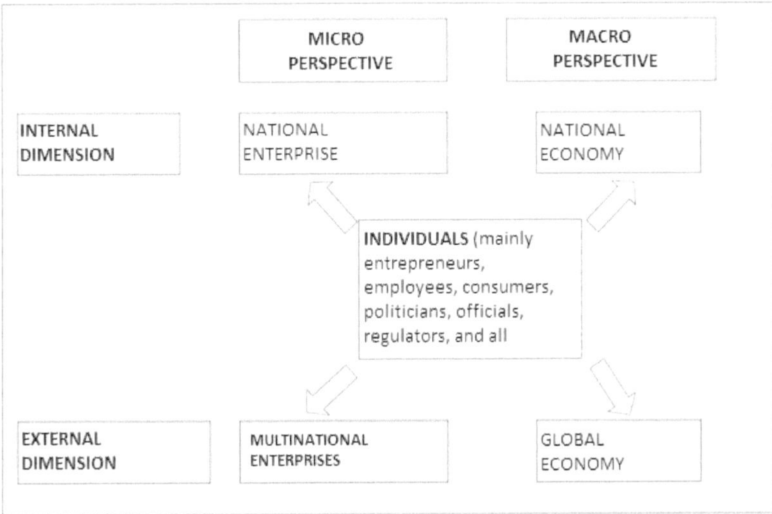

In the first case, it will be important to examine the contribution of the sector of culture to the generation of state GDP and how states promote the cultural values conducive to economic development.[47] In the second case, in turn, we should verify what type of actions are undertaken by states regarding the use of culture to promote their economic interests abroad (e.g. activity concerning the foreign cultural policy of states[48]), how effective they are and whether this allows the states to support economic development.

On the other hand, while applying the micro perspective, one should examine the extent to which culturally conditioned attitudes and actions of individuals translate into broadly understood entrepreneurship (or its lack) and on the

47 Valuable information concerning the European sector of culture is provided by the report *The Economy of Culture in Europe…* It is also worth performing an analysis of the publications of UNESCO, which deals with global promotion of culture, among others. From the point of view of individual states, the source of information can be the publications of the institutions responsible for supporting and developing culture domestically and abroad.

48 An interesting discussion on this topic is presented by S. Parzymies in his article 'Zagraniczna polityka kulturalna Francji w procesie reform' (France's Foreign Policy in the Period of Reforms), *Stosunki Międzynarodowe – International Relations*, vol. 46, no. 2, 2012.

process of internationalisation of the activity of national business entities. After all, it depends on individuals whether the enterprises they represent will be able to develop their activity in foreign markets, thus contributing to the economic growth of the state they represent. The most important issue in this respect is the ability to adapt and to overcome the cultural barriers encountered while entering foreign markets and conducting business activity in them. This includes, among others, the ability to meet the needs of the clients, as well as to take into account the needs and specific behaviour of employees.[49] Another important problem is the overcoming of cultural differences in the processes of international fusions and takeovers.

Do the tools at the disposal of researchers and the current state of knowledge, however, allow them to identify the influence of culture on these issues? The proponents of the thesis that 'culture matters' concur. Looking at them from the perspective of individuals and their 'cultural background', they attempt to:

- show the cultural foundation for the development of values, attitudes and models of conduct;
- identify the values, attitudes and models of conduct facilitating or hampering economic development;
- determine how to best deal with cultural differences (by identifying the characteristics typical of individual national cultures).

For most researchers, the starting point in their search for the foundations of the development of economic attitudes is the classical theory of Max Weber – regardless of whether they accept or reject it.[50] According to Weber, the key element that provided the basis for the development of attitudes conducive to the development of capitalism was Protestant ethics (the religious factor as an important element of culture). In his opinion, in accordance with the rules of Protestant religion, the goal of the individual was work, and the accumulated wealth reflected its quality. Furthermore, individuals were exhibiting a particular combination of views and beliefs, which contributed to the development of the attitude commonly referred to as the 'spirit of capitalism'. The promoted values were honest and hard labour (for the glory of God), accumulating capital while retaining moderation and an ascetic lifestyle, as well as reliability, trust and fulfilling one's commitments in trade

49 This type of issues and relations are studied by a relatively new variety of marketing – the so-called ethnic marketing.

50 M. Weber, *The Protestant Ethic…*; M. Weber, *Economy and Society: An Outline of Interpretive Sociology*, 4th ed., University of California Press, 1978 (the original edition titled *Wirtschaft und Gesellschaft* was published in 1922).

relations. Laziness and idleness were frowned upon (and both considered sins). Additional factors conducive to the development of capitalism were also: respect for private property and entrepreneurship as well as trust.[51] This was the source of the advantage that Protestant countries had over the Catholic ones. This way of thinking provided the foundation for many interpretations of the economic development and success of the Western European countries (e.g. the UK, Germany) or the United States. The proponents of Weber's theories include Harrison and Landes. The latter is even convinced that 'Max Weber was right'.[52] Looking for an answer to the question about the reasons of the quick economic development of Western Europe in the modern area, Landes referred to the concepts of the German scholar and confirmed that it was Protestant ethics that shaped the type of personality (rational, ordered, diligent, productive) which contributed to the establishment of a new economic system – capitalism.[53] However, Weber's approach has often been criticised for being too narrow (disregarding the other factors conducive to the development of capitalism), based on wrong assumptions (e.g. Amintore Fanfani claimed that it was rationalism rather than Protestantism that was the source of capitalism), and even not entirely consistent with history (e.g. Hector M. Robertson argued that there were signs of capitalism already in the Middle Ages).[54] Furthermore, critics of the approach also point out that Weber's theory was inadequate for explaining the economic success of Confucian societies (initially, this concerned the so-called Asian Tigers and now the PRC).[55] One of the most well-known criticisms of Weber is the work by Davide Cantoni titled *The economic effects of the protestant reformation*, in which the author does not

51 The scholars who assign particular importance to trust as the basis of creating social capital include F. Fukuyama (see e.g.: *Social Capital…*).

52 For more see: D. Landes, 'Culture Makes…', p. 2.

53 D. Landes, 'The Wealth and Poverty of Nations…', pp. 177–179; for more on Weber's concepts see pp. 174–179.

54 A discussion of the criticism of M. Weber's theses can be found in Sandra Pierotti, 'Backup of "The protestant Ethic and the Spirit of Capitalism": Criticisms of Weber's thesis', *Georgia Tech*, 14 September 2003, available at: http://www.csudh.edu/dearhabermas/weberrelbk01.htm (accessed on 23 April 2013); see also: F. Fukuyama, *Culture and Economic Development…*, pp. 3130–3134.

55 M. Weber addressed this issue himself as well in the book titled *Die Wirtschaftsethik der Weltreligionen: Konfuzianismus und Taoismus*, Tübingen 1920 (*Economic Ethics of the World Religions: Confucianism and Taoism*), where he stated that Confucianism was unfavourable to the development of capitalism, e.g. due to the role of familial ties in the society, which facilitated nepotism. F. Fukuyama writes about this in *Culture and Economic Development…*.

confirm the influence of Protestant ethics on the economic development of the German countries in the analysed period.[56]

Regardless of later criticism, however, Max Weber's theory is still among the most frequently cited theories and a source of inspiration for further discussions and studies. The proponents of the religious factor (in this meaning, in fact the 'focus' of *culture*) having key importance for the shaping of attitudes facilitating economic development of states stress also that despite focusing on Protestantism and failing to appreciate the importance of other religions, Weber was not wrong. Citing the research conducted under the aforementioned CMRP project, Harrison claims that – comparing only highly developed countries – 'Protestant countries do substantially better than Catholic countries with respect to prosperity, trust, and corruption.'[57] Furthermore, Harrison's research shows that in economic terms not only Protestants but also 'Jewish, and Confucian societies do better than Catholic, Islamic, and Orthodox Christian societies'.[58] This could explain the economic successes of countries such as, for instance, the United States or Canada, Western European countries, Japan, the so-called Asian Tigers – that is Hong Kong, Singapore, South Korea and Taiwan as well as Jewish, Chinese, Japanese and Vietnamesediasporas dispersed around the world.

The second important issue here is the problem of identification of the values, attitudes and models of conduct that facilitate or hamper economic development. Regardless of the fact that this is a very difficult task in terms of methodology and one giving rise to much controversy regarding its scientific nature, researchers make repeated attempts to deal with it.[59] Examples of different approaches to this problem can be found in the first part of the joint publication *Culture Matters*, dedicated to the relations between culture and the economy. In the chapter titled *Culture Makes Almost All the Difference*, David Landes focuses on cultures

---

56 D. Cantoni, *The Economic Effects of the Protestant Reformation: Testing the Weber Hypothesis in the German Lands*, Harvard University, 10 November 2009, available at: http://www.people.fas.harvard.edu/~cantoni/cantoni_jmp_2_7_1.pdf (accessed on 23 April 2013); and D. Cantoni, 'Godly Business: The End of the Protestant Work Ethic', *Foreign Policy*, March–April 2010, available at: http://www.foreignpolicy.com/articles/2010/02/22/godly_business (accessed on 14 January 2013).

57 L. Harrison, *Culture and economic development*, CATO Unbound, 4 December 2006, available at: http://www.cato-unbound.org/2006/12/04/lawrence-e-harrison/culture-and-economic-development/ (accessed on 23 April 2013).

58 *Ibid.*

59 See e.g.: L. W. Pye, 'Asian Values: From Dynamos to Dominoes?', in S. Huntington, L. Harrison (eds.), *Culture Matters...*, pp. 244–255.

conducive to development (he points out the economic success of ethnic minorities of Chinese people, Lebanese people, Jews, or Calvinists) and on the factors which hamper development (here he refers to e.g. the attitude of the Russians in the post-Communist period). He also analyses the problem more broadly on the example of the failure of Brazil and the success of Japan. He furthermore shows that regardless of the other factors, the preferred attitudes and values have a great influence on whether the given country has a chance to succeed (Japan) or not (Argentina).[60] A different approach is proposed by Michael E. Porter. He defines the term 'economic culture'[61] and explores 'the complex links between economic culture and economic progress'.[62] At the same time, he refers to his classical concept of competitive advantage and argues that the level of prosperity in countries depends exactly on such advantage developed by the societies. He assumes that the values and attitudes conducive to increasing competitiveness of societies and states include: diligence, enterprise, confidence in education as well as the inclination to economise and invest (although he believes that the most important one is productivity). Porter also highlights the fact that in the age of globalisation, the positive model of economic culture spreads freely in the world and gradually becomes universal. This does not mean, however, that economic cultures of societies will be vanishing.[63]

The analyses conducted by two other authors – Carlos Alberto Montaner and Daniel Etounga-Manguelle – concern particular regions (Latin America and Africa, respectively) and show how cultural factors can cause a slowdown of economic development. The first author, when analysing Latin American countries, focuses on the role of six elite groups[64] and their attitudes and values as barriers

---

60 In his research, when comparing Japan and Argentina, Landes highlighted the passivity and fatalism of Argentinians (originating largely from the dependency theory) as the factors hampering the development of the country and as their antithesis, he pointed to the active and humble attitude of the Japanese, who while acknowledging their weaknesses used their assets to make a huge civilisational leap in the Meiji period. For more see: D. Landes, 'Culture Makes…', p. 4–10.

61 M. Porter defines economic culture as 'the beliefs, attitudes, and values that bear on the economic activities of individuals, organisations, and other institutions'; cf.: M. Porter, 'Attitudes, Values, Beliefs, and the Microeconomics of Prosperity', in S. Huntington, L. Harrison (eds.), *Culture Matters…*, p. 14.

62 *Ibid.*, p. 15.

63 *Ibid.*, pp. 27–28.

64 According to Montaner, these are: the politicians, the military, businessmen, clergy, intellectuals, and leftist groups; cf.: C. A. Montaner, 'Culture and the Behavior of Elites in Latin America', in S. Huntington, L. Harrison (eds.), *Culture Matters…*, pp. 56–64.

hampering progress. At the same time, he notes however, that the elites alone cannot be blamed for the lack of progress and that within the elites there are people who think and behave differently and who try to invoke change.[65] Daniel Etounga-Manguelle, in turn, looks for the internal (cultural) reasons for the economic backwardness of Africa. First of all, he focuses on the problem of identifying the characteristics of African culture (which is a very hard task given the diversity of this continent) and then he points out the areas in which cultural revolutions should be conducted to improve the economic and social situation of the continent (namely: education, politics, economy, and social life).[66]

The most comprehensive and consistent concept, however, is presented by Mariano Grondona. Referring to Weber's ideas and analysing the characteristics of the American society (as a pro-development society) and the Argentine society (as an anti-development society), he presents an original set of cultural characteristics/factors which facilitate or hamper economic development of states (see Table 1). He also stresses, however, that the list of attributes he presents is not closed and that the 'positive' and 'negative' sets cannot be fully assigned to particular societies. In his opinion, these tools – forming a certain theoretical basis – 'facilitate analysis because they offer two poles of reference that help us locate and evaluate a given society'.[67]

Although we can intuitively list certain universal values and attitudes that facilitate entrepreneurship and the development of the economy (such as e.g. initiative, respect for and a positive attitude to work, honesty, openness to change, observance of laws), it is very hard to name one that would be equally effective in all and any circumstances. Michael E. Porter recommends that we should not consider these attributes dogmatic and unambiguous – what works in a given place, time and case will not always have the same effect in other circumstances.[68]

65 *Ibid.*

66 D. Etounga-Manguelle, 'Does Africa Need a Cultural Adjustment Programme?', in S. Huntington, L. Harrison (eds.), *Culture Matters…*, pp. 65–79.

67 M. Grondona, 'A Cultural Typology for Economic Development', in S. Huntington, L. Harrison (eds.), *Culture Matters…*, p. 53. It is also worth noting that Grondona's typology served as the basis for further studies and development of a more refined concept by the CMPR project team.

68 M. Porter, *Attitudes, Values…*, pp. 14–15.

Table 1. The set of cultural factors that influence economic development according to Mariano Grondona

Factors/effect	Progressive cultures	Conservative cultures
	Yes, they are favourable to development	No, they are resistant to development
Religion	Protestantism (the Calvinistic branch)	Publican religion
Trust in the individual	Faith in the individual	Mistrust in the individual
The moral imperative	Consistent laws and norms, not totally exigent and therefore realisable	Two worlds out of touch with each other: exalted ideals and highest standards that are difficult to enforce vs. furtive immorality and generalised hypocrisy
Two concepts of wealth	Creating what does not yet exist – striving after innovation	Using what already exists (the land and what derives from it)
Two views of competition	Competition is the way to success	Striving after utopian equality, rejecting competition
Two notions of justice	Distributive justice puts an emphasis on the future – involves the interest of future generations	Distributive justice puts an emphasis on the present – concerned with those who are alive now
The value of work	Respect for every kind of work	Work is not highly valued
The role of heresy	The open, questioning mind able to negate the given state of affairs creates innovation	Orthodox societies suppress innovation
To educate is not to brainwash	Education helps individuals discover their own truths, does not dictate what the truth is	Education transmits dogma, producing conformists
The importance of utility	Eschewing unverifiable theories (utilitarianism)	Grand cosmovisions with no real use
The lesser virtues	Esteeming a job well done, tidiness, courtesy, punctuality	Lesser virtues are virtually irrelevant
Time focus	Focus on the future that is within reach	Exaltation of the past
Rationality	Progress – the consequence of a vast sum of small achievements	Great visions and grandiose projects – unfinished and with no real effect
Authority	The rule of law	The rule of force

Factors/effect	Progressive cultures Yes, they are favourable to development	Conservative cultures No, they are resistant to development
Worldview	The world is seen as a setting for action	The world is a vast entity in which irresistible forces manifest themselves and people have to save themselves from them (fanaticism and fatalism)
Life view	Life is something that people make happen, they are the protagonists	Life happens to people and they must accept it
Salvation from or in the world	Salvation depends on the success of one's efforts in transforming this world	Salvation is the goal of one's life and can be achieved by resisting temptations in this world
Two utopias	Progressing slowly toward a distant utopia through creativity	Seeking an early utopia that is beyond reach of the individual
The nature of optimism	The optimist is the person who is resolved to do whatever is necessary to assure a satisfactory destiny	The optimist is the person who expects that luck, the gods or the powerful will favour him or her
Two visions of democracy	Liberal constitutional democracy (J. Locke, Montesquieu, J. Madison)	Heir of the tradition of absolutism, even when it takes the form of popular democracy (J. J. Rousseau)

Source: own compilation on the basis of M. Grondona, *A Cultural Typology...*, pp. 47–53.

The third noteworthy issue which can be of help in studying economic effectiveness is the problem of dealing with cultural differences in the international sphere. This is particularly important in the context of internationalisation of business activity by enterprises (external activity of enterprises) and functioning within the framework of international organisational structures (transnational corporations). In the first case, the issue of key importance for improving the effectiveness of actions is, regardless of the form of internationalisation,[69] becoming familiar, as thoroughly as possible, with the cultural determinants in the target country and finding ways to deal with the differences. What can be very helpful in this regard are publications of public institutions concerning the promotion of their country abroad (e.g. of the ministry of foreign affairs and specialised institutions dealing with external promotion of the country). Other excellent sources include the studies and papers cited in

69 Internationalisation of business activity can take the form of: export, granting a franchise or license, joint-venture, and foreign direct investments (FDI).

the previous fragment, as well as the aforementioned World Values Survey, which comprehensively presents the cultural differences between countries.

In the second case, in turn, regarding the functioning within the framework of international organisational structures, very useful for the identification and overcoming of cultural barriers, are the aforementioned studies by Geert Hofstede as well as Hampden-Turner and Trompenaars. Hofstede, after long-term studies among almost a hundred thousand IBM employees in several dozen countries identified the essential cultural differences between the various countries (national cultures) that influence the functioning of enterprises in business relations and the possibilities of cooperation within an organisation and between organisations. In his research, he identified four basic categories which he called 'national cultural dimensions' – power distance, individualism versus collectivism, masculinity versus femininity, and uncertainty avoidance.[70] Hampden-Turner and Trompenaars, in turn, analysed surveys conducted among fifteen thousand managers from various countries all over the world and developed a typology for seven capitalist countries (the US, the UK, Japan, Germany, Sweden, the Netherlands, France). The results of their research show that while the economies of these countries function according to similar general principles, there are considerable differences between them in terms of specific cultural characteristics. The dilemmas identified by the researchers are the basis for developing a system of values. These dilemmas are: universalism vs particularism; analysis vs synthesis; individualism vs collectivism; internal vs external control; time sequential vs synchronic; ascribed status vs achieved status. The researchers have determined that 'in any culture, a deep structure of beliefs is the invisible hand that regulates economic activity. These cultural preferences, or values, are the bedrock of national identity and the source of economic strengths.'[71]

Conclusions

The approaches presented in this article show that the problem of relations between culture and the economy can be studied in many different ways and with diverse tools. Every researcher focuses on the approach native to his or her specialty or on a certain portion of reality and the analysis of selected phenomena which are often to become the basis for generalisations. However, the formulation of universal conclusions and theorems is hampered by the lack of appropriate research tools and a uniform methodology. In this context, the following recommendation by Lawrence Harrison seems particularly apt: 'A comprehensive theoretical and

70 G. Hofstede, G. J. Hofstede, M. Minkov, *Cultures and Organizations…*

71 Ch. Hampden-Turner, A. Trompenaars, *The Seven Cultures…*, p. 4.

applied research programme should be undertaken with the goal of integrating value and attitude change into development policies.'[72] This shows that Harrison is not only convinced that culture influences the broadly understood development but also believes that it is possible to develop instruments that would use it for pro-development actions. The necessity to conduct considerable historical work and develop a sound theoretical framework is also pointed out by Jeffrey Sachs.[73]

Before this project is implemented, however, we should address the current state of research. What we can observe is that the common element of all approaches is that they take into account, in the context of economic processes, the role of the individual and his 'cultural baggage'. Authors attempt to explain the influence that individuals (as representatives of societies) exert on various elements important in economic processes – e.g. on production, consumption, and on the approach to work and its efficiency. Some, for example Mariano Grondona, attempt to present a set of culturally conditioned factors facilitating or hampering economic processes. Research shows, however, that just as there are no universal sets of attributes ensuring economic success, there are also no ideal models that would be effective in all circumstances. The cultural factor is only one of many variables contributing to economic success but one which surely cannot be disregarded, even though some researchers might negate it. One of the scholars who advise caution in judging the influence culture has on the economy is Jeffrey Sachs. He stresses that analyses should be based on comprehensive approaches – taking into account culture as well as factors such as geographical location, politics and the economy.[74] Thus, we could say that 'culture matters but is not decisive'. We should also remember that while on the one hand, culture is among the key factors of economic development (which can either considerably increase it or dramatically limit it), on the other hand, economic development is conducive to changes which can contribute to cultural transformations in societies.[75] We are, therefore, dealing with a complex interrelation – culture influences economic processes and these processes change culture.

The original version of this text was published in the academic journal "Społeczeństwo i Polityka", no. 4, 2012.

---

72 L. Harrison, 'Why Culture Matters', in S. Huntington, L. Harrison (eds.), *Culture Matters…*, p. xxxii. In this chapter, the author describes in detail what particular elements should be included in this kind of a research project.

73 J. Sachs, 'Notes on a New Sociology of Economic Development', in S. Huntington, L. Harrison (eds.), *Culture Matters…*, p. 43.

74 For more see: *Ibid.*, pp. 29–43.

75 This issue is also pointed out by, for example, R. Inglehart, in *Culture and Democracy…*, pp. 80–97.

Stanisław Bieleń

Culture in International Negotiations

Key words: negotiation cultures, cultural differences and determinants, the topography of culture, international diplomatic culture

Abstract: Culture plays both a positive and a negative role in negotiations. On the one hand, it is conducive to establishing certain universal foundations that constitute a catalyst for agreements owing to the skill and experience of professional negotiators. On the other hand, however, culture can hamper negotiations, contributing to disharmony and interfering with the development of mutual understanding. This work considers the relative rather than absolute influence culture has on international negotiations.

Role of culture in international relations

Culture is an indispensable element of the motivating power of states.[1] It generates people's readiness to organise international life according to set rules and delimits the boundaries across which various relations are established. There relations, however, are not necessarily cooperative. For example, the recurring outrage in the Islamic world regarding offensive drawings and films showing the prophet Muhammad in a bad light prove how culture can generate conflicts in contemporary international relations.[2]

Culture can be treated as a set of universal values, norms and practices to which large communities aspire but it can also be a set of specific characteristics that differentiate individual groups of people. On the one hand, it has cementing functions for civilisations, and on the other hand, it is an instrument for diversifying people. Culture is especially conducive to identification; it allows to distinguish large communities, but at the same time to exclude others, and deny them the right to otherness.[3] Consequently, two logics collide here, one of them pointing

---

1 For more see: J. S. Nye, Jr., 'The Future of Power', *Public Affairs*, New York 2011; cf.: S. Bieleń, *Polityka w stosunkach międzynarodowych* (*Politics in International Relations*), Warszawa 2010, pp. 42–43.

2 A. Chludziński, *Karykatury Mahometa – prowokacja czy profanacja?* (*Muhammad's Caricatures – Provocation or Profanation?*), available at: http://kk.php/kk.php/s,4649/q,Karykatury.Mahometa.8211.prowokacja.czy.profanacja (accessed on 20 April 2013).

3 In the academic literature on the subject we find many attempts at defining culture as fully as possible. The first attempt to summarize these efforts was made already in 1952

to the participation of culture in the universal process of civilising the world and the other to the divisions of the world and the rise of particularistic tendencies. On the one hand culture fosters divisions, and on the other hand it facilitates 'transversality' of the world (interpenetration, participation in the same time and space).[4] Multiculturalism, which highlights the equal importance of cultures, is perhaps a reaction to such limitations.[5] It is worth bearing these observations in mind while analysing the processes of negotiation.[6] It turns out that in the 'global village' or the 'flat world' there is no escape from differences and the behaviours that were shaped through centuries and are now as integral a part of local life as indigenous flora and fauna.[7] Globalisation does not necessarily imply cultural homogenisation. The ability to speak English does not imply thinking in this language or, more broadly, belonging to Anglo-Saxon culture. The multitude of cultural differences, especially regarding systems of values and styles of communication, causes misunderstandings at the negotiating table, even between partners who are positively predisposed towards each other. Another important factor in this context is the system of inculturation and upbringing of the negotiators.[8]

---

in the context of anthropology, in the book by A. Kroeber, C. Kluckhohn, *Culture: A Critical Review of Concepts and Definitions*, New York 1952.

4 P. Katzenstein, 'A World of Plural and Pluralist Civilizations: Multiple Actors, Traditions, and Practices', in P. Katzenstein (ed.), *Civilizations in World Politics. Plural and Pluralist Perspectives*, London 2010, pp. 1–40.

5 W. J. Burszta, *Antropologia kultury. Tematy, teorie, interpretacje* (*Anthropology of Culture. Topics, Theories, Interpretations*), Poznań 1998, p. 152; W. Daszkiewicz, 'Wielokulturowość a ideologia multikulturalizmu' (Multiculturalism and Multiculturalist Ideology), *Cywilizacja*, no. 33, 2010, pp. 196–199.

6 Experts dealing with this issue stress that perception of culture, as part of a dynamic discourse, is subject to conflicting interpretations. Culture is always defined in opposition to something else (A. Kuper, *Culture: The Anthropologists' Account*, Cambridge, MA 1999, p. 14).

7 M. McCrum, *Going Dutch in Beijing: The International Guide to Doing the Right Thing*, London: Profile Books, 2007, p. viii.

8 Inculturation is a mechanism of transmission of culture under which cultural heritage is transferred. It takes place through direct guidelines which are realised in the process of raising and education, through conscious observation and imitation, as well as through involuntary imitation and absorption. It refers to a given cultural system but in certain situations can cover elements of two or even several cultures, or include content foreign to a given culture. A new cultural reality requires re-inculturation in a new culture. See: T. Prywer, *Inkulturacja jako składowa procesu socjalizacji* (*Inculturation as a Component of Socialisation*), available at: http://www.edukacja.edux.

Regardless of semantic misunderstandings, in international relations countries often intentionally include culture as an element of their strategies and an instrument of their foreign policy. Culture constitutes an important tool for promotion and image management and we have to admit that various global powers, such France, the United Kingdom or the United States, have long considered this means of international influence very important. Even for small countries such as Austria or Finland, culture is a very important instrument of drawing attention and interest of others. There is also a belief that culture has a modifying effect on the international image of states. For example, the perception of Russia through its ruling elite does not yield the same effect as the perception through the country's cultural heritage.[9] One can dislike Russia for political reasons yet cannot help but be enchanted by its culture. The countries established after the dissolution of the USSR or Yugoslavia started building their international identity through cultural specificity because they either had no other assets or had only assets that were of no use for the development of a new international image. The force of attraction of the European Union is based not only on its economic achievements but also on cultural and civilisational heritage and there is no doubt that the so-called return to Europe of the countries of Central and Eastern Europe has strong cultural connotations.[10]

Cultural sensitivity is also manifested in the clash of hegemonic tendencies with inclinations to defend one's identity (imperialisation of the world vs. sovereignisation). It is obvious that representatives of smaller nations or weaker countries (which often have great cultures and traditions, e.g. India, Mexico, also Poland) are particularly sensitive about their pride and status in relations with such global powers as the US or Russia, which try to impose their will on them. For example, the martyrological and heroic culture of Poles interferes with establishing pragmatic relations with the neighbours and with defining Polish national interest in the spirit of realism.[11]

---

pl/p-9546-inkulturacja-jako-skladowa-procesu-socjalizacji.php (accessed on 20 April 2013).

9 Cf.: S. Bieleń (ed.), *Wizerunki międzynarodowe Rosji* (*International Images of Russia*), Warszawa 2011.

10 J. Bátora, M. Mokre (eds.), *Culture and External Relations. Europe and Beyond*, Farnham 2011; R. Krawczyk, *Podstawy cywilizacji europejskiej* (*Foundations of European Civilisation*), Warszawa 2006.

11 For more see: S. Bieleń, 'Szanse na pojednanie polsko-rosyjskie w świetle wyzwań geopolitycznych' (Chances for Reconciliation Between Poland and Russia in Light of Geopolitical Challenges), in S. Bieleń, A. Skrzypek (eds.), *Geopolityka w*

Role of culture in international negotiations

One has to admit that the precise identification of the influence of culture on international negotiations is not an easy task.[12] There is a common belief that negotiators are more aware of the significance of culture when negotiations fail than when they are successful for all parties involved. As a matter of fact, next to cultural elements, psychological and ideological determinants, which are often very hard to differentiate, carry great weight as well.[13] Misinterpretation, for example, can be a consequence of false convictions with an emotional and psychological basis as well as a result of ideological, e.g. religious attitudes.[14] In the Cold War period, barely anyone recognised the significance of culture.[15] Everyone - both theoreticians and practitioners - focused on factors resulting from ideological hostility and calculations concerning the risk of a nuclear conflict.[16]

The end of the Cold War confrontations saw an emergence of the belief that Western standards, serving peace and security of all the participants of international relations, would gain the upper hand.[17] Once again, everyone disregarded

---

stosunkach polsko-rosyjskich (*Geo-Politics in Polish-Russian Relations*), Warszawa 2012, pp. 197–217.

12 Ch. Jönsson, 'Diplomacy, Bargaining and Negotiation', in W. Carlsnaes, T. Risse, B. A. Simmons (eds.), *Handbook of International Relations*, London 2003, pp. 219–220.

13 For more see: J. W. Salacuse, *Making Global Deals. Negotiating in the International Marketplace*, Boston: Houghton Mifflin, 1991.

14 While observing the so-called 'Smolensk syndrome' in Poland, caused by the catastrophe of the presidential Tu-154 plane, one might get the impression that all these determinants are reflected in it. Psychology has pointed out long ago that in group thinking, maintaining coherence and solidarity of the group is more valued than realistic weighing of facts. This phenomenon can also affect people's conduct during negotiations. See: I. L. Janis, *Victims of Groupthink: A Psychological Study of Foreign-Policy Decisions and Fiascoes*, Boston 1972.

15 As a part of the commitments adopted in the Helsinki Final Act in 1975, the so-called third basket included issues related to cooperation and exchange in the area of culture. In practice, however, this issue was subject to far-reaching ideologisation. For more see: F. Gołembski, *Współpraca kulturalna w procesie budowy europejskiego ładu pokojowego* (*Cultural Cooperation in the Process of Building European Peace Order*), Warszawa 1979; F. Gołembski, *Uwarunkowania współpracy kulturalnej między państwami o odmiennych systemach polityczno-społecznych* (*Determinants of Cultural Cooperation Between Countries Having Different Political and Social Systems*), Warszawa 1989.

16 For more see: A. Cassels, *Ideology and International Relations in the Modern World*, New York–London 1996.

17 F. Fukuyama, *The End of History and the Last Man*, New York: Free Press, 1992.

the importance of cultural differences, forgetting that in this regard, the world was more heterogeneous than homogenous. The increased role of the cultural factor in international negotiations is also the effect of dynamic identification processes taking place in various parts of the world. Never before have nations so openly demonstrated their identity and the striving to emphasise their otherness.[18]

As a result of all this, the very nature of international negotiations is being redefined. Although they are treated as an important legal and diplomatic instrument, it is exactly for cultural reasons that they are becoming the key to understanding the complexity of the globalised world and especially to legitimising the changes which take place in it.[19] Therefore, the stress in the understanding of international relations falls not on the decision-making processes but rather on the process of communicating.[20]

In their book of 1982, Ira William Zartman and Maureen Berman said that negotiations are universal regulatory processes but they are diversified in terms of the means of communicating in the international environment.[21] The richness of negotiation styles makes negotiators aware of how difficult of an art this is, and how much knowledge, experience, sensitivity, and empathy it requires.

18 Cf.: A. D. Smith, *The Cultural Foundations of Nations. Hierarchy, Covenant and Republic*, London: Blackwell, 2008; A. D. Smith, *The Ethnic Origins of Nations*, Oxford: Basil Blackwell, 1986.

19 For a negotiation to take place the following conditions (necessary and sufficient) are required: 1) the existence of at least two protagonists who have the desire to employ negotiations in order to overcome the problem and find the solution to it; 2) identification of the problem as well as the possibilities and means of overcoming it; 3) impossibility (objective) or inability (subjective) of the parties to solve the problem in another way, using other means; 4) the parties considering the agreement on certain actions beneficial or even necessary for their own interest. See: J. Pańków, *Negocjacje jako sposób rozwiązywania konfliktów społecznych* (*Negotiation as a Way of Solving Social Conflicts*), Warszawa 1987.

20 In classical approaches, negotiations are treated as: 1) a type of social interaction which take place by means of verbal communication between the representations of social entities according to certain rules specified and accepted by their participants; 2) a difficult and complex process of decision-making in which each participant – regardless of whether the talks are bilateral or multilateral – tries to lead the parties to a common decision ensuring, first of all, the realisation of its own interests. Cf.: K. Kocot, *Rokowania dyplomatyczne. Prawnomiędzynarodowe sposoby regulowania sporów* (*Diplomatic Negotiations. Methods of Dispute Resolution Applied in International Law*), Wrocław 1969.

21 I. W. Zartman, M. R. Berman, *The Practical Negotiator*, New Haven, CT: Yale University Press, 1982, p. 226.

Sometimes, negotiators are compared to physicians, who while educated in one culture, venture to different parts of the world to heal patients in entirely different environments. At that time, they have to face the problem of cultural dissonancethat concerns, for instance, diagnosing disease symptoms, describing pain, or applying the right therapy. It has been observed that physicians educated in Western culture need a lot of time to adapt to the new environment of non-Western countries.[22]

In this culturally complex world, negotiations help in progressing from one social situation to another, facilitate becoming accustomed to new models of behaviour. The most obvious case is the process of peace talks after acts of war or armed conflicts. Abandoning hostility, recognising the arguments of the opposing parties and accepting the new order are often more of a challenge than just agreeing on the precise wording of an international agreement. This is because it requires the parties to apply the principles of reciprocity and equal treatment, and makes them give up the desire to impose their own will on others. Due to cultural differences, these seemingly obvious attributes of diplomatic negotiations are not necessarily perceived in the same way in different parts of the world, especially in the context of the preferred negotiation strategies. These strategies depend not so much on the negotiation style conditioned by culture as on particular interests and needs, the power relation between the parties, the bargaining position, the severity of the conflict of interests, the conflicting values (including preferences concerning the perception of justice, perception interference caused by bad communication, emotions, prejudice, stereotypes, information gaps, or misinterpretations), personal preferences and attitudes of the negotiators, and finally, external pressure and instructions from the superiors.[23]

Geert Hofstede, an expert and classic in the field of studying the influence of culture on organisations, stresses that 'effective intercultural negotiations demand an insight into the range of cultural values to be expected among partners from other countries'.[24] Apart from values, it is also the rituals, symbols, beliefs,

---

22 Cf.: M. Weingarten, *Changing Health and Changing Culture: The Yemenite Jews in Israel*, Westport, CT: Praeger, 1992.

23 Negotiation strategies are the most broadly formulated plans referring to the entirety of the process of negotiation and taking into account the means which a party has at its disposal in order to realise its intended goals. Cf.: D. G. Pruitt, 'Strategy in negotiation', in V. A. Kremenyuk (ed.), *International Negotiation. Analysis, Approaches, Issues*, San Francisco–Oxford: Josey-Bass Elsevier Publishers, 1991, pp. 78–89.

24 G. Hofstede, G. J. Hofstede, M. Minkov, *Cultures and Organizations: Software of the Mind*, 3rd ed., Maidenhead: McGraw-Hill, 2010, p. 400.

and superstitions adopted by groups of people and passed on from generation to generation that play a huge role.[25] In negotiations, attention is paid to these aspects of culture that concern meanings, conventions and presuppositions (assumptions). They constitute a kind of grammar for identifying various allegories, interpretations and signs (e.g. reading between the lines, recognising the 'spirit' of agreements, identifying the psychological atmosphere). Without them, communication between people, or any coordinated action for that matter, is impossible. Probably, many of them are connected with religious upbringing. The beliefs in daemons, spirits, phases of the Moon, the Wheel of Fortune, oracles, fate, healers, soothsayers, and prophets are elements of many contemporary societies that affect people's perception of the world – even enlightened and educated ones. The superstition connected with the 'unlucky thirteen' (possibly related to the thirteenth participant in the Last Supper, Judas Iscariot, who betrayed Jesus) or with the 'lucky seven' in European culture, or with the 'eight' in China, has a bearing on everyday thinking. Consulting horoscopes and astrologists is not a rare practice, even among politicians of such high calibre as the late US President Ronald Reagan.[26] The Chinese ancient practice of feng shui,[27] that is planning the

---

25 W. Hernández Requejo, J. L. Graham, *Global Negotiation. The New Rules*, Basingstoke: Palgrave Macmillan, 2008, pp. 39–49.

26 Presidents capable of self-mockery handle governing better. Ronald Reagan was the first one to laugh at his own weaknesses. Sometimes he even turned them into strengths and with his warm humour he won himself more sympathy than an entire team of PR experts ever could. Reagan was accused of being a president between 9 am and 7 pm and of not overworking himself. He replied: 'It's true, hard work never killed anybody but I figure, why take the chance?' He was so loved for his humorous attitude to himself that the media forgave him many eccentricities which would have destroyed others. One of the most intriguing habits of the White House was to consult everything with an astrologist. Nancy Reagan would set the schedule of her husband's meetings and duties only after consulting the horoscope specialist Joan Quigley. The White House Chief of Staff, Donald Reagan, devised the calendar of the White House according to these arrangements. The influence of astrology on Reagan's calendar was so great that Nancy managed to reschedule the date of the history-making Treaty on Intermediate-range Nuclear Forces (the INF Treaty) in 1987 from prime time in TV to the afternoon, as this was what the astrologist suggested. Cf.: M. Fita-Czuchnowska, *Grecjanie atakują!* (*Grecians are attacking!*), available at: http://www.wprost.pl/ar/111588/Grecjanie-atakuja/#an_949251846 (accessed on 12 November 2012).

27 Pronounced 'fung shwei', literally 'wind and water'; wind, which cannot be seen – the invisible, water, which cannot be taken hold of – the intangible; therefore, feng shui is life-force, an invisible and intangible essence. People and the universe are linked by the *chi* energy, which flows through their entire being. The goal is to take advantage of

surroundings and seeking harmony with the natural environment, can be considered a superstition but given its longevity in the Chinese society, one simply cannot disregard it in figuring out the motives for human behaviour. Feng shui is sometimes called geomancy,[28] as it also covers issues such as protecting buildings from evil spirits, the influence of shape on the surroundings or the arrangement of dates in the calendar.

Rituals are models of behaviour connected with important events in life. They are conducive to coordination of relations between people both in everyday life and on special occasions. In order to understand the rituals of a given culture and their history, a very thorough knowledge of this culture is needed.[29] The greatest obstacle in understanding the rituals of the other party during negotiations is in fact not ignorance but rather ethnocentrism, which clouds the parties' cognitive abilities.[30]

Symbols are related to communication. They are naturally ambiguous, thus often even contradictory meanings are brought together under a single symbol. While the ambiguity of spoken or written signs can be eliminated or mitigated by adding further signs and by observing the rules of grammar, the ambiguity of a symbol can always be expressed only partially or unclearly by related descriptions; in the end, the complete symbolical image remains inexpressible, reserved to internal perception.[31] The problem of graphical representations, allegories and various superstitious speculations concerns every language. What adds to it are various images, myths or metaphors, which often require far-reaching expertise

---

it in increasing happiness and prosperity and to counteract the negative force *sha chi*. See: L. Matela, *Geomancja. Formy Feng Shui. Pozytywne energie* (*Geomancy. Feng Shui Forms. Positive Energies*), Białystok 1998.

28 In India, geomancy exists in an analogous system called *vastu vidya*.

29 Cf. e.g.: G. Althoff, *Die Macht der Rituale. Symbolik und Herrschaft im Mittelalter*, Darmstadt: Primus, 2003, Polish edition: *Potęga rytuału. Symbolika władzy w średniowieczu*, tłum. A. Gadzała, Warszawa 2011.

30 Raymond Cohen refers to the famous affair involving the US Navy ship USS *Astoria*, which President Franklin D. Roosevelt sent in 1939 with a mission to carry the ashes of the deceased Japanese ambassador Hirosi Saito from Washington to Yokohama. Despite the strained relations between the US and Japan, the Japanese perceived this gesture as a sign of extraordinary importance, a new leaf being turned in their relations, while the Americans had nothing more in mind than fulfilling a diplomatic obligation. See: R. Cohen, *Negotiating Across Cultures. International Communication in an Interdependent World*, Washington DC: United States Institute of Peace, 1997, pp. 3–8.

31 M. Oesterreicher-Mollwo, *Lexikon der Symbole*, Herder, 1990, Polish edition: *Leksykon symboli*, transl. by J. Prokopiuk, Warszawa 1992, p. 5.

to be properly identified and understood.[32] Aesthetical impressions provide many meanings as well. 'A picture is worth a thousand words', Confucius is believed to have said. Painting, music, folklore, drama, and dancing can tell a lot about human emotions and experiences. Perhaps we should also add film to this list.[33] Therefore, linguistic skills require knowledge of the cultural context of the negotiating parties.[34] It is often the case that the same words in a given language are differently understood by different nations. For example, the Spanish word *tambo* denotes a roadside inn in Bolivia, Columbia, Ecuador, and Peru, dairy in Argentina and Uruguay, and a brothel in Chile.[35] The understanding of linguistic contexts is facilitated by close relations between some languages. For example, the Romance languages or the Slavic languages allow for a better mutual understanding than languages that are very distant from each other. Consequently, the Japanese and Chinese understand the concept of 'saving face' much better among themselves, while Americans and Europeans do not pay much attention to it, even though they know of this notion.[36]

The meaning of words referring to fundamental objects such as 'sun', 'tree' or 'foot' does not become distorted in translation into other languages. But translation of abstract terms such as 'justice', 'sovereignty' or 'leadership' is conditioned by an entire system of meanings and associations which are difficult to recognise for someone unfamiliar with them. Lorand Szalay showed semantic differences on the example of the word 'corruption', which is understood differently in the United States and in Korea. In the US, corruption is considered an immoral act with criminal repercussions (just as it is the case in most Western countries). However, while Koreans recognise its consequences as unfortunate, they do not

32 See: M. J. Gannon, *Understanding Global Cultures: Metaphorical Journeys through 23 Nations*, Thousand Oaks, CA: Sage Publications, 2001.

33 M. F. Gawrycki, *Uwikłane obrazy. Hollywoodzki film a stosunki międzynarodowe* (*Entangled Images. Hollywood Film and International Relations*), Warszawa 2011.

34 People transmit to each other some semantic codes, words or expressions being patterns of sound or print. Thus, the true meaning of a message depends on the mind of the recipient, who ascribes specific content to it according to his or her own knowledge, experience, interests, within a framework of reference delimited by the sender. The prerequisite for understanding between the sender and the recipient is, therefore, the agreement between the intentions of the sender and the meaning ascribed by the recipient. See: L. B. Szalay, 'Intercultural communication: A process model', *International Journal of Intercultural Relations*, no. 5, 1981, pp. 133–146.

35 W. Hernández Requejo, J. L. Graham, *Global Negotiation…*, p. 45.

36 O. Kazuo, 'How the "Inscrutables" Negotiate with the "Inscrutables": Chinese Negotiating Tactics vis-à-vis the Japanese', *China Quarterly*, vol. 79, 1979, p. 549.

consider corruption morally wrong. Differences in the perception of this concept result from a different philosophy underlying the functioning of the society and the public services. In the United States, they are supposed to be impartial and serve the entire society, so they cannot be susceptible to bribery. In Korea, in turn, gifts for functionaries are accepted and the functionaries' commitments to friends and relatives take precedence over some abstract duties to the society.[37]

'A worldwide survey was conducted by the UN. The only question asked was: "Would you please give your honest opinion about solutions to the food shortage in the rest of the world?" The survey was a failure. In Africa they didn't know what "food" meant; in India they didn't know what "honest" meant; in "Europe" they didn't know what "shortage" meant; in China they didn't know what "opinion" meant; in the Middle East they didn't know what "solution" meant; in South America they didn't know what "please" meant; and in the US they didn't know what "the rest of the world" meant'.[38] This joke shows the paradox of the contemporary world, which often cannot reach an agreement on the most fundamental matters, despite the information revolution.

Differences in the system of preferences and expectations lead to different ways of describing reality. Asians focus more on the whole and perceive the details and facts in a broader context, while Westerners register events taking place in the foreground and do not pay attention to the broader background. Exploring this geography of thinking allows for a better understanding of negotiation behaviour of representatives of different cultures, especially with regard to designing the future.[39]

It is sometimes assumed that the most important prerequisite for understanding others is understanding oneself, because the awareness of one's own culture determines the sensitivity to cultural differences and tolerance – the readiness to accept and even adjust. The basis for developing sensitivity to others is understanding one's own cultural heritage, the influence of geopolitics on group thinking, consolidation of the national character when facing other religions and mental influences.[40]

---

37 L. B. Szalay, *Intercultural Communication...*, pp. 140–141.

38 M. McCrum, *Going Dutch in Beijing...*, p. vii.

39 R. Nisbett, *The Geography of Thought: How Asians and Westerners Think Differently... and Why*, New York, NY: Free Press, 2004.

40 R. J. Lewicki et al., *Essentials of Negotiation*, 5th ed., Boston-Dubuque-Madison: McGraw-Hill, 2010.

The 'Great Divide' between negotiation cultures

Of course, culture is not the sole factor determining attitudes. However, it creates predispositions of people from given cultural groups to act in a particular manner in particular circumstances.[41] Disregard for cultural differences is common and usually leads to *faux pas*, mistakes and eventually failures. Cultural differences not only affect behaviour, reactions, motivations, and expectations but also determine the negotiation style, its pace, language, expectations and methods. Therefore, every negotiator brings to the table their deeply rooted opinions and experiences. Consequently, negotiations with representatives of other cultures differ considerably from the style of negotiations within one culture.[42]

While talking about cultural determinants, we should pay particular attention to:

- The nature of linguistic differences (understanding of words and their semantic contexts);
- The meaning of body language (silence, pauses, speed or spontaneity of reactions);
- The need to identify the cultural (religious, ethnic) group that the partner belongs to;
- That there is no basis for the generalisation that representatives of the given population negotiate in the same way;
- The means of learning the culture of the partner (usefulness of professional counselling, ability to pose questions).

The factors that have the greatest influence on the course of negotiations with foreigners are:

- The sense of individual and group identity, defining oneself against the background of others;
- The degree of organisation of the negotiations, the attachment to rules and rituals;
- The different meaning of time in different cultures;
- The methods of exchanging information.

---

41 M. J. Gelfand, J. M. Brett (eds.), *The Handbook of Negotiation and Culture*, Stanford: Stanford Business Books, 2004.

42 R. J. Janosik, 'Rethinking the Culture–Negotiation Link', *Negotiation Journal*, no. 3, 1987, pp. 385–395.

Taking into account these criteria, the following dichotomies of negotiation cultures are distinguished:[43]

- Deal-focus vs. relationship-focus;
- Informal vs. formal;
- Rigid-time vs. fluid-time;
- Expressive vs. reserved.

Deal-focus cultures are characterised by focusing on performing the task at hand; they exist in a relatively small part of the world: Northern Europe, North America, Australia, and New Zealand. Relationship-focus cultures (the Arab world, most African, Latin-American and Asian countries) emphasise creating bonds, interpersonal relations, trust, which requires patience and time. They exhibit an ambiguous, oblique style of speech, high contextuality of communication, limited openness to foreigners; the intermediaries are important, as are agreements and personal connections as well as preserving harmony, refraining from embarrassing or confusing the other party, hiding negative emotions; the contract does not finalise the negotiations.

Informal cultures (Australia, New Zealand, the US, Canada, Denmark, Norway, Iceland) are characterised by egalitarianism, paying little attention to proprieties, status or hierarchy. Ceremonial cultures (typical of most European and Asian countries, the Mediterranean Basin and the Arab world as well as Latin America) emphasise showing respect, the importance of social and professional hierarchy, formality in addressing the other party, protocol rituals, conventions regarding dress and attire, the proprieties.

Rigid-time cultures (the Nordic and other Germanic European countries, North America, Japan) stress punctuality, 'clock worship', importance of the agenda, the schedule, the order of day, adversariality, observance of the order of speaking. Fluid-time cultures (typical of the Arab world, most African, Latin American, South Asian and Southeast Asian countries) have a relaxed attitude to the clock and calendar, promote a flexible order of the day and exhibit aversion for setting fixed dates and deadlines.

Expressive cultures (characteristic of Romance European countries, other Mediterranean countries and Latin America) are distinguished by directness, openness, overlapping of speakers, low-context language. Reserved cultures (typical of East and Southeast Asia, the Nordic countries and other Germanic European countries) exhibit great composure, importance of silence, the order of speaking,

---

43 See: R. R. Gesteland, *Cross-Cultural Business Behavior: Negotiating, Selling, Sourcing and Managing Across Cultures*, Copenhagen: Copenhagen Business School Press, 1999.

significant spatial distance, avoiding looking into the eyes of the other party, limited gesticulation.

The above division, proposed by Richard Gesteland, shows that every participant in negotiations in international relations must first of all learn the local customs and practices applied during diplomatic and business talks in order to avoid awkwardness and offence, but more importantly, become sensitive to the differences existing in the contemporary world.

The individualist and the collectivist ethos

In international relations, culture is associated with spatial location. The topography of culture determines changes in people's thinking, in how people perceive each other, in people's diversity, independence and identity.[44] These characteristics are naturally not conducive to successful communication during negotiations, which requires empathy and understanding of the other party's arguments. Communities that had the opportunity for spatial dispersal, for example North Americans – developed an individualist style of negotiations, which defines their conduct even today. The Japanese, in turn, crowded on a relatively small area, had to learn to coexist in a group and acquire compromise. Thus, the cooperation-oriented attitudes that characterise them have been a prerequisite for their survival. In the past, people had to cross vast distances to obtain supplies and it did not create favourable conditions for long negotiations. Later, numerous ideological determinants were added to it. The cultures that developed under the influence of various factors were so different that people meeting at the negotiating table are unable to comprehend the fundamental semantic codes characteristic of the other party.[45]

From the perpective of defining one's identity against the background of others, the assessment of contemporary negotiation cultures is dominated by a division into the individualist ethos and the collectivist ethos. This division may seem simplified as it does not reflect certain differences existing within the same reference groups. For example, between India and Japan, whose cultures are both collectivist, there can be as many disparities as between any single one of these countries and the United States.

Individualist cultures, with the most characteristic example of American negotiation culture,[46] have arisen from the Protestant tradition that originated in the

---

44 M. Kendik, *Negocjacje międzynarodowe* (*International Negotiations*), Warszawa 2009.

45 E. T. Hall, *The Silent Language*, New York: Fawcett, 1959, p. 26.

46 S. Bieleń, 'Północnoamerykański styl negocjacji' (North American Negotiation Style), in S. Bieleń (ed.), *Historia. Stosunki międzynarodowe. Amerykanistyka. Księga*

Reformation. The destiny of the human, who experienced God's grace, is salvation, so it is only up to him to achieve this goal. Discovering the right and true path to salvation by studying the Bible is a result of the effort of the individuals themselves. Consequently, the foundation of the individualist culture is free will, development of one's own personality and self-actualisation. Thus, all social affiliations depend exclusively on personal choices. Belonging to various groups is conducive to satisfying various needs but is not a permanent attribute of an individual. Social mobility and changing affiliations is valued instead. In social life, people value equality and status that is acquired rather than inherited. Authority and power are a consequence of the position held. They can easily be questioned but they are respected nonetheless. Rights and obligations are specified by law. Individual obligations are derived from agreements, not customs. Disputes are settled by law (in court) and not by the general public or communal methods of mediation. The dominating approach is an adversarial one, under which each party defends its rights on an equal footing and presents arguments in a persuasive and logical manner. All these characteristics connected with individual mobility and initiative are typical of the Anglo-Saxon immigrant societies (US, Canada, Australia). Basing economies and political systems on the liberal doctrine was conducive to promoting such human capabilities that within 200 years these societies achieved the highest level of development in the world. This undeniable civilisational success resulted in the common North American belief that the American lifestyle deserved universal application and promotion all over the world.[47]

The collectivist, communal ethos originates with the initial domination of rural agricultural communities, in which the need to support each other while working the land, harvesting or doing irrigation works determined the relations between the individual and the group. In collectivist cultures, the primacy of the family, clan or caste (as well as class or nation) determines a rigid social and religious hierarchy. The well-being of the group is placed above that of individuals. Individual identity is set against the background of group affiliations and individual needs are determined by the interest of the community. Therefore, the perception of an individual by the group is the most precious value. Losing one's good name (face) in the eyes of the group is worse than death. Dishonour demands revenge. Individual freedom is thus limited by the obligations to the family and community. Group affiliations are acquired by birth and are not determined by personal preferences.

Jubileuszowa na 65-lecie Profesora Wiesława Dobrzyckiego (*History. International Relations. American Studies. A Jubilee Book for the 65th Anniversary of Prof. Wiesław Dobrzycki*), Warszawa 2001, pp. 51–72.

47 R. Cohen, *Negotiating Across Cultures…*, pp. 29–30.

The fundamental relations and ties of loyalty are inherited within the group and often last entire life. There is no respect for abstract law. All decisions are personal, based on group wisdom; personal commitments mean much more than contracts. Everyone has an assigned role and the resulting social status. Hierarchy is part of the natural order of things and education shapes respect for authority and power rather than individual autonomy. Truth is not sought in intellectual deliberations or disputes, it can be found in collective tradition. Cooperative and non-confrontational attitudes are valued. Disputes are solved by conciliation, in the name of preserving group harmony, not abstract law and justice.[48]

The characteristics presented briefly above show how differently the two ethoses can shape behaviours at the negotiation table; first of all, how they influence the forms of expression, the attitude to hierarchy or the manner of conducting debates.

Linguistic dissonance

The language of every social group contains specific meanings referring to the notion of truth or the raison d'être. Words are often affective and involve a multitude of metaphorical connotations characteristic of the given reference group. When negotiations are conducted between various cultures, linguistic dissonance is common and hampers mutual understanding. However, in the long-lasting negotiation process certain notions and categories have been developed to allow effective communication despite cultural differences. These include: 'proposals', 'interests', 'positions', 'concessions', 'compromise', 'contract', which mean approximately the same in different cultures. However, it is also worth to look for their equivalents in every language in order to avoid misunderstandings. Thus, the cultural context is important and becoming familiar with it is a prerequisite for the successful use of these terms. Therefore, contrary to what we might believe, 'contract' or 'agreement' mean something else in the United States – or generally in Western culture – than it does in Japan, where these terms are denoted by the word *keiyaku*. For Western negotiators, a contract usually means an official document,

48 *Ibid.*, pp. 30–31. Wenyu Xu, a researcher studying contemporary Chinese literature, points out that China is in need of a change and an awakening of the awareness of citizenship. Chinese history lacks modern awareness of citizenship; for thousands of years, China only had common people but no citizens. After a couple thousand years of feudal patriarchal awareness, the relations between people still have the same character. The legal awareness is low and connections or customary rules are often more important than law. W. Xu, 'Cesarz to nie cały świat' (The Emperor Is Not the Whole World), *Gazeta Wyborcza*, 3–4 November 2012.

an agreement of the parties to enter a relation of mutual commitments (rights and obligations), while in Japan *keiyaku* means the stage of making promises as the basis for further proceedings in order to establish mutually beneficial relations. Another example is the Chinese term *guanxi*, which refers more or less to connections or relationships, while Western people perceive it as a 'bargaining coin'.[49] Misunderstandings between Israelis and Arabs were often caused by different understanding of the same words by the two parties, for example 'normalisation', 'peace', 'withdrawal', or even 'water' or 'land'. In most cases, the factor preventing mutual understanding was the mythologisation of these terms or assumptions made on the basis of negative attitudes, prejudice or ideologies.[50]

These few examples already show that there are no established simple models of behaviour in negotiations. They require extensive cultural knowledge, which is reflected in languages and behaviours. Linguistic analyses are a good starting point for examining cultural phenomena in international negotiations as language is the cornerstone of cultural identity, it constitutes a treasury of meanings gathered and passed on from generation to generation. At the same time, it is a dynamic medium of social evolution, making it possible to register the changes taking place. It is the cement of national cultures that allows people to maintain a community of meanings and behaviours.

The American anthropologist Edward T. Hall that bore in mind people's communication over the boundaries of cultures introduced a division into 'low-context' and 'high-context' cultures.[51] The former are characteristic of communication in collectivist societies, where there is an obligation to 'save face' and to maintain group harmony (East Asian and Southeast Asian countries). The meaning of what negotiators say at the table can be found in the context in which words are used rather than in the words themselves.[52] Communication is highly nuanced, allusive, mosaic (Aesopian language), indirect. The goal is to maintain the image of the group, not to convey information. The message is conveyed by the context (allusions, remarks, implicit statements) rather than by words. Body language plays a very important role here. Weighing words, cautiousness, focusing on politeness and courtesy, avoiding obtrusiveness and dissonance – for example by never openly saying 'no' – are the typical attributes of high-context communication.

49 D. Y. Lee, P. L. Dawes, 'Guanxi, Trust, and Long-Term Orientation in Chinese Business Markets', *Journal of International Marketing*, no. 2, 2005, pp. 28–56.

50 See: K. Bojko, *Izrael a aspiracje Palestyńczyków 1987–2006* (*Israel and the Aspirations of Palestinians 1987–2006*), Warszawa 2006.

51 E. T. Hall, *Beyond Culture*, New York: Anchor Books, 1976.

52 R. R. Gesteland, *Cross-Cultural Business Behavior…*, p. 41.

Truth is not the most important value. It can and will be sacrificed as the price for preserving a pleasant atmosphere. More attention is paid to rhetorical expressions than to conveying information. Consequently, in such cultures emphasis is put on establishing personal relations, which are the prerequisite of trust and honesty. A façade of politeness hides the all-important intent to maintain harmony, which prevents the parties from using rhetoric that could lead to embarrassment and confusion (disapproval). Cautiousness in formulating judgements, being economical with words and exercising self-restraint are the desired traits of every participant in the negotiation process.

Low-context cultures (the Scandinavian countries and other Germanic European countries, North America, Australia, and New Zealand) have a different style of expression. The message conveyed is direct and overt, there is no beating about the bush, people speak bluntly and straight from the shoulder. Allusions and gestures are secondary to the content transmitted verbally. Calling spade a spade is valued, so that no time is wasted on evasive and non-committal arguments. Language performs an informative function, accuracy and precision of the verbal message is important. Conclusion of transactions does not require friendship, although politeness and courtesy are not discarded completely. Separating professional roles from social roles is essential. Individual freedom is not restricted by commitments to groups and differences of opinion do not evoke a sense of disharmony and are not treated as getting ready for an attack. On the contrary, in low-context cultures, arguing, persuading and driving a hard bargain is everyday practice. Being delicate about expressing one's interests or intentions is considered a weakness, not a virtue.

The division presented above is slighlty simplified. In the contemporary world, cultures mix and blend, hence the described types should be considered idealised. Furthermore, regardless of the cultural background, negotiators always develop a certain 'chemistry' in mutual interactions; in the end, they refer to each other's offers and try to reach a win-win situation. However, particular assets often gain the upper hand, instead of impressions resulting from cultural differences.

Approach to time as the difference between rigid-time and fluid-time cultures

Diplomacy has always been an art of using time. Agreements have been evaluated from the perspective of the time spent on negotiations, their pace, delaying tactics and synchronisation with other events. Employing historical arguments or using the so-called historical policy to justify contemporary relations is absolutely not a recent development. In international negotiations, we can find numerous examples of referring to events long past and expecting compensation for bygone injustices (China–Japan, France–Germany). Poles are definitely a nation that uses historical time in the diplomatic game.

As a result of different approaches to time, in international negotiations cultures that stress punctuality, time discipline and observing agendas meet cultures that have a relaxed attitude to punctuality and do not pay attention to schedules. Therefore, we differentiate between rigid-time (monochronic) cultures and fluid-time (polychronic) cultures. The former can be found in North America, the Nordic and Germanic countries, and in Japan. Their characteristic feature is a focus on bargaining, which is to result with a successful solution of the problem. In fluid-time cultures, characteristic of the Arab world, most African countries, Latin America, South and Southeast Asia, the pace and result of negotiations are not all-important. The goal is instead to establish an atmosphere of understanding and interpersonal relations. The approach to time determines the perception of history, the present and the future. What is considered to be remote past in one culture, in another seems just like 'yesterday'. Thus, perception of time determines the social reality, and contrasts rigidity with flexibility. In rigid-time cultures, time is a measurable phenomenon; it is linear, and it can be divided into sections and delimited forwards. Consequently, it is possible to plan the future, which helps to avoid unnecessary losses and limit risk. Schedules are rigid and serve to maintain discipline in order to allow for the fulfilment of the intended goals. In fluid-time cultures, the emphasis is on the rhythm of life set out by nature, rituals and customs. Bonds and understanding of the problem are much more important factors than observing the calendar. Academic literature on the subject provides us with numerous examples of the American party's frustration and impatience during the negotiations with the People's Republic of China in the 1970s, which resulted in failure. Putting pressure on the schedule often proved ineffective because the Chinese needed time to understand the intentions of the other party and defend their arguments.[53] The general conclusion regarding high-context and fluid-time cultures is that their representatives try to understand and get to know their partners or opponents, while representatives of low-context and rigid-time cultures believe that the whole world follows the rules they believe in and, consequently, that there are no problems with understanding the other party.[54]

53 R. Cohen, 'Negotiating Across Cultures', in Ch. A. Crocker, F. O. Hampson, P. Aall (eds.), *Turbulent Peace. The Challenges of Managing International Conflict*, Washington DC 2003, pp. 476–478.

54 W. Hernández Requejo, J. L. Graham, *Global Negotiation...*, p. 19.

Is there an international diplomatic culture?

The perception of negotiations is influenced by various historical experiences, the level of development and social prosperity. Looking at negotiations through culture, we can notice that in Western societies, which have attained a high level of prosperity, negotiations are a synonym of decency and justice; they are the basis of a peaceful and stable social order. Negotiations always suggest the skill and proficiency of the participants, their ability to overcome problems and take care of things safely and effectively despite unfavourable circumstances. Cooperation and solidarity between people and organisations appear as the condition *sine qua non* of their survival in the society, which can no longer be governed by simple force.[55]

In authoritarian or totalitarian societies, such as in the USSR/Russia, the notion of negotiations based on decency or justice has not developed at all. There has been no place in this country for such art and knowledge.[56] In many collectivist cultures, negotiations are a manifestation of brotherly and familial behaviours; in Africa, for example Sudan, they are associated with reconciling feuding parties (Christians and Muslims, the North and the South).[57]

It is undoubtedly a just warning that in the approach to various cultural determinants of international negotiations one should not venture into far-reaching generalisations as these always imply simplification. Due to the growing internationalisation of social life, as well as the participation of nations and states in the processes of globalisation, the values of traditional perception of culture are subject to redefinition. Cultural diffusion affects negotiation styles as well.

In every culture, there are proponents of strategies of cooperation, rivalry and/or accommodation. There are the popular dichotomies reflecting the division of negotiators into 'hard' and 'soft', 'ideological' and 'matter-of-fact', into 'hawks' and 'pigeons', 'sharks' and 'dolphins'. Due to specific determinants, however, we can state with a substantial dose of probability that Russian negotiators are more belligerent that, for example, the Chinese ones. The same observation is rather hard to apply to American negotiators because they can be both John Wayne-style 'cowboys' and patient 'missionaries', who model their behaviour on promoting values of pioneers and settlers (a good example of exceptional patience and empathy is the former US President Jimmy

55 M. Cathelineau, *Négocier gagnant*, Paris: Inter Editions, 1991.

56 Cf.: S. Lovell, A. Rogachevskii, A. Ledeneva (eds.), *Bribery and Blat in Russia. Negotiating Reciprocity from the Early Modern Period to the 1990s*, Basingstoke: Palgrave Macmillan, 2000.

57 J. D. Leach, *War and Politics in Sudan: Cultural Identities and the Challenges of the Peace Process*, London: I. B. Tauris, 2011.

Carter). There is, however, a pattern where negotiators from individualist cultures tend to exhibit inclinations for applying rivalry-based strategies, while representatives of collectivist cultures tend to seek compromise and cooperation.

Regardless of cultural 'genotypes', in the international arena, diplomats are a kind of a guild, which observes similar behaviour patterns. Having comparable professional training, guided by similar pragmatics, based on the rules of international law and mutual loyalty, international negotiators exhibit a natural ease in using well-tried procedures and a semantic code they all understand. In a sense, they are cosmopolitans who understand the significance of national differences but can subordinate them to universal standards and the requirements of the negotiation process.[58] Martin Wight once observed that it was the emergence of such common culture of behaviour that was the original requirement for the development of the system of states, starting with Ancient Greece.[59] The international system that emerged, however, has been dominated by the values of the Western world, originating in Europe. This is perhaps why Harold Nicolson, in his famous work *Diplomacy*, pointed to the existence of a universal diplomatic code that allows communication between people.[60] In Nicolson's time (1886–1968), it was a natural thing that Western culture was absolutely dominant in the world. For some time now however, we have been dealing with a tendency towards pluralisation of this system, with the emergence of new dynamic centres of influence, which demand equal treatment in negotiations.[61] Not long ago, barely anyone would imagine that Iran could be sitting at the negotiations table as an equal to Western powers. But now, it seems increasingly more necessary if peace is to be preserved.[62] Even Israel is aware of the fact that the problem of Palestine cannot be solved only by military measures and that at some point they will have to commence talks even with representatives of Hamas.

In the age of globalisation, all participants in international relations are connected by the awareness of the challenges and threats to the international community.

---

58 I. W. Zartman, M. R. Berman, *The Practical Negotiator...*, pp. 224–229.

59 M. Wight, *Systems of States*, Leicester: Leicester University Press, 1977.

60 H. Nicolson, *Diplomacy*, 3rd ed., London 1969, Chapter 10.

61 See: Ch. A. Kupchan, *No Ones World. The West, the Rising Rest, and the Coming Global Turn*, Oxford 2012.

62 In his book, George Friedman predicts that in the next decade, the most desired effects in relations with Iran will be achieved by making a move that seems unacceptable at this moment. He means negotiations. (G. Friedman, *The Next Decade. Where We've Been... and Where We're Going*, Doubleday 2011; Polish edition: *Następna dekada. Gdzie byliśmy i dokąd zmierzamy*, trans. by M. Wyrwas-Wiśniewska, Kraków 2012, pp. 141–142).

These, in turn, spur people to develop the sense of responsibility and to look for solutions and remedial measures. In this context, it is worth mentioning the emergence of common 'cognitive maps' or 'mental models', which reflect people's 'beliefs about the importance of the issues and about the cause and effect relationships between them'.[63] 'People tend to construct a shared understanding of the world by interacting with each other within a group over an extended period of time. By exchanging interpretations of what they see, it is said that they *enact* a shared reality. The resulting shared cognitive map is variably referred to as the group's dominant logic, common paradigm or belief system. [...] As individuals can belong to different groups, they can be influenced by different belief systems simultaneously. As members of a national culture, their cognitive maps will to a certain extent be influenced by the beliefs dominant within the nation. [...] In the same manner, people can be impacted by [...] any other groups in which they interact with others.'[64]

We can observe both growing standardisation and diversification (decomposition) of behaviour patterns, expectations and preferences. One factor that is conducive to their standardisation is, for example, the propagation of English as the language of negotiations. The scholars who monitor this phenomenon emphasise that cultural values related to egalitarianism and individualism have been expanding. For example, the simple use of the word *you* by a Chinese, Spanish or even Polish person constitutes a departure or blurring of the social context of status, which is related to hierarchy.[65]

Another factor conducive to standardisation is treating international negotiations as an analytical challenge, or a joint research.[66] This phenomenon is connected with an intensive joint effort towards analysing the views and positions of parties that regards many important global problems, for example those concerning difficult and new issues such as the consequences of uncontrolled financial flows, exploitation of ocean resources, technological problems of disarmament, or the consequences of global warming. This requires all participants in international relations to present a more rational approach, apply the logic of co-responsibility and to abandon egoistic particularisms. Before proceeding to the stage of proper agreement building, it is necessary to take advantage of specialist knowledge and have the situation examined in detail. Therefore, the majority of negotiations are

---

63 B. de Wit, R. Meyer, *Strategy Synthesis: Resolving Strategy Paradoxes to Create Competitive Advantage*, Cengage Learning EMEA, 2010, pp. 31–32.

64 *Ibid.*, p. 32.

65 W. Hernández Requejo, J. L. Graham, *Global Negotiation...*, p. 46.

66 B. I. Spector, 'Metaphors of International Negotiation', *International Negotiation. A Journal of Theory and Practice*, no. 1, 1996, pp. 1–9.

conducted on the expert, working level. These groups (specialists, professionals) develop a new international awareness, which provides an opportunity to strengthen the international negotiation culture.

The exclusiveness and elitism of international diplomatic culture are, however, subject to decomposition due to the participation of a rising number of non-professional diplomats in negotiations – politicians and functionaries of various public and private agencies, who do not care to observe the established standards of conduct. On the one hand, this creates the risk that the quality of the negotiation processes in terms of professional knowledge of procedures, rules and even language will decrease but on the other hand, it facilitates dissemination of knowledge about the universal character of negotiations and the specific measures applied in them. The result of this phenomenon is a fashion for training negotiators in a sensitivity to differences in negotiation styles and cultural differences but also a hope for civilising local politicians who acquire some 'international polish' by being active in extranational structures. In this context, there are more and more observations about Polish politicians becoming more 'civilised' while working in EU negotiation groups.[67]

International diplomatic culture will never be as coherent as national cultures because all diplomats acting in the international arena carry within them some elements of their national cultures, which they internalise since early childhood in the process of socialisation. No later experience can supplant what has been acquired in childhood with regard to the mental attitudes to various encountered phenomena. Furthermore, diplomatic negotiators – even at the level of international functionaries – are not entirely free of pressures or instructions on the part of their superiors as well as of certain limitations resulting from loyalty, moral commitments and simple concern for their own future. Once they finish working for international agencies, national negotiators need to have a place in their countries. Therefore, there are numerous ties limiting their independence of thought and boldness of action.[68]

---

67 Cf.: B. Curyło, *Negocjacje w procesie rozszerzenia Unii Europejskiej na Wschód: uwarunkowania, aktorzy, przebieg* (*Negotiations in the Process of Eastward Enlargement of the EU: Determinants, Actors, Course of the Negotiations*), Toruń 2012.

68 G. Fisher, *Mindsets. The Role of Culture and Perception in International Relations*, Yarmoth, ME: Intercultural Press, 1988, pp. 68–69.

Conclusions

To sum up, one should bear in mind the relative rather than absolute influence of culture on international negotiations. It is hard to speak of any cultural determinism, if only for the aforementioned standardisation of the diplomatic behaviour patterns. It will always be the case that many successes and failures in negotiations will be mainly the result of coinciding or opposing objective interests of the parties, not only of their subjective perception. However, if the parties to negotiations fail to recognise the benefits of mutual concessions, all other measures are of secondary importance.

The regularities that have been observed in the long history of diplomatic contacts cannot be disregarded. Culture conditions mutual perception, rejects information which do not fit or are inconsistent with one's own point of view, and 'provides an interpretative filter or perceptual screen'.[69] It is conducive to assigning meanings to words and behaviours of the other party and conditions attributing errors, related to improper reading of signals in communication with the other party.[70] Culture turns international negotiations into a complex conglomerate of linguistic, procedural and ritual games, every one of which is based on specific rules and conventions. Only highly experienced negotiators can master the challenge – as shown by numerous memoirs – and avoid misunderstandings and faux pas in terms of understanding and observing them.

Culture thus plays both a positive and a negative role in negotiations. On the one hand, it is conducive to establishing certain universal foundations that constitute a catalyst for agreements owing to the skill and experience of professional negotiators. On the other hand, however, culture can hamper negotiations, contributing to disharmony and interfering with the development of mutual understanding.

The original version of this text was published in the academic journal "Społeczeństwo i Polityka", no. 4, 2012.

---

69 B. de Wit, R. Meyer, *Strategy Synthesis…*, p. 32.

70 G. Fisher, *International Negotiation: A Cross-Cultural Perspective*, Yarmouth, ME: Intercultural Press, 1980.

Dorota Heidrich

Culture and International Organisations

Key words: international organisations, world culture, organizational culture, United Nations, UNESCO, League of Arab States, European Union

Abstract: This article analyses different aspects of the impact of culture on international organisations (IOs). Its principal arguments concentrate on the influence of cultural determinants characteristic of particular state members of IOs, on understanding the significance of culture vs. other determinants in IOs and on how globalization processes influence IOs.

Introduction

The notion of 'culture' is one the most popular terms in the humanities and social sciences, as well as in colloquial language.[1] There are multiple definitions of culture and they differ depending on the main field of interest of their authors. Today, many social and economic processes taking place within states or in the international arena are explained through culture. We can define culture by quoting its first scientific definition, by Edward B. Tylor: 'that complex whole which includes knowledge, belief, art, law, morals, custom, and any other capabilities and habits acquired by man as a member of society.'[2] Thus defined, culture influences the development of nations, which subsequently create states. States in turn establish international organisations (IOs) through which they attempt to pursue their actions according to their cultural background. Cultural values shape states' interests realized in international organisations' fora.

The analysis of the influence of culture on the establishment and activity of international organisations[3] yields more questions than answers. Finding regularities that would apply to all IOs is a challenging task. The multitude and diversity of these structures (IOs) form highly heterogeneous institutional and legal solutions conditioned by the will of the members of these organisations. It is likewise

1 Cf. the entry for 'Kultura' (Culture) in *Nowa encyklopedia powszechna PWN*, vol. 3, Warszawa 1998, p. 618.

2 E. B. Tylor, *Primitive Culture*, London 1871; see also: A. Kłoskowska, *Socjologia kultury* (*Sociology of Culture*), Warszawa 2007, p. 22.

3 For the sake of the present analysis, only intergovernmental organizations will be taken into account, leaving behind international non-governmental organizations (INGOs). The influence of culture on the latter ones requires separate research and discussion.

difficult to reveal a pattern of relation between cultural, political and economic determinants in the process of IOs creation. These determinants overlap and influence one another. As this paper will argue, cultural values coming from three distinct levels influence IOs. The first ones are values of national states that form IOs. The second ones are cultural determinants characteristic of the international community (universally or regionally). The last one is the organisational culture that develops in each particular international organisation.

The purpose of this analysis is to present different aspects of the impact of culture on IOs. The following discussion is formed around three principal arguments: First, cultural determinants characteristic of particular states might prove extremely important both in the process of establishing international organisations and in their everyday activities, however they do not need to be the only factor responsible for an efficient functioning of an IO. Second, motives other than culture and ideology may cement international cooperation with much stronger bonds than cultural similarities, even if the latter form a solid base at the initial stageof cooperation. Thirdly, because of globalisation processes, IOs are becoming more and more similar from the point of view of their architectural schemes but, at the same time, member states of IOs tend to put forward their particular cultural values.

With regard to the first argument, a particular emphasis needs to be placed on the fact that particular members' cultures influence interstate cooperation, but also lead to the creation of the so-called organisational culture[4] of IOs. Conflicting cultural factors may prove constructive if tackled properly by an organisation's institutional capabilities, determined by the organisational culture. At the same time, contradictions between cultural values may lead IOs to deadlocks that hurt their credibility and ability to act. Overcoming such damaging circumstances hugely depend on the type of organisation as well as its subjective and objective competences. At the same time, external political, ideological or economic determinants might influence the overall performance of IOs. For example, it was politics and ideology that determined the cooperation between countries during the Cold War era. Members of international organisations, often belonging to the same civilisation[5] but divided by the Iron Curtain, were unable to agree on certain

4 The term 'organizational culture' will be explained further in the analysis.

5 For the purpose of this paper, I shall understand 'civilisation' as the distinguishing characteristic of great and more complex cultures – while being fully aware that the relation between the concepts of 'culture' and 'civilisation' is not entirely clear. In the opinion of Samuel Huntington, it is cultures that create civilisations and not the other way round, and 'the major differences in political and economic development among

policies and actions, however, they did cooperate in fields that they considered more important than ideological divergence. The question that arises around this first argument is thus whether there exists a "world culture" that would be applicable to at least organisations of universal membership and subject matter mandates.

In relation to the second principal argument of the paper, it would be far-fetched to claim that cultural determinants of international cooperation are the most influential; however they do matter, especially in IOs that act beyond ideology-free agendas. This is true especially for organisations with a broad subject matter mandate. The line of analysis presented in this paper to a certain extent disagrees with Samuel Huntington's claim, who argued that ideology or historical circumstances have significantly less cementing qualities than civilisation and culture:

> *Countries with cultural affinities cooperate economically and politically. International organisations based on states with cultural commonality, such as the European Union, are far more successful than those that attempt to transcend cultures.*[6]

The EU represents a particular case for the sake of this analysis because of its unique, *sui generis* character that is related with the depth and width of social, political, economic and cultural integration. This uniqueness limits the possibility of membership of culturally different states. The author of this paper argues that it is predominantly for this reason that Turkey has not become a EU Member State yet, and it is rather unlikely to happen in the foreseeable future. Cultural otherness of this country, the fact that it belongs to another civilisation precludes Turkey's membership in this integration-oriented organisation. It needs to be emphasised though that political and economic determinants of Turkey's relations with EU bear importance as well. There are well-founded doubts concerning Turkey's fulfilment of the minimum requirements for membership specified in Article 2 of

---

civilisations are clearly rooted in their different cultures'. See: S. Huntington, *The Clash of Civilizations and the Remaking of World Order*, Simon & Schuster, New York 2011, p. 29. See also: G. Michałowska, 'Porządek międzynarodowy w perspektywie paradygmatu cywilizacyjnego' (International Order in the Context of Civilizational Paradigm), in R. Kuźniar (ed.), *Porządek międzynarodowy u progu XXI wieku* (*International Order at the Beginning of the 21st Century*), Warszawa 2005, p. 175; R. Zenderowski, 'Czym jest kultura? Kultura a cywilizacja. Spór o definicje podstawowych pojęć' (What Is Culture? Culture Versus Civilization. A Dispute about the Definitions of the Basic Concepts), in R. Zenderowski, K. Cybul, M. Krycki, *Międzynarodowe stosunki kulturalne* (*International Cultural Relations*), Warszawa 2010, p. 96.

6 S. Huntington, *The Clash of Civilizations...*, p. 28.

the Treaty on European Union.[7] At the same time, economic issues, such as the fear of EU nations that Turkey's membership may prove detrimental to the labour market of these countries play a significant role as well. Notwithstanding the very recent events in Turkey (an attempted coup against President Erdogan on 15th July 2016 r. and the backlash of his government that followed), the EU due to political reasons continues cooperation and negotiations with Ankara. This approach also results from the significance of Turkey in dealing with the refugee crises by the EU and its member states. Regardless of cultural differences, Turkey is a member of the North Atlantic Treaty Organization (NATO), as well as of other organisations, such as the Council of Europe (CoE) and the Organisation for Security and Cooperation in Europe (OSCE). For NATO, Turkey's membership was crucial in achieving its goals, i.e. the establishment of an effective and efficient military alliance. Cultural factors were of lesser importance; as a matter of fact, they lost to political, strategic and ideological arguments.

Efficient cooperation in IOs does not always require the use of a standardised cultural code; specialised, technical or coordinative organisations can successfully act with the participation of countries of various cultures and even from different civilisational environments. The Organisation for Economic Co-operation and Development (OECD) has 34 members, including countries from the Western civilisation, as well as Japan, Korea and Turkey. At the same time, members of organisations sharing the same cultural values at the time of an IO creation may later fall apart on political, ideological and economic grounds. This is a phenomenon observed at present within the European Union, which challenges Huntington's argument.

The third argument of the present paper claims that IOs are becoming more and more similar in structure from the perspective of their architectural schemes and organisational culture, but at the same time member states of IOs tend to emphasise their particular cultural values. This is happening because of globalisation processes that lead to superficial homogeneity in values around the globe, values which are being rejected by various non-Western cultural systems. This rejection leads to a deepening amplification of cultural differences. Countries that feel inundated by foreign values tend to move back from the previous stance

7 Article 2 TEU: 'The Union is founded on the values of respect for human dignity, freedom, democracy, equality, the rule of law and respect for human rights, including the rights of persons belonging to minorities. These values are common to the Member States in a society in which pluralism, non-discrimination, tolerance, justice, solidarity and equality between women and men prevail.'

of acceptance of values previously seen as common[8]. Such developments might have a potentially negative impact on policies and activities of IOs. The crucial challenge both for IOs and their members is to uphold the effectiveness of an organisation. That would only be possible if the involved parties refrained from actions aimed at undermining the values of cultures and ruining their internal structure, and if they retained respect even for the differences which are hard to understand.[9] If they do the opposite, the growing resistance to homogeneity may be detrimental to mutual trust and respect; without it effective international cooperation is difficult.

The forthcoming parts of the paper are structured in the following way: Firstly, the idea of "world culture" in IOs is discussed. This part relates also to the third principal argument of the paper, i.e. the universalisation of cultural values. The next part concentrates on the notion of "organisational culture". What follows is the analysis of the influence of culture's impact, which differs in case of the two types of IOs: universal membership organisations (UN and its specialized agencies) and limited -membership organisations (League of Arab States and EU). The case studies present the extent to which culture has an impact on these two types of IOs. They also show, following the second principal argument of this paper, that other determinants of IO functioning, such as politics, ideologies and economy frequently overlap.

The significance of world culture

World culture, as defined by John Boli and George M. Thomas, is 'a unitary social system, increasingly integrated by networks of exchange, competition, and cooperation, such that actors have found it "natural" to view the whole world as their arena of action and discourse'.[10] It constitutes the world polity, i.e. 'a set of

8 A good example here might be a shift in approach of some African Union countries towards the International Criminal Court and of these states, together with others from other parts of the world in the Assembly of State Parties of the International Criminal Court.

9 G. Michałowska, *'Porządek międzynarodowy…'*, p. 196.

10 J. Boli, G. M. Thomas, *Constructing World Culture: International Non-Governmental Organizations since 1875*, Stanford 1999, p. 14. Explaining the processes of institutional cooperation between states by means of the concept of world culture proposes viewing the existence of organisations not from the perspective of state interests – as both in realism and liberalism – but from the perspective of the system of common values. According to Jacek Czaputowicz, the latter is the foundation, on which the world models of human society which provide guidelines as to how to behave in given circumstances

fundamental principles and models, mainly ontological and cognitive in character, defining the nature and purposes of social actors and action'.[11] An exhaustive answer to questions regarding the very existence of world culture would require complex analysis of the phenomena linked to the processes of globalisation. Such analysis however exceeds the scope of this paper. It is rather obvious that the age of globalisation has led to spreading of material products around the globe which allow people (at least some of them) to eat the same food, drink the same coffee, wear similar shoes or use similar mobile phones. However, it is uncertain whether we can speak about an equally advanced globalisation of values and if so, can we say that all values spread at a similar pace? It seems much easier to disseminate ideas in the fields of economy, finance and institutions.[12] Consequently, it is surely much easier to point out the elements of global culture that facilitate cooperation in technical and economic areas than in political or social spheres. At this point, it should also be stressed again that these 'worldwide' or 'universal' values – as the Western states like to perceive them – are rejected by some states as ideas imposed by external powers, unsuitable for internalisation in societies and political systems of other civilisations. Nonetheless, we may assume that universal norms appear more and more commonly even in parts of the world that are entirely different in terms of culture and civilisation. These values are part of IOs, as international organisations are definitely structures of the world polity.

---

are based. The adoption of patterns of behaviour by countries takes place by imitation. Consequently, the countries that follow the logic of correctness and the principles considered appropriate as being a part of world culture are becoming isomorphic. Such behaviour can result in the emergence of a collectivist culture of friendship which assumes the existence of three factors: co-interrelationship, a sense of common fate and homogeneity. Cf.: J. Czaputowicz, *Teorie stosunków międzynarodowych. Krytyka i systematyzacja* (*Theories of International Relations. Critical Remarks and Systematisation*), Warszawa 2008, p. 318.

11 J. Boli, G. M. Thomas, 'World Culture in World Polity: A Century of International Non-Governmental Organizations', *American Sociological Review*, vol. 62, no. 2, 1997, p. 172.

12 In an interview for the weekly *Polityka*, while commenting on his experience as an economic consultant working for undemocratic regimes, Marek Dąbrowski, the co-founder and former president of the Center for Social and Economic Research (CASE), said: 'Most recommendations were gradually implemented, but this was not the case with the recommendations concerning institutional and political changes; undemocratic tendencies were resurfacing even despite the subsequent revolutions' (J. Żakowski, 'Przy uchu władzy' ['Wispering in the Ear of the Authorities'], interview with M. Dąbrowski, *Polityka*, no. 4, 2013, p. 36).

According to Martha Finnemore, the values constituting the culture of the world polity can involve contradictions and ambiguities, which translate into pathologies in these organisations. Among these pathologies, Michael N. Barnett and Martha Finnemore list one factor: the blind faith vested in legitimacy given to certain values by the international community, without any critical analysis of the context of the objectives and principles of the organisation concerned. This in turn can lead to actions that are inconsistent and ineffective.[13] Assuming that world culture is an existing phenomenon, its values should influence IOs, at least to a certain extent. This would also mean that there is a certain meta-level of cultural values in IOs; a level on which values are not questioned by any member, as they are viewed as obvious. Part of the notion of world culture would also be the very existence of international cooperation in the form of IOs. The emergence and development of these institutions date back only to the 19th century. Before the first international organisation could be created (Central Commission for the Navigation on the Rhine, formally constituted in 1815 but in fact dating back to 1804), states needed to acknowledge that their interests are realised better through cooperation rather than hostile use of military power. Since then, the process of establishing basic values of world culture constituting the world polity as we know them now could have begun.

The significance of organisational culture

Another concept that requires some clarification is the term "organisational culture". For IOs it may be defined as 'the rules, rituals, and beliefs that are embedded in the organisation'.[14] The notion of organisational culture has been developed in the studies of the significance of cultural differences in enterprise management, mainly in the works of Geert Hofstede, but also by other authors, such as Fons Trompenaars and Charles Hampden-Turner.[15] The results of studies of organisational culture of enterprises, understood as 'the collective programming of the

13 M. N. Barnett, M. Finnemore, 'The Politics, Power, and Pathologies of International Organizations', *International Organization*, vol. 53, no. 4, 1999, pp. 717–718.

14 *Ibid.*, p. 719.

15 Cf.: G. Hofstede, G. J. Hofstede, M. Minkov, *Cultures and Organizations: Software of the Mind*, 3rd ed., McGraw-Hill, 2010; F. Trompenaars, Ch. Hampden-Turner, *Riding The Waves of Culture: Understanding Diversity in Global Business*, 2nd ed., McGraw-Hill, 1997.

mind that distinguishes the members of one organisation from another',[16] prove useful in the analysis of the internal determinants of functioning of international organisations. This is especially true when we treat an international organisation as a bureaucratised whole, susceptible to various pathologies and mistakes as proposed by Michael N. Barnett and Martha Finnemore.[17]

In international organisations, the development of organisational culture is often influenced by the domination of one professional group among the organisation's functionaries. One of researchers to point this out is Galit A. Sarfaty, in her analysis of the process of including human rights-related issues in the agenda of the World Bank.[18] The author noted that the many years of disregarding human rights in the Bank's programmes were a consequence of the fact that the majority of the employees of that organisation were economists. Their education and experience steered the Bank towards thinking about development in purely economic terms, as the only objective aspect, and consequently treating human rights issues as a political field by definition. In the opinion of the World Bank, the inclusion of this field in its development programmes could constitute an infringement of its statutory principles. The dominance of a single way of thinking could lead to a distorted perception of reality.[19] Perhaps cultural values, the models of behaviour of individuals can also influence the form of culture in an international organisation, although compared to employees of international enterprises, the functionaries of these organisations are a rather unique professional group. By definition, they often operate in the international environment, which forces them to adjust their individual cultural models to their surroundings. Regardless of whether the officials from the United Nations Secretariat in New York comes from a country with a large Power Distance Index (PDI) or from a cultural area where the PDI is low, they will act in the same way because this is what is required for functioning in a multicultural environment. However, the very same Secretariat can struggle with considerable challenges in managing personnel employed in an office located on the other side of the planet. Moreover, the implementation of humanitarian and development projects using local workers whose cultural 'programming' tends

16 G. Hofstede, G. J. Hofstede, M. Minkov, *Cultures...*, p. 344. As a starting point, the author takes his earlier definition of culture as 'collective programming of the mind that distinguishes the members of one group or category of people from another' (*Ibid.*).

17 M. N. Barnett, M. Finnemore, *The Politics...*, p. 718.

18 G. A. Sarfaty, 'Why Culture Matters in International Institutions: The Marginality of Human Rights at the World Bank', *The American Journal of International Law*, vol. 103, no. 4, 2009; see also: M. N. Barnett, M. Finnemore, *The Politics...*, p. 706.

19 Cf.: M.N. Barnett, M. Finnemore, *The Politics...*, p. 723.

to complicate the work of organisations can be particularly problematic. Similar challenges may also appear during, for example, the execution of peacekeeping operations when an additional complicating element is the specific organisational culture of the armed forces, which is different in each country of origin of the peacekeepers.[20] The need for UN functionaries to adjust to common standards was emphasised already in 1954 in the Standards of Conduct in the International Civil Service[21] adopted by the International Civil Service Advisory Board. The document states that personnel employed in the UN System are obliged to act in accordance with the common standards, the observance of which cannot be made conditional on cultural values. On the other hand, however, their conduct may not in any way infringe on the cultural values of other functionaries through a lack of tolerance for other nations, religions or cultures. In other words, the document highlights certain values common to all UN civil service officials and puts those values above individual beliefs, while at the same time respecting cultural diversity of the functionaries of the organisations and institutions of the UN System. These values include: peace, respect for fundamental human rights, economic and social progress, international cooperation, social justice, human dignity, and non-discrimination. Among the guiding principles the document includes: loyalty to the organisation in which the given person is employed, honesty, impartiality, tolerance and respect for others, which in order to be achieved 'in a multicultural setting calls for a positive affirmation going well beyond passive acceptance'.

Michael N. Barnett and Martha Finnemore show that the culture of international organisations, which they understand as the principles, rituals and beliefs rooted in the given organisation, can also contribute to the development of negative models of conduct of the institution itself. In this context, the authors enumerate three mechanisms which, having been shaped within the framework of the active bureaucratised structure, can indicate the existence of 'pathology' in an organisation. These are: irrationality of rationalisation, bureaucratic universalism, normalisation of deviance, organisational insulation, and cultural contestation.

20 Cf.: H. Schreiber, 'Kultura organizacyjna wojska i jej wpływ na efektywność operacji wielonarodowych' (Organisational Culture of the Armed Forces and Its Influence on the Effectiveness of Multinational Operations), in A. Czupryński, L. Elak, H. Schreiber (eds.), *Bezpieczeństwo dla rozwoju. Komunikacja międzykulturowa w operacjach reagowania kryzysowego* (*Security for Development. Intercultural Communication in Crisis Response Operations*), Warszawa 2012.

21 See: *Standards of Conduct in the International Civil Service*, United Nations, available at: http://www.un.org/en/ethics/pdf/StandConIntCivSE.pdf (accessed on 26 April 2013).

At the same time, they stress that 'the connection between these mechanisms and pathological behaviour is probabilistic, not deterministic'.[22]

Irrationality of rationalisation occurs when the principles and procedures adopted by an organisation in order to fulfil its tasks become a goal in itself, that is when international organisations attempt to apply previously adopted bureaucratic premises at all costs and do not revise them to adjust to the circumstances. The authors refer to the example of UN activities regarding the organisation of elections and peacekeeping operations. With regards to elections, the authors argue that the 'objective' of the UN activity in countries that needed rebuilding was the establishment of some form of stable and just government. Democratic elections were considered necessary for this, as a successful conclusion of the operational activity. As a result, UN functionaries would work towards holding elections even when such a procedure was premature or even counterproductive. The authors point to Bosnia and the African countries, where the actions of the international community caused an increase in ethnic tensions, which is exactly what a democratically elected government was supposed to cure. With regards to peacekeeping operations, the authors believe that the UN also made grave mistakes caused by the fact that the personnel was not adequately prepared for their task. Members of the Blue Helmets were not prepared to take on crisis management tasks and mediation between parties in internal conflicts. Consequently, it was impossible for them to fulfil their mandate and the activity proved counterproductive.

An example of the internal mechanism of bureaucratic universalism are the actions of the International Monetary Fund (IMF) in relation to the financial crisis in Asia in 1997–1998, when the IMF applied remedial measures similar to those recommended previously to some countries of Latin America, thus causing the situation in Asia to deteriorate. In this context, we should also note that similar criticism regarding the activities of the Fund had appeared even earlier, in the 1980s and 1990s, when it promoted the introduction of the Washington Consensus in developing countries, which had essentially meant drastic liberalisation, deregulation and privatisation of the economy. In some cases, the policy completely failed – being utterly unsuitable to the local conditions and state of the economy and disregarding the inexistence of institutions necessary for the supervision of proper implementation of the programmes.[23] As a result, the post-Washington Consensus

---

22 M. N. Barnett, M. Finnemore, *The Politics...*, p. 719.

23 Cf.: R. Piasecki, *Rozwój gospodarczy a globalizacja* (*Economic Development in the Context of Globalisation*), Warszawa 2003, p. 51 ff.

was developed, this time taking into account cultural and other factors.[24] Another example of bureaucratic universalism is the direct application of experience from peacekeeping operations conducted in one part of the world to countries located in a different region.

Normalisation of deviance is noticeable in situations when international organisations start behaving at variance with internal legal and non-legal rules of conduct adopted earlier and when they start treating such deviance as the norm. Michael N. Barnett and Martha Finnemore use the example of the attitude of the officials from the office of the United Nations High Commissioner for Refugees (UNHCR) towards the repatriation of refugees and – in this context – the UN agency's respect for the principle that returns must be voluntary and should be safe for repatriated people. Otherwise, they would infringe on the principle of non-refoulement, which is at the very core of refugee law.[25] In the authors' opinion, the slow departure from observing these principles and sanctioning the change by means of internal UNHCR documents prove the existence of the mechanism of 'normalisation of deviance'.

Insulation of an international organisation is a consequence of its wrong decisions due to a lack of analysis of actions from the perspective of their practical effectiveness. Such a situation can be caused by an organisational culture which does not allow for the possibility of questioning the knowledge of the organisation's functionaries and for an impartial evaluation that would show the potential shortcomings. Copious examples – fortunately largely corrected by now – are provided by international organisations' development assistance and humanitarian aid.

Finally, in the opinion of Michael N. Barnett and Martha Finnemore, cultural contestation refers to the rivalry between individual internal organisational cultures developed within a single bureaucratic order. These subcultures emerge particularly in organisations which like, for example the UN, have a relatively general mission, broad and politically conditioned membership, and numerous

24 *Ibid.*, p. 66. The author quotes the economist Douglas C. North, who stated in a lecture delivered on the occasion of receiving the Nobel Prize in 1993 that culture was the key to understanding how the past influences the present and the future (*Ibid.*). The aforementioned examples of the mechanism of 'bureaucratic universalism' in the IMF can also be used for 'irrationality of rationalisation' because in the perception of the IMF's decision-makers, the goals set in the Consensus have overshadowed the broader context of the implemented solutions.

25 Pursuant to the principle of non-refoulement, it is not allowed to send persons who are applying for refugee status (as well as persons who have been refused this status) to places where they would be at risk of being persecuted.

internal structural units. The conditions for the emergence of internal organisational subcultures are education, previous professional experience and personal determinants of the personnel of various departments, offices and agencies. They create their own models of conduct, worldview and instruments used to pursue the organisation's goals. Due to the existing differences, they often exhibit a contesting attitude towards the organisational subcultures of the 'Others'. Such mechanisms can be observed within the UN, where the mission of providing humanitarian aid collides with the principle of non-interference and impartiality in armed conflicts. In this context, the authors quote the words of Shashi Tharoor, a former high official of the UN Secretariat: 'It is extremely difficult to make war and peace with the same people on the same territory at the same time.'[26]

To sum up, each and every organisation has its organisational culture that significantly influences the activities of an IO. Taken together with the culture of the international community (world culture) that may be of regional or universal character, we may see that civilisational and cultural determinants influence organisations on two different levels. The third one that can be observed is the influence of national cultures of member states on IOs. As already noted, all these types of influence may be different in various types of organisations, whether they are universal or with limited membership. It is worth looking into examples of these two types of organisations. Their analysis reveals not only the influence of culture itself but also the relations between cultural and other determinants (political, economic, etc.).

Culture in universal organisations

Nowadays, United Nations is the most universal organisation. The sources of the international cooperation that culminated in the signing of the Charter of the United Nations can be traced back to long before the Dumbarton Oaks Conference (August–October 1944). The decision to establish the UN, made at the conference of four world powers in Moscow on 30 October 1943, was conditioned by political interests of that time, as well as by the historical experience of World War I and the League of Nations. The representatives of the Allies recognised the need to establish 'a general international organisation, based on the principle of the sovereign equality of all peace-loving states, and open to membership by all such states, large and small, for the maintenance of international peace and security'.[27]

26 Cited after: M. N. Barnett, M. Finnemore, *The Politics…*, p. 725.

27 *The Moscov Conference; October 1943. Joint Four-Nation Declaration*, The Avalon Project, available at: http://avalon.law.yale.edu/wwii/moscow.asp (accessed on 26 April 2013).

The decisions made later at the conference in Dumbarton Oaks regarding the goals and principles of the organisation, membership, organisational structure, and rules of cooperation in the area of maintaining peace and security in the world and regarding economic and social issues confirmed the ideas expressed in the Atlantic Charter and in the United Nations Declaration.

The establishment of the UN (San Francisco, 26 June 1945) was a result of cooperation between the members of the anti-Nazi coalition.[28] The organisation was created thanks to the determined efforts towards common goals of protecting future generations from the disaster of war, reaffirming faith in fundamental human rights and uniting forces in order to preserve international peace and security. Both cultural and civilisational differences were overcome as the future UN member countries had converging political goals. Even if it was soon to turn out that the cementingof the community that participated in the UN was not resistant to erosion, San Francisco was the cornerstone of the new agreement. The UN Charter was adopted unanimously and its most controversial provisions, e.g. regarding membership in the Security Council together with its competences, were worded according to the wishes of the global powers, which had been joined by France and which each received a permanent seat on the Council.

The provisions included in the Preamble and in Article 1 of the Charter – concerned issues such as faith in human rights, dignity and value of the individual, as well as respect for these values; fundamental freedoms for all without distinction as to race, sex, language, or religion; equal rights for man and women as well as for all nations small and large; support of economic and social development of all nations. These points were all proof that certain universal values were emerging. The Charter contributed to the promotion of these values and became something of a constitution of the international community.[29] Its norms are absolute and binding to all members of the international community but nonetheless, in the history of the UN they have been repeatedly infringed upon by member countries. The UN has drawn up many documents that elaborate upon the goals and principles stated in the Charter and reaffirm them. For the purpose of this article, particularly important are the ones concerning issues that are perceived

28 J. Symonides, 'Organizacja Narodów Zjednoczonych: geneza, powstanie, cele i zasady funkcjonowania, struktura, organy główne i pomocnicze, system Narodów Zjednoczonych' (UN: Genesis, Establishment, Objectives and Rules of Operation, Main and Auxiliary Bodies, the UN System), in J. Symonides (ed.), *Organizacja Narodów Zjednoczonych. Bilans i perspektywy* (*United Nations. Assessment and Future Prospects*), Warszawa 2006, p. 20.

29 *Ibid.*

ambiguously or differently by various members, for example human rights and freedoms, the rule of law, or good governance.

As an organisation in which all the great civilisations and cultures participate, the UN has many times dealt with cultural diversity – on the one hand confirming its importance, and on the other hand, acting towards the development of a broad catalogue of universal norms and rules of conduct. The adoption of some decisions by the UN has been often blocked by cultural and civilisational differences as well as different political and economic conceptions. These determinants have been interrelated. The unity within the blocks of the Cold War period was the consequence of political and ideological choices; borders have not always coincided with the lines dividing cultures and civilisations. The changes started in 1989 clearly highlighted the weakness of the blocs; they fell apart and many of their members changed sides. Some countries of the Eastern Bloc joined the western structures and started speaking the political language of the countries which have grown from the same civilisational roots. Others remained in the sphere of influence of the Russian Federation or arrived at crossroads, left to themselves, unimportant in terms of strategic influence of contemporary superpowers (e.g. Cuba, Angola). The bloody conflicts of the 1990s were a challenge to the international community and the UN Charter itself as it was drawn up for the reality of 1945. The violent crimes committed in Europe, Africa and in Asia, however, have shown that the disrespect for certain universal values can constitute a threat to peace and security in the world. New challenges for the UN emerged as the process of globalisation was progressing.[30] As Joseph Stiglitz puts it, globalisation 'has reduced the sense of isolation felt in much of the developing world and has given many people in the developing countries access to knowledge well beyond the reach of even the wealthiest in any country a century ago,'[31] but at the same time, it has failed to bring the promised economic benefits to many of them. In the axiological dimension, globalisation contributed to people relishing the values transmitted by new technological devices, which in turn led to growing discontent and tendencies towards protection of local values.

---

30 Cf.: D. Heidrich, 'Debata na temat globalizacji w Narodach Zjednoczonych' (Debate on Globalisation in the UN), in E. Haliżak, R. Kuźniar, J. Symonides (eds.), *Globalizacja a stosunki międzynarodowe* (*Globalisation and International Relations*), Bydgoszcz–Warszawa 2003; D. Heidrich, A. Jarczewska, 'ONZ wobec ekonomicznych i społecznych wyzwań globalizacji' (UN against the Economic and Social Challenges of Globalisation), in J. Symonides (ed.), *Organizacja…*

31 J. Stiglitz, *Globalization and its Discontents*, Penguin, London 2002, p. 4.

A breakthrough moment in the functioning of the international community was the event of 11 September 2001, which for many people constituted proof for the aptness of Huntington's vision of the clash of civilisations and an end of naïve divagations about end of history. The struggle for values, protection of own culture from being dominated by the Western pap of McDonalds, pop culture and a liberal vision of man and the world was reflected in the UN, for instance in the form of numerous debates on the problems of globalisation.[32] These conflicts highlighted not only the differences between civilisations but also the cracks in them, especially heatedly discussed in relation to the changes in the trans-Atlantic order. The differences in perception of international problems led Robert Kagan to the conclusion that 'Americans are from Mars and Europeans are from Venus.'[33] This metaphor, used very often in the debate on the differences between the nations of the Western civilisation, was a reflection of the weightiness of the debate between the allies. Some countries of Western Europe tried to clearly distance themselves from the policy pursued by George W. Bush under the so called 'War on Terror', that they considered contrary to European values as well as universal values such as multilateralism, faith in international law, the rules governing the use of force pursuant to Article 2(4) of the UN Charter, etc. The influence of this conflict on the UN was considerable – not only because the Security Council was bypassed in the process of making the decision by the US to invade Iraq in March 2003, but also because of the intensification of the debate started in 1999 on a redefinition of the notion of sovereignty in the context of humanitarian intervention, which led to the emergence of the concept of 'responsibility to protect' (RtoP or R2P). The debate on the changes taking place in the UN after the Cold War also led to changes in the conduct of operations in the fields of humanitarian aid, development assistance, peacekeeping, promotion of human rights, and many others. Thus, it contributed to the development of new norms and extra-legal standards of the culture of the world polity.

Culture in the material sense and its significance for international cooperation became one of the reasons to establish the United Nations Educational, Scientific and Cultural Organisation (UNESCO) in November 1945. The UNESCO Constitution stresses that 'ignorance of each other's ways and lives has been a common cause, throughout the history of mankind, of that suspicion and mistrust between the peoples of the world through which their differences have all too

32 Cf.: D. Heidrich, 'Debata...'

33 R. Kagan, *Of Paradise and Power: America and Europe in the New World Order*, Vintage, New York 2004, p. 1.

often broken into war' and World War II 'was a war made possible by the denial of the democratic principles of the dignity, equality and mutual respect of men, and by the propagation, in their place, through ignorance and prejudice, of the doctrine of the inequality of men and races.'[34] Pursuant to the provisions of this document, 'wide diffusion of culture, and the education of humanity for justice and liberty and peace are indispensable to the dignity of man' and 'peace based exclusively upon the political and economic arrangements of governments would not be a peace which could secure the unanimous, lasting and sincere support of the peoples of the world.'[35] Today, the organisation has 195 members; the most recent one is Palestine (2011).

UNESCO has repeatedly been a field of ideological struggles. In the Cold War period, the countries of the Eastern and the Western Bloc were leaving UNESCO to demonstrate their displeasure with the direction its development was taking. Poland, for example, quit in December 1952, the US – in December 1984 and the United Kingdom – only a year later.[36] Today, UNESCO is one of the most important forums for international cooperation in the area of culture. The organisation focuses on promoting cultural diversity through the protection of heritage and improving the means of expressing culture, encouraging social cohesion through the support of pluralism, intercultural dialogue and culture of peace, as well as stressing the central importance of culture in reaching sustainable development and other issues. The organisation also works towards preservation of the products of culture as world heritage. However, the scope of its activity exceeds the area of interest of this article and shall not be covered here. For the same reason the author has intentionally left out organisations such as the Council of Europe and numerous EU cultural cooperation programmes.

---

34 *Constitution of the United Nations Educational, Scientific and Cultural Organization*, available at: http://portal.unesco.org/en/ev.php-URL_ID=15244&URL_DO=DO_TOPIC&URL_SECTION=201.html (accessed on 26 April 2013).

35 *Ibid.*

36 The UNESCO Constitution does not provide for a possibility of withdrawal. The absence of the People's Republic of Poland was treated as failing to pay its contribution. Poland returned to UNESCO in 1954, after the USSR joined the organisation. These events prompted the organisation to introduce changes to Article 2 of the Constitution in 1954 in the form of Section 6, which regulated the withdrawal from the organisation. Cf.: G. Michałowska, 'Polska w Organizacji Narodów Zjednoczonych do spraw Oświaty, Nauki i Kultury' (Poland in United Nations Educational, Scientific and Cultural Organization), in S. Parzymies, I. Popiuk-Rysińska (eds.), *Polska w organizacjach międzynarodowych* (*Poland in international organisations*), Warszawa 2002, p. 194. The US returned to UNESCO only in 2003 and the UK in 1997.

Cultural determinants of the establishment and functioning of limited membership organisations

The influence of cultural and civilisational factors on limited membership organisations is important and particularly visible in the case of those in which subjective competences include political and social issues. Case studies of the League of Arab States and the European Union are discussed below.

League of Arab States

The League of Arab States (often called the Arab League) was established already during World War II; the Pact of the League of Arab States was signed in Cairo on 22 March 1945.[37] The establishment of this organisation was connected with the belief that Arab countries had common interests and that there was a need to deepen the cooperation between them. The Preamble to the Pact refers to the principle of respecting independence and sovereignty of the member countries.[38] In 1946, the countries of the Arab League signed the Cultural Treaty on cooperation in the field of education, student and employee exchange, availability of mutual cultural achievements, and other areas of mutual support.[39]

The common values of the Arab countries are particularly evident in the Arab Charter on Human Rights, which was adopted for the first time in 1994 but did not enter into force at that time.[40] The document was later modified and signed once again in 2004.[41] The Preamble to the Charter refers to universal documents on human rights and condemns Zionism, which it considers, alongside racism to be a violation of human rights and a threat to international peace and security. Article 2.3 of the Charter once again refers to Zionism, this time listing it

---

37 For more on the origins of the League see: T. Fryzeł, *Liga Państw Arabskich* (*League of Arab States*), Warszawa 1981.

38 *Pact of the League of Arab States*, The Avalon Project, available at: http://avalon.law.yale.edu/20th_century/arableag.asp (accessed on 26 April 2013).

39 *Cultural Treaty of the Arab League*, Jewish Virtual Library, available at: http://www.jewishvirtuallibrary.org/jsource/Peace/arabcult.html (accessed on 26 April 2013).

40 The Permanent Arab Commission on Human Rights was founded in 1968 as the first step towards building a regional, multilateral system of human rights protection in the Arab countries. In 1990, the Cairo Declaration on Human Rights in Islam was signed. The Charter on Human Rights was its formal extension and, in contrast to the legally non-binding Declaration, was an international agreement.

41 *Arab Charter on Human Rights*, Human Rights Library, University of Minnesota, available at: http://www1.umn.edu/humanrts/instree/loas2005.html?msource=UNWDEC19001&tr=y&auid=3337655 (accessed on 26 April 2013).

next to 'all forms of racism […] and foreign occupation and domination.' These provisions of the Charter became the reason for its criticism. In 2008, when the document entered into force, the United Nations High Commissioner for Human Rights at that time, Louise Arbour, spoke very highly of it, which spurred a heated response.[42] Critics of the Charter point out that some of its wordings constitute proof of the existence of relativism (Islamisation) in the Arab League regarding universal human rights, which have been adjusted to the regional cultural, ethnic and religious conditions.[43]

The Charter assumes that the Arab world is coherent. The Preamble includes references to 'the Arab nation' and Article 1 notes that the Arab States have a 'sense of belonging to a common civilisation'. In contrast to the Pact of the League, the Charter refers to values common to all Arab countries: dignity of the human person exalted by God and having the right to a decent life based on freedom, justice and equality; the eternal principles of fraternity, equality and tolerance; the humanitarian values; the unity of the Arab nation, which struggles for its freedom and defends the right of nations to self-determination, to the preservation of their wealth and to development and sovereignty. The approach to human rights in the Arab League clearly shows that the civilisation and culture of the Arab countries – through religion, which essentially regulates all aspects of social life – effectively limits the capabilities of the organisation. International law, regardless of whether the rest of the world considers it universal or not, will not be able to shift the borders set by faith.[44] In the opinion of Roman Kuźniar, the Islamic civilisation is so different from the Western one that liberal concepts and categories of human rights simply do not fit in with this world.[45] The regional document does not mention, for example, the right to convert to a different faith and it does not prohibit in absolute terms the use of capital punishment on people

42 Following protests, the High Commissioner issued a statement in which she distanced herself from some provisions of the Charter, including the references to Zionism. Cf.: *Statement by UN High Commissioner for Human Rights on the entry into force of the Arab Charter on Human Rights*, Office of the United Nations High Commissioner for Human Rights, available at: http://www.unhchr.ch/huricane/huricane.nsf/view01/6C211162E43235FAC12573E00056E19D?opendocument (accessed on 26 April 2013).

43 Cf. e.g.: *UN Rights Chief Must Clarify Endorsement of Arab Charter with Anti-Semitic Provisions*, UN Watch, available at: http://www.unwatch.org/site/apps/nl/content2.asp?c=bdKKISNqEmG&b=1316871&ct=4981963 (accessed on 26 April 2013).

44 B. Banaszak *et al.* (eds.), *System ochrony praw człowieka* (*Human Rights Protection System*), Kraków 2003, p. 286.

45 R. Kuźniar, *Prawa człowieka. Prawo, instytucje, stosunki międzynarodowe* (*Human Rights. Law, Institutions, International Relations*), Warszawa 2004, p. 212.

under the age of eighteen (which, of course, is not unique to the Arab countries). Nonetheless, we should note that the Islamic civilisation does give in to external influence regarding human rights. The 1994 version of the Charter did not include the prohibition of slavery, among others, while the current version does.

European Union

The significance of civilisation, identity and culture, in both its material and axiological dimensionis the subject of many scientific reflections for European integration and its offspring – the European Union.[46] As a result, this issue is rather well described (although it cannot be said of other international organisations). The EU is the only international organisation with such extent of integration in virtually all areas of life. The influence of European culture (if we were to assume that such a culture indeed exists) and the cultural diversity of the individual EU Member States on the emergence of the first integration projects is indisputable. However, we should also remember that the implementation of the plan to integrate Western Europe saw the light of day in the form of the European Coal and Steel Community in 1951 and a few years later in the form of the European Economic Community and the Euratom, which seem to be the realisation of the functional vision of integration. The attempt to establish the European Defence Community and the European Political Community has failed, and the activities of the Council of Europe – an organisation whose competences are only coordinative – have proved insufficient to offset this fiasco. Of course, the achievements of the Council of Europe are unquestionable, as is its contribution to uniting the

46 A very interesting analysis of how culture has been used in the European project is offered by Cris Shore in his seminal book *Building Europe. The Cultural Politics of European Integration*, Routledge, London, New York 2002. See also: F. Gołembski, *Kulturowe aspekty integracji europejskiej* (*Cultural Aspects of European Integration*), Warszawa 2008; F. Gołembski, 'Kulturowe aspekty studiów europejskich' (Cultural Aspects of European Studies), in K. A. Wojtaszczyk, W. Jakubowski (eds.), *Studia europejskie. Zagadnienia metodologiczne* (*European Studies. Methodological Problems*), Warszawa 2010; K. Łastawski, 'Wpływ tożsamości kulturowej Europy na proces integracji' (Influence of Europe's Cultural Identity on the Process of Integration), in I. Stawowy-Kawka (ed.), *Czynniki stabilizacji i destabilizacji w stosunkach międzynarodowych na początku XXI wieku* (*Stabilising and Destabilising Factors in International Relations at the Beginning of 21st Century*), Kraków 2009; A. Ziętek, 'Kultura w procesie globalizacji i integracji europejskiej' (Culture in the Process of Globalisation and European Integration), in J. Rokicki, M. Banaś (eds.), *Naród, kultura i państwo w procesie globalizacji* (*Nation, Culture and State in the Process of Globalisation*), Kraków 2004.

continent and strengthening European identity, but in the 1950s it became evident that the idea of building a Europe based on more than just efficient economic cooperation would have to be postponed. The functional theory explaining the integration processes essentially did not consider the problem of the cultural and civilisational community of Western Europe. In the opinion of David Mitrany, international organisations are created because the countries participating in them expect to gain certain benefits from them.[47] At the same time, Mitrany stresses that in the process of integration, states do not give up their sovereignty but instead decide to carry it out jointly.[48] Hence, in this theoretical model, there is no issue of rivalry between cultures or domination of one culture or another, and it is also of no importance whether the community is cemented by a single culture or civilisation. Likewise, this problem is not discussed in neo-functionalism, which perceives European integration as a testing ground for integration of other regions, eventually leading to a global federation composed of many institutions with supranational competences anyway.[49] The founding fathers of the European community, in turn, believed that establishing an organisation which would focus on integrating the production of coal and steel in the initial six European countries would contribute to their further integration and perhaps, as Mitrany wanted it, eventually even the establishment of a political federation. In a declaration of 9 May 1950, Robert Schuman clearly stated that 'the pooling of coal and steel production should immediately provide for the setting up of **common foundations** for economic development as a **first step in the federation of Europe**, and will change the destinies of those regions which have long been devoted to the manufacture of munitions of war, of which they have been the most constant victims. [...] In this way, there will be realised simply and speedily that **fusion of interest which is indispensable to the establishment of a common economic system**; it may be the leaven from which may grow a wider and **deeper community between countries** long opposed to one another by sanguinary divisions [emphasis – DH].'[50]

One of the attempts to understand what the European Union is today is undertaken by the so-called English school, which deals with the analysis of the international community. According to Jacek Czaputowicz, initially, the representatives of

---

47 J. Czaputowicz, *Teorie...*, p. 118.

48 *Ibid.*, p. 119 ff.

49 *Ibid.*, p. 125.

50 Cf.: *The Schuman Declaration – 9 May 1950*, European Union, http://europa.eu/about-eu/basic-information/symbols/europe-day/schuman-declaration/index_en.htm (accessed on 26 April 2013).

this school were not interested in the process of European integration and treated it as an unimportant local phenomenon, limited in functionality and time and, consequently, possesing no greater influence on the structure of the expected universalist society. However, their deliberations can be used for its explanation because the European Union can be treated as a society in which elements of international and global (that is, supranational) community coexist. In more recent studies of the English school, in the works by Barry Buzan, we can find an explanation of integration exactly through the model of the transnational community, with one path to its establishment leading through the European integration model, where countries grow similar to each other and become, among others, a community in the axiological sense, functioning within the framework of a given normative order.[51]

As observed by Franciszek Gołembski, the Treaty of Rome signed in 1957 has broadened the scope of cooperation in Europe, partially focusing on culture, even though its aim was not to improve cultural cooperation and promote the cultural heritage of Europe but rather to protect local values so that cultures of the individual states would not be impoverished in consequence of the progressing integration.[52] After the establishment of the European Union, cooperation in the field of culture was intensified and a framework of the EU cultural policy was created (its beginnings lie as early as in the 1980s), in which culture is used as a tool to deepen European integration.[53] The turning point in the debate on the existence and significance of European identity and culture was the Treaty establishing a Constitution for Europe signed on 29 October 2004 in Rome, which, however, has not been ratified by all EU Member States due to numerous doubts consequently, never entered into force. One of the most controversial points was the Preamble, which has shown how much Europe was divided in the perception of what 'common European values' should be included in the document. In the end, the reference to the culture of ancient Greeks and Romans and to the French

51 J. Czaputowicz, *Teorie...*, p. 285. According to Czaputowicz, an additional explanation of European integration should be the transferring of national competences to supranational institutions. Mutual uniformisation of the countries will cause the 'thickening' of their societies, up to the moment when further possibilities of the development of European integration as a result of processes inspired at the national level will be exhausted. In order for the integration to proceed, there is a need to cross the boundaries towards a global society ('supranationality'). Thus, there appears a need to transfer the sovereign power of states to supranational institutions (*Ibid.*).

52 F. Gołembski, *Kulturowe aspekty...*, pp. 195–196.

53 *Ibid.*, p. 196.

Revolution was abandoned because it was especially unacceptable to catholic countries, including Poland. However, there was also no agreement regarding the reference to Christian values, even though it can be argued thatit was the Christian tradition that has formed what we nowadays can guardedly refer to as European culture or civilisation. Following a compromise agreement, it was decided to include a reference to the cultural, religious and humanist heritage of Europe.

This wording has been confirmed in the Treaty on European Union (TEU), in the version changed by the Treaty of Lisbon: 'Drawing inspiration from the cultural, religious and humanist inheritance of Europe, from which have developed the universal values of the inviolable and inalienable rights of the human person, freedom, democracy, equality and the rule of law.' Furthermore, the Treaty refers in numerous articles to the common cultural heritage of Europe and the EU Member States. The Treaty on the Functioning of the European Union also stresses the importance of cooperation in the area of culture. The Treaties use expressions such as '(European) culture', 'cultural heritage of European significance', 'cultural traditions and regional heritage', but there is no mention of a 'European civilisation' (although there is a reference to 'European identity' in the Preamble). It should be emphasised that while one of the objectives of the EU mentioned in Article 3 TEU is to promote its values, listed in Article 2 TEU,[54] the EU shall also 'respect its rich cultural and linguistic diversity, and shall ensure that Europe's cultural heritage is safeguarded and enhanced' (Article 3 TEU).[55] Consequently, common values do not imply a unification of the cultures of the Member States. It even seemsthat the EU can only function effectively and enjoy support for its continued existence if it also admits cultural diversity and tolerance for this diversity, at the same time adopting a non-negotiable set of values. The answer to the question about the extent of the supreme values is contained in Article 7 TEU, which provides the possibility of organisational sanctions against a Member State that infringes upon the values enumerated in Article 2. Consequently, we should assume that these values are common to all the members and the organisation itself. However, there still remainsa problem of interpreting the conduct of states in relation to the obligation to observe these values. So far, only once steps were taken against a Member State to penalise it for failing to observe the common values of the EU: it was Austria, when the Austrian Freedom Party of the late

54 Cf.: footnote 7.

55 Article 167 of the Treaty on the Functioning of the European Union emphasises that: 'The Union shall contribute to the flowering of the cultures of the Member States, while respecting their national and regional diversity and at the same time bringing the common cultural heritage to the fore.'

Jörg Heider took power. There were many doubts regarding the justness of this decision, and consequently the present version of the TEU provides for a modified procedure of imposing these kinds of sanctions by EU bodies. Respect for the values listed in Article 2 TEU is also a condition *sine qua non* for applying for membership in the organisation (the so-called Copenhagen criteria). The protection of the values common for the entire EU and stemming from the cultural and civilisational heritage of Europe is also one of the objectives of EU's actions in the international arena, both under the Common Foreign and Security Policy (CFSP) and the Common Security and Defence Policy (CSDP). 'In its relations with the wider world, the Union shall uphold and promote its values and interests [...]' (Article 3(5) TEU). Apart from the ones mentioned, these values include: basing international relations on peaceful cooperation, security, lasting development of the world, solidarity and mutual respect between nations, free and fair trade, combating poverty, protection of human rights, and faith in international law, first of all in the principles of the UN Charter.

The League of Arab States and the European Union are, undeniably, organisations established largely for the purpose of nurturing the common values and material achievements of the participating countries, owing to the cultural and civilisational cement that binds them. The common history of the member countries, and to a certain extent their historical experience, their common language, ethnic similarities, Christianity and Islam are the theoretical basis for cooperation. However, as it turned out on several occasions, they were not always sufficient to ensure efficient functioning and achievement of their objectives. The deep cracks in the Arab League are connected with the attitude of the member countries towards the Arab–Israeli conflict, the war in the Persian Gulf of 1991 and with the inability to influence the current events in Syria. The European Union, in turn, is today in the deepest crisis since the Treaty of Maastricht. And this crisis is not only economic and financial – it is also a crisis of ideas, in which there is no vision of future development because the members cannot find a common language in the issues tied to the very existence of the EU. Yet, the EU still remains a unique institution, carrying the weight of European identity in its heritage but its actions are not always satisfactory. The European values developed over centuries, which are important in external activities, do not always give direction to foreign policy as they are superseded by political and economic interests of the Member States.

As presented in the paper, culture inevitably plays a role in international organisations, especially in those that deal with political or ideological issues or require common grounds for deep integration processes. The influence of culture on IOs comes from three levels: the level of national cultures of member states whose interests and actions in an organization are shaped by their cultural background; the level of culture of the world polity (world culture) and the level of culture present in the organisation as a bureaucratic whole. On top of that, certain external circumstances and other determinant factors may shape the power of impact of cultural values on all three levels.

The original version of this text was published in the academic journal "Społeczeństwo i Polityka", no. 4, 2012.

Justyna Nakonieczna-Bartosiewicz

Culture and Nation-State's Reputation

Key words: nation-state reputation, nation-state image, nation branding, cultural diplomacy, public diplomacy

Abstract: The article focuses on the role of culture and cultural diplomacy in nation branding, which is assumed to be one of the factors influencing the creation of a nation-state's image and reputation. It deconstructs the terms image and reputation. Then, it searches for how culture is used in constructing a state's image and reputation strategies.

Referring to the publication on soft power by Joseph Nye, Simon Anholt wrote that 'there are times when only coercion can achieve the aims which a government [...] wishes to pursue, and this is hard power; other ends can only be attained through the exercise of cultural, intellectual or spiritual influence'.[1] While analysing the foundations on which, according to Nye, soft power rests, we can see that each of them approaches culture from a different perspective. The resources that Nye lists in this context are culture (both high and popular), as well as the political values of the given state and a normative evaluation of the state's foreign policies.[2] Thus a reflection on the aspects of culture in foreign activities of a nation state and its importance in these activities is by all means justified, especially regarding its most culturally determined area – the construction of a state's image and reputation in the international arena.

If we treat culture as a collectively agreed upon 'set of values and practices that create meaning for a society',[3] then culture becomes the key element shaping the international activity of states. After all, as Martina Topić and Cassandra Sciortino aptly note, the power of attraction and seduction works only when its attributes are interpreted as attractive and enticing.[4] Even the effective power of a threat

1 S. Anholt, *Brand New Justice: How Branding Places and Products Can Help the Developing World*, Routledge 2005, p. 13.

2 J. Nye, *Soft Power: The Means to Success in World Politics*, New York 2005, p. 11 ff.

3 Ibid., p. 11; see also: G. Hofstede, G. J. Hofstede, M. Minkov, *Cultures and Organizations: Software of the Mind*, Revised and expanded 2nd edition, New York: McGraw-Hill, 2004.

4 See: M. Topić, C. Sciortino, *Cultural Diplomacy and Cultural Imperialism: A Framework for the Analysis*, in M. Topić, S. Rodin (eds.), *Cultural Diplomacy and Cultural Imperialism. European Perspective(s)*, Frankfurt am Main 2012, p. 16.

is culturally determined. The character of the relations between states depends largely on how they perceive and interpret each other's power and interests, and on their intentions towards each other.[5] How states behave towards one another is, therefore culturally determined and at the same time, constitutes a cultural action. Hence, culture itself can be both the subject of state actions and their carrier.

One of the reasons why the international community has become aware of this fact is the radical change of the conditions under which international interactions take place. This change was caused mainly by the communication revolutions of the late 20th century, which have increased the possibilities of communication between various entities (also without the participation of the nation state), including access to current information from diverse channels of communication.[6] The international community is now more responsive and oriented towards communicating. We could say that it is a great age of communication; there is an awareness of the need to speak and to constantly monitor how it has been received.[7] Public issues exist mainly in the media, and thus become publicity. This means it involves sending and decoding meanings in the public sphere – thus, it is cultural. Moreover, nation-states face the need to stand up to the problems of identity of their societies, on which they used to exert a much greater influence.[8] The traditionally understood nation-state identity has been challenged because new backgrounds of identity extending beyond the term 'nation' have been discovered. Globalisation that has led to the democratisation of international relationshas enhanced the role of culture in the protection and expression of these identities. We can see it especially in the articulation of 'new identities', which do not fit neatly into the classic categories of the nation state such as locality, region

5 M. Sułek, J. Symonides, 'Wstęp' (Introduction), in M. Sułek, J. Symonides (eds.), *Państwo w teorii i praktyce stosunków międzynarodowych* (*State in the Theory and Practice of International Relations*), Warszawa 2009, p. 14.

6 E. Gilboa, 'Searching for a Theory of Public Diplomacy', *The Annals of the America Academy of Political and Social Science*, vol. 616, 2008; see also: A. Ziętek (ed.), *Międzynarodowe stosunki kulturalne* (*International Cultural Relations*), Warszawa 2010, pp. 134–135.

7 See: E. Gilboa, 'Public Diplomacy in the Information Age', transl. into Polish by M. Miłkowski, in B. Ociepka, (ed.), *Dyplomacja publiczna* (*Public Diplomacy*), Wrocław: Wrocław University Press, 2008, pp. 37–58.

8 See: Z. Bauman, 'O tarapatach tożsamości w ciasnym świecie' (On the Problems of Identity in the Cramped World), in W. Kalaga (ed.), *Dylematy wielokulturowości* (*Dilemmas of Multiculturality*), Kraków 2004, pp. 28–32.

or even the planet Earth.[9] Finally, the number of nation states existing in current times is also significant. Epecially the small and medium-sized ones, which are not very recognisable, look for new ways to present themselves in the international arena.[10] One of these ways is managing their image and reputation. However, large and widely recognisable states need to look after their reputation as well. It might seem that superpowers such as the United States do not have to pay any particular attention to nurturing their image and monitoring how culture affects it. It turns out otherwise, however, and the North American motto 'to know us is to love us' has proven illusory; what is more, this 'knowledge' is based on stereotypical and superficial perception of North America from the perspective of popular culture.[11]

Image and reputation of a state

The image and reputation of a state are directly related to how the state is perceived by its neighbours. Looking after the positive image and, in the long run, reputation is one of the classic tasks of diplomacy.[12]

An image is a subjective mental picture; an idea a person has about a given entity,; the common opinion about it or a mosaic of its mental depictions. Such a mosaic is also created by people's ideas about the given state.[13] According to researchers who study public relations, the image is a product of three constituents:

---

9 Cf.: J. Kukułka, *Wstęp do nauki o stosunkach międzynarodowych* (*Introduction to International Relations Scholarship*), Warszawa 2003, pp. 179–182.

10 Simon Anholt believes that the fact that many small and medium-sized states are unrecognisable is one of the main reasons for the need to create state brands. He claims that nowadays, the situation in which countries find themselves resembles that in a crowded bar where in order to draw attention to yourself, you have to present yourself briefly and simply (S. Anholt, *Brand New Justice...*, p. 133).

11 Studies conducted by Boston University in 2002 among Muslim teenagers on the image of Americans were concluded by, among others, the statement that 'pop culture, rather than foreign policy, is the true culprit of anti-Americanism'. S. Anholt, J. Hildreth, *Brand America: the Mother of All Brands*, Cyan Communications, 2005, p. 150.

12 B. Ociepka, 'Dyplomacja publiczna jako forma komunikowania międzynarodowego' (Public Diplomacy as a Form of International Communication), in B. Ociepka (ed.), *Dyplomacja publiczna...*, p. 26.

13 As a matter of fact, we should be talking about images, as any entity can have many of them, depending on how it is perceived by different groups. Cf.: S. Bieleń (ed.), *Wizerunki międzynarodowe Rosji* (*International Images of Russia*), Warszawa 2011.

the situation of an entity, the manner of communication and the social resonance.[14]

The situation of an entity has its characteristics. These are, first of all, the declared values and norms that are the principal constituents of its identity. For a country, it regards mainly its national and state identity.[15] Its image is further influenced by the degree of fulfilment of its declarations because it affects how much the citizens identify themselves with it.

The second important component of the image is the intensity and quality of information on its situation, manifested in the communicational activity of states,[16] usually conducted as part of public diplomacy. This activity can take the form of unilateral sending (for example, propaganda) or of a multilateral communication in which the state and the recipients of the communication interact (this form is taken by new public diplomacy).

This approach can be observed in the way public diplomacy is defined. It is described, first of all, as communication that aims at ensuring a positive image of the state, which in turn is the object of these actions.[17] However, there are no forced limitations as to who can be the sender of the communicated message. Usually governments representing states are expected to be senders (as suggested by the term 'diplomacy') but it can also be any other foreign or national entity, including non-governmental organisations, the private sector and ordinary citizens. This inclusion of non-state actors in the process of international public communication is a characteristic feature of modern public diplomacy, which, for this exact reason, is referred to as 'new' public diplomacy. Researchers who deal with these issues underline the multilateral nature of this type of activity. It goes beyond unilateral informational communication controlled by state authorities, which we are dealing with in the case of propaganda or the early public diplomacy in the United States. In academic literature we find the opinion that public diplomacy covers a broad and changeable range of processes and activities – from government actors communicating with

---

14 For more see: K. Wojcik, *Public relations. Wiarygodny dialog z otoczeniem* (*Public Relations. A Reliable Dialogue with Those Around Us*), Warszawa 2005, pp. 38–43.

15 J. Kukułka, *Wstęp do nauki…*, p. 180.

16 Cf.: *ibid.*, p. 157.

17 According to Beata Ociepka, public diplomacy is a bilateral, dialogue-based form of international political communication addressed to foreign recipients and executed primarily through the media and through direct channels. Its aim is to shape and promote a positive image of a given country and society abroad, including encouraging positive attitudes towards the sender country by influencing the public opinion (B. Ociepka, 'Dyplomacja publiczna jako forma…', p. 12).

people through media, to interpersonal contacts such as the academic exchange of researchers from various countries. Thus, on the one hand, public diplomacy is the process of communication between the government of a country and foreign audience in order for the latter to understand the values and ideals of the given nation, its institutions and culture, as well as its goals and the policies it pursues. On the other hand, its second aim is to influence the actions of another country by affecting its public opinion.[18] It is believed that public diplomacy is also more successful in a network environment, with numerous multidimensional relations, in which the traditional state-centric model stumbles upon communicational limitations. It allows for coordination of activity between government departments and non-governmental organisations involved in the process of communication.[19]

Figure 1: Levels of international communication.

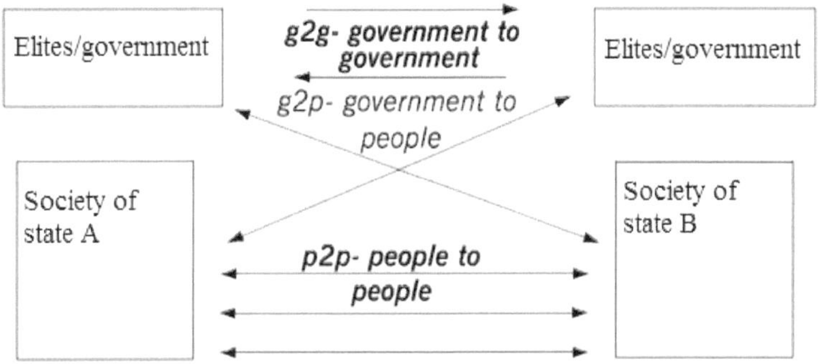

Source: On the basis of: W. Ph. Davison, *Mass communication and Diplomacy*, in J. Rosenau, K. Thompson, & G. Boyd (eds.), *World Politics*, New York, Free Press, 1974, p. 388–403; J. Olędzki, *Komunikowanie w świecie* (*Communication in the World*), Warszawa 2001, p. 25.

The subjective area of international communication executed as a part of public diplomacy is illustrated by the model originally devised by W. Phillips Davison (see Fig. 1), who identified its three levels.

The first level is comprised of the interactions between governments (referred to as government-to-government, g2g). They are elite, undertaken by designated

18 Cf.: M. Topić, C. Sciortino, *Cultural Diplomacy…*, p. 10.

19 Cf.: M. Leonard, C. Stead, C. Smewing, *Public Diplomacy*, London 2002, available at: http://fpc.org.uk/fsblob/35.pdf (accessed on 4 May 2013), pp. 9–10; B. Ociepka, 'Nowa dyplomacja publiczna – perspektywa teorii stosunków międzynarodowych i komunikowania politycznego' (New Public Diplomacy – The Perspective of the IR Theory and the Theory of Political Communication), *Przegląd Strategiczny*, no. 1, 2012, p. 137.

state officials within the framework of traditional diplomacy. Their principal aim is to represent the state in international relations, realised through a mechanism described as the triad: *observer–négocier–protéger* (i.e. monitoring important political and social events in another country, conducting international negotiations and protecting state interests by reacting to events that are unfavourable to the state, as well as providing assistance to its citizens staying abroad).[20] A communication in which elites of one country reach the society of another country (referred to as government-to-people communication, g2p) involves information activities conducted by the first country, taking the form of propaganda or public diplomacy in the traditional sense.[21] There is no common agreement between scholars as to which actions undertaken by the actors of international relations can be called propaganda and which ones are already public diplomacy. Initially, public diplomacy was treated as a purely informational activity (that is, as a rather unilateral communication) that uses the instruments of classic cultural diplomacy aimed at foreign recipients and as such, it could easily be considered propaganda. Beata Ociepka[22] believes that when there is interaction ('dialogue form of political communication') and the action goes beyond unilateral conveying of information, in which a reaction is not expected, then it goes beyond propaganda. What is more, in contemporary democratic systems it is rather hard to conduct propaganda because citizens have free access to many sources of information and therefore able to verify the messages they receive.[23]

The third level is the communication between the societies of two countries, manifested primarily in the cilvilisational and cultural influence of the societies on each other (referred to as people-to-people, p2p). It can be described by the vivid metaphor of 'citizen diplomacy', which suggests that all citizens staying abroad are 'ambassadors' of their countries. However, the expression 'citizen

20 See: R. Kuźniar, 'Międzynarodowe stosunki polityczne' (International Political Relations), in E. Haliżak, R. Kuźniar (eds.), *Stosunki międzynarodowe. Geneza, struktura, dynamika* (*International Relations. Genesis, Structure, Dynamics*), Warszawa 2006, pp. 135–136.

21 One of the traditional definitions of public diplomacy describes it as activity which covers government-sponsored cultural, scientific and informational programmes, citizen exchange and sending activity. These actions are dedicated to promoting mutual understanding and influencing foreign recipients in order to further the state's national interest (cf.: E. Wolfson, 'Dyplomacja publiczna z amerykańskiej perspektywy' ['Public Diplomacy from the US Perspective'], in B. Ociepka (ed.), *Dyplomacja publiczna...*, p. 202).

22 B. Ociepka, 'Dyplomacja publiczna jako forma...', p. 12.

23 B. Ociepka, 'Nowa dyplomacja publiczna...', pp. 132–134.

diplomacy' emphasises the influence of individuals (citizens) on the images of countries – their conscious and unconscious behaviour abroad contributes either to consolidating or abolishing the stereotypes regarding their home country.[24] For example, the leaflet issued in 2007 by the US Department of State and titled *10 Things Americans Can Do to Support Public Diplomacy*[25] shows how citizen diplomacy can be directed in a way that it supports the realisation of the goals of public diplomacy. The document recommends activities such as: participating in international student exchanges (including hosting foreign students and encouraging one's children to participate in programmes of studies abroad); encouraging children to learn foreign languages, to discover the histories of other countries and follow news from the world, to maintain relations with their peers from other countries; active participating in non-governmental organisations which conduct programmes addressed to other countries; partaking in provision of humanitarian aid to countries suffering from the effects of natural disasters; encouraging participation in intercultural dialogue, and other activities.

The consolidation of a positive image and reputation requires the state to be active on every level of communication. A good example of a situation when all subjects of communication need to be taken into account is one of Poland's image-related problems, publicised in 2010, regarding the manner in which Poles were presented in European history textbooks.[26] The research conducted by Adam Suchoński[27] shows that in many textbooks, Poland's image was distorted – first of all, it was shown as a backwater country inhabited by victims of wars, oppression and failed national uprisings. In the scholar's opinion, this image is the result of many years of negligence by Polish authorities, who do

---

24 J. Mikułkowski Pomorski, *Jak narody porozumiewają się ze sobą w komunikacji międzykulturowej i komunikowaniu medialnym* (*How Nations Communicate Between Each Other in Intercultural and Media Communication*), Kraków 2007, pp. 58–62.

25 U.S. Department of State, *10 Things Americans Can Do to Support Public Diplomacy*, 19 IV 2007, available at: http://www.dfwworld.org/Document.Doc?&id=27 (accessed on 1 February 2013).

26 J. Dziadul, 'Polska? A co to?' (Poland? What Is That?), interview with Prof. Adam Suchoński, *Polityka*, 9 May 2010, available at: http://www.polityka.pl/kraj/wywiady/1505364,1,rozmowa-z-prof-adamem-suchonskim.read#ixzz2MgUJFnUT (accessed on 1 February 2013); B. Łabutin, 'Widły nam już zbrzydły' (We're fed up with the pitchfork), interview with A. Suchoński, *Gazeta Wyborcza*, 18 August 2011, available at: http://wyborcza.pl/1,76842,10136285,Widly_nam_juz_zbrzydly.html (accessed on 1 February 2013).

27 Adam Suchoński – expert of the Polish Ministry of National Education for history textbooks.

not monitor textbooks for issues related to their country as other countries do. For years, no official materials about the events and people that are important to Poland have been prepared or published to be used by foreign textbook authors.[28] Moreover, Polish historians do not participate in the development of European textbooks. This means that for years, there has been no flow of information between experts and no permanent institutionalised communication monitoring conducted by state authorities.

The last component of the image is reception (resonance) among these actors with whom the given state wants to establish a positive image of itself. Social resonance, in turn, is the resultant of three variables: the area of reason, i.e. the state of knowledge about the given country; the emotional area, i.e. impressions, feelings or sentiments, including expectations, ideas, fears, desires, prejudice, sympathies; as well as social norms – norms of the group that people feel attached to and which provide them with guidelines for normative interpretation of information about the given country. The significance of this component is very well illustrated by the failed promotional campaign of the US broadcasted on television in 2002, titled 'The Shared Values Initiative' and addressed to Muslim communities[29] after the terrorist attacks of 11 September 2001 – the event which made Americans aware to what extent the United States was not accepted.[30] Wally Olins[31] commented on that rather harshly by saying that while the United States was undeniably the most well-known country in the world, as well as the strongest and most influential one, it discovered with great astonishment that it is not the most loved one; in fact, in

28 Such documents should be included in the Georg Eckert Institute in Brunswick, where authors gather the materials for textbooks and can become acquainted with how a given country is presented in other textbooks.

29 The spots shown in local television channels broadcasted in Pakistan, Malaysia, Kuwait, Kenya, and Tanzania, as well as in the Pan-Arab Television viewed in Saudi Arabia, Kuwait, the United Arab Emirates, Bahrain, Oman, Qatar, Jordan, Lebanon, and Egypt had an audience of 288 million people (S. Anholt, J. Hildreth, *Brand America...*, pp. 142).

30 While in various parts of the world people were sympathising with Americans because of the tragedy that they had suffered, many Muslim communities were reluctant to share that feeling. For example, one TV transmission showed how on the West Bank and in Lebanese refugee camps crowds were dancing and joyfully celebrating what they considered the fall of Satan. See: *Arafat Horrified by Attacks, but Thousands of Palestinians Celebrate; Rest of World Outraged*, 12 September 2001, available at: http://www.foxnews.com/story/0,2933,34187,00.html#ixzz2KL271aAh (accessed on 1 February 2013).

31 W. Olins, *Wally Olins. On B®and*, Chapter 8: 'Branding the Nation', Thames & Hudson, 2004.

some parts of the world there is a profound aversion for the US. He subsequently concludes that for a nation which believes that its values and lifestyle are the best in the world and assumes that the rest of the world agrees with that, this is a very shocking and disturbing opinion, one all the more devastating and hurting as it is a nation that craves and expects admiration and sympathy.[32]

The aim of the said campaign was to reduce the bad reception of the United States. It was comprised of five mini-documentaries about the life of Muslims in America which were to be published during the Ramadan. The campaign was aimed to convince Muslims that the US was a place where they could lead a peaceful and happy life in accordance with the rules of their faith. However, the advertisements failed to achieve the expected results and were criticised for an overly aggressive promotion of US foreign policy under the cover of religious tolerance.[33] The marketing form of this campaign did not win approval either, as it was considered a sign of arrogance and an example of the United States' cultural and economic imperialism.[34] What is more, the campaign itself was discontinued in an atmosphere of a scandal when Charlotte Beers, who was responsible for its development, resigned.[35]

A change of views and preferences automatically entails a modification of the image and therefore, it is innately not a static and lasting notion.[36] A good example of the volatility of the image is the radical change in the attitude of the Dutch nationals towards Polish immigrants. In early 2012, anti-Polish sentiments soared, stimulated by the actions of Geert Wilders, the leader of the xenophobic Party for Freedom (PVV). For example, he created a website where Dutch people could report and file complaints regarding bothersome behaviour of Poles working in the Netherlands. In 2012, however, Wilders lost the elections and his party got no seats in the parliament. As a result, his voice was marginalised in the public debate. Within a year, the attitude of the Dutch towards Poles improved considerably,

---

32 See: W. Olins, *Wally Olins. On B®and*, Thames & Hudson, 2004. Simon Anholt, another promoter of nation branding, commented on the same issue in similar words, saying 'America just isn't used to being hated' (S. Anholt, J. Hildreth, *Brand America...*, p. 146).

33 Every piece ended with a sentence which stated that it was a message from the Council of American Muslims for Understanding and from the American nation.

34 S. Anholt, J. Hildreth, *Brand America...*, pp. 144–145; M. Goldberg, *To know America is to love America?*, 20 December 2002, http://www.salon.com/2002/12/20/beers/ (accessed on 1 February 2013).

35 Charlotte Beers officially resigned her post as Under Secretary for Public Diplomacy and Public Affairs due to health reasons (cf.: S. Anholt, J. Hildreth, *Brand America...*, p. 125).

36 B. Rozwadowska, *Public Relations. Teoria. Praktyka. Perspektywy* (*Public Relations. Theory. Practice. Prospects*), Warszawa 2009, p. 55.

even though neither the number of Poles staying in the Netherlands nor their behaviour (as we may assume) has radically changed.[37] According to a report published by the Institute of Public Affairs on the perception of Poland and Poles in the Netherlands, as many as 40 percent of Dutch nationals surveyed believe that Poles obey the law and almost 50 percent do not see any problem in Poles becoming permanent residents and citizens of the Netherlands.[38]

While countries have the capability to manage their image more or less successfully, it is not exactly the case with their reputation.[39] Although the terms 'reputation' and 'image' are often used interchangeably to refer to the same phenomenon, reputation is the result of a consolidated normative evaluation of image. Reputation is the good name; the way it is renowned – the part of image that seems unchanging despite the changing circumstances and which has to be earned by consistent strengthening of the image in the long-term perspective. This is the reason why countries are constantly looking for more effective instruments for strengthening their reputation. One of the latest is state branding, the promoters of which believe that it is the job of responsible governments to maintain the reputation of their countries by managing their brands.[40]

It is believed that states are interested in managing their image and looking after their reputation for two main reasons – first, in order to increase international community's acceptance of their goals and means applied to achieve them, and second, in order to minimise the effects of the factors that distort the desired image and that could negatively affect this acceptance.[41] In the 'crowded environment' in which modern states have to function, for many of them, seeking

37 J. Pawlicki, K. Pawłowska-Salińska, 'Cud w Hadze, czyli Holendrzy (już) nas kochają' (Miracle in the Hague – the Dutch Already Love Us), *Gazeta Wyborcza*, 12 December 2012, available at: http://www.wyborcza.pl/1,75477,13033596,Cud_w_ Hadze__czyli_ Holendrzy__juz__nas_kochaja.html (accessed on 12 December 2012); W. Olins, *Wally Olins. On B®and…*

38 Instytut Spraw Publicznych, *Wizerunek Polski i Polaków w Holandii. Główne wnioski z badania* (*The Image of Poland and Poles in the Netherlands. Main Survey Conclusions*), available at: http://www.isp.org.pl/uploads/filemanager/Gwnewnioskizbadania-WizerunekPolskiiPolakwwHolandiiPL1.pdf (accessed on 1 February 2013).

39 G. Szondi, 'Filary zarządzania reputacją: dyplomacja publiczna w Europie Wschodniej z perspektywy public relations' (Pillars of Reputation Management: Public Diplomacy in Eastern Europe from the Public Relations Perspective), transl. into Polish by M. Miłkowski, in B. Ociepka (ed.), *Dyplomacja publiczna…*, p. 69.

40 S. Anholt, *Competitive Identity: The New Brand Management for Nations, Cities and Regions*, Palgrave Macmillan, 2007, p. 2.

41 See: J. Kukułka, *Wstęp…*, p. 159.

attention has become the most important activity. This is especially true of the small and medium-sized countries as they have to put the largest effort into gaining acceptance of the international community. They do not possess many 'hard tools' at their disposal and often, they are not particularly well-known. For them, active public diplomacy including the strategy of state branding with the use of their cultural potential is an opportunity to become known as reliable actors of international relations.[42] The way these tools are used is determined by the nature of the international community, which has both competitive and cooperative characteristics. States will act differently depending on which type of factors is perceived as dominant. When cooperative factors are dominant or when the state does not have to engage in direct rivalry, there is a greater inclination for the soft approach in communicating one's needs, plans and actions. When there is no hostile attitude – or as Roman Kuźniar described it, in a 'normal situation' – then countries are more willing to use culture, science, information, the attractiveness of their ideology or social model in their promotional, propagandist and informative activities conducted in particular to enhance their prestige, to sway other societies to their side and improve their image. This, in turn makes it easier for them to exert political influence.[43] On the other hand, if there are more circumstances causing rivalry (for material resources, ideas, and especially for who is right), the competitive approach will be applied more often, which can result in a 'harder' approach of states in using culture to impose their point of view.[44]

Methods of image and reputation management

Both image and reputation are reflections of the impressions and opinions of external entities. Because of this, the essence of their management lies in communicative activities undertaken by states in order to influence long-term reputation. This is possible through promoting the image that is considered desirable.[45] It is a challenge, because in the present times people have incomparably easier and greater access to information regarding all countries than ever before. On the one hand, the greater the volume of information forming the basis of perception of the image, the more complete and consistent with the actual state of affairs

42 B. Ociepka, 'Nowa dyplomacja publiczna…', p. 137.
43 R. Kuźniar, 'Międzynarodowe stosunki polityczne…', p. 128.
44 E. Wolfson, 'Dyplomacja publiczna…', pp. 207–228.
45 G. Szondi, 'Filary zarządzania reputacją…', p. 72.

it becomes.[46] On the other hand, an excess of information results in a greater inclination to become acquainted with it only superficially, and thus develop and consolidate only a stereotypical perception of reality.

The tools which allow exerting influence on image include, first of all, methods that allow the state to perform its communicative activity. It is difficult to classify them clearly. This group includes actions considered as part of public relations of states, psychosocial instruments, information activity, as well as psychological warfare and propaganda. These are the most common instruments used in cultural diplomacy or public diplomacy. As of late, the list also includes the country-of-origin effect and the resulting nation branding. The reason why all these instruments are applied is the belief that state reputation is important in international activity.

It is assumed that the oldest tool for facilitating image management is cultural diplomacy. Most generally speaking, it considers exchange of ideas, information, art, and other aspects of culture between nations and people in order to enhance mutual understanding.[47] Cultural diplomacy, in the classic meaning of this term, involves the possibility of conducting intercultural dialogue and developing cultural relations, which both are within the competence of diplomatic services.[48] There are a number of authors who state outright that the aim of cultural diplomacy is to manage the image of the state and that culture is an effective tool used in this process.[49] On the other hand, even within one country, cultural diplomacy can have different goals and tools depending on the target country, as exemplified by how cultural diplomacy is perceived in France. The country's approach towards Austria, the Netherlands and Sweden should be rather referred to as foreign cultural policy, which can be understood as an export of cultural values

---

46 See: J. Kukułka, 'Postrzeganie międzynarodowe' (International Perception'), *Stosunki Międzynarodowe*, no. 16, 1992, p. 94.

47 M. Topić, C. Sciortino, *Cultural Diplomacy...*, p. 10.

48 L. Łukaszuk, 'Wykonywanie funkcji misji dyplomatycznej a dialog i współdziałanie międzykulturowe – w świetle prawa i praktyki' (Performing the Functions of a Diplomatic Mission – Dialogue and Intercultural Cooperation, Law and Practice), in Z. Galicki, T. Kamiński, K. Myszona-Kostrzewa (eds.), *50 Lat Konwencji Wiedeńskiej – aktualna kondycja uregulowań dotyczących stosunków dyplomatycznych* (*50 Years of the Vienna Convention – the Present Condition of Regulations Concerning Diplomatic Relations*), Warszawa 2012, p. 119.

49 B. Bojarczyk, J. Olchowski, A. W. Ziętek, 'Od dominacji kulturowej do soft power. Kultura w promocji państwa' (From Cultural Domination to Soft Power. Culture in Country Promotion), in A. W. Ziętek (ed.), *Międzynarodowe stosunki kulturalne* (*International Cultural Relations*), Warszawa 2010, p. 135.

(primarily promotion of language, supporting foreign appearances by artists and presentation of their works, sport events, exchange of students and academics, international congresses and establishment of cultural and information centres abroad).[50] With regard to Australia, Canada, Singapore, and the UK, in turn, it resembles cultural relations more.[51]

Cultural diplomacy helps, first of all, in the promotion of a country through culture and allows for opening up to cultural contacts. Under this approach, state authorities establish institutions with the task of improving the cultural recognisability of their country.[52] Hence the typical institutions of cultural diplomacy are cultural attachés at diplomatic missions and cultural centres or institutes established in foreign countries. Among the most well-known are the British Council, the German Goethe-Institut, the Alliance Française, and the Chinese Confucius Institute. In Poland, the Adam Mickiewicz Institute performs this type of activity. The primary aim of these institutions is presenting the cultural achievements and promoting the artistic life of their countries, as well as teaching their language. They organise and co-organise artistic events, which give foreign citizens the opportunity to familiarise with the cultural achievements of the institutes' home countries. They are centres of cultural life in their host countries. Their activities are directly and institutionally sponsored and supervised by state authorities.

Cultural diplomacy is considered to precede public diplomacy.[53] However, there is no agreement as to how it is meant to be placed in the context of public diplomacy. Generally, we can understand public diplomacy as a communication of states with foreign audiences, which is aimed at informing and persuading the foreign audience on foreign policy goals and nation interests.[54] There is a strong tendency to consider cultural diplomacy a part of public diplomacy as the aim of the latter is primarily to coordinate the communication activities of a state, including the ones directly related to culture (done by cultural diplomacy). This approach is also justified by the goal of cultural diplomacy: promotion through culture, which isrealised by providing information and disseminating knowledge

---

50 See: J. Mikułowski Pomorski, *Jak narody...*, p. 63.

51 This has been pointed out by M. Topić and C. Sciortino (*Cultural Diplomacy...*, p. 10).

52 L. Łukaszuk, 'Wykonywanie funkcji...', p. 119.

53 See: B. Bojarczyk, J. Olchowski, A. W. Ziętek, 'Od dominacji kulturowej...', p. 135.

54 See: E. Gilboa, 'Diplomacy in the Media Age. Three Models of Uses and Effects', *Diplomacy & Statecraft*, no. 12 (2), 2001, p. 4.

about culture, civilisational achievements and history.[55] However, there are scholars who believe these two instruments are equally important.[56]

As a fundamental issue, culture appears also in other instruments that are used to manage the reputation of a country. Actions such as these can be considered part of a broad spectrum of actions in the sphere of public diplomacy.[57] The notion of state brand and nation branding is the subject of a lively discussion and gives rise to many controversies.[58] It should be noted that the very idea of creating state brands has very strong cultural connotations as it is consistent with the cultural standard of the United States. The state brand can be treated as a cultural artefact of the US – a way of thinking and expressing that stems from the language of marketing and advertising, the birthplace of which are indeed the United States. However, there is a common conviction among scholars studying state brand that this term denotes something different than commercial brand and refers to creating an outline for describing the identity of the branded entity. State brand is presented as reputation and authority of a country and its image – together with the visual symbols and ideas that constitute it and briefly present the nature and idea of the country (nation), its reason for existence and the system of recognised values – or the sum of the beliefs about the country and its nation.[59] In

55 This is how the goals of the Polish cultural diplomacy are defined (M. Mickiewicz, 'Polska dyplomacja kulturalna' [Polish Cultural Diplomacy], in B. Ociepka (ed.), *Dyplomacja publiczna…*, pp. 117–118).

56 See: G. Szondi, 'Filary zarządzania reputacją…', p. 77.

57 However, there is no agreement whether nation branding is a part of public diplomacy or vice versa. Simon Anholt, a promoter of nation branding, believes that public diplomacy is one of the elements of branding, as it is considered an instrument of shaping the nation brand. Beata Ociepka does not agree with him. She claims that public diplomacy is a broader notion than state branding, and is not an element of nation brand management or an instrument of the state branding campaign; she believes that public diplomacy should be viewed as an instrument coordinating many areas, including the economy. According to Ociepka, brading focuses on showing uniqueness, while public diplomacy can strive to show similarities (e.g. during the processes of accession to an organisation or in integration processes); public diplomacy does not treat the recipient solely as a consumer but also as a citizen, and a participant of social relations (B. Ociepka, *Dyplomacja publiczna jako forma…*, pp. 28–29).

58 S. Anholt dedicated a chapter to a discussion on why branding has a bad brand (see: S. Anholt, *Competitive Identity…*, pp. 10–11; cf.: J. Nakonieczna, 'Znaczenie marki państwa w geoekonomicznej przestrzeni' ['The Importance of State Brand in Geoeconomic Space'], in E. Haliżak (ed.), *Geoekonomia* [*Geoeconomics*], Warszawa 2012).

59 M. A. Boruc, M. Kłoczko, 'Posłowie' (Afterword), in W. Olins, *Wally Olins. On B®and…*, p. 250.; S. Anholt, 'The Anholt Nation Brands Index. Special Report on

other words, state brand involves a reference to the immaterial, symbolical and emotional attributes of a country and on the specific processes of communication relating to them; this, in turn, leads to a positive reception of image and in the long run, reputation.[60] In a sense, brand simultaneously supplants and ties together terms such as identity, image and reputation.

Thus, analysing the proposed methods of state brand management allows us to see that its principal element is culture, essentially believed to be the only truly unique and characteristic constituent of state brand.

In one of the best-known models, proposed by Anholt (the Nation Brand Hexagon), most constituents refer either directly or indirectly to culture or to the national heritage of the country concerned. Since Anholt believes that brand is the sum of perceptions concerning a country, he isolated six basic elements of brand which are measured among respondents which speak about a given country, as well as the way and the intensity in which they are perceived.[61] The intensity of perception of each element is illustrated on a special diagram that depictsthe country's brand. The constituents are:

- tourism
- export (brand export);
- governance – especially the perception of the government's actions in the international arena and towards solving global problems; investment and immigration, which allows to estimate the perception of the country as a potential place to work and invest in;
- culture and heritage – referring to the perception of the national heritage of the country as well as the overall recognition of the country's cultural activity;
- people – especially how the nationals of the country are perceived, whether they are considered hardworking, kind and friendly but also whether any famous and internationally recognisable individuals are associated with the country.

The key importance of culture for the management of state brand is also stressed by the second leading promoter of nation branding – Wally Olins. First of all, he notes that culture is both the basis of a sense of pride (of the society's national heritage) and the driving force behind initiating cooperation with other countries (reference to common history or cultural identification can be helpful in establishing relations). Olins also believes that internationally recognisable

Europe's International Image, Q2 2006, plus an Update on the Status of "Brand Denmark"', *Place Branding*, vol. 2, no. 3, 2006.

60 J. Nakonieczna, 'Znaczenie marki państwa…', pp. 266–267.

61 S. Anholt, *Competitive Identity…*, pp. 39–41.

individuals are important as well (artists such as Pedro Almodóvar, who is associated with Spanish cinema, but also fictional characters such as James Bond, who is the epitome of a British gentleman) and considers them ambassadors of culture. Secondly, Olins notices the cultural aspect of the state's participation in international events, such as international expos or sports events, which help consolidate a positive image of the organiser or a very capable participant of such events. Thirdly, culture is an important element of visual identification of a country. For example, the logo used by Spain includes a sun by Joan Miró or the logo of the British public services website gov.uk includes a royal crown.

To sum up, while describing the nature of the state brand, promoters of nation branding stress the considerable significance of culture in its shaping and management. In their opinion, culture is as important in this respect as economy and trade. In brand management, culture can be used as:

- national heritage (especially artistic heritage), which is a source of pride. Therefore, it is also easy to promote;
- an original identifying element – it is primarily through culture than one can show the uniqueness of a country;
- cultural recognisability in the international arena, which has been supported for many years, e.g. through the activity of UNESCO and its World Heritage List, established under the conventions of 1972 and 2003.

Conclusion

Should all countries look after their reputation? On the one hand, it is obvious that first of all, the ones that do not have any particular distinguishing features should consciously manage their images. Since they usually do not have particularly developed 'hard' resources, their own culture is their best support. It is through culture that they can become recognised by other people. On the other hand, the standards of promotion are set by the largest and most active entities of international relations and it is they who decide what is desirable and acceptable. The growing popularity of nation branding is a manifestation of this very fact because it is considered a successful method of promotion developed in Western culture, particularly in the United States.

Countries want to be not only recognisable but also respected in the international community. To this end, they apply many diverse communication strategies. The key element, however, is always culture – whether it is through direct reference to national heritage or through the awareness of cultural determinants in the interpretation of the way in which they are perceived. Taiwan presents itself as the guardian of the national heritage of the Chinese civilisation. Poland wants to be seen as the heart of Europe and while joining the EU it justified its membership as a due return to Europe. Switzerland, in turn, has for years been seen as symbol of discretion, precision and reliability.

Wiesław Lizak

Cultural Determinants of Conflicts

Key words: international conflicts, nationalism, religion, fundamentalism, political culture

Abstract: The article analyses how cultural factors determine the emergence and evolution of international conflicts. Specific cultural factors, such as national ideologies, nationalism, religions, religious denominations, and political culture, are considered when evaluating international conflicts.

In the contemporary world, conflicts are most often caused by several parallel reasons. Regardless of the external (most visible) manifestations of the phenomena and processes conducive to conflicts, which often dominate the information flow reaching the recipients and influence their perception and judgement, in practice, at the bottom of every conflict there is a number of interrelated contradictions originating with local social, political, economic and cultural processes and phenomena. Hence, cultural determinants are among many factors influencing the emergence and evolution of conflicts in the contemporary world. However, this influence is very special, due to their consciousness-based nature. Specifically, it is a function of the existing social values, attitudes, religious beliefs as well as ideological convictions and outlooks on life. As a result, they refer to the fundamental determinants that shape the identity of nations, social groups and individuals, and, consequently, they become very hard to 'negotiate' at the stage when contradictions and different interests arising in the processes of social interaction are revealed. The compromise necessary for peaceful resolution of disputes or conflicts arising on such grounds requires both parties to make concessions and accept the reasoning of the opponent (partner) in the dialogue.

The ideas, social norms, visions of own place and role in the broader community of analogous entities, convictions and religious beliefs as well as (auto) stereotypes existing within social groups are at the very core of the development of own image (identity) and the image of other social groups. Protection of own identity and the values that constitute it is the fundamental paradigm that defines the behaviour of collectives in crisis situations. All this results in the fact that the emergence of contradictions on these grounds entails emotional reactions which are difficult to control but which are often taken advantage of by the ruling classes in order to achieve particularistic political goals (it is not uncommon to see intentional provoking and fuelling social emotions in order to acquire political support). In this way, consciousness-based forms of social life become an instrument used to pursue political goals by a mobilisation of supporters. In this situation, we are often dealing with symbolical or real violence, when the advantage held by a social group in the cultural sphere entails attempts at domination over other social entities and consolidation of the existing state of affairs. At that time, contradictions in the cultural sphere become the source of permanent conflict-generating antagonisms. They arise on the basis of various elements constituting the cultural context of the contemporary everyday life, such as the sense of ethnic ties, membership in religious groups, or models of social behaviour referring to the functioning of the socio-political system. It is precisely these factors that play a special role in the process of building social ties, in formulating demands regarding the expectations of one's own group and other social groups, and in determining the means to realise them. Thus, they become the basis for conflict-generating processes. Therefore, further in the article, the author shall attempt to present their specific role in this process.

National ideologies and nationalisms

National ideas, which emerged as a consequence of the social transformations taking place due to modernisation processes caused by the industrial revolution, play an essential role within the framework of broadly understood consciousness-based determinants. Some of the consequences of the said modernisation include the establishment of new social groups on the rubble of feudal class societies as a result of the development of capitalist free market-based economy. The emergence of new forms of social consciousness in these circumstances led to the development of modern nations, based on common language, culture, history, and often political community as well. The 19th and 20th centuries witnessed fundamental transformations of the nature and character of social ties between people living in developing industrial societies. Of course, this process did not progress at the same pace in all regions and parts of the world, just as uneven were the modernisation-related transformations caused by the industrial revolution – not only in the global scale but also, for instance, within Europe.[1]

The emergence of modern nations, based on lasting social ties, gave birth to the idea of self-determination of nations, which has led to radical geopolitical changes

---

1 Cf.: K. Pomian, *L'Europe et ses nations* (*Europe and Its Nations*), Editions Gallimard 1990, Polish edition: *Europa i jej narody*, Warszawa 1990, pp. 151–164; A.D. Smith, *Nationalism and Modernism: A Critical Survey of Recent Theories of Nations and Nationalism*, London 1998, pp. 47–69.

in the global scale taking place in the last two centuries. The origins of this idea can be traced to the first half of the 19th century, when national independence movements were emerging almost everywhere in Europe, taking the form of attempts to overthrow the yoke of foreign rule (e.g. Poles and the nations living within the borders of the Ottoman Empire) and of unification aspirations of nations living across several different countries (such as Germans, Italians or Romanians). It is the epic struggle for political unification of the Apennine Peninsula or the German lands that led to the coining of the catchphrase that every nation has a right to live in a separate country – which in later years became the symbol of transformations caused by national movements. This gave birth to nationalist ideas, which obviously placed the nation in the focal point of the political debate on the future of the given group of people who felt they shared a common history and language.[2]

The principle of self-determination of nations was constituted as a regulatory principle of the international order during the period of World War I. Two events had a particular impact on it becoming an element of international law; first, the announcement of the Declaration of the Rights of the Peoples of Russia by Soviet Russia's authorities in November 1917, which included the obligation to respect the national rights of the peoples inhabiting the former empire of the Tsars;[3] and second, the statement made by the US President Thomas Woodrow Wilson (the Fourteen Points) in January 1918, in which, as one of the leaders of the winning coalition, he called for respect for the national rights of the peoples living in the multi-ethnic European empires (he mentioned the right of the Polish nation to rebuild an independent state, among others). At that time, the defeat of Germany and Austria-Hungary and the revolutionary transformations in Russia

2 However, the emerging nationalisms called upon various political reference platforms and as a consequence, are sometimes classified as political nationalisms,where the state is the point of reference for the birth of the national idea (e.g. in France or postcolonial America); and folk nationalisms, under which the birth of national identity bases on historical determinants of social identity, often in opposition to (unaccepted) political authorities (Central and Eastern Europe, where nations took form under multiethnic monarchies – Austrian, Russian or Turkish). See: N. Davies, *Europe: A History*, Oxford: Oxford University Press 1996, Polish edition: *Europa. Rozprawa historyka z historią*, trans. by E. Tabakowska, Kraków 1998, pp. 863–887.

3 Despite provisions on the individual nations' right to break away from Russia and establish independent countries, in later practice, however, the binding interpretation of this principle narrowed down its meaning. It was pointed out that it should be understood in the context of the rights of the working class and its vanguard – the communist party (see: L. Bazylow, P. Wieczorkiewicz, *Historia Rosji* (*The History of Russia*), Wrocław 2005, p. 409).

opened the way for the establishment of new countries in Europe, pursuant to the principle of self-determination, although some of them eventually developed as multinational states (Czechoslovakia and the Kingdom of Serbs, Croats and Slovenes, which later became Yugoslavia). The binding force of this principle, as one of the fundamental rules of the contemporary international order, was further confirmed in the provisions of the United Nations Charter of 1945 (Article 1) and the Declaration on Principles of International Law Concerning Friendly Relations and Cooperation among States in accordance with the Charter of the United Nations of 24 October 1970 (it refers to it as the 'principle of equal rights and self-determination of peoples').[4] The inclusion of this principle in international law became the basis for legitimising the processes of national independence, as confirmed by the UN General Assembly of 14 December 1960 titled 'Declaration on the Granting of Independence to Colonial Countries and Peoples'.[5]

The development of regulations concerning the right of nations to determine their own international status was an answer to the emergence of certain social needs resulting from the freedom aspirations of the peoples which desired political subjectivity. In terms of ideas, this took the form of nationalism as a set of beliefs and social attitudes concerning the role and place of the given social group in the global geopolitical space. Nationalisms, however, proved to be highly diverse. Very often, they were becoming carriers for freedom-oriented content for nations still struggling to achieve subjectivity, but in some cases they turned into a call to build one's own identity in opposition (or even hostility) to other nations. In extreme cases this even led to chauvinism (e.g. Nazism).[6] However, regardless of the content and form, nationalisms (carrying both freedom-oriented and aggressive content) were becoming the source of disturbances shaking up the existing territorial and political order and giving rise to many conflicts.

Wars for national independence – a consequence of these processes – are usually assessed as positive. By increasing the number of entities benefiting from the principle of self-determination of nations, conflicts arising as a result of nations

---

4 United Nations General Assembly Resolution 2625 (XXV): *Declaration on Principles of International Law Concerning Friendly Relations and Cooperation among States in accordance with the Charter of the United Nations*, 24 October 1970, http://www.stosunkimiedzynarodowe.info/dokument,8,Deklaracja_zasad_prawa_miedzynarodowego_24_X_1970.html4 (accessed on 5 January 2013).

5 United Nations General Assembly Resolution 1514 (XV): *Declaration on the Granting of Independence to Colonial Countries and Peoples*, 14 December 1960 r., http://www.grocjusz.edu.pl/Documents/dekl2514.html (accessed on 5 January 2013).

6 Cf.: A.D. Smith, *Nationalism...*, pp. 82–84.

striving to free themselves from foreign domination help stabilise the international order in the long term perspective, even though they can have a destructive effect while they last. National independence-based conflicts are thus always a consequence of authorities that administers the territory inhabited by an ethnic group aspiring for self-determination, but lacks the political will to respect the subjective rights of this group.

Nationalisms were at the source of the decolonisation processes which resulted in the establishment of approximately 130 new countries after World War II (mainly in Asia and Africa but also in the Pacific and the Caribbean). This process, coinciding with the Cold War era, has considerably changed the shape of the political world map. In most cases, it was peaceful but in a number of countries the colonial authorities' resistance to any concessions to native people led to outbreaks of national independence wars. Just after the end of World War II, the processes of decolonisation engulfed Asia, where they turned into an armed conflict in Indonesia, Vietnam and Malaya. A bloody conflict in North Africa also preceded Algeria's independence.[7] Long decolonisation-based conflicts arose in Southern Africa as well, where racist regimes established by settlers of European descent and Portuguese colonialism managed to create an empire of the white man which strived to protect the region from freedom aspirations of the native peoples. Such were the intensive conflicts in Angola, Mozambique, Namibia, Rhodesia (present-day Zimbabwe), and in South Africa. Furthermore, armed colonial conflicts also broke out in two other African countries, namely Portuguese Guinea (present-day Guinea-Bissau) and Kenya (the Mau Mau Uprising in the 1950s). In each case, the clash of liberation-oriented nationalisms with colonial forces resulted in the ultimate victory of the former.[8]

Nationalisms are also a source of processes which destabilise multi-ethnic states, especially when one of the nations constituting the state has a privileged position in it (or at least is perceived as privileged by the other ethnic groups living there). The emergence of a separate identity in the colonial period in the area of Eritrea caused a secessionist conflict which ended in 1993, resulting with that area

---

7 In this case, due to internal legal determinants and Algeria's status within the French state, this was more a secession than decolonisation. See e.g.: M. Connelly, *A Diplomatic Revolution: Algeria's Fight for Independence and the Origins of the Post-Cold War Era*, New York 2002; A. Kasznik-Christian, *Algieria*, Warszawa 2006, pp. 265–361; I. S. Lustick, *Unsettled States, Disputed Lands: Britain and Ireland, France and Algeria, Israel and the West Bank-Gaza*, Ithaca 1993, pp. 239–301.

8 For more see: I. F. W. Beckett, *Modern Insurgencies and Counter-Insurgencies: Guerillas and Their Opponents since 1750*, New York 2001, pp. 121–147.

breaking away from Ethiopia to form a separate state.[9] In neighbouring Sudan, after a civil war against the Arab and Arabised north which lasted for about half a century, in July 2011 the South, mostly inhabited by peoples culturally different from the ones in the north, seceded as South Sudan.[10] Decentralist tendencies conditioned by ethnic and cultural differences between various peoples caused civil wars leading to secessions – of East Pakistan in 1971 (the establishment of Bangladesh)[11] and East Timor in 1999 (secession from Indonesia).[12]

The weightiest events of this type, however, having most influence on international order, took place in Europe. Following a crisis of the so-called real socialism, three multi-ethnic countries broke up – the USSR, Yugoslavia and Czechoslovakia. The processes which led to the collapse of Yugoslavia were the most dramatic. Nationalisms showed their absolutely negative side there as they turned into chauvinist ideologies and pursued the idea of ethnically pure statehood. Initially, the idea of 'Greater Serbia' became the source of aspirations to preserve the Yugoslavian state within its borders but when this proved impossible, it turned into the idea to keep all ethnically Serbian lands in a single state. With the political borders being fundamentally different from the ethnic borders, civil wars broke out in the territories of Croatia and Bosnia and Herzegovina.[13] At the same time, the nationalisms of the other nations of former Yugoslavia manifested themselves as well in the form of a desire to gain interdependence within historical borders, even though they had not reflected the ethnic and cultural landscape shaped by several centuries of migrations and cultural and religious transformations. Thus, the Yugoslav Wars of the 1990s turned out to be the bloodiest conflicts that Europe has witnessed since the end of World War II. Local nationalisms led to the emergence of as many as seven new states in the next two decades (Slovenia, Croatia,

9 Cf.: T. M. Woldemikael, *Eritrea's identity as a cultural crossroads*, in P. Spickard (ed.), *Race and Nation: Ethnic Systems in the Modern World*, New York 2005, pp. 337–353.

10 Cf.: J. Vidmar, 'South Sudan and the international legal framework governing the emergence and delimitation of new states', *Texas International Law Journal*, vol. 47, no. 3, 2012, p. 541 ff.

11 See: C. Baxter, *Bangladesh: From a Nation to a State*, Boulder, CO 1997, pp. 61–79.

12 See: I. Martin, *Self-Determination in East Timor: The United Nations, the Ballot, and International Intervention*, Boulder, CO 2001, pp. 15–34.

13 Bassam Tibi calls Serb's attitude towards other nations of former Yugoslavia (especially the Bosnians) 'ethnofundamentalism' (see: B. Tibi, *Der religiöse Fundamentalismus im Übergang zum 21. Jahrhundert*, Bibliographisches Institut, Mannheim 1995).

Bosnia and Herzegovina, Serbia, Montenegro, Macedonia, and Kosovo – although the last one is not recognised by all other countries).[14]

Nationalisms became also the power which brought about the collapse of the Soviet Union. Revealed in the second half of 1980s as a result of the liberalisation of the real socialist system in the USSR, they became an alternative to communist ideology as a form of identity-building of ethnic groups inhabiting this country. This national revival eventually led to the negation of the need to continue maintaining the Soviet federation and all attempts made by the central authorities to control these processes (in some cases going even as far as suppression) were only conducive to the emergence of new tinderboxes (Lithuania, Georgia, Kazakhstan, Nagorno-Karabakh). However, in contrast to what happened in Yugoslavia, the process of dissolution of the USSR was ultimately peaceful, mainly because the political leaders of the largest constituent republic, that is Russia, also participated in the process of deconstructing the Soviet empire. This allowed for a swift legitimisation of the successor states. However, the nationalisms which awoke at that time became the source of contradictions within the newly established states, the borders of which did not always reflect the ethnical landscape, just as was the case in Yugoslavia. Especially the Caucasus region was characterised by a large degree of instability, caused by nationalisms in the following years (Chechnya, Dagestan, Nagorno-Karabakh, South Ossetia, Abkhazia).[15]

Even today, nationalisms continue threatening the stability of the existing international order. As ideas expressing the interests of ethnic groups through the principle of self-determination, they can lead to further geopolitical changes. The number of countries in existence nowadays (below 200) is far less than the number of ethnic groups which have a fully formed identity and potentially show independence-oriented tendencies. In Europe, separatist movements can be observed in, among others, the United Kingdom (Scots, the Irish), France (Corsicans), Spain (Basques, Catalans), Belgium (the Flemish, Walloons). In Asia, similar phenomena can be observed in, among others, China (Tibetans, the Uyghurs),

---

14 For more see: V. Meier, *Yugoslavia: A History of Its Demise*, London 1999; S. P. Ramet, *Balkan Babel: The Disintegration of Yugoslavia from the Death of Tito to Ethnic War*, 2nd ed., Boulder, CO 1996; M. Waldenberg, *Rozbicie Jugosławii: jugosłowiańskie lustro międzynarodowej polityki* (*The Disintegration of Yugoslavia: The Yugoslavian Reflection of International Politics*), 2nd ed., Warszawa 2005; W. Walkiewicz, *Jugosławia: byt wspólny i rozpad* (*Yugoslavia: the Common Existence and the Disintegration*), Warszawa 2000, pp. 234–270.

15 For more on geography of conflicts in the post-Soviet area see: G. I. Mirsky, *On Ruins of Empire: Ethnicity and Nationalism in the Former Soviet Union*, Westport, CT 1997.

India (the Assamese, Punjabis, Sikhs), Sri Lanka (Tamils), Myanmar (the Karen, the Shan), Indonesia (West Papuans), Turkey, Iraq, Syria, and Iran (Kurds).[16] In consequence of the Arab-Israeli conflict related to the division of Palestine (in the territorial shape determined during the period of the British Mandate), a separate Palestinian nation has eventually formed. The logic of local contradictions makes the implementation of the Palestinians' right to self-determination seem the necessary condition for the final solution of the conflict which has been destabilising the situation in the Middle East virtually from the beginning of the 20th century. At this point, we should note that the establishment of Israel was also a manifestation of the development of a modern national idea among the Jewish Diaspora in Europe, and Zionism became the ideological manifestation of the aspirations to rebuild the Jewish national homeland in the historical cradle of that nation.[17]

The situation regarding the status of ethnic groups is very specific in Africa. While colonialism has initiated modernisation processes (and consequently also transformations of the forms of ethnic consciousness), on the continent, it was negated too soon (alter only 50–60 years) for it to reorganise its ethnical map. African nationalisms united local ethnic groups under the banners of struggle for political independence and called for an establishment of modern nations within postcolonial borders once liberty was achieved. However, mistakes made by the ruling elites (authoritarianism, failures in the strategy of economic development, tribalisms, ineffectiveness of the state) led to the consolidation of the dominant forms of ethnic identities (tribes). The multi-ethnic nature of these countries seems to be one of the most important determinants of the conflicts which tore these states apart from the inside. If we were to compose a list of countries which have experienced, to a greater or lesser extent, contradictions arising from ethnic and cultural diversity, among others, it would have to include most countries of the region. They were the most dramatic in countries such as Rwanda, Burundi, Sudan, Democratic Republic of the Congo, Liberia, Sierra Leone, Angola or Chad.

---

16 Cf.: L. De Winter, H. Türsan (eds.), *Regionalist Parties in Western Europe*, London 1998; A. I. Singh, *Democracy, Ethnic Diversity, and Security in Post-Communist Europe*, Westport, CT 2001, pp. 36–47; see also: J. R. Rudolph, Jr. (ed.), *Encyclopedia of Modern Ethnic Conflicts*, Westport, CT 2003, passim.

17 See: D. J. Gerner, *One Land, Two Peoples: The Conflict over Palestine*, 2nd ed., Boulder, CO 1994; D. J. Gerner, *Middle East – The Palestinian Issue*, in J. R. Rudolph, Jr. (ed.), *Encyclopedia...*, pp. 161–168; B. Morris, *Righteous Victims: A History of the Zionist-Arab Conflict, 1881–2001*, New York 2001; J. A. Reilly, *Middle East – The Arab-Jewish Struggle for Palestine to 1948*, in J. R. Rudolph, Jr. (ed.), *Encyclopedia...*, pp. 137–149.

Some of them experienced ethnicity-based acts of genocide (e.g. Rwanda).[18] These examples show how in the process of formation of national identity, individual groups can develop stereotypes regarding other groups, which in turn affects their ability to understand each other and communicate, leading to viewing each other as 'aliens' and to behaviours and views of others valued on the basis of a simplified perception of reality.[19]

There were also situations in Africa where nationalism caused destabilisation of the relation between states. In this context, we can cite the various concepts of 'greater nations' – the ideas of Great Somalia and Greater Morocco – as the source of disturbance to stability and peace. The idea of Greater Somalia arose from the idea of Pan-Somalism – a specific form of nationalism which propagated the thesis of a 'mature' Somali nation and demanded the establishment of a state based on ethnic borders.[20] Somalis, however, inhabit not only Somalia but also territories in Djibouti, Ethiopia and Kenya (in consequence of colonial divisions imposed on Africa by European powers), Somalia and as a result, Somalia voiced territorial claims against its neighbours, which caused an outbreak of armed conflicts. An analogous situation took place in Northwest Africa, where Moroccan nationalism postulated a need to return to the borders of the country's Golden Age. This has resulted in tensions and conflicts between Mauretania and Algeria, and an unsolved conflict concerning the status of Western Sahara.[21]

Ideologies based on the idea of racial supremacy are closely related to nationalisms. Africa was the region where institutionalised manifestations of racist

---

18 See: J. M. Burr, R. O. Collins, *Africa's Thirty Years' War: Libya, Chad, and the Sudan, 1963–1993*, Boulder, CO 1999; J. B. Forrest, *Subnationalism in Africa: Ethnicity, Alliances, and Politics*, Boulder, CO 2004; S. Y. Hameso, *Ethnicity in Africa: Towards a Positive Approach*, London 1997; G. K. Kieh, Jr., I. R. Mukenge (eds.), *Zones of Conflict in Africa: Theories and Cases*, Westport, CT 2002.

19 Cf.: Ł. Łotocki, *Obcość etniczna w perspektywie socjologiczno-politologicznej* (*Ethnical Otherness from a Socio-Political Perspective*), Warszawa 2009; Ł. Łotocki, 'Obcość jako kategoria analityczna stosunków międzynarodowych' (Otherness as an Analytical Category of International Relations), *Stosunki Międzynarodowe – International Relations*, vol. 41, no. 1–2, 2010; E. Nowicka (ed.), *Swoi i obcy* (*Ours and Others*), Warszawa 1990.

20 Cf.: I. M. Lewis, *A Pastoral Democracy: A Study of Pastoralism and Politics among the Northern Somali of the Horn of Africa*, New York 1961, pp. 266–295; A. Mrozek-Dumanowska, *Islam a naród w Afryce: Somalia, Sudan, Libia* (*Islam and Nation in Africa: Somalia, Sudan, Libya*), Warszawa 1973.

21 Cf.: Y. H. Zoubir, D. Volman (eds.), *International Dimensions of the Western Sahara Conflict*, Westport, CT 1993; J. Żebrowski, *Maroko: współczesność a historia* (*Morocco: Today and Yesterday*), Warszawa 2001, pp. 78–92.

conceptions survived the longest. Southern African ideology of apartheid was the basis for the political system in South Africa even until the early 1990s. The principles of apartheid were also put into force in the territory of Namibia which was occupied by the neighbouring South Africa (in this case, decolonisation took place in 1990). Another attempt to establish a political system based on similar principles was made by European settlers in Rhodesia (present-day Zimbabwe; the Rhodesian Crisis lasted from 1965 to 1980). In all the aforementioned cases, the attempts to establish legal racial barriers preventing emancipation of the coloured (native) people resulted in armed conflicts. As the domination of groups of European origin was at the source of the processes shaping the local nationalisms, these nationalisms were becoming radical, both in terms of measures and the manner of realising their freedom-related demands.[22] We should also remember that conflicts conditioned by racial differences can be found in the other parts of the region as well. They are most visible in the Sahel area, where the spheres of domination of Arab-speaking and Berber peoples (who dominate the north of the continent) meet the sphere of the Negroid peoples (Sub-Saharan Africa). Internal destabilising processes occurred in almost all the countries located in this geographic area (Sudan, Chad, Niger, Mali, and Mauretania), proving the existence of negative stereotypes which remaina legacy of the cultural differences between the 'white' and the 'black' Africa.[23]

The role of denomination and religion

The factor of denomination and religion usually coexists with ethnic differences but is nonetheless an important element conditioning the emergence of contradictions which lead to conflicts (e.g. it was the cause of many religious wars). Differences in terms of denomination and religion can affect both the relations between individual states – especially when the socio-political powers dominant in them refer to religious values as axioms – and the relations between individual ethnic groups in multinational countries if religion is an important element of their identity. They can also determine the shape of relations within large social

22 J. Balicki, *Apartheid: studium prawno-polityczne rasizmu w Afryce Południowej* (*Apartheid: A Legal and Political Case Study of Racism in South Africa*), Warszawa 1967; D. Grinberg, *Geneza apartheid* (*The Genesis of Apartheid*), Wrocław 1980; P. E. Louw, *The Rise, Fall, and Legacy of Apartheid*, Westport, CT 2004; P. O'Meara, *Zimbabwe: The politics of independence*, in G. M. Carter, P. O'Meara (eds.), *Southern Africa: The Continuing Crisis*, 2nd ed., Bloomington 1982, pp. 18–56.

23 Cf.: J. M. Burr, R. O. Collins, *Africa's Thirty Years' War...*

groups if they constitute a separate criterion of self-identification in such a group. By referring to the transcendent aspect of human life, religious content shapes people's worldview, the system of preferred values – especially the moral ones – and through that also the manner of perceiving and defining the world around them. These values often lead to absolutisation of the content they carry, also in relation to the various manifestations and dimensions of social life. Religious and moral content thus serves the legitimisation of the behaviour of individuals and social groups.[24] In extreme cases, this also takes place when minority groups claim to know a 'revealed truth' and their deep conviction of the unique nature of the 'knowledge' they hold can lead to the justification of violence used in order to promote it. Such situations take place both when new religious movements arise and when there is a reinterpretation of the existing and commonly accepted religious dogmas (as is the case with fundamentalisms). In the latter situation, these processes are more likely to occur in religions which do not have a formalised institutional structure and a hierarchy keeping a vigil over the followers' observance of orthodox dogmas.

In contemporary world, the regions particularly susceptible to the emergence of contradictions of religious nature are the ones in which religious differences are a significant element of social self-identification, strengthening other influences on the development of group identity, in opposition to other social groups. In Europe, there are essentially two key regions to be mentioned in this context. The first one is the Balkans, where religious differences have been a very important element influencing the development of nationalisms, as manifested by the Yugoslav Wars of the 1990s. This is symbolically reflected in Bosnia and Herzegovina, inhabited by three separate nations for whom self-identification on the basis of denomination and religion has been an essential element of the development of their own identity – Serbs are Orthodox Christians, Croats are strongly connected with Roman Catholicism, while Bosnians were called Muslims in Yugoslavia, which clearly pointed to Islam as the factor differentiating them from the other South Slavs. The last example additionally illustrates the thesis that the religious factor plays an important role in the processes of ethnogenesis taking place in the contemporary world. The conflicts between these nations were worsened (in Bosnia and Herzegovina and in Croatia) by inveterate stereotypes born of the historical ties of each of these nations with separate cultures. The cultural and

---

24 Cf.: H. Schreiber, *Religia jako element 'zwrotu kulturowego' w stosunkach międzynarodowych* (*Religion as an Element of a 'Cultural Turn' in International Relations*), in A. M. Solarz, H. Schreiber (eds.), *Religia w stosunkach międzynarodowych* (*Religion in International Relations*), Warszawa 2012, pp. 62–68.

religious borders in the Balkans are historically conditioned because the division into Roman Catholic and Orthodox nations coincides with the borders dividing the Roman Empire into the Latin West and the Greek East (Byzantium). The influence of Islam, in turn, is related to the expansion of the Ottoman Empire into the Balkans (and to the Islamisation of some Slavs and Albanians). It is worth stressing that the sympathy with the parties to the conflict shown by other countries often coincided with a similar cultural and historical context.[25]

The second area where contradictions arising from religious and cultural differences in Europe are concentrated is the Caucasus. In this case, one of the sources of local conflicts was the division into Muslims and Christians. This factor affected, among others, the relations between Chechens and Russians, as well as between Armenians and the Azeri. A revival of Islam during the collapse of the Soviet empire had a significant effect on the entire region, by shaping the freedom moods in many local ethnic societies following Islam (the peoples of Dagestan, Abkhazians, Adjarians, and others). This gave rise to the idea (rather Utopian from the modern perspective) of uniting the peoples living in the region and establishing a Caucasian state.[26]

Examples of how the religious factor affects relations between various conflicted social groups can be found in other regions of the world as well. The lasting antagonism between Hindus and Muslims in British India became the basis for the decision to eventually divide the country during decolonisation into two states – India and Pakistan. Even within independent India, religion plays an important role in the country's political system by shaping the relations with religious and ethnic minorities and with Pakistan. Religious contradictions were also an important factor (together with ethnical differences) during the civil war in Sri Lanka (the Sinhalese are followers of Buddhism, while the Tamil people are Hindus). Religion formed the basis for separatism in the southern Philippines as well. The inhabitants of this part of the archipelago are mostly Muslims, while the majority of Filipinos are Roman Catholics. The separatist movement in southern Thailand had a similar basis (Muslims struggling against the domination of a Buddhist

25 For more see: J. A. Haught, *Holy Hatred: Religious Conflicts of the '90s*, Amherst, NY 1995, pp. 25–43; S. Majstorovic, *Religion and collective identity: The ethnopolitical barriers to democratization in the Balkans*, in W. Safran (ed.), *The Secular and the Sacred: Nation, Religion, and Politics*, London 2003, pp. 169–183; V. Perica, *Balkan Idols: Religion and Nationalism in Yugoslav States*, New York 2002, pp. 3–16.

26 See: J. A. Haught, *Holy Hatred...*, pp. 131–135; see also: C. Zürcher, *The Post-Soviet Wars: Rebellion, Ethnic Conflict, and Nationhood in the Caucasus*, New York 2007, passim.

majority). In the PRC, the highest degree of separatist activity is exhibited by two minorities, the identity of which is mostly shaped by religion: Tibetans, who follow Lamaist Buddhism, and the Muslim Uyghurs.[27]

In the Middle East, an attempt to establish a political system based on confession was made in Lebanon. Changes in the demographic structure and rivalry for influence between various religious groups eventually led to a civil war in 1975. The dominance of the followers of Islam in these countries was often the factor that initiated discrimination practices against religious minorities, particularly Christians. During crises, this often turned into organised acts of violence (e.g. in Iraq, against the minorities representing the Eastern Churches of Christianity, and in Egypt, against Coptic Christians). In some countries of the region (e.g. in Saudi Arabia), the monopoly of the dominant religion was institutionally decreed.

Similar contradictions arising from religious differences or consolidated by them can be found in Africa as well. The long-lasting internal conflict in Sudan was determined by the attempts of the Arabic-speaking ruling elites to islamise the country and by the discrimination practices against the people of the southern regions, who were followers of either Christianity or traditional African religions. The contradictions which led to the outbreak of a civil war in Nigeria (the Biafran War) were a consequence of similar differences between the north (Islam) and the south (Christianity and traditional religions) of the country. Such differences also attributed to deepening the contradictions during the civil war in the Ivory Coast.[28]

Religion is one of the main determining factors of a civilisation (Samuel Huntington).[29] In ideologised form, religion takes the shape of fundamentalism, which, by nature, strives after exclusive determination of group membership, leaving 'infidels' below the horizon of its own vision of the world. As a political ideology, fundamentalism sometimes becomes the source of practices aimed at

---

27 See: D. Allen (ed.), *Religion and Political Conflict in South Asia: India, Pakistan, and Sri Lanka*, Westport, CT 1992; M. Dillon, *Xinjiang – China's Muslim Far Northwest*, New York 2004, pp. 51–71, 156–162; A. T. Grunfeld, *The Making of Modern Tibet*, Armonk, NY 1996, pp. 25–33; J. A. Haught, *Holy Hatred…*, pp. 47–58, 107–111; L. G. Noble, *The Philippines: Autonomy for the Muslims*, in J. L. Esposito (ed.), *Islam in Asia: Religion, Politics, and Society*, New York 1987, pp. 97–124.

28 Cf.: C. A. Quinn, F. Quinn, *Pride, Faith, and Fear: Islam in Sub-Saharan Africa*, New York 2003, pp. 33–88; G. R. Warburg, U. M. Kupferschmidt (eds.), *Islam, Nationalism, and Radicalism in Egypt and the Sudan*, New York 1983.

29 Cf.: S. P. Huntington, *The Clash of Civilizations and the Remaking of World Order*, Touchstone, New York 1996.

controlling the political system of a given country, accepting violence (justified by, for example, a specifically interpreted concept of jihad) as an effective way of pursuing one's goals and implementing one's vision of the world and its development (a goal formulated not only for one's social group but for the entire mankind as the subject of influence of those who know the 'revealed truth').

Indeed, the role of religion in the contemporary international relations is often perceived from the perspective of Muslim fundamentalism. By calling upon radicalism, both in terms of the content of the promoted doctrine and the means serving the fulfilment of political goals, the proponents of the fundamentalist interpretation of Islam became a threat to the security of many modern countries. This is true of both Muslim countries, the political elites of which do not – in the opinion of the adherents of these views – sufficiently meet the requirements posed by religious norms, and of the highly developed Western countries, which are believed to be the source of inacceptable ideas to be countered and fought with all determination.[30]

Muslim fundamentalism was born mainly in response to the situation in the Arab and Muslim world in the 20th century. Confronted with the political domination of the West in the colonial and postcolonial era, the memory of a glorious past, political power and civilisational achievements of Muslims during the Arab Caliphate (the time of the Umayyad and Abbasid dynasties) created a need for an ideology which would refer to tradition and put forward emancipation-related demands. The belief that the reason for the domination of the Islamic world by external powers is the departure of Muslims from religious values and the truth revealed in the holy books of that religion, created circumstances conducive to the emergence of the idea of a necessary return of Muslims to religious purity, to the 'foundations' of the religion set forth when prophet Muhammad still walked the earth. Thus, Muslim fundamentalism is an attempt to return to these forms of religion which, thirteen centuries ago, allowed the followers of Islam to establish

---

30 At the same time, we should remember that this phenomenon is not limited solely to the Islamic world and can be found in other religious systems as well. See: B. Tibi, *Der religiöse Fundamentalismus...* For more on the genesis and nature of Muslim fundamentalism see e.g.: J. Danecki, 'Fundamentalizm i teokracja. Próba charakterystyki współczesnego islamu' (Fundamentalism and Theocracy. Towards a Characteristics of the Modern Islam), *Euhemer*, no. 3, 1991, pp. 63–72; J. Danecki, *Podstawowe wiadomości o islamie* (*Elementary Information on Islam*), vol. 2, Warszawa 1998, pp. 51–163; B. Milton-Edwards, *Islamic Fundamentalism since 1945*, New York 2004; D. R. Springer, J. L. Regens, D. N. Edger, *Islamic Radicalism and Global Jihad*, Washington 2009.

a powerful empire on three continents and which – as the proponents of these conceptions believe – will allow a revival of the Muslim civilisation, negating the primacy of the Western civilisation. However, since the political elites of the postcolonial Arab and Muslim countries cooperate with the Western powers, political violence used by some fundamentalist groups is directed against their own political regimes as well.[31]

An additional factor providing a social base for such views was the crisis of the dominant form of a postcolonial state in the Arab and Muslim world. The failures of modernisation undertaken by the ruling elites, the fact that political authoritarianism was the dominant form of political regime and the lack of strong development impulses (except for the oil-producing countries) contributed to delegitimisation of state institutions and created a natural demand for alternative visions organising the social order. The radicalism of fundamentalist groups in the Arab world is further strengthened by the fact that the countries of this region were unable to oppose the establishment and rise to the military and economic power of Israel, considered a representative of Western interests in the Middle East.[32]

Muslim fundamentalism threatens international security mainly because some of its proponents are willing to accept violence as a justified means of pursuing political goals. However, the proponents of such actions, who strive after establishing a 'global caliphate' in the future, are a decisive minority even in those countries in which the conservative interpretation of Islam is predominant. As a result, terrorism becomes the means of fighting for the implementation of the desired vision of evolution of the world. The organisations following the idea of 'militant Islam' are dangerous not only because of their size and influence but primarily because of their willingness to apply 'blind' violence in order to draw the world's attention to their objectives, hoping that this will allow them to expand their own social and political base. That is why spectacular actions are very important for terrorism motivated by Muslim fundamentalism and a large number of accidental victims only strengthen the propaganda effect.[33]

There was a particular escalation of actions of groups representing this vision after the end of the Cold War, when an accumulation of negative socio-political phenomena erupted, creating favourable conditions for the emergence of political radicalism. The most significant and most dangerous terrorist organisation

---

31 Cf.: J. Danecki, *Fundamentalizm i teokracja....*

32 See: D. R. Springer, J. L. Regens, D. N. Edger, *Islamic Radicalism...*, pp. 18–27.

33 See: D. R. Springer, J. L. Regens, D. N. Edger, *Islamic Radicalism...*, pp. 168–200.

calling upon an ideologised religious concept is the Al-Qaeda, which was led by the figure symbolical for fundamentalist movements, Osama bin Laden. Al-Qaeda proved to be a network of radical Muslim groups, often with only very loose ties to each other, which focuses mainly on the promotion of fundamentalist ideas and training of new members/followers. A number of radical organisations with similar profiles maintained contacts with Al-Qaeda, retaining full organisational independence and freedom of operation at the same time. Therefore, the success of the antiterrorist strategy implemented by some countries, led by the US, was not sufficient to completely eliminate the existing threat. While Al-Qaeda bases were successfully limited to the borderland between Afghanistan and Pakistan, there are still active clone organisations, such as the Al-Qaeda in Iraq, the Al-Qaeda of the Arabian Peninsula or the Al-Qaeda of the Arab Maghreb, as well as a series of more or less organised militant groups in various parts of the world which draw upon the ideology symbolised by the Al-Qaeda (e.g. Al-Shabaab in Somalia, Ansar Dine in Mali, or Boko Haram in Nigeria).[34]

The resulting threats manifest themselves in many different forms. The most spectacular terrorist operations (e.g. the bomb attacks in American embassies in Kenya and Tanzania of 7 August 1998, the attack on the American cruiser USS Cole in Yemen of 12 October 2000, the airplane attacks on the World Trade Center and the Pentagon of 11 September 2001) are only some of them. In countries struggling with internal conflicts (usually generated by local conditions), such as Afghanistan, Iraq or Somalia, local fundamentalist groups attempted to take control of the entirety or parts of the country in order to introduce a socio-political order based on their own concepts. A relatively significant threat are also individuals or small conspiratorial groups operating in isolation, as their plans are hard to uncover and they can independently attempt assassinations, bomb attacks, etc., inspired by the calls for a jihad. The religious inspirations of such undertakings imply ruthless action, and often a will to pay the highest price, like in suicide bombings. This seems yet another manifestation of the cultural specificity of this part of the world, in which human life can be easily subordinated to other values.

34 E. Gearon, 'The Al Qaeda enigma: There is not one but many different Al Qaedas, most of whom have little connection to their supposed ideological partners elsewhere in the world', *The Middle East*, no. 418, 2011, p. 8 ff; S. Piłaszewicz, 'Ferment w życiu religijnym Nigerii. Ruch Boko Haram' (Ferment in the Religious Life of Nigeria. The Boko Haram Movement), *Afryka*, vol. 35, 2012, pp. 27–40; A. Le Sage, 'The Evolving Threat of Al Qaeda in the Islamic Maghreb', *Strategic Forum*, no. 268, 2011, p. 1 ff; M. Scheuer, 'The Zawahiri era', *National Interest*, no. 115, 2011, p. 18 ff.

Conflicts vs. political culture

An important element influencing the stability of contemporary societies and the ability to solve conflicts which could arise in them is the type and character of the political culture predominant in a society. This refers both to entire societies (e.g. the attitude towards national, religious and racial minorities, openness to other cultures) and the ruling elites (ability to solve social tensions and conflicts, resistance to the temptation to monopolise power, or susceptibility to pathogenic phenomena such as corruption, tribalism and nepotism). Two important factors in this context are the political regime (democracy, authoritarianism, totalitarianism) and the ability to settle opposing social interests arising within it.

The functioning of democratic political systems shows that their functional structure includes elements that increase the chances for a peaceful solution of tensions and contradictions, which essentially constitute an inherent element of every society with differences arising on the basis of different places and roles of individual groups within the social stratification system. Mechanisms of representative democracy, rules of settling interests, an inclination towards compromise, typical of a dialogue-based culture, the existence of mechanisms of protecting the rights of minority groups within the society, mechanisms of counterbalancing and controlling the individual segments of public authority, freedom of organisation under the principles of autonomy and self-government within the framework of the civil society institutions – all this is conducive to compromise-based forms of regulatory action and has a stabilising effect on the political system of the given state. The lack of mechanisms mitigating social contradictions creates conditions favourable for possible use of force in crisis situations in the given country or society.[35]

An important question in this context is whether democracy is the best type of political system for every society in terms of solving social conflicts. This depends on, for instance, whether there is an appropriate political culture and the will in to include the interests of all important social entities in multi-ethnic societies in the processes of decision-making. In a conflicted society (such as in Rwanda), where ethnic affiliation is what determines political loyalty, the democratic system will prefer the majority group and cast the minority group or groups to the margins of the society, possibly making violence the only way for the latter to pursue their rights. This example illustrates the specific phenomenon of 'ethnic democracy', in which the principal basis for the development of social divisions are ethnic ties, as is the case with many countries in Africa, where most states

35 Cf.: A. I. Singh, *Democracy...*, pp. 1–7.

are multi-ethnic, where the development lag in relation to the highly developed world is considerable and where the threat of the existence of 'ethnic' parties is high. However, it should be noted that phenomena of this type can occur in highly developed countries as well. Belgium and Spain are good examples. In such cases, the democratisation processes can, paradoxically, result in increasing social contradictions – especially when this process shakes the established social hierarchy and can lead to a consolidation of social groups around their particularistic interests.[36] The aforementioned example of Rwanda follows this pattern: democratisation forced by external pressure violated the interests of the previously dominant (majority) ethnic group. This, together with strong negative stereotypes established and consolidated in earlier periods, and with the Hutus' fear of a return of to the state of affairs from the pre-colonial period during which the Tutsi were the privileged social group, led to an escalation of animosities and a full-scale conflict in which ethnic purges were considered a way to finally solve inveterate problems marking the relations between the opposing ethnic groups. The example of Yugoslavia shows a certain aspect of this phenomenon as well – the process of state collapse and the outbreak of ethnic conflicts occurred (paradoxically) at the time when the democratisation processes started.

Political culture also forms the hierarchy of social values; it conditions forcing rules and norms of conduct on others, and determines the dominant standards of behaviour. In many countries and societies, it is still customary for the majority to force their preferred values on the rest of the society, as for instance, the attempts to impose *sharia* upon the non-Muslim minorities in many countries with a Muslim majority (e.g. in Sudan or in northern Nigeria). Democracy has its limitations and they resurface wherever the majority does not respect the rights of minority groups and marginalises them within the social order. As a result, despite politics being ruled by democratic principles, violence can prove to remain the only way for these groups to pursue their rights. Democracy can also facilitate the dissemination of nepotism and corruption, thus weakening the economic system and the state's development potential. Consequently, its forms and significance for the society should be perceived from the perspective of the dominant cultural values which condition the practical functioning of the game of interestsplayed by the various groups existing in the given political community.

Nondemocratic political systems, in turn, through the very fact of limiting civil liberties can stimulate the emergence of freedom movements in opposition to the

36 See: B. D. Jones, *Peacemaking in Rwanda: The Dynamics of Failure*, Boulder, CO 2001, pp. 164–165.

existing rules of politics and, consequently, of conflicts.[37] Social conflicts basedon this factor frequently break out when the ruling elites are not willing to make concessions and can take the form of mass riots, demonstrations, protests, and – in extreme cases – lead to civil wars (the most recent examples can be found in the Arab world – Libya, Yemen and Syria are countries in which internal conflicts broke out as a consequence of the societies' attempt to end unaccepted dictatorships). At the same time, examples of many countries prove that revolutionary changes do not necessarily have to lead to an improvement in terms of political liberties. The newly appointed regime can be equally prone to applying authoritarian or even totalitarian solutions in formulating the principles of the new socio-political order as the one that was overthrown. Democratisation is a very complex process and without an appropriate political culture in the society, it is not difficult to negate its achievements or – while retaining the formal regulations characteristic of democratic regimes – fill them with the wrong content. Examples can be found in all the regions of the contemporary world (some post-Soviet countries in Europe and Asia, Middle Eastern countries such as Iran or Egypt, and many African countries). Furthermore, by their very nature, authoritarian systems draw upon the idea of elitism. In this case, the society is subject to the influence of the elites, which are prepared to make important decisions in the name of the state. Consequently, authority operates outside social control. This facilitates the escalation of internal controversies in the socio-political system and makes it easier for the authorities to use violence when the political status quo is threatened, thus generating further controversies which threaten the stability of the social order. As a result, the political culture which develops in such circumstances can accept violence as a form of dealing with social controversies.

Conclusion

The influence of the cultural factor on the course of processes conducive to conflicts is a complex process. Parallel to other factors (political or economic), culture very often modifies the processes of emergence and evolution of controversies that stand at the source of these processes. It is in the field of culture that we most often find the answer to the question of why the behaviours of individuals or groups take the forms they do, and why in certain circumstances the differences arising in the sphere of social roles or positions generate violence, while in others they are solved peacefully. The cultural factor is like an optical prism influencing people's

37 Cf.: A. I. Singh, *Democracy...*, pp. 8–10.

perception of the surrounding world, thus affecting their beliefs and expectations. Furthermore, culture provides the instruments which shape the world in accordance with the interests and expectations of social groups. All this considered, culture has a decisive influence on how the emerging differences in interests, antagonisms and contradictions will be solved.

The original version of this text was published in the academic journal "Społeczeństwo i Polityka", no. 4, 2012.

Jakub Zajączkowski

India as a Multicultural State: Political Theory and Practice

Key words: multiculturalism, 'sacred geography', Hindu nationalism, Mahatma Gandhi

Abstract: The article analyses the multicultural state model using the example of India in the context of international relations scholarship. It presents the sources and reasons of the development of this model and its specificity. Ultimately, the article argues that political fragmentation and the emergence of numerous social movements do not weaken Indian democracy but in fact strengthen it.

Methodological principles

An analysis of the multicultural state model on the example of India in the science of international relations requires that we address both methodological and practical issues. In order to perform this analysis and show the nature of the Indian model of multicultural state, as well as present the sources and reasons of the development of this model and its specificity, we need to examine these issues in four dimensions, which at the same time will constitute research questions:

a) Taking into account the cultural and civilisational uniqueness of India, the specificity of the political system and the role of state institutions, we need to examine to what degree the Indian model of multicultural state follows the example of Anglo-Saxon capitalism and liberal democracy, and to what extent it follows Asian capitalism and illiberal democracy;
b) Can the Indian model of multicultural state be implemented in the Asia-Pacific Region and in other developing countries;
c) The key question, however, is how important the Indian model of multicultural state is for India's foreign policy and whether it can be considered one of the pillars of soft power;
d) Does multiculturalism weaken or strengthen India's statehood?

By answering these questions, we will fulfil the following research objectives:

a) A comprehensive and multidimensional reconstruction of the values constituting the Indian model of multicultural state and presentation of the role that it plays in India's foreign policy;

b) Presentation of the debate between representatives of various research and political currents in India on the multicultural state model, as well as of the main topics of the dispute.

Discussing these determinants will allow us to show the extent to which the multicultural state model in India is unique and innovative.

Usefulness of the classical and alternative research approaches in the study of the multicultural state model on the example of India

Due to the complexity of the issues related to the Indian multicultural state model and its specificity, its multidimensionality as well as the challenges facing India, using only a single research approach in the study of India's multiculturalism would result in a very narrow view. Research pluralism in the analysis of the vision of this state is further justified by India's cultural and civilisational diversity. Furthermore, since the beginning of the 1990s, new concepts of state have been emerging, as an alternative to the Nehruvian model.

Therefore, the multicultural state model should be analysed in the context of the liberal, constructivist and postcolonial paradigm. This will allow us to identify the elements and attributes which, on the one hand, prove India's uniqueness, and on the other hand, will show what India shares with traditional Western thought. At the same time, it needs to be emphasised that multiculturalism and democracy form the foundation of the Indian state. The keywords characterising the Indian state model, the so-called New Delhi consensus, are:

a) Democracy and federalism;
b) Secularism;
c) Responsibility;
d) Sustainable and lasting economic growth;
e) Gradual and evolutional reforms.

The genesis and specificity of the multicultural state model should be associated with the cultural and civilisational conditions in India. In this context, the theory of constructivism proves to be an increasingly useful research approach. Many Indian scholars agree with this thesis. Just as Indian politicians, they point out that India is not simply a country but a civilisation-state. They stress that no analysis of the Indian vision of state is complete or true unless it takes into account the political, social and cultural roots of Indianness.[1]

At the same time, in examining India's multiculturalism, we should take note of the postcolonial factor, and in this context, we should refer to the principles of postcolonialism. Homi K. Bhabha contested the thesis of homogeneity of postcolonial states. In his book *The Location of Culture* (1994) he discussed the concept of hybridity, that is the complexity of relations between the Western and the postcolonial countries. The relations between a colonial power and its colonies were very complex, the two sides influencing and interpenetrating each other. This was especially visible in the sphere of culture. Homi K. Bhabha's concept of hybridity was further discussed by Gayatri Ch. Spivak, who in the essay *Can the Subaltern Speak?* opposes the simple division between the coloniser and the colonised.[2]

Multiculturalism in India should be discussed not only in the cultural and civilisational context but in the socioeconomic context as well. Consequently, an analysis of the multicultural state model in India in the context of the liberal approach would indeed be justified, one which is based on three key notions: democracy, institutions and international law and economic interdependencies.

In the early 21st century, the most important concept is the economic one. The factors that prove the usefulness of liberal paradigm include the economic dynamism of the Indian economy, its opening up to the world, the emerging interdependencies between it and the economies of the West. The priorities of India's internal and international strategy are development, overcoming socioeconomic problems, and attracting foreign investment. The success of political and economic elites of India depends mainly on economic success, which is in turn influenced by the development of international cooperation.[3] India abandoned the principles of central planning, the ideology of non-involvement, in favour of the principles and rules of market economy. It accepts the present international order as it is optimal for its development needs.[4] Traits such as adaptability and

---

1 P. R. Chari, P. I. Cheema, S. P. Cohen, *Perceptions, Politics and Security in South Asia: The Compound Crisis of 1990*, London and New York: Routledge, 2003, p. 4.

2 G. Ch. Spivak, *A Critique of Postcolonial Reason: Toward a History of the Vanishing Present*, Harvard University Press, 1994.

3 S. Haggard, *Pathways from Periphery: the Politics of Growth in the Newly Industrializing States*, Ithaca: Cornell University Press, 1990.

4 F. Mengzi, 'Tackling Challenges in the Global Economy and Building a New World Order – China's Influence and U.S. Factors', *Contemporary International Relations*, no. 2, 2010, pp. 1–10.

the will to preserve the *status quo* are characteristic of India's policy as well as of the model of the Indian state in general.

Multicultural state model in Indian political tradition

Cultural, historical and identity-related determinants

The idea of multicultural state has been shaped in the Indian political tradition by conditions such as: cultural and linguistic diversity, social structure and the lack of political unity.[5] In this context, we should point out India's specificity in terms of its social structure, ideas and the concept of state in Indian political thought. India has never been a political unity although several times it was subject to a single ruler. What is more, there has always been a strong sense of separate identity among the various groups– social, ethnic, etc. The Indian society is thus a patchwork of various societies which is only now gradually forming into a modern society. India is therefore a country where the particularisms of individual ethnic groups are the rule and universalism is an exception.[6]

Despite this diversity, civilisation and tradition are the cementing elements of the Indian society. India's 'sacred geography' is a metaphorical notion.[7] It comes down not as much to geography as to stressing the role of the Indian civilisation and culture in shaping the identity of the Indians. All the more so as there are currently few Indians who – regardless of their denomination or ethnic background – are not proud of their ancient heritage. India's civilisation, culture and history, based on broad cultural symbolism and spiritual values, are important ingredients in the establishment of the foundations of the Indian state. Many Indians are convinced that their country, culture and tradition are unique.[8]

The Indian civilisation and culture have influenced the foundations of Indian statehood as well.[9] Indians stress that, already in the oldest Indian texts dialogue,

---

5 'Conservations in "International Relations": Interview with Bhikhu Parekh', *International Relations*, no. 3, 2004, p. 381.

6 S. Dutt, 'Identities and the Indian State: An Overview', *Third World Quarterly*, 1998, p. 413.

7 S. Chaturvedi, 'Representing Post-Colonial India', in K. Dodds, D. Atkinson (eds.), *Geopolitical Traditions*, London and New York: Routledge, 2000, p. 213.

8 See: S. Sarkar, 'Indian Democracy: The Historical Inheritance', in A. Kohli (ed.), *The Success of India's Democracy*, Cambridge: Cambridge University Press, 2001, pp. 45–46.

9 See: R. Cassen, T. Dyson, L. Visaria (eds.), *Twenty-First Century India: Population, Economy, Human Development and the Environment*, Oxford: Oxford University Press, 2004, p. 15–25.

contemplation and public discourse were presented as highest values. Dogmas and radical proposals were rejected, and compromise has been sought instead. In the opinion of Nalini Kant Jha, since the ancient times, India has been seeking 'the golden mean'.[10] Referring to this tradition, Jawaharlal Nehru stressed that it was India's objective to help reconcile the conflicting ideologies.[11] In this context, he also cited the old Indian saying that development is achieved through dialogue and debate.[12]

This attitude was surely a result of the deeply rooted Indian tolerance. Indians accept that there are many worldviews, philosophies and religions in the world. They recognise and acknowledge all these views, even if they are contrary to their principles and vision of the world. 'Generally speaking, we cannot find in any Indian religion the conception of "heretic" in any sense of Western usage [...] Such a tolerant attitude is found not only in religious teachings but in the fundamental policies of administration taken by many kings and rulers throughout the history of India.'[13]

Learning the complexity and divergence of the Indian civilisation allows us to understand the fact that in their policies, Indian kings and rulers (e.g. Ashoka) drew both upon principles preached by Buddha and those taught by Chanakya. Pragmatism, idealism and realism have been coexisting in India for centuries. One needs to take this into consideration when performing an analysis of the principles and foundations of India as a multicultural state because it is characterised by inexplicitness and multidimensionality. At the same time, despite the increase of pragmatism at the turn of the 20th and 21st centuries, elements of culture, history and tradition still play an important role in shaping the principles of the Indian vision of statehood.[14]

---

10 N. K. Jha, *Domestic Imperatives in India's Foreign Policy*, Colorado Springs: International Academic Publishing, 2002, p. 42.

11 K. Bajpai, A. Mattoo, *Securing India: Strategic Thought and Practice*, New Delhi: Manohar, 1996, pp. 49–50; Cf.: J. Nehru, *The Discovery of India*, New Delhi: Penguin Books, 2004, pp. 35–37.

12 *Ibid.*

13 Quoted after: H. Nakamura, Ph. P. Wiener, *The Ways of Thinking of Eastern Peoples: India, China, Tibet, Japan*, revised ed., University of Hawaii Press, 1964, p. 170.

14 S. S. Chaulia, BJP, 'India's Foreign Policy and the "Realist Alternative" to the Nehruvian Tradition', *International Politics*, no. 1, 2002, pp. 215–234.

Development of the multicultural state – principles and goals

On the verge of independence India had to face the challenge of building a new state and defining its identity. For India, independence brought with it an entirely new geopolitical situation, much different from what it used to have under the British rule, when it was divided into 562 principalities and nine provinces. India had to choose the shape and structure of this new state. After 1947, the most important issue was the unity of the state's territory. This striving went beyond the practice of the British raj and the Mughal tradition.

However, the main leaders of the national liberation movement, Mahatma Gandhi and Jawaharlal Nehru, had different concepts and visions of the state. Mahatma Gandhi presented a concept of India as a community of many independent and autonomous societies. Jawaharlal Nehru, on the other hand, was a proponent of a strong multicultural state based on pluralism, secularism and democracy. It was reflected by the principle of 'unity in diversity', which he strongly promoted. Consequently, Gandhi rejected the concept of a strong central government, although Nehru and Gandhi both agreed on the idea of a federal India. He believed that drawing on Western experience was as dangerous as British imperialism, and that Indian democracy should for this reason be based on the experience of Indian civilisation. Moreover, according to him, only autonomous villages (*ashrams*) could be the foundation of democracy. Thus as we can see, on the verge of independence India faced not only economic and social challenges but also political ones, as well as the problem of identity.

After 1947 however, Nehru's concept gained the upper hand. It was a response to challenges such as migrations, clashes between Muslims and Hindus (communalism), the threat from Pakistan, the process of unification and uniformisation of territories, and separatism. One of the elements of this response was the adoption of the European concept of nation-state. The state's foundations were to be: secularism, federalism, democracy, and in the economic dimension – modernisation, which was to be achieved through carefully planned industrialisation. This strategy was confirmed in the Constitution of India of 1950 and in the subsequent five-year plans. At the same time, the state was to become an all-powerful guardian of each and every citizen, reflected by centralism, bureaucracy and centrally planned economy.[15] The Indian constitution granted limited rights to the provinces, establishing a 'quasi-federal' system with the domination of the centre, which was also described as a federal system with a high degree of unitarisation.

---

15 T. Gerlach, *Indie w świadomości Indusów* (*India in the Minds of the Indians*), 1st ed., Wrocław 1988.

A uniform bureaucratic machine was to guarantee the cohesion of the state. At the same time, Nehru wanted India's history to be rewritten in order to combat the deformations in the vision of India's history introduced by the historians of the age of colonialism. Stanisław Tokarski and Surender Bhutani point out that in the 1950s India's leaders chose the category of nation and broadly understood nationalism, building a vision of critical reconstruction of history based on the development of historical studies.[16] According to Mobashar Jawed Akbar, these foundations constituted India.[17]

The state became the central category of the Indian society, what it was supposed to unite. Jawaharlal Nehru placed the state at the very core of the Indian society. 'The state was enlarged, its ambitions inflated and it was transformed from a distant, alien object into one that aspired to infiltrate the everyday lives of Indians, proclaiming itself responsible for everything they could desire […]'.[18] By referring to India's tradition, to the compromising attitudes deeply rooted in Indian custom, to the dialogue between cultures which, for centuries, has been characteristic of the Indian subcontinent, Nehru attempted to create a multicultural and democratic state, to combine opposing ideas and concepts, both in the political sphere and in the economic sphere. He combined idealism and the principle of *Ahimsa* with realism, liberalism with protectionism and socialism, tradition with modernity.

The guarantor of a multicultural state was to be the principle of secularity, which in India translates into equal treatment of all religions. It is based on two concepts: *sarva dharma samabhava* (that all religions are treated equally) and *dharma nirapekshata* (religious neutrality). The constitution guarantees the equality of all citizens before the law, regardless of their denomination.[19] The election law prohibits political parties from inciting religious hatred or using religious symbols to provoke unrest. Indian Secularity, however, does not mean that the sacred aspect is removed from the life of the individual or the society.[20] Gary Jeffrey

16 S. Tokarski, S. Bhutani, *Nowoczesne Indie. Wyzwanie rozwoju* (*Modern India. A Challenge of Development*), Warszawa: Askon, 2007, p. 50.

17 M. J. Akbar, *Nehru. The Making of India*, New Delhi: Roli Books, 2002, p. 7.

18 S. Khilnani, *The Idea of India*, London and New Delhi: Penguin Books, p. 41.

19 For more see: L. I. Rudolph, S. H. Rudolph, 'Living with Multiculturalism: Universalism and Particularism in an Indian Historical Context', in R. Schweder, M. Minow, H. R. Marcus (eds.), *Engaging Cultural Differences: The Multicultural Challenge in Liberal Democracies*, New York: Russel Sage Foundation, 2002, pp. 43–62.

20 K. Dębnicki, *Konflikt i przemoc w systemie politycznym niepodległych Indii* (*Conflict and Violence in Independent India's Political System*), Warszawa: Wydawnictwo Akademickie Dialog, 2000, p. 140.

Jacobsohn considers India an example of a state with a so-called positive secularism (the term is also used by nationalists but in a different meaning) because the state actively works to prevent inequalities resulting from religious practice (in Hinduism) from overshadowing the main goal of the Indian constitution, that is universal equality and building a welfare state.[21]

The 1950s and 1960s saw the creation of the foundations of the multicultural Indian society in the institutional and legal sphere. At the same time, the armed forces were expanded and the internal and external threats were highlighted. India was presented, especially in the 1970s and 1980s, as a besieged fortress. Having a common threat and a common enemy helped to consolidate the society and shape the identity of Indians.

In the period of the Cold War however, India lacked a debate and reflection on the Indian society and state model. The vision of the state adopted by Nehru was to guarantee a unity of the society. In the 1970s and 1980s, Indian leaders failed to see many limitations and aberrations. The problem of poverty was not solved. Although the constitution abolished the caste system, it still remained a characteristic feature of the Indian political scene. India was faced with many caste, socioeconomic (in the northeast) and ethnic conflicts. These conditions spurred a debate on the Indian vision of the state and society. All the more so, the manner in which the problems of Kashmir and the Sikhs had been solved revealed the crisis of the idea of multicultural state.

The challenges to multicultural democracy in India on the verge of the 21st century: a crisis of the concept of multicultural democracy?

Political and socioeconomic challenges

The socio-cultural and political-economic processes taking place after the end of the Cold War influenced the internal and external policy of India and, consequently, its vision of the state. We should mention here the increasing importance of communalism, and the evolution of the political system and economic reforms. The years 1989–1991 were characterised by instability, frequent breakups of coalitions and weak governance.[22] Parliamentary elections confirmed that

21 For more see: G. J. Jacobsohn, *The Wheel of Law: India's Secularism in Comparative Perspective*, Princeton: Princeton University Press, 2003, pp. 51–72.

22 For more see: A. Kohli, *Democracy and Discontent: India's Growing Crisis of Governability*, New York: Cambridge University Press, 1991.

regional parties were growing in importance and that there was a need to establish a broad coalition in order to win the elections.[23] The role of caste parties, drawing their electorate from lower layers of society, was growing as well. Alongside the transformation of the party system from one-party to multi-party, the relations between the central government and the provinces evolved as well.[24] India abandoned 'quasi-federalism' or 'centralised federalism' for federalism in which the provinces play a rather important role, especially in the area of economy and investments.[25]

At the same time, particularly in the early 1990s, India had to face several socioeconomic challenges. A number of scholars emphasise the phenomenon of economic polarisation in India at the beginning of the last decade of the 20th century. The authors of the article *A Tale of Two Indias* stress that economic reforms have created billionaires living among the poorest people in the world.[26] The ineffectiveness of the affirmation policy, especially in terms of economy, became one of the key topics in the early 1990s. It was pointed out that the most poverty stricken layers of society still had no chance for social advancement. Moreover, there was a significant intensification of violence, directly connected with the caste divisions.[27] Subrata K. Mitra even writes about an institutionalisation of riots, a 'riot system' as a permanent element of the election campaigns in India. Politicians tried to take advantage of caste and ethnic divisions and other similar divisions to mobilise their electorate. The political scene was thus polarised.[28]

Consequently, ethnic conflicts overlapped with the socioeconomic ones. It even seems that the latter are now becoming a greater challenge to Indian democracy than the former, as proven by the activity of the Naxalites – Indian radical Maoists. The intensification of their activity after 2004 justifies the claim that they are currently one of the prime threats to the Indian state. The attacks on representatives

---

23 A. Sinha, *The Regional Roots of Developmental Politics in India*, Bloomington 2005; M. Weiner, 'The Regionalization of Indian Politics and Its Implications for Economic Reform', in J. D. Sachs, A. Varshney, N. Bajpai (eds.), *India in the Era of Economic Reforms*, Oxford: Oxford University Press, 1999, pp. 261–295.

24 For more see: R. Cassen, T. Dyson, L. Visaria (eds.), *Twenty-First Century India...*, pp. 15–25.

25 L. Saez, *Federalism without a Center: The Impact of Political and Economic Reform on India's Federal System*, New Delhi: Sage Publications, 2002, p. 5.

26 A. Perry, H. S. Zaidi, 'A Tale of Two Indias', *Time International*, Asia Edition, 6 December 2004, p. 18.

27 For more see: A. Prasad, *Reservation Policy and Practice in India*, New Delhi 1991.

28 S. K. Mitra, 'The Morality of Communal Politics: Paul Brass, Hindu-Muslim Conflict, and the Indian State', *India Review*, no. 4, 2003, pp. 15–30.

of Indian parties in 2013 only confirm the magnitude of the threat posed by this ideology. However, it should also be stressed that the above political or economic and social determinants did not directly undermine the concept of multicultural state, although they did so indirectly by weakening the state and its institutions, which are the basis for the concept of multiculturalism in India.

An alternative to multiculturalism: the concept of Hindu India

At the beginning of the 21st century, the concept of multicultural state faced many challenges. India's party system was changing, and the political and social tensions and conflicts were accompanied by an increasing significance of Hindu nationalism, which formed an alternative to the idea of multicultural and democratic India.[29] Hindu nationalists (from organisations such as: *Rashtriya Swayamsevak Sangh*, RSS,[30] *Vishwa Hindu Parishad*, VHP, that is the World Hindu Council, and the Indian People's Party, *Bharatiya Janata Party*, BJP, established in 1981) emphasised the need to consolidate the unity of Hindus and to clearly state their separateness. The means to achieve this was to be the *Hindutva* ideology, which involved certain principles and norms derived from Hinduism. Referring to Vinayak Damodar Savarkar, one of the fathers of Hindu nationalism, they highlighted the importance of the three fundamental elements of *Hindutva*, that is: fatherland (*pitrabhoomi*), caste (*jati*) and culture (*sanskriti*).

Hindu nationalists proposed an alternative to multicultural democracy. The aim of *Hindutva* was to strengthen Hinduism, overcome the various divisions in it, and consolidate the *Hindu Rashtra*. In the past, internal divisions made India suffer numerous invasions by foreign armies. Thus, the uniformisation of Hinduism and an emphasis on the identity of the Hindu nation was to help overcome the greatest weakness of Hindus as compared to Muslims and Christians – their doctrinal and social fragmentation.

For Hindu nationals, the most crucial issue is not the territorial and ethnic unity but first of all a cultural one. They say that this notion is broader than religion (admitting that Hinduism, its mythology and religious tradition are essential elements of Hindu culture). Therefore, they stress that *Hindutva* should rather

---

29 R. Bhargava, 'The Crisis of Secularism in India', in R. Bhargava (ed.), *Secularism and its Critics*, New Delhi: Oxford University Press, 1998, pp. 418–453.

30 For more on the RSS and its importance see: W. K. Andersen, S. D. Damle, *The Brotherhood in Saffron: The Rashtriya Swayamsevak Sangh and Hindu Revivalism*, Boulder: Westview Press, 1987; K. Jayaprasad, *RSS and Hindu Nationalism*, New Delhi: Deep & Deep Publications, 1991.

be considered cultural nationalism than religious fundamentalism.[31] Nationalists believe that when India – or, to be precise, Hindus – 'bound together by ties of a common blood and common culture can dictate their terms to the whole world.'[32]

It should be noted, however, that what Hindu nationalists meant by this is only the Hindu culture, which is the only Indian culture they accept and recognise. Consequently, their notion of the Indian nation was restricted to Hindus. Some authors believe that Hindu nationalists based their assumptions on an imagined, artificial community that is socially and politically unified.[33] Hindu nationalists negate the separateness of other religious groups in India. They believe that the Hindu culture should be recognised as fundamental, that its superiority should be respected and its chief principles adopted by everyone. When trying to answer the question: who is a Hindu, Hindu nationalists clearly define them as those citizens of India whose ancestors have been living in India since ancient times, who recognise their culture, language and religion as originating in India, and whose outlook on the world is inseparably connected with the Hindu tradition. Indian patriotism is thus limited solely to Hinduness; it is rooted in Hindu civilisation, culture and history.

While presenting threats to the state, Hindu nationalists call on the classic dichotomy: own vs. foreign, own vs. other. They also interpret the history of the Indian subcontinent in the same way. Hindus are presented as the majority group among the inhabitants of India, one which is constantly 'under siege', threatened by minorities, especially the Muslims. In this context, an interesting expression has evolved, which is frequently used by nationalists when they refer to the situation of Hindus in India: a majority with a minority complex.[34]

The main threat to Hindus are Muslims. Muslim invasions on the territory of the present-day India, taking place since the 8th century, the division of the Indian subcontinent and the situation in Kashmir can be considered proof that Muslims do not want assimilation with Hindus, and that they are in fact only a threat to

---

31 In several judgements of 1995, the Supreme Court of India recognised *Hindutva* to be not a religious movement or current but rather a traditional 'way of life'. For more see: B. Cossman, R. Kapur, 'Secularism: Bench-marked by Hindu Right', *Economic and Political Weekly*, no. 31, 1996, pp. 1613–1630.

32 V. D. Savarkar, *Hindutva: Who is a Hindu?*, Bombay: Veer Savarkar Prakashan, 1969, p. 141.

33 B. Cossman, R. Kapur, *Secularism…*, p. 1615.

34 A. T. Embree, 'Who Speaks for India? The Role of Civil Society in Defining Indian Nationalism', in R. Dossani, H. S. Rowen (eds.), *Prospects for Peace in South Asia*, Stanford: Stanford University Press, 2005, p. 179.

the integrity of India and its superpower aspirations. At the same time, Muslims are presented as the fifth column, as a minority which works with Pakistan to undermine New Delhi. The Muslim threat has often been exaggerated by Hindu nationalists through various myths concerning, among others, the Islamic demographic bomb on the Indian subcontinent. According to some forecasts promoted by radicals, in 2281, or even sooner, Muslims will constitute the majority of the Indian society.[35] At the same time, they create the image that through a high birth rate, conversions, establishment of religious Islamic schools and mosques financed from funds provided by the Arab states (the so-called Gulf money), Muslims are already a serious challenge and a threat to Hindus. Therefore, nationalist organisations call for the consolidation of Hindus and a ban on conversions.

Consequently, in the last decade of the 20th century, a real alternative to multicultural democracy appeared – a renaissance of the *Hindutva* ideology, which was caused by, among other things, the ineffectiveness of the concept of secular state and the lack of a peaceful solution to the conflicts in Kashmir and Punjab. At the same time, it was also, to a large degree, the result of the activity of radical organisations of Sikhs and Muslims. What gave rise to conflicts between Muslims and Hindus and also strengthened the separate Hindu identity was the issue of special rights for ethnic minorities. To explain the phenomenon of the revival of Hindu nationalism, Rajeev Bhargava lists more than a dozen conditions and determinants such as: the preservation of certain forms of Hindu nationalism in the society, the colonial heritage, new social processes and the fear of destruction of the traditional social hierarchy, institutionalisation of majority democracy (under Indira Gandhi, and later under Rajiv Gandhi as prime minister), that is pro-Hindu democracy, the elements of communalistic policy in the 1980s, the political and economic crisis in India in the late 1980s and early 1990s, skilled use of religious symbolism by nationalist organisations and their effective use of the dispute concerning the Babri Mosque in Ayodhya, the Shah Bano case, the situation in Kashmir.[36]

The above factors all contributed to the revival of the *Hindutva* ideology. It should be noted, however, that it happened in two phases. The first phase was the period before 1993. At that time, the dominant vision was radically nationalistic. It focused mainly on the threats to India and emphasised the conflict with the Muslims. It promoted a nationalistic, centralised India and rejected the notions

35 For more see: N. DeVotta, 'Demography and Communalism in India', *Journal of International Affairs*, nr 3, 2002, p. 53–70.

36 R. Bhargava, 'Liberal, Secular Democracy and Explanations of Hindu Nationalism', *India Review*, no. 3, 2002, pp. 72–74.

of secularism and federalism as the foundations of the Indian state. The second period were the years of BJP governance (preceded by a period of internal debate and departing from fundamentalism towards realism and pragmatism), that is the years 1999–2004. After the riots in Ayodhya in 1992, the support for the BJP in the elections to state assemblies in 1993 and 1995 fell. Therefore, the Hindu nationalists, particularly the leaders of the BJP – aware of the feelings of Indians – tried to present themselves as a moderate party that did not try to challenge the fundamental principles of the multicultural state.[37]

Nationalist concepts and the *Hindutva* still play an important role in India's political life. After the lost elections in 2004 and 2009, it seemed that it would not be able to find any significant support among the Indian society but corruption scandals, lack of decisive economic reforms (third generation) or any solutions to the problems in the field of agriculture, as well as a crisis of leadership in the Indian National Congress made a victory of the BJP in the 2014 elections conceivable. It should be stressed, however, that the BJP now tries to emphasise economic issues in its strategy instead of ideological ones (a return to the successful elections campaign of 1999). In this context, the party points out, for example, the economic successes of the Gujarat State, the Chief Minister of which (since 2001) is Narendra Modi. His opponents accuse him of idleness during the bloody riots in Gujarat in 2002 (more than a thousand Muslims died in communalistic fights). Although Modi considers himself to be the leader of Hindu nationalists and often referred to nationalist ideas in the past, since mid-2013 – when he became the BJP's main candidate for prime minister of India after the May 2014 elections – he has been presenting himself as a proponent of economic reforms. He is aware that limiting himself to ideological issues and undermining the principles of multicultural state will not allow him to become the prime minister.[38]

Significance of the multicultural democracy model in the 21st century India – towards an assessment

As a result of India's political fragmentation as well as caste and communalistic conflicts, many researchers declared a crisis of the multicultural state. Surander Bhutani, an Indian political scientist, points out that the current political system

37 S. K. Mitra, 'Making Local Government Work: Local Elites, Panchayati Raj and Governance in India', in A. Kohli (ed.), *The Success…*, pp. 103–126.

38 *The Economist*, 14–20 December 2013, p. 14, pp. 24–26.

of India requires essential reforms.[39] T. N. Madan explains the ineffectiveness of the Indian political system with the inadequacy of Western-style democracy in the Indian reality.[40] This opinion, however, seems unjustified.

Multiculturalism, which is deeply rooted in the social, institutional and legal dimensions, is neither a trap nor a threat to India. The rules and principles of the multicultural state have proven durable and are a guarantee of relative stability. It is noteworthy that in 1998–2004, contrary to what it had led its voters to believe, the BJP did not introduce any laws that would threaten the Indian democracy (before the elections, the BJP had announced that it would, for example, change the constitution, establish a presidential system, change the status of Jammu and Kashmir). Under its governance, in 2000, three new States were established (Uttaranchal, Chhattisgarh and Jharkhand) and four new official languages were recognised. In addition, the candidate for Prime Minister in 2014, N. Modi, tried to disassociate himself from his earlier radical statements.

The reason for this is that Hindus are so diversified – due to their languages, customs, castes – that it would be hard for them to follow Nehru's main motto and build unity on uniformity instead of diversity. Since 2002, there have been no riots in India of a magnitude comparable to those of the 1990s in Ayodhya. A large majority of Indians accepts the democratic system, the principles of free elections, advocates a peaceful solution of the Kashmir issue, objects to the establishment of a uniform civil code for all citizens of India, and condemns the destruction of the Babri Mosque.

The Indian society opposes revolutions and extremist views. This does not mean, of course, that India is free of violence. This violence, however, is not systemic. The persecution of Christians in August and September 2008 was in fact part of a political election campaign (related to the elections to the Indian parliament in 2009); they were meant to mobilise the electorate. The important thing, however, is that they were local, limited to the states inhabited by proponents of the *Hindutva*. On the pan-Indian scale, such actions are not accepted.

Looking for the golden mean and compromise has always been characteristic of Hindu culture and tradition. Since the establishment of independent India, since Mahatma Gandhi and Jawaharlal Nehru, it has been the foundation of the country's internal and foreign policy. In principle, Indians are against any revolutions, they identify themselves with the ostensible static of the elephant, and they

---

39 S. Bhutani, 'The 2004 Elections in India: What Mandate? And, What Change?', *Acta Asiatica Varsoviensia*, no. 17, 2004, pp. 13–16.

40 T. N. Madan, *Modern Myths, Locked Minds*, New Delhi: Oxford University Press, 1997.

advocate evolution in economy and politics.[41] Permanence, survival and invariability are as important as progress and development. India rationally assumes that an elephant cannot be a tiger. The elephant cannot jump like the tiger because it is not a tiger. But it has a great strength which will tear down all obstacles. In the Indian vision of development, the idea of small steps supported by reason gains the upper hand.[42] This is exactly what the Indian elephant does. It ostensibly remains static for years but once it gains momentum, no one can stop it.[43]

Subrata K. Mitra notes that India is an example of successful development of multicultural democracy[44] based on federalism, constitutionalism as well as on giving civil and political rights to individuals (e.g. Article 16 of the Constitution of India) and to religious, linguistic and ethnic minorities (Article 29). Some scholars believe that the strengthening of Indian federalism (e.g. by a judgement of the Supreme Court of India of 1994 concerning the dissolution of state governments by the president) and of local and court authorities justifies the thesis that we are not dealing with a collapse of Indian democracy but rather with its revitalisation.[45] The multicultural state model has also grown stronger, owing to the end of the absolute dominance of the political scene by two largest parties (1984 was the last time when a single party won more than 50 per cent seats in the parliament – it was the Indian National Congress, or INC in short). The need for coalitions between the BJP and the INC strengthens the importance of regional parties, castes and ethnic groups on both State and national levels. It also facilitates the development of the civil society, as shown by, among others, the success of the newly established Aam Aadmi Party (Common Man Party) in the Delhi Assembly election in December 2013.[46] Its programme focused primarily on criticising the corruption and the previous political elites (both the BJP and the INC).

The ability to form a coalition and the need to take into account the requests of the coalition partners influences India's foreign and internal policies. The Indian National Congress and the Indian People's Party (BJP) have to abandon their more radical ideas and promises and adopt pragmatic solutions (as, for example, in the

41 S. Tokarski, 'Edukacja, rozwój, demokracja. Indie na progu XXI wieku' (Education, Development, Democracy. India at the Verge of the 21st Century), *Afryka, Azja, Ameryka Łacińska*, vol. 83, 2006, p. 48.

42 S. Tokarski, S. Bhutani, *Nowoczesne Indie…*, p. 58

43 *Ibid.*

44 For more see: S. Mitra, *Constitutional….*

45 J. Manor, 'Political Regeneration in India', in D. L. Seth, A. Nandy (eds.), *The Multiverse of Democracy: Essays in Honour of Rajni Kothari*, New Delhi: Sage Publications, 1996.

46 *The Economist*, 14–20 December 2013, p. 51.

elections programme of the coalition National Democratic Alliance headed by the BJP, in which the party no longer advocates amending Article 370 of the Constitution of India, which now grants a broad autonomy to Jammu and Kashmir) or are forced to work for a consensus in the key issues (e.g. regarding the *Comprehensive Nuclear-Test-Ban Treaty*, CTBT). Consequently, Political fragmentation and the emergence of numerous social movements paradoxically is not a trap; it does not weaken democracy but in fact it strengthens it instead. Political and social changes activate the lower social groups – previously politically idle, they are now included in the political discourse. Therefore, the Indian vision of the state cannot be solely a Nehruist vision or a Hindu vision (advocated by the proponents of *Hindutwa*). It is not only the result of these two but of a dozen different visions, and it had to take into account the visions of various regional groups, castes, individuals active on the national and state level and on the levels of *panchayats* and municipal councils.

Part III. Culture in International Law

Bogusław Lackoroński

Culture in the Making of Public International Law – Custom and General Principles of Law Recognised by Civilised Nations

Key words: Regional customs, general principles of law, culture, public international law, source of law.

Abstract: The role of culture in the creation of public international law depends on many variables. The analyses carried out in this article show that while the impact of culture on the creation of public international law derived from special regional customs can be considered relevant, the influence of culture on the creation of rules based on the general principles of law recognised by civilised nations is now becoming less important.

Since 'culture' is defined in diverse ways,[1] discussing its role in the creation of public international law requires the adoption of a particular understanding of this notion. The adopted definition has been selected to correspond as best as possible to the issues connected with the creation of public international law.

The mechanisms of the making of public international law and its functioning differ depending on the sources of this law. Depending on which source of public international law we are dealing with, the analysis of the mechanisms of its development and functioning should be performed using a set of instruments developed largely or solely either under 1) the linguistic approach (treaty law); or 2) the sociological and 3) the psychological approaches[2] (customary law); or

1 Cf.: A. Kłoskowska, *Socjologia kultury* (*Sociology of Culture*), Warszawa 1983, pp. 11–37; J. Pruszyński, 'Kultura – kultura prawa – dziedzictwo kultury' (Culture–Legal Culture–Cultural Legacy), in W. Czapliński (ed.), *Prawo w XXI wieku. Księga pamiątkowa 50-lecia Instytutu Nauk Prawnych Polskiej Akademii Nauk* (*Law in the 21st Century*), Warszawa 2006, p. 670.

2 The psychological approach to law treats it as a psychic experience manifested in internal conviction of the existence of a certain obligation and the resulting right of another person to demand the fulfilment of this obligation (cf.: L. Petrażycki, *Wstęp do nauki prawa i moralności. Podstawy psychologii emocjonalnej* [*Introduction into the Study of Law and Morals. Principles of an Emotional Psychology*], J. Lande (ed.), Warszawa 1959, p. 14; T. Chauvin, T. Stawecki, P. Winczorek, *Wstęp do prawoznawstwa* [*Introduction to Jurisprudence*], Warszawa 2012, p. 28). The application of this approach in the study of public international law, which concerns primarily legal entities instead of natural persons, may

4) the axiological approach[3] (general principles of law recognised by civilised nations). It would seem to be a justified claim, however, that one of these concepts of law completely displaces the others in relation to the rules originating with the individual sources of public international law. When we attempt to answer the question about the instruments and methods of analysing the mechanisms of creation and functioning of public international law in general, we should support the application of methods and instruments developed under the multidimensional approach. According to this approach, law is a social phenomenon and all four aforementioned concepts of law are useful in studying it. However, due to the key significance, in the process of creating and in the functioning of public international law, and considering the attitude and behaviour of its subjects[4] and the bodies which apply its rules,[5] we should stress the special importance of the sociological approach in the study of these issues, an approach assuming that law is a set of rules and principles of conduct which reveal their true existence through the mass, repetitive behaviour of entities.[6] The domination of this approach does not absolutely determine the adoption of the sociological definition of 'culture' but sufficiently justifies it.

Sociology perceives culture as a set of beliefs, convictions, ideas, and values, as well as objects, symbols and tools which represent them.[7] This definition makes it possible to distinguish two aspects of culture: the non-material, referred to as the cultural content, and the material, comprising the carriers of this content. *Prima facie*, it seems that both aspects play a certain role in the creation and functioning of international law. However, while the non-material aspect of culture can affect the process of creation of public international law and influence its content,

seem surprising and wrong. However, as the science of international relations takes into account the psychological factors which determine the behaviour of the participants in international relations, such as personality psychology, the inclusion of the psychological approach in the study of public international law is justified. (cf.: R. N. Lebow, *A Cultural Theory of International Relations*, Cambridge 2008, pp. 562–567).

3 T. Chauvin, T. Stawecki, P. Winczorek, *Wstęp...*, pp. 26–27; see also: L. Morawski, *Wstęp do prawoznawstwa (Introduction to Jurisprudence)*, Toruń 2006, pp. 17–20; A. Korybski, L. Leszczyński, A. Pieniążek, *Wstęp do prawoznawstwa (Introduction to Jurisprudence)*, Lublin 2001, p. 17.

4 J. Makowski, *Prawo międzynarodowe (International Law)*, Warszawa 1922, p. 60.

5 M.Ch. Bassiouni, 'A Functional Approach to "General Principles of International Law"', *Michigan Journal of International Law*, vol. 11, 1990, p. 769.

6 T. Chauvin, T. Stawecki, P. Winczorek, *Wstęp...*, p. 28.

7 A. Giddens, *Sociology*, transl. into Polish by A. Szulżycka, Warszawa 2007, p. 45; see also: A. Kłoskowska, *Socjologia...*, p. 34.

it seems that the material aspect can be of significance primarily in the context of its functioning, that is application and effect, as it is the elements of material culture that are most often subjected to regulations of public international law and their protection can be an indirect inspiration to create this law. One could attempt defending the view that in this way, the material aspect of culture also has a certain degree of influence on the process of creation of public international law.[8] However, this impact is largely quantitative and indirect rather than qualitative. The material aspect of culture seems to be important when decisions are made to create or extend legal measures for the protection of cultural heritage. A good example of the influence of culture on the creation of public international law is the way in which indigenous cultures affect the establishment of legal measures to protect themselves.[9] The material aspect of culture, in turn, has no direct influence on the development of qualitatively new rules of public international law. For this reason, the subject of interest of this article is limited to the role of the non-material aspects of culture in the meaning specified above.

The influence of non-material aspects of culture on the creation of public international law is not the same for all the rules in this field of law. The extent of their influence depends on the source of the analysed rule and on its spatial, personal and substantive scope. By definition, culture affects treaty rules, the content of which is fully dependent on the will of the parties, however, in a different manner and to a different degree than customary rules or general principles of law recognised by civilised nations. It seems that culture can be of key significance also in the creation of public international law, to the extent to which this law can be derived from auxiliary sources, that is established legal theories of international law or case law. Due to the essential importance of culture in shaping the way in which legal theorists and judges of international courts perceive the international reality and international law,[10] the influence of culture on public international law

8 Cf. the remarks concerning culture in the material and non-material aspect as the subject of regulations of public international law in L. Łukaszuk, 'Wielokulturowość a prawo traktatów' (Multiculturality and the Law of Treaties), in Z. Galicki, T. Kamiński, K. Myszona-Kostrzewa (eds.), *40 lat minęło – praktyka i perspektywy Konwencji wiedeńskiej o prawie traktatów* (*40 Years Later – the Practice and Prospects of the Vienna Convention on the Law of Treaties*), Warszawa 2009, pp. 253–257; Declaration on the Rights of Indigenous Peoples adopted by the United Nations General Assembly during its 61st session at UN Headquarters in New York City on 13 September 2007.

9 L. Łukaszuk, 'Wielokulturowość…', pp. 255–256.

10 Cf. the remarks made by A. Buss concerning the judges of the ICJ disregarding the approach to territorial sovereignty in Buddhist culture in the Judgement of 15 June 1962

arising from these sources seems obvious and natural, and sometimes we can even clearly see the imprint left by individuals whose views affect the content of public international law arising from these sources.[11]

The manner and extent of cultural influence on the content of general rules of law is different than its influence on the content of regional rules. Finally, it seems that the manner and extent of culture's influence on the creation of public international law may depend on the subject of regulation. Following this line of thought, we can also arrive at the conclusion that culture may be of a different significance in the process of creating rules of public international law which regulate political or economic relations than in the creation of rules which regulate technical issues regarding international telecommunications, aviation or space cooperation.

Due to the extensiveness and complexity of the role of culture in the creation of public international law, the limited framework of this article does not allow for it to be exhaustively analysed and presented here. Thus, the article shall present an analysis of the role of culture in the creation of international law limited to selected rules based on custom – especially regional custom – and the general principles of law recognised by civilised nations. The choice of these two sources of international law is based on the hypothesis that they might be particularly susceptible to the influence of culture, one which the author of this article seeks to verify.

In this context, we should also clearly state that the role of culture in the process of interpretation of public international law is an entirely separate issue.[12] Its

---

in the case concerning the Temple of Preah Vihear and its influence on the content of the judgement (A. Buss, 'The Preah Vihear Case and Regional Customary Law', *Chinese Journal of International Law*, vol. 9, no. 1, 2010, p. 126). A. Buss does not directly put forward this thesis, but his deliberations lead to the conclusion that one of the reasons for failing to take into consideration the regional customs and principles of significance for the solution of *The Preah Vihear* Case was possibly the ICJ's judges' culturally-determined focus on the Western approach to territorial sovereignty.

11 In the past, theorists of international law rejected the opinion that legal doctrine could become a source of law (see: J. Makowski, *Prawo...*, p. 45; W. Góralczyk, S. Sawicki, *Prawo międzynarodowe publiczne w zarysie* [*Public International Law – An Outline*], Warszawa 2009, pp. 65–66). Currently, however, the predominant position is that the legal doctrine can constitute an auxiliary source of public international law (see: R. Bierzanek, J. Symonides, *Prawo międzynarodowe publiczne* [*Public International Law*], Warszawa 2011, pp. 110–11; W. Czapliński, A.Wyrozumska, *Prawo międzynarodowe publiczne. Zagadnienia systemowe* [*Public International Law. Systemic Issues*], Warszawa 2004, pp. 30–31).

12 Cf.: M. Romanowicz, 'Zasady interpretacji prawa traktatowego jako źródło konwergencji kultur prawnych' (Rules of Interpretation of Treaty Law as the Source of

key significance in this regard is a consequence of the fact that it influences the manner in which normative content is perceived by the interpreting entity. This issue, however, does not fall within the scope of the discussion determined by the subject of the present article.

An analysis of selected judgements of the International Court of Justice (ICJ) and academic literature on the subject shows that in the process of creating public international law based on custom and the general principles of law recognised by civilised nations, culture can be important as: 1) a factor identifying the values and established situations which should be subject to protection by public international law; 2) the basis for determining the subjective or geographic scope of application of the regional (particular, also called special or local) rules of public international law which are regional, and differentiating them from universal (general) rules; and 3) the source of opposition of individual entities or groups against new rules of public international law. Some of the roles of culture highlighted and described in this article have been identified as a result of observation of the present state of development of public international law and the views of legal theorists in this respect, while others are only proposed roles that culture could play in public international law, thus influencing the process of creation of its rules[13].

Role of culture in identifying the values and established situations subject to protection by public international law

To discuss the influence of culture on the creation of public international law based on custom and the general principles of law recognised by civilised nations we have to consider the changes in the traditional approach to each of these sources of law in legal science. The influence of culture on the process of creating international law resulting from each of these sources is not equal. It seems that culture has more potential influence on those rules of public international law that are established and shaped by statements of intent or knowledge of subjects of international law than it has on those that are based on their actual conduct. The actual conduct of subjects of public international law is less directly determined by

Convergence of Legal Cultures), in O. Nawrot, S. Sykuna, J. Zajadło (eds.), *Konwergencja czy dywergencja kultur i systemów prawnych?* (*Convergence or Divergence of Legal Cultures?*), Warszawa 2012, pp. 281–292.

13 See how French (continental) and American (Anglo-Saxon) legal cultures may influence international law – its making and understanding – in a different manner: E. Jouannet, 'French and American Perspectives on International Law: Legal Cultures and International Law', *Maine Law Review*, vol. 58, no. 2, 2006, pp. 291–336.

cultural factors than by interests, on which culture has a more indirect influence,[14] as the interests of subjects of public international law are largely a direct consequence of their current or potential international situation and/or political, economic or social position. The latter depends to a large extent on the given situation in international relations, conditioned, in turn, by so many factors that even if culture is among them, its influence is most often very hard to discern. This does not mean that culture is a new factor influencing the content of public international law. Its role in the creation of international law with customary character has been noticed for a long time, particularly with regard to international humanitarian law[15] and especially concerning the approach to the status of civilians during armed conflicts, as well as the manner and goal of conducting armed conflicts,[16] as well as the evolution of the idea of the just war[17] or the legal use of force in international relations.[18] It seems, however, that cultural influence on the content of public international law which is largely the consequence of the actual conduct of subjects of public international law proceeds in a different, indirect manner – and thus harder to discern – than on the creation of rules of public international law which are respectively the consequence of statements of intent or knowledge of subjects of public international law.

Means and manifestations of cultural influence on the content of rules derived from special regional customs

As a result of a changing approach to custom as a source of public international law, there has been a gradual departure from the descriptive concept towards a normative one.[19] According to a position well-established in the legal doctrine[20]

---

14 As proven by the fact that the research currents in international relations focusing primarily on the actual conduct of the subjects of international relations ignore the role of factors such as personality (cf.: R. N. Lebow, *A Cultural...*, p. 558).

15 J. Makowski, *Prawo...*, p. 480.

16 *Ibid.*, pp. 473–479.

17 Cf.: P. Grzebyk, 'Idea wojny sprawiedliwej – od starożytności po czasy nowożytne' (Idea of Just War – from the Antiquity to the Modern Times), *Forum Prawnicze*, no. 2, 2010, pp. 56–73.

18 R. Bierzanek, J. Symonides, *Prawo...*, pp. 383–390.

19 A. E. Roberts, 'Traditional and Modern Approaches to Customary International Law: A Reconciliation', *The American Journal of International Law*, vol. 95, 2001, pp. 760–761.

20 See: R. Bierzanek, J. Symonides, *Prawo...*, pp. 106–107; W. Czapliński, A. Wyrozumska, *Prawo...*, p. 77; W. Góralczyk, S. Sawicki, *Prawo...*, p. 98; P. Marcisz, 'Custom in European Union Law', *Studia Iuridica*, vol. 54, 2012, pp. 144–149.

and in the case law of international courts,[21] only a custom which meets two requirements can be a source of public international law. The first one is its general and widespread practice (*diuturnus usus*). Legal theoreticians refer to this requirement as the objective one. The second requirement is the acceptance of this general and widespread practice as obligatory (*opinio juris sive necessitatis*). This requirement is referred to as subjective.

Under the traditional approach, while examining whether a given custom is a source of public international law, the main focus was placed on the objective requirement. It determined the values and circumstances subject to protection under public international law. The fulfilment of this requirement did not settle conclusively that the custom was a source of public international law; however, it increased the probability of confirming the subjective requirement. As a result of this division of focus between the two requirements for recognising a custom as a source of public international law under this approach, the content of the custom, and especially the spectrum of values and established situations subject to protection under the rules based on the custom, largely reflected the general and widespread practice, and was only to a lesser degree the consequence of the belief in the existence of a legal obligation to obey it. Under this approach, custom is the reflection of the current state of affairs in international relations and not the ideas of how it should look like; therefore it is called the 'descriptive approach'.[22] It seems that under the descriptive approach, cultural influence on the creation of rules of public international law based on custom is limited, since those rules are largely a result of the actual conduct of the subjects of public international law, and culture has only an indirect effect on them, and it is only one of many factors in this regard.

Under the contemporary approach to custom in public international law, referred to as the 'normative approach' or the 'prescriptive approach', there is a greater emphasis on the subjective requirement.[23] The shape of the customary rules of public international law, especially the spectrum of values and established situations subject to protection under these rules, is no longer determined mainly by the practice of the subjects of international law; now it is also influenced by the declarations regarding the statements of intent or knowledge of the subjects –

21 See: ICJ Judgment of 20 February 1969 in the *North Sea Continental Shelf* Cases, ICJ Reports 1969, pp. 43–44; ICJ Judgement of 3 June 1985 in the case concerning the Continental Shelf between the Libyan Arab Jamahiriya and Malta, ICJ Reports 1985, pp. 29–30.

22 A. E. Roberts, 'Traditional...', pp. 761–762.

23 *Ibid.*, pp. 762–763.

especially states – which are much more conditioned by their own cultures. One of the possible reasons for this state of affairs is the change in the way international relations have been developing – nowadays they reflect both the actual interests and the possibilities of realising them and, to an almost equal extent, the statements of intent and knowledge of the participants in these relations, which are a manifestation of their perception of a given state of affairs in international relations.[24] Treating custom as a source of public international law contributes significantly to 'opening up' the process of creatingpublic international law regulations stemming from this lawto the influence of culture. With the growing importance of the subjective requirement for recognising custom as a source of international law, it is only natural that we are observing a growing significance of all factors – especially cultural ones – that drive the development of the conviction that there is a legal obligation for behaving in a particular way in international relations.

Regardless of the influence of the above changes in the approach to general international customs exerted on the possibility of cultural influence on the content of rules derived from these customs, we should stress that culture has naturally always had an influence on the creation of rules derived from special regional customs.[25] These customs are distinguished in an opposition to general customs in public international law.[26] What is more, the fact that legal rules derived from regional customs usually indicate a different behaviour than the one required by general customs naturally gives rise to a question of the applicability of the *lex*

24 Cf.: R. N. Lebow, *A Cultural...*, pp. 535–537, 558–560. The author notices and analyses the role of spirit, understood in a particular way, as a need for self-acceptance, higher self-esteem and recognition from the participants in international relations, in the development of modern states and international relations. The discussion contained in this work leads to the conclusion that culture plays an essential role in the process of shaping the spirit of states as a determinant of their behaviour in international relations.

25 The name 'special custom' or 'particular custom' is broader than 'regional custom', as it may also include special customs of universal nature, therefore it will be more adequate to use the name 'special regional custom' further in this article, as it shows both the limited personal and geographic scope of application of rules based on it and its place in the hierarchy of rules of public international law.

26 This distinction is not only between the personal or geographic scope of application of rules stemming from general and special customs but also between the approaches to the way of identifying the subjective requirement *opinio juris sive necessitatis*. For some legal theorists assume, in reference to special customs, that *opinio juris sive necessitatis* should be expressly stated (cf.: P. Marcisz, 'Custom...', p. 147, which reports the views of A. A. D'Amato on this issue).

specialis derogat legi generali principle for settling the conflicts between them. In the legal doctrine, there is no explicit answer to this question. However, looking at the case law of international courts, it is believed that in a situation where a special regional custom is unquestionable and there is no explicit general rule which contradicts it, the custom should be taken into account as a basis for settling a dispute or determining the required behaviour of entities in a given situation.[27] In my opinion, rules derived from regional customs which are considered binding without doubt should always prevail over rules derived from general customs,[28] unless the latter are *ius cogens*. Moreover, the primacy of particular regional rules should not depend on the level of explicitness of the general rule.

As according to ICJ case law, a special regional custom which is a source of international law may be established both in multilateral and bilateral relations,[29] and the content of the rules resulting from it may be largely determined by cultural factors. These factors may influence both the practice of the entities, particularly states participating in the creation of a customary rule, and their belief that they are legally required to obey this practice in the future.

In ICJ, the judgements concerning special regional customs, and the culture of the entities (states) that participate in the process of their development is not directly indicated as a factor which has influenced this process, thus it is directly considered by the ICJ. *Prima facie*, it may lead to the conclusion that the statement about the influence of culture on the creation of particular international customs of regional nature and the rules derived therefrom is incorrect. It seems, however, that this conclusion would not be entirely justified. The fact that ICJ judgements on this matter do not include any direct reference to culture does not mean that it has had no role at all in shaping the practice which is the basis for the rulings. It does mean, however, that it would be difficult to identify its role and importance.

The most important ICJ judgements that refer to special regional customs are the Colombian-Peruvian *Asylum* Case and the *Right of Passage* Case concerning Portugal's right of passage through Indian territory.[30] According to these judgements, the circumstances that according to the parties proved the existence of a special regional custom, are largely a consequence of the cultural context in which they function. The importance of the cultural context reveals itself in two aspects:

27 A. A. D'Amato, 'The Concept of Special Custom in International Law', *The American Journal of International Law*, vol. 63, no. 2, 1969, p. 219.

28 See: *Right of Passage* Case, ICJ Judgement of 12 April 1960, ICJ Reports 1960, p. 44.

29 See: *ibid.*, p. 39.

30 *Asylum* Case. ICJ Judgement of 20 November 1950, ICJ Reports 1950, pp. 266–389; *Right of Passage* Case, pp. 6–46; cf.: A. Buss, 'The Preah…', pp. 118–119.

in the first one, which can be called 'behavioural', the cultural context influences the behaviour of subjects of international law that is their reaction to the given reality; in the second one, which can be called 'axiological', the cultural context justifies the thesis that given behaviours of subjects of public international law, although inconsistent with the rules derived from general customs, are not a violation of public international law. Consequently, we could say that cultural context in its axiological aspect is the basis for identifying values and established situations that should be respected due to some special cultural determinants existing in the examined relations and deserves to be protected by public international law.

Both the behavioural and the axiological aspects of the role of the cultural context in the development of special regional customs can be observed in the Colombian-Peruvian *Asylum* Case, in which Colombia, when defending its decision on granting diplomatic asylum, and in particular its conformity with a special regional custom, invoked the practice of granting diplomatic asylum allegedly existing and justified in the context of Latin American governments' attitude towards political opposition.[31] It should be stressed that due to the lack of evidence, the ICJ did not agree with the arguments of Colombia on the existence of a special regional custom in this case. However, it is worth noting that when referring to Colombia's position, the ICJ stressed that the Latin American practice of granting diplomatic asylum and the observance of this practice are a consequence of extra-legal considerations, such as good-neighbourliness and different political interests of states. These considerations, in turn, can be seen as an element of the broadly understood cultural context in which states operate. After analysing the ICJ judgement in the *Asylum* Case, it seems justified to say that extra-legal circumstances, such as cultural context, were important factors for identifying the values and established situations that, according to at least one of the parties in the dispute, should be protected. At the same time, the judgement shows that the fact that certain behaviours are justified in given cultural contexts cannot itself replace the evidence of an actual existence of a uniform and long-standing practice or the belief that such practice results from a legal obligation. As indicated by the weight of evidence for the existence of a binding rule derived from a special regional custom, it is the state that invokes such a rule that has to prove its existence.[32]

A much more difficult issue is the analysis of the influence of culture on the emergence of a special regional custom in the case concerning Portugal's right of

31 *Asylum* Case, pp. 285–286.

32 A. A. D'Amato, 'The Concept...', p. 216 and the ruling in *Asylum* Case quoted therein, pp. 276–277.

passage through Indian territory to its enclaves Dadra and Nagar-Aveli. According to the ICJ judgement, the decisive argument was that Great Britain had respected the right of Portugal to pass through Indian territory although none such right had been granted under the draft treaty prepared in 1779 by Portugal and the ruler of Maratha, nor could it be inferred from its provisions. The ICJ considered the treaty to be concluded *per facta concludentia*, as the Maratha authorities had been referring to it in their internal laws of 1783 and 1785, suggesting that it had been indeed in effect.[33] The motives for respecting Portugal's right by Great Britain were not directly indicated in the ICJ judgement,[34] therefore any categorical opinions on this subject may be considered groundless. It seems probable, however, that one of the factors causing Great Britain to respect Portugal's right of passage to the enclaves through the Indian territory was the principle *par in parem non habet imperii*, deeply rooted in European culture, as well as the principle of sovereign equality of states, both being the key principles of the Westphalian system, governing the relations between states even today.[35] For it is stated in the judgement in the *Asylum* Case that despite a lack of a basis for it in the treaty of Maratha, Great Britain treated Portugal as an entity exercising its sovereign power over the said enclaves, and the right of passage through the Indian territory is connected with this power.

It is hard to say precisely to what extent this attitude of Great Britain was resulting from an ignorance of the rights of Portugal to the said enclaves, and to what extent it was a consequence of a special *iunctim* in Western legal culture between territorial sovereignty and the sovereign power of the entity holding such sovereignty. It seems, however, that the behaviour of Great Britain which led to the development of a special regional custom in bilateral relations with Portugal was indeed influenced by its approach to territorial sovereignty and to the scope of powers associated with it, characteristic of the Western approach to sovereignty and related attributes.[36] According to this approach, first of all, the authority of the state exercising sovereignty over a particular territory is indivisible and is not subject to any other authority. A different approach to this issue is represented by countries influenced by Buddhism, in which sovereign power is

33 *Asylum* Case..., p. 37.

34 *Ibid.*, p. 39.

35 Cf.: *Jurisdictional Immunities of the State, Germany v. Italy*. ICJ Judgement of 3 February 2012, ICJ Reports 2012, par. 57, http://www.icj-cij.org/docket/files/143/16883.pdf (accessed on 1st May 2013).

36 The approach and its genesis have been described by A. Buss ('The Preah...', pp. 123–124).

related primarily to the people, and not to a strictly delimited territory, defined by precisely outlined borders.

Consequently, it can be assumed that if Great Britain had treated Portugal in accordance with the Buddhist paradigm of sovereignty, it would most likely have not considered it an entity holding sovereign power over the enclaves. Portugal had in fact limited power in relation to the population of Dadra and Nagar-Aveli and executed it under instructions from the Maratha government, which according to the Buddhist approach to sovereignty would preclude recognising the Portuguese sovereignty over the enclaves. Considering the existence of these two different approaches to sovereign power and its attributes in the context of the *Right of Passage* Case, it seems even more justified to claim that the development of a special regional custom between Portugal and Great Britain which was the source of Portugal's right to pass through Indian territory had been affected by the cultural factor in the form of Great Britain's Western approach to sovereignty and its attributes. However, whereas in the Colombian-Peruvian asylum case the cultural context was important in both the behavioural and axiological sense, in the case concerning the right of passage over Indian territory the cultural factor seems to have played a mainly behavioural role, primarily as a determinant of the behaviour and position of Great Britain against Portugal's right to pass through this territory.

Means and manifestations of cultural influence on the content of rules derived from general principles of law recognised by civilised nations

The last part of the term 'general principles of law recognised by civilised nations' can be a starting point in the studies on the role of culture in the creation and recognition of individual general principles as a source of law.[37] It seems that the concept of 'civilised nations' allows, first of all, to take cultural factors into account when identifying the values and established situations to be protected by public international law. The general clause 'civilised nations' refers, inter alia, to the condition of the cultural heritage of communities functioning in international

37 Although culture is not synonymous to civilisation, it remains in close relation with it (cf.: J. Pruszyński, 'Kultura…', p. 671). Therefore, we can safely claim that a reference to civilisational development may justify taking cultural factors into account in the process of identifying the general principles of law that are the source of public international law in the traditional approach to this law.

relations.[38] Although the general clause 'civilised nations' in the traditional sense referred to a small group of selected countries,[39] the legal rules that were derived from it were so universal that they corresponded with the legal systems of other states as well. These rules include, in particular, the principle of full compensation for damages resulting from a breach of international law[40], the principle of good faith, *estoppel*[41] and equity principles,[42] *nullus commodum capere potest de injuria sua propria.*[43]

It should be stressed that the final part of the term 'general principles of law recognised by civilised nations' is nowadays subject to significant reinterpretation. As a result, we have departed from the traditional, exclusive meaning of the phrase 'civilised nations', stemming from the historical context in which it had emerged and had been introduced first to the Statute of the Permanent Court of International Justice and then to the Statute of the International Court of Justice. It can probably be assumed that since the establishment of the United Nations, the expression 'civilised nations' has been interpreted in an inclusive manner.[44] According to the inclusive interpretation, the phrase 'general principles of law recognised by civilised nations' does not mean the rules created and applied by a specific group of nations characterised by a higher level of development in terms of civilisation but rather principles common to most legal systems of the world[45] and forming a part of public international law.[46] The content of the general principles of law recognised by civilised nations is reconstructed primarily using the comparative method, taking into account not only the legal systems of the Western countries but also those based on other models, such as Muslim or Hindu

38 Cf.: H. Schreiber, *Koncepcja «sztuki prymitywnej». Odkrywanie, oswajanie i udomowienie Innego w świecie Zachodu* (*The Concept of 'Primitive Art'. Discovering, Adapting and Domesticating the Other in the Western World*), Warszawa 2012, pp. 134–136.

39 F. T. Freeman Jalet, 'The Quest for the General Principles of Law Recognized by Civilized Nations – A Study', *UCLA Law Review*, vol. 10, 1963, pp. 1044–1045.

40 M. Ch. Bassiouni, 'A Functional...', p. 794.

41 A. Kozłowski, *Estoppel jako ogólna zasada prawa międzynarodowego* (*Estoppel as a General Principle of International Law*), Wrocław 2009, pp. 39–51, 349.

42 W. Czapliński, A. Wyrozumska, *Prawo...*, pp. 98–108.

43 M. Ch. Bassiouni, 'A Functional...', p. 793.

44 Cf.: *Ibid.*, p. 768.

45 A. Buss, 'The Preah...', p. 119; M. White, 'Equity – A General Principle of Law Recognised by Civilised Nations?', *Queensland University of Technology Law Journal*, vol. 4, no. 1, 2004, p. 108.

46 M. Ch. Bassiouni, 'A Functional...', pp. 771, 788.

legal systems.[47] This new approach to the general principles of law recognised by civilised nations corresponds to their role in the system of sources of public international law. These rules are in fact treated as a supplementary source of public international law, justifying the validity of norms such as customs, which cannot be derived from any other source of law due to the lack of an objective or subjective premise.[48]

The current approach to the general principles of law recognised by civilised nations reduces the degree and extent of influence of cultural factors from selected countries, regions or sub-regions of the world and opens the process of developing norms derived from this source based on the common cultural heritage of all the subjects of international law,[49] although it is difficult to determine what is within its scope. The importance of such a general, common denominator and the principles derived from it in the situation of an increasing role of international organisations and transnational and supranational institutions was acknowledged already in the mid-20th century.[50] Given that the former understanding of the term 'general principles of law recognised by civilised nations' was the basis for the standards commonly accepted in most legal systems in the world, regardless of their provenance, the reinterpretation of the final part of this phrase is not likely to have any practical significance. It seems that it will strengthen the existing tendency to think of general principles of law recognised by civilised nations as principles common to all or most legal systems in the world.

The above analysis leads to the conclusion that culture is one of the factors influencing the selection of values and established situations to be protected by the rules of public international law, with their source in custom and the general principles of law recognised by civilised nations. Naturally, this does not mean that the impact of cultural factors on the process of creation of law derived from both these sources is visible at first sight and always the same. Culture often indirectly affects the content of the rules of public international law derived from custom

---

47 W. Friedmann, 'The Use of "General Principles" in the Development of International Law', *The American Journal of International Law*, vol. 57, 1963, p. 285; see also the comments, including the critical ones, on the application of the comparative method in the reconstruction of general principles of law (F. T. Freeman Jalet, 'The Quest...', pp. 1075–1083).

48 M. Ch. Bassiouni, 'A Functional...', pp. 768–769, 774–779.

49 Cf.: *ibid.*, p. 783.

50 R. Schlesinger, 'Research on the General Principles of Law Recognized by Civilized Nations', *The American Journal of International Law*, vol. 51, 1957, p. 737; cf. also: W. Friedmann, 'The Use...', p. 282.

and the general principles of law recognised by civilised nations, allowing the identification of values or conditions that deserve protection.

The change in the approach to these two sources has an impact on the manner and degree of cultural influence on the process of creating rules of public international law derived from custom. The mentioned change suggests that the result will be an increased intensity of the impact of culture on the process of creating rules of international law derived from this source.

However, with regard to the general principles of law recognised by civilised nations, the assessment of this change in approach to the sources of public international law may lead to contradictory conclusions. On the one hand, the change could theoretically result in a greater democracy in creating the rules of public international law and ensure that more actors have influence on the content of standards derived from this source. It may lead to taking into account cultural factors common to a larger number of subjects of international law than before. On the other hand, it could theoretically lead to hegemony over the process of creating international law of those subjects of public international law who are the most active and who have the greatest potential to impose legal standards and solutions applied in their national laws, thus making them a part of public international law. Since the general principles of law recognised by civilised nations will be understood as the legal solutions used in most legal systems in the world, the content of the rules of public international law can be shaped by the countries that 'export' successful national legislative solutions. Consequently, rules based on the general principles of law recognised by civilised nations may be the result of influence of one country or group of countries and the values promoted by them instead of a natural influence of legislative solutions applied in various countries, with the reception of these solutions resulting from individual and natural development of their legal systems. In practice, however, due to the current interpretation of the term 'general principles of law recognised by civilised nations', the change in approach to this source of law is not likely to have any significant consequences.

Culture as the basis for identifying the scope of the regional (special) rules of public international law and distinguishing them from the universal (general) rules

The impact of cultural factors on the process of creating international law may lead to either a universalisation or a particularisation of the emerging rules. The impact of national and regional cultures will most frequently cause particularisation of the rules of public international law, while the impact of the common cultural heritage of humanity on the law-making process can lead to the universalisation of law.

Classifying rules as either universal or regional may have essential practical implications. On the one hand, for a universal rule to be binding it does not have to be accepted by all parties covered by it, in particular by all countries, on the other hand, with respect to regional rules there are views according to which their applicability is subject to the consent of all the parties concerned.[51]

The importance of the cultural factor as the basis for distinguishing between universal (general) and particular (special) rules will also have practical significance when it comes to the rejection of the requirement to gain the consent of all countries for a special rule to be binding. In such a case, the cultural factor can be an important basis for identifying the subjective and geographical scope of application of a given rule of public international law. The role of the cultural factor will then become more important than it is now. This is because in such a situation, the subjective and geographical scope of application of a special regional rule will be identified not on the basis of the relatively easily verifiable criterion of 'consent' but on the basis of parameters such as religion, language and political system of the entities in relation to which the applicability of the rule of public international law is discussed.

This leads to the conclusion that the change in the approach to the role of consent expressed by the intended addressees of a rule derived from a special regional custom as the requirement for the application of the rule may be highly relevant to the role of culture in the process of reconstructing its subjective and geographical scope of application. In the case of departure from the requirement of consent of all the parties concerned as the condition for it to be binding for all of them, the subjective and the geographical scope of application would be influenced by the cultural factors that have shaped its content. In the context of the functioning of the subjects of international law, the existence of cultural factors is very likely to justify the application of rules derived from special regional customs to these entities.

The doctrine of international law distinguishes between situations where a special regional custom is in conflict with the general practice and those where a special regional custom is the source of a rule unrelated to any other rule of public international law, in particular with any general rule.[52] In the situation where a certain issue is regulated exclusively by rules deriving from a special regional

51 A. A. D'Amato, 'The Concept...', pp. 211–223.

52 Cf.: *ibid.*, p. 219.

custom, it can be questioned whether the rule actually has a limited scope in terms of subjects of application or geographical area, or it is in fact a general rule. To solve this problem, which especially today has considerable practical significance, when consent of all subjects of customary rules having subjectively or geographically limited scope of application is required, the impact of particular cultural factors on the development of their content will have to be taken into account. Recognising that particular cultural factors influence the content of international law can justify accepting them as rules of a limited subjective or geographical scope of application with all its consequences, particularly with regard to the basis of their validity.

Culture as a source of opposition of individual entities or groups to the rules of public international law

The theoretical and practical roles of culture in the creation of public international law seem to highlight the importance of culture as a unifying factor for the entire international community or for various groups formed by its members. In the reflections presented so far in this article, culture has appeared to be a factor that infuses rules of international law with content corresponding with the values shared by the international community and thereby grants legitimacy to their compliance with public international law.

However, attempts to infuse rules of international law with cultural content, which is supposed to be a part of universal law, can also divide the international community. Such situations occur, for example, during discussions on human rights, which give rise to doubts as to whether the values subject to protection under these rights are indeed universal. Culture can, therefore, be an 'obstacle' in the creation of universal international law, if the rules of this law are created in a way that takes into account the cultural background of one civilisation, leaving out the others. It seems, however, that as long as the opposition to the establishment of a universal rule of public international law is actually rooted in the culture of a country and not dictated by short-term political interests of its current government, the role of culture as an 'obstacle' in the development of rules that are culturally alien to some members of the international community should be assessed positively. Creating universal rules of international law that are culturally alien to some members of the international community can lead to international conflicts and lower the authority of international law. Moreover, in legal sciences, it is believed that the authority of the law in general, which naturally also includes public international law, is reduced by rules that will be complied with as a result of external obligation instead of rules of conduct internalised by most of its subjects, which condemns the enforcement of these rules to failure.

Conclusion

To sum up, it should be emphasised that the role of culture in the creation of public international law is a function of many variables. In particular, the degree and manner of cultural influence on the creation of international law depends on the source from which a given legal rule is derived.

The analyses carried out during the compilation of this article show that whereas the impact of culture on the creation of international laws derived from special regional customs can be considered relevant, the influence of culture on the creation of rules based on the general principles of law recognised by civilised nations is now becoming less important. It seems that in the latter case, the quantitative criteria such as the number of countries whose legal systems have adopted certain principles, seem to be more important than the criteria that are deeply rooted in cultural content that is an element of the context of functioning of the various subjects of international law.

Given the extent of the problem of the role of culture in international law, it is clear that there is a need for research on the role of culture not only in the creation of public international law but also in its application, especially interpretation. In the application of public international law, the role of culture may manifest itself particularly clearly when culture becomes the basis of the potentially controversial argument referred to as 'cultural defence'.[53] Culture serving as justification of the behaviour that is objectively at variance with general international law may then be an important factor leading to the development of a special regional rule. If a behaviour that objectively infringes on general public international law is effectively justified by using cultural arguments, it can define a practice to be commonly used by entities falling within the scope of influence of the same cultural background. It is therefore only natural that, given the opportunity, such entities will seek to act in a way that agrees with their cultural background to the greatest possible extent and that is, at the same time, justified in the light of public international law, though not entirely compliant with it. For this reason, if

53 The argument is often used in the application of national laws in countries having a large number of immigrants, especially in criminal proceedings. Cf.: L. Łukaszuk, 'Wielokulturowość…', pp. 264–265; J. Zajadło, 'Prawo kontra obyczajowość' (Law Versus Morality), in J. Zajadło (ed.), *Fascynujące ścieżki filozofii prawa* (*Fascinating Paths of the Philosophy of Law*), Warszawa 2008, pp. 68–79.

cultural defence is ever to be a valid argument in the application of international law, it should lead to the development of a consistent practice that will transform into a regional custom, provided that the subjective condition *opinio juris sive necessitatis* is fulfilled.

Depending on the direction of the development of international law, the role of culture in the process of its creation may grow. This growth in importance may be particularly strongly influenced by the implementation of hermeneutical conceptions in international law, applied even more in the legal theories of individual states. From the hermeneutical perspective, law is a cultural object, a set of meanings, a special act of communication.[54] Even if the current trends in the development of public international law do not lead to a greater role of culture in the shaping of the rules of public international law, the current rate and extent of this factor's influence makes it worthwhile to conduct more thorough studies on its meaning.

The original version of this text was published in the academic journal "Społeczeństwo i Polityka", no. 4, of 2012.

54 M. Zirk-Sadowski, *Prawo a uczestniczenie w kulturze* (*Law and Participation in Culture*), Łódź 1998, pp. 45–92.

Agnieszka Bieńczyk-Missala

Cultural Determinants of the Development and Observance of Universal Human Rights

Key words: Universality of human rights, cultural relativism, United Nations, Islam, Asian values, African values

Abstract: The article analyses the importance of cultural factors in the following phases: conceptualisation of human rights, creation of universal standards, and their implementation. It presents intergovernmental discussion on the universality of human rights and shows examples of culturally-motivated human rights violations.

The term universal human rights refers to the standards of human rights developed and adopted by the United Nations after World War II. With the creation of international law in this field, certain institutions have been established with the task to promote human rights and monitor their observance, such as the United Nations Commission on Human Rights (UNCHR), later replaced with the United Nations Human Rights Council (UNHRC), the United Nations High Commissioner for Human Rights (UNHCHR), the UN treaty bodies, and others. Human rights are an important element on the agendas of all the major UN bodies, including the Security Council.

At the same time, no other branch of international public law, except for the international humanitarian law, also known as the law of armed conflicts, knows such drastic infringements on the commitments taken by countries. This is due to political, economic and cultural determinants but even more importantly, because of the extremely asymmetrical nature of the relations between the state and the individual.

The aim of this article is to analyse the importance of cultural factors in the following phases: conceptualisation of human rights, creation of universal standards in this field, and their implementation.

Conceptualisation of human rights

The conceptualisation of human rights took place in Europe and in the Anglo-Saxon countries. This long process was the result of a search for balance between privileges of authorities and the rights of individuals. It was taking place in conditions of considerable social inequalities (e.g. problems of religious and ethnic minorities, slavery, discrimination against women) and it was also the result of historic processes (e.g. the industrial revolution, which contributed to the development of workers' rights).

The concept of human rights would not have come into existence if not for the achievements of European philosophers, lawyers and specialists in the humanities, who have been pondering since antiquity over the meaning and nature of freedom, equality, justice and the desired character of the relations between authorities and citizens. These scholars included such eminent figures as Seneca, Cicero, Thomas Aquinas, Hugo Grotius, Paulus Vladimiri, Thomas Hobbes, John Locke, Jean Jacques Rousseau, Thomas Paine, and many others who contributed to the development of the idea of human rights.[1]

The principal reasons for the actions undertaken by those who struggled for the abolition of slavery or for women's or workers' rights was the objection to affronting human dignity, injustice and exploitation. This would not have been possible without moral or religious principles and without the courage to stand up against those who were holding power, whether they were factory owners, privileged groups of men, dominant ethnic and cultural groups, or simply governments. Most often, this courage led them todeath penalty or another arbitral form of execution, because the introduction of human rights was at variance with the interests of the authorities. This is equally true today.

The codification of human rights in internal law was an important stage. The first achievement in this respect was King John of England's signing of the Great Charter of the Liberties of England (1215), which has ever since remained a source of constitutional law in Great Britain, also in terms of human rights. Later crucial documents include the Habeas Corpus Act (1679), the Bill of Rights (1689), the American Declaration of Independence (1776), the French Declaration of the Rights of Man and of the Citizen (1789)[2] and the United States Bill of Rights (1791), i.e. the ten first amendments to the American constitution of 1787. In

---

1 See especially: M. Piechowiak, *Filozofia praw człowieka* (*Human Rights Philosophy*), vol. 1–2, Lublin 1999; F. J. Mazurek, *Godność osoby ludzkiej podstawą praw człowieka* (*Human Dignity as the Basis of Human Rights*), Lublin 2001, pp. 17–75.

2 See: R. Kuźniar, *Prawa człowieka. Prawo, instytucje, stosunki międzynarodowe* (*Human Rights. Law, Institutions, International Relations*), Warszawa 2000, pp. 19–33; J. Machowski, 'Wprowadzenie' (Introduction), in J. Machowski, *Prawa człowieka. Zagadnienia współpracy międzynarodowej* (*Human Rights. Problems of International Cooperation*), Warszawa 1968, pp. 13–14; K. Motyka (ed.), *Prawa człowieka. Wprowadzenie. Wybór źródeł* (*Human Rights. Introduction. Selected Documents*), Lublin 1999, pp. 22–23.

this context, it is also worth mentioning Polish legislation, such as the privileges granted to the Polish nobility – the Privilege of Czerwińsk (1422) and the Privilege of Jedlnia (1430), which granted the nobles, respectively: inviolability of property and immunity from prosecution unless a proper warrant was issued by a court of justice – as well as the documents of Casimir III the Great which guaranteed freedom of denomination to Orthodox Christians (1341) and Armenian Monophysites (1356), and the act of the Warsaw Confederation (1573), which established freedom of religion and a prohibition of discrimination on grounds of denomination for nobles, royal burghers and other free people.

The proponents of the universalism of human rights call upon the common values shared by all great religions of the world, such as the sanctity of life, respect for human dignity and a moral responsibility for others, assuming that they constitute the basis of human rights. They cite the Code of Hammurabi (ca. 1772 BC), the Cyrus Cylinder (539 BC) and the Edicts of Ashoka (238 BC) as examples of non-European legislation containing rules concerning selected human rights.[3]

The modern concept of human rights emerged, however, in the countries of what we nowadays call the West. What contributed to this was the idea of natural laws and the period of Enlightenment, which brought forth the aforementioned documents that guaranteed political and civil rights in France and the US. In the later period, the development of international humanitarian law has been particularly important, as well as the progressing abolition of discrimination against various social groups in the internal systems of respective states. Furthermore, World War II was an event of profound importance in this context. The scale and atrocity of the crimes committed at that time ultimately made the international community aware that an individual should not be helpless against authorities. Thus, through internal and international law states had to adopt rules that would guarantee the people that their rights would be observed.[4]

The emergence of the universal system of human rights protection was made possible by the provisions of the Charter of the United Nations, adopted on 26 June 1945, that established the United Nations. In the preamble to the document, the members of the organisation jointly committed to 'reaffirm faith in fundamental human rights, in the dignity and worth of the human person, in the equal rights of men and women and of nations large and small.'[5] Furthermore, the Charter

---

3 D. Shelton, 'An Introduction to the History of International Human Rights Law', *Documentary File*, 34st Study Session, 30 June–25 July 2003, Strasbourg, vol. 1.

4 Cf.: L. Henkin, *The Rights of Man Today*, London 1978, p. 95 ff.

5 *Charter of the United Nations*, available at: http://www.un.org/en/documents/charter/ (accessed on 15 December 2013).

states that one of the purposes of the UN was to achieve co-operation in promoting and encouraging respect for human rights and for fundamental freedoms for all without distinction as to race, sex, language, or religion (Article 1.3), and in Articles 55 and 56 makes the respect for these rights and their observance the subject of cooperation of its members. During the ratification of the Charterno country, regardless of its culture, religion or political system, voiced any reservations on the articles concerning human rights.[6] Despite their limited character, the Charter of the United Nations has become a solid basis for the development of international law in this respect.

Adoption of the Universal Declaration of Human Rights

The fathers of the Universal Declaration of Human Rights (UDHR) of 10 December 1948 enscribed in it provisions stating that 'all human beings are born free and equal in dignity and rights [...]' (Article 1) and 'everyone is entitled to all the rights and freedoms set forth in this Declaration, without distinction of any kind, such as race, colour, sex, language, religion, political or other opinion, national or social origin, property, birth or other status [...], no distinction shall be made on the basis of the political, jurisdictional or international status of the country or territory to which a person belongs, whether it be independent, trust, non-self-governing or under any other limitation of sovereignty' (Article 2).[7]

As we can see, it was assumed that human rights were universal, and everyone was entitled to them from birth regardless of various circumstances, for example cultural and political ones. At that time, the notion of universalism of human rights was not the subject of intergovernmental disputes.[8] Nonetheless, in June 1947, the Executive Board of the American Anthropological Association submitted a statement to the UN Commission on Human Rights which was working on the Declaration and cautioned it against disregarding the differences between

---

6 For more see: K. Drzewicki, 'Prawa człowieka w Karcie NZ i w Powszechnej Deklaracji Praw Człowieka' (Human Rights in the UN Charter and in the Universal Declaration of Human Rights), *Sprawy Międzynarodowe*, no. 3, 1998.

7 *The Universal Declaration of Human Rights*, available at: http://www.un.org/en/documents/udhr/index.shtml (accessed on 15 December 2013).

8 J. Morsink, *The Universal Declaration of Human Rights: Origins, Drafting, and Intent*, Philadelphia 1999; M. Glendon, *A World Made New: Eleanor Roosevelt and the Universal Declaration of Human Rights*, New York 2002.

cultures, emphasising that 'standards and values are relative to the culture from which they derive' and thus, universal human rights do not in fact exist.[9]

At that time, the United Nations Educational, Scientific and Cultural Organization (UNESCO) sent a questionnaire concerning the universalism of human rights to a group of philosophers who, after consulting with spiritual authorities of Confucianism, Hinduism, Islam and Christianity, agreed that certain fundamental principles exist in all religions and cultures.[10]

The work on the preparation of the Universal Declaration of Human Rights involved representatives of many schools, traditions and cultures, including Charles Malik from Lebanon and Peng Chun Chang from China, who all contributed to the final text of the Declaration.[11] Due to this, for example, the Preamble does not include a reference to God because this was the position of the proponents of the positivist school and the delegation of socialist countries, what is more,the representatives of different religions had different visions of the origin of human rights.

A very problematic issue concerned the representation of Africa because at that time the continent consisted mostly of colonies; the only UN members from Africa were Egypt, Ethiopia, Liberia, and South Africa. In the entire process of compiling the text, Western inspirations were dominant. They were the result of, among others, European philosophical concepts as well as the experience of Nazism and Stalinism. The creators of the Declaration wanted to prevent situations from happening ever again in the future, where the rights of individuals would be secondary to collective interests, which historically led to the development of totalitarianism.

The final text agreed upon by the parties and the subsequent adoption of the Declaration on 10 December 1948 were considered a great success; a beginning of a world founded on 'freedom, justice and peace'.[12] In the vote on the Universal Declaration of Human Rights, out of 56 present delegates only the representatives

9 The Executive Board, American Anthropological Association, 'Statement on Human Rights', *American Anthropologist*, vol. 49, no. 4, October–December 1947, part 1, pp. 539–543. The Association retracted this Statement in 1999, by adopting the Declaration on Anthropology and Human Rights.

10 W. Osiatyński, *Prawa człowieka i ich granice* (*Human Rights and Their Limits*), Kraków 2011, pp. 239–240.

11 Professor Michael Ignatieff, a researcher of human rights from Harvard University, points out that the secularist approach was not a sign of the cultural domination of Europe but only of its pragmatism. Cf.: M. Ignatieff, *Human Rights as Politics and Idolatry*, Princeton, NJ 2001, pp. 53–95.

12 *The Universal Declaration....*

of eight countries abstained (two countries were not at all present at the meeting of the UN General Assembly)[13] and later all but one of them – Saudi Arabia – withdrew from the earlier position and accepted the provisions of the Declaration (Saudi Arabia did not agree to making no reference to God in the declaration and to the right to change religion). During the work on the UDHR, upon the motion of a Christian delegate from Lebanon, a clause guaranteeing the freedom to change religion was added to Article 18. Several Muslim countries spoke against this provision but only Saudi Arabia eventually abstained during the voting on the resolution. It is an interesting fact that the Lebanese motion was seconded by the Pakistan delegate. This delegate was a member of the Islamic reform movement Ahmadiyya.[14]

Saudi Arabia would also not accept the provisions concerning equal status of men and women included in Article 16 of the Declaration. Under this article, men and women entering into a marriage and founding a family should be of full age; it also provided for the principle of 'free and full consent of the intending spouses', as well as for them having 'equal rights as to marriage, during marriage and at its dissolution'.

The position of Saudi Arabia was a herald of future attempts to contest some universal human rights by certain Arab states. At the same time, the situation has shown that there were differences concerning the interpretation of Islam between Muslim countries.

States' attitudes to the universal human rights instruments

In the later years, cultural differences still did not play the decisive role in the process of developing universal standards of human rights. The line of disagreement was determined by the divisions resulting from the reality of the Cold War and concerned the meaning of the individual categories of human rights. It was impossible to adopt a single legally binding instrument containing the catalogue of human rights. As a result, in 1966 two Pacts were adopted: the International Covenant on Civil and Political Rights (ICCPR) and the International Covenant on Economic, Social and Cultural Rights (ICESCR).

13 These were: the Byelorussian SSR, Czechoslovakia, People's Republic of Poland, Saudi Arabia, the Soviet Union, the Ukrainian SSR, the Union of South Africa and, Yugoslavia.

14 In 1974, the Ahmadiyya community was deemed non-Muslim in Pakistan and was subsequently subjected to discrimination and persecution.

During the work on the International Covenant on Civil and Political Rights, Saudi Arabia and Egypt attempted to remove the provision that guaranteed freedom to change religion. In the end, a compromise proposed by Brazil and the Philippines was adopted and the phrase 'everyone has the right to [...] freedom to change his religion or belief', as found in Article 18 of the UDHR, was replaced with 'everyone has the right to [...] freedom to have or to adopt a religion or belief of his choice'.[15]

For both Covenants, several reservations resulting from cultural differences were voiced. Bahrain reserved the right to implement certain articles of the ICCPR – Article 3 (concerning equal rights of men and women) and 23 (concerning equal rights and responsibilities in marriage) to the extent to which they are not at variance with the Sharia law. Qatar committed to observe the general non-discrimination clause in Article 2.1 and the clause concerning men and women in Article 3 only within the framework of internal law. Mauretania filed a reservation to Article 18, concerning the freedom of religion, and the aforementioned Article 23. Pakistan, in turn, restricted the implementation of Article 3.[16]

In the case of the International Covenant on Economic, Social and Cultural Rights, reservations were voiced by Bangladesh, which declared that it would implement Article 2 (principles concerning the implementation of the Covenant), Article 3 (equal rights of men and women to enjoy the rights set forth in the Covenant) and Article 7 (the right to enjoy just and favourable conditions of work) only within the framework of internal law.

There was also a heated discussion during the process of drafting the Convention on the Elimination of All Forms of Discrimination against Women (CEDAW), adopted in 1979.[17] The aim of the provisions to be adopted was to eliminate discrimination against women understood as 'any distinction, exclusion or restriction made on the basis of sex which has the effect or purpose of impairing or nullifying the recognition, enjoyment or exercise by women, irrespective of their marital status, on a basis of equality of men and women, of human rights

15 Article 18, *International Covenant on Civil and Political Rights*, General Assembly resolution 2200A (XXI) of 16 December 1966, available at: http://www.ohchr.org/EN/ProfessionalInterest/Pages/CCPR.aspx (accessed on 15 December 2013).

16 The reservations voiced by various states to UN conventions can be found on the UN website, available at: http://www.un.org/en/rights/ (accessed on 20 December 2013).

17 See:. H. J. Steiner, P. Alston, *International Human Rights in Context: Law, Politics, Morals: Text and Materials*, 2nd ed., Oxford–New York 2000, p. 439 ff.

and fundamental freedoms in the political, economic, social, cultural, civil or any other field' (Article 1).[18]

Although human rights concern primarily the relations between the state and the individual, in the Convention states have committed to undertake measures aimed at eliminating discrimination against women by persons, organisations as well as enterprises. States are to take, among others, 'all appropriate measures, including legislation, to modify or abolish existing laws, regulations, customs and practices which constitute discrimination against women' (Article 2).[19]

Many countries, primarily Muslim ones, decided that they would be unable to force individuals to abandon their cultural traditions and customs even if they infringe on universal women's rights. Consequently, they filed reservations to the said article, claiming its inconsistence with the Sharia law, as well as with their constitutions and internal legislations (Algeria, Bangladesh, Qatar, Libya, Morocco, Niger, Syria and the United Arab Emirates). India declared that, as a state, they supported the requirement to register marriages but at the same time, it admitted that in such a large country with such great diversity of customs, religions and different levels of literacy, this was not in fact practiced.[20]

Furthermore, Article 5 requires states to take all appropriate measures to 'modify the social and cultural patterns of conduct of men and women, with a view to achieving the elimination of prejudices and customary and all other practices which are based on the idea of the inferiority or the superiority of either of the sexes or on stereotyped roles for men and women.'[21] India declared that it would implement the said obligations but only in agreement with the policy of non-interference in the private affairs of the members of communities, upon their initiative or their consent. The representative of Niger pointed out that the proposed changes could not be implemented immediately as they were at variance with the customs applied at that time but he did not preclude their implementation in a longer time-frame, following evolution of attitudes in the society. The representative of Qatar, in turn, cautioned that the implementation of the said

18 *Convention on the Elimination of All Forms of Discrimination against Women*, available at: http://www.un.org/womenwatch/daw/cedaw/text/econvention.htm#article1 (accessed on 15 December 2013).

19 *Ibid.*

20 The reservations entered by various states to this Convention are available at: http://www.un.org/womenwatch/daw/cedaw/reservations.htm (accessed on 15 December 2013).

21 *Convention on the Elimination of All Forms of Discrimination...*

principles could be construed as encouraging women to abandon their roles as mothers and child-bearers, as this could undermine the family structure.[22]

Some countries voiced reservations concerning granting women the right to choose their residence and domicile under Article 15 of the Convention (Algeria, Morocco, Qatar, Syria, and the United Arab Emirates). Niger declared that it would recognise this right only in relation to unmarried women.

Some anxiety was also caused by Article 16, which concerns equal rights and responsibilities of men and women regarding marriage, including entering into it and dissolving it. Reservations to these provisions were entered by Algeria, Bangladesh, Brunei, Egypt, India, Iraq, Jordan, Kuwait, Lebanon, Libya, Niger, Oman, Malaysia, Qatar, Syria, Tunisia, and the United Arab Emirates. In some cases, they concerned the making of decisions regarding children. Kuwait, Lebanon, Malaysia, Oman, Qatar, Syria, Tunisia, and the United Arab Emirates did not recognise equal rights of men and women with respect to the nationality of their children (Article 9).

Such a large number of reservations entered by Arab states met with severe criticism from the other members of the UN. Official objections were filed by, among others, Belgium, Canada, Czechoslovakia, Denmark, Estonia, Finland, France, Greece, Hungary, Ireland, Latvia, Mexico, the Netherlands, Norway, Poland, Portugal, Romania, Spain, Sweden, and the United Kingdom.[23] Pursuant to Article 28.2 of the Convention, reservations that are incompatible with its object and purpose, that is elimination of discrimination, are not permitted. Similar rules have been included in the Vienna Convention on the Law of Treaties (VCLT) and constitute a part of customary international law. The extensive reservations voiced in relation to the aforementioned articles obviously imply that discrimination of women in fact exists. In light of the purpose of the Convention, it was especially difficult for the international community to accept the reservations filed by Saudi Arabia and Mauretania, which announced that they intended to observe only those parts of the Convention which were not at variance with the Sharia law and with their internal laws. Such a position makes it impossible to determine which provisions of the Convention the countries actually consider binding.

Cultural differences could also be observed in the context of the discussion on the Convention on the Rights of the Child (CRC) of 1989. Taking into account

---

22 'Konwencja w sprawie likwidacji wszelkich form dyskryminacji kobiet' (Convention on the Elimination of All Forms of Discrimination against Women), in A. Bieńczyk-Missala (ed.), *Międzynarodowa ochrona praw człowieka. Wybór dokumentów* (*International Protection of Human Rights. Selected Documents*), Warszawa 2008, pp. 85–86.

23 *Ibid.*

the number of actual ratifications (196 as of 26 June 2016), we could consider this instrument a truly universal one. However, the reservations voiced by some countries prove that many of them were in fact not ready to truly implement its provisions. Afghanistan, Kuwait, Mauretania, Qatar, and Saudi Arabia all voiced extensive reservations declaring that they would only obey those rules of the Convention that were compliant with Sharia law. Iraq, Jordan, Kuwait, the Maldives, Morocco, Oman and Syria announced that they would observe Article 14.1 concerning freedom of religion in accordance with Sharia law or internal law (Malaysia). Furthermore, in this context the Vatican stressed the inalienable rights of parents and Poland declared it would perform this provision with respect to parental authority and in accordance with Polish customs and traditions. The Polish declaration also questioned Articles 12 and 13, concerning children's freedom to express their own views and their access to information, as well as Articles 15 and 16, concerning the rights of the child to freedom of association, peaceful assembly and privacy.[24]

Article 21, which regulates adoption, also proved problematic to Arab states. Jordan, Kuwait, the Maldives, and Oman declared that the notion of adoption was at variance with the principles of Sharia law. Algeria stated that it would interpret Article 13, concerning the freedom of expression, Article 16, on access to information, and Article 17, on access to the mass media, taking into account its internal law.[25]

It is worth stressing that, indeed, the creators of the Convention took into account the natural immaturity of children. Many provisions include clauses allowing a restriction of the exercise of the rights they refer to. Usually, however, this concerns situations when this is needed to protect national security or public order, public health or morals, as well as the fundamental rights and freedoms of others (Articles 13, 14 and 15).

24 *Convention on the Rights of the Child*, General Assembly resolution 44/25 of 20 November 1989, available at: http://www.ohchr.org/en/professionalinterest/pages/crc.aspx (accessed on 15 December 2013); cf.: A. Bieńczyk-Missala (ed.), *Międzynarodowa ochrona....*

25 The reservations voiced by various states to UN conventions can be found on the UN website, available at: http://www.un.org/en/rights (accessed on 20 December 2013).

Cultural aspects at the World Conference on Human Rights in Vienna

The goal behind the organisation of the 1993 global summit in Vienna was to discuss the new challenges in the field of human rights and develop a work programme for the United Nations. In the post-Cold War reality, this was an opportunity to manifest negative attitudes to the universal human rights adopted by the UN.

While reservations to the universal human rights instruments were voiced mainly by Arab countries, at the World Conference on Human Rights it was especially the East Asian countries, experiencing a particularly strong economic development at that time, that manifested their different opinions. They tried to point out that they had achieved their economic success due to limited democracy and the Asian values,[26] among which social and personal values were distinguished. The former are, among others, social order and good organisation, harmony, ensuring the responsibility of public state officials, freedom of self-expression and respect for the authorities, while the latter are, among others:intensive labour, respect for science and education, honesty, relying on oneself, self-discipline and fulfilling one's commitments towards others. It was also pointed out that in contrast to the values preferred by the Western societies (freedom of expression, rights of individuals, personal freedoms, open debates on political issues, looking after oneself, relying on oneself, personal achievements, intensive labour, achieving success in life and helping others), Asian values concern primarily the social dimension.[27] Furthermore, the Confucian idea was also brought up. According to Confucianism, man is the part of a certain group and only within this group he can fully realise himself. The relationships between people are thus founded on the principle of hierarchy, so relations within a group are always subject to

26 The concept of Asian values was promoted by: Malaysia, Singapore, China, Burma (Myanmar), the Philippines, Indonesia, North Korea, Cambodia, Laos, Thailand, and Vietnam. The most involved officials were the prime ministers of Malaysia and Singapore: Mahathir bin Mohamad and Lee Kuan Yew. For more see: A. Bieńczyk-Missala, 'Non-European Ideas of Human Rights', in M. F. Gawrycki *et al.* (eds.), *Re-Visions and Re-Orientations. Non-European Thought in International Relations*, London–New Delhi–New York–Sydney: Bloomsbury, 2014, pp. 191–207.

27 Mahathir bin Mohamad referred to, for example, the results of the systematic quantitative research conducted by David Hitchcock to compare East Asian and American values (cf.: M. bin Mohamad, 'Wartości azjatyckie' [Asian Values], *Res Publica Nowa*, no. 3, 2003).

dependency. Obedience to one's seniors, both in age and hierarchy, submitting to control and full confidence in the authorities are therefore considered natural.

At the regional meeting held before the World Conference, on 29 March 1993 in Bangkok, Asian countries adopted a declaration in which they expressed their opinion on the international system of human rights protection. First of all, they confirmed the commitments resulting from the UN Charter and the Universal Declaration of Human Rights, they expressed their support for the process of ratification of the UN treaties that were most important for this field: the International Covenant on Civil and Political Rights and the International Covenant on Economic, Social and Cultural Rights, and they also recognised the need for further international cooperation aimed at respecting human rights.

They noted that the instruments adopted in the field of human rights largely concerned only one category of rights, namely civil and political rights, and at the same time they underlined the interdependence and the inalienable character of all the categories. Asian countries considered the universal and inalienable character of the right to development an integral part of fundamental human rights and observed that the main reason for the difficulties in exercising this right lays in international macroeconomy, which reflected the gulf between the rich North and the poor South.[28] They called poverty the main barrier to a full exercise of human rights.

Furthermore, the Asian states expressed their opposition to using human rights as an instrument of political pressure and emphasised the principles of respecting national sovereignty, territorial integrity of states and non-interference. They called for avoiding the use of double standards and pointed out the need for objectivity and non-selectivity in the approach to human rights. They themselves, however, did not observe these principles, as in their Declaration they referred only to the lack of respect for human rights in Palestine, the Golan Heights and the territories occupied by Israel.

The 1993 Bangkok Declaration was an important voice in the discussion on the universalism of human rights. Enshrined in it was the conviction that human rights were universal and it also highlighted the significance of national and regional particularisms, as well as the historical, cultural and religious determinants of the observance of human rights. This was one of the most important

28 The Declaration on the Right to Development was adopted by the UN General Assembly on 4 December 1986, A/RES/41/128.

foundations of the relativism theory, which conditioned the extent and observance of human rights on cultural or religious issues.[29]

The Bangkok Declaration partially coincided with what was expressed in the Tunis Declaration, summing up the regional meeting for Africa held in Tunis on 2–6 November 1992. African countries agreed that it was impossible to establish a single model of observing human rights because this could be construed as disrespect for the historical and cultural determinants of states, as well as their traditions, standards and values. Nonetheless, they also confirmed the indisputability of the universal nature of human rights and stated that their protection and promotion was the duty of all countries, regardless of their political, economic and cultural systems. They also recognised that the responsibility for the implementation of human rights lay mainly with governments.

During the World Conference in Vienna, the issue of cultural differences was primarily raised by Asian countries, which wanted their requests concerning the restriction of the principle of universalism through recognition of freedom of interpretation of human rights to be taken into account and implemented in a manner that would reflect the specific conditions – including cultural determinants – of individual states.[30] African states, in turn, focused more on developing the concept of the right to development and on the need to increase financial assistance provided by developed countries to the developing ones.[31]

Western countries were rather critical of the requests made by the Asian countries because they believed that the human rights developed by the United Nations should not be relativised.[32] In the end, after a consensus was reached, the Vienna

---

29 *Asian States Stress Regional Specificity of Human Rights at Preparatory Meeting for World Conference*, United Nations Information Service, UNIS/HR/109, 1 April 1993.

30 *International Herald Tribune*, 19 May 1993 and 19–20 July 1993.

31 Nonetheless, the notion of 'African Values' has been developed in academic discourse, see e.g.: B. Ibhawoh, 'Cultural Relativism and Human Rights: Reconsidering the African Discourse', *Netherlands Quarterly of Human Rights*, vol. 19, no. 1, 2001; K. Quashigah, 'The Philosophical Basis of Human Rights and Its Relation to Africa', *Journal of Human Rights Law and Practice*, vol. 1, no. 2 and 3, 1991; J. Cobbah, 'African Values and the Human Rights Debate: An African Perspective', *Human Rights Quarterly*, vol. 9, no. 3, 1987; D. Shiman, 'An African Perspective on Human Rights', *Update on Law-Related Education*, vol. 16, no. 3, 1992. For more on the determinants and the state of the observance of human rights in Africa see: G. Michałowska, *Problemy ochrony praw człowieka w Afryce* (*Problems of Human Rights Protection in Africa*), Warszawa 2008.

32 The discussion on the meaning of the concept of 'Asian values' quieted down with the decline in the region's economic development. It was also subjected to criticism. See e.g.: A. Sen, *Human Rights and Asian Values*, New York 1997; J. Donnelly, 'Human

Declaration and Programme of Action confirmed the international standards of human rights in an unchanged form. The document states: 'all human rights are universal, indivisible,interdependent and interrelated'; 'the universal nature of these rights and freedoms is beyond question'; at the same time: 'while the significance of national and regional particularities and various historical, cultural and religious backgrounds must be borne in mind, it is the duty of States, regardless of their political, economic and cultural systems, to promote and protect all human rights and fundamental freedoms.'[33] To a certain extent, the requests of Asian countries to show understanding of their regional or cultural differences was taken into account, although at the same time, it was noted that they cannot be a pretext for infringing upon human rights but only the reason for another way of implementing them.[34]

In the final Declaration, the participant states also referred to culturally-conditioned discrimination and violence against women. Eliminating all discrimination on grounds of gender is a primary objective for the international community.[35] It was also stated that violence resulting from discrimination on grounds of gender, including all its forms stemming from cultural prejudice, needs to be eliminated. This was to be achieved through legal instruments such as national and international measures in the field of economic and social development, education, motherhood protection, health protection, and welfare work.

Culturally conditioned infringement on human rights

Infringements on human rights motivated by cultural differences occur on all continents. They can be identified by excluding the political and economic determinants of infringements, although in some cases – such as abortions of female embryos and murders of new-born female babies in India – both cultural and

---

Rights and Asian Values: A Defence of "Western Universalism"', in J. R. Bauer, D. A. Bell (eds.), *The East Asian Challenge for Human Rights*, Cambridge, UK–New York 1999, pp. 60–87.

33 The above passage was a reference to the situation in Singapore, which called its political system an 'Asian style democracy' (Cf.: D. P. Forsythe, *Human Rights in International Relations*, Cambridge 2000, p. 47).

34 See: 'Deklaracja Wiedeńska i Program Działania' (Vienna Declaration and Action Plan), in A. Bieńczyk-Missala, *Międzynarodowa ochrona...*, p. 183 ff; see also: Z. Kędzia, 'The Vienna World Conference on Human Rights: Failure or Milestone in Human Rights History?', *International Geneva Yearbook*, vol. 8, 1994.

35 'Deklaracja Wiedeńska i Program Działania...', p. 188.

economic reasons should be taken into account.[36] Historically, in Europe, the most serious cases of such infringements involved discrimination of minorities, including Jews, infidels and women. The development of the idea of human rights, internal and international law as well as efforts towards implementation of law took place alongside cultural transformations. They were accompanied by promotion of tolerance and respect for diversity, which led to reducing discrimination and violence motivated by cultural factors. Nonetheless, even in Europe, there are culturally motivated infringements on human rights, such as child marriage, polygamy, as well as discriminatory practices and behaviours towards women.

In Europe and in the Anglo-Saxon countries however, the acceptance and implementation of human rights were a much quicker process than in the other regions of the world. This was possible, among others, due to philosophical achievements, legal traditions, well-developed individualism, strong ties between the individual and the law, as well as the acceptance of the idea of human rights by the Christian Church.

The cultural determinants hampering the implementation of human right include: collectivism, a deep belief in power derived from God, the notion of obedience, a weak relation between the individual and the state, as well as contradictions between some human rights and the rules and convictions resulting from religion or beliefs.[37]

Culturally motivated infringement on human rights may include the discrimination against women in South Asia and in Muslim countries. However, we should take into account that there is no single interpretation of Islam and that as a result, different Islamic countries employ different practices.

India is a very interesting example in this regard, as it has abolished the caste system and the institution of the dowry in its internal law; what is more, it has introduced a legal ban on performing examinations to reveal the sex of an unborn baby, a ban on child marriage and sati – the ritual of self-immolation of widows – but it has been, nonetheless, unable to overcome the deeply rooted social norms. Thus still, depending on caste membership, women have limited opportunities to exercise human rights. They are frequently harassed and molested in public

---

36 The need to provide a considerable dowry while marrying off one's daughter, no possibility for women to inherit.

37 See e.g.: B. A. Ackerly, *Universal Human Rights in a World of Difference*, Cambridge 2008; P. V. Ness, *Debating Human Rights. Critical Essays from the United States and Asia*, London–New York 1999; K. Przybyszewski, *Prawa człowieka w kontekstach kulturowych* (*Human Rights in Cultural Contexts*), Poznań 2010.

places (so-called 'Eve teasing'), forced to enter into marriage before the age of 18,[38] and widows are usually excluded from participation in the social life.[39] Women struggle with similar problems in Nepal as well.

The typical infringement on human rights, rooted in social tradition but inconsistent with the established standards, is female genital mutilation. Most countries have outlawed this practice but as the World Health Organisation points out, itis still practiced in 28 countries, including the Muslim part of Indonesia, Egypt, Somalia, Mali, Eritrea, Sudan, Sierra Leone, and Ethiopia as well as among immigrant groups in Europe, North America or Australia.[40]

The United Nations have expressed a negative opinion on the practice of female genital mutilation. On 20 December 2012, the UN General Assembly unanimously passed a resolution which called on states to condemn this practice regardless of whether it is performed in hospitals or not and to implement all available measures – legal and educational – to protect women and girls. The resolution was supported by a 2/3 of states, including a group of African countries,[41] and stressed the fact that genital mutilation posed serious health risks. 18th December 2014, the UN General Assembly adopted without a vote a resolution devoted to intensifying global efforts for the elimination of female genital mutilation. Member states were called to develop and implement national strategies to prevent this practice, including the training of medical personnel, social workers and community and religious leaders[42]. Considerable effort in this regard was undertaken by: Mauritania, Yemen, Burkina Faso, Kenya, Ethiopia, Mali, Somalia, Uganda, Egypt and Eritrea.

Other culturally motivated practices includethe so-called honour killings. They affect mostly young women who are believed to have brought shame to their family or community by premarital or extramarital sexual intercourse, homosexuality,

---

38 According to UNICEF, 47 percent of surveyed women aged 20–24 married before they were 18, UNICEF Report: The State of the World's Children 2009, available at: http://www.unicef.org.

39 For more on the determinants of the approach to human rights in India see e.g.: J.W. Elder, 'Hindu Perspectives on the Individual and the Collectivity', in I. Bloom, J. P. Martin, W. L. Proudfoot (eds.), *Religious Diversity and Human Rights*, New York 1996, pp. 54–86, M. Juergensmeyer, *Hindu Nationalism and Human Rights*, in I. Bloom, J. P. Martin, W. L. Proudfoot (eds.), *Religious Diversity...*, pp. 243–261.

40 *Eliminating Female Genital Mutilation*, An interagency statement OHCHR, UNAIDS, UNDP, UNECA, UNESCO, UNFPA, UNHCR, UNICEF, UNIFEM, WHO, World Health Organization, 2008.

41 UN General Assembly Resolution, A/RES/67/146 of 20 December 2012.

42 UN General Assembly Resolution, A/RES/69/150 of 18 December 2012.

refusal to accept an arranged marriage, or apostasy from Islam. In many societies, there is traditional consent for such killings. This is especially true of countries such as Egypt, Jordan, Morocco, Pakistan, Syria, Turkey, Yemen, but others as well.[43] There is also, however, a considerable number of cases of honour killings in Europe and in the United States, where large communities of immigrants exist. In 2009, the Parliamentary Assembly of the Council of Europe (PACE) issued Resolution 1681, in which it called on its members to develop and implement national action plans aimed at combating this practice.

One of the greatest rifts between the universal system of human rights protection and the Sharia law is the freedom of religion.[44] According to the predominant interpretation of the Quran, apostasy from Islam should be punished by death, hence in many Muslim countries it is either punishable or illegal. The penal codes of Mauretania (1984) and Sudan (1991), for example, provide for capital punishment for committing apostasy from Islam although in the periodic report to the UN Human Rights Committee under the International Covenant on Civil and Political Rights Sudan declared that it was not conversion from Islam itself that was considered a crime but rather manifestation of this conversion in a manner that poses a threat to public security.[45] Capital punishment can also be pronounced by Sharia courts in countries which have given them the relevant competences: Saudi Arabia, Yemen, Afghanistan, the Comoros, Iran, and Pakistan.

The second major rift between the universalist concept and Islam concerns expressing criticism of religion. According to Islamic law, blasphemy is one of the most serious offences. If the perpetrator is a Muslim, then it partially overlaps with apostasy. Since 1999, the members of the Organisation of the Islamic Conference have been systematically proposing in the Committee, and then in the UN Human Rights Council, a resolution calling for protection of religion from defamation. Their efforts were further intensified by the criticism of Muslims in relation to the terrorist attacks of 2001. The Western states have strongly opposed this initiative because they considered such a prohibition a threat to the freedom of speech.[46]

---

43 See e.g.: Report of the Secretary-General of 2002, Working Towards the Elimination of Crimes Against Women Committed in the Name of Honour, A/57/169.

44 See e.g.: D. Little, A. Sachedina, J. Kelsay, 'Christianity, Islam and Religious Liberty', in I. Bloom, J. P. Martin, W. L. Proudfoot (eds.), *Religious Diversity* ..., pp. 213–242; S. Akbarzadeh, B. MacQueen (eds.), *Islam and Human Rights in Practice*, London–New York 2008.

45 M. A. Baderin, *International Human Rights and Islamic Law*, New York 2003, p. 125.

46 The texts of the subsequent resolutions are available on the UN website: www.un.org.

In the context of the aforementioned actions, it should be noted that while in Muslim countries the relations between religion and the state are diverse, the Islamic tradition rejects the separation of the sacred and the profane. It is a Muslim's duty to obey the ruler who acts in accordance with the principles of Islam. Political thought is ordered theocratically, which has certain consequences for the social and political system and for the understanding of the individual. Therefore, it is hard for them to adopt the Western concept of the human being as an independent individualthat has free will and independently chooses his means of self-actualisation. In Islam, God towers over human sovereignty. Man is a part of God's creation and he is to be completely subordinated to its Creator. Consequently, human freedom is limited by the will of God.[47]

Yet another plane of disagreement is equality. The problem concerns primarily (although not solely) discrimination against women. The Quran allows a man to have up to four wives, provided that they are treated justly. The Human Rights Council has deemed polygamy at variance with the principle of equal rights in marriage and called for its removal from those legal systems which still recognise it.[48] Polygamy, however, is legal in most Muslim countries. Furthermore, it is also practiced by some Muslims living in Western countries.

What is alien to universalist thought – polygamy, certain forms of isolating women from men, a strict dress code, and others – in Islam is perceived as a protection of morals and a means of safeguarding the biological role of women.[49] On the other hand, some Muslims claim that according to the Quran, the legal status of men and women is equal and that the discrimination present in some Arab countries is the result of traditions and customary law, which sometimes are not at all related to the message conveyed by the Quran.[50]

While discussing the relation between the principles of Islam and human rights, we have to point to the considerable diversity of thought and practice in Muslim societies, the reason for this being, among others, the freedom of interpretation of the Quran. There exists no single universally binding interpretation

47 J. Danecki, *Podstawowe wiadomości o islamie* (*Basic Information on Islam*), vol. 1–2, Warszawa 1997.

48 M. A. Baderin, *International Human Rights...*, p. 138.

49 M. A. Nowicki, 'Szarijat niezmienny i święty' (Sharia Law – Unchangeable and Sacred), *Rzeczpospolita*, 5 June 1999.

50 Cf. also: K. Barcikowska-Gruchalska, 'Uwarunkowania realizacji koncepcji uniwersalizmu praw człowieka' (Determinants of the Realisation of the Universalist Concept of Human Rights), *Sprawy Międzynarodowe*, no. 3, 2003.

of this book.[51] As a result, the situation of women in various Muslim countries is different. There are, of course, numerous scientific papers attempting to prove the existence of synergy between human rights and the principles of Islam.[52] On the other hand, however, many traditions practiced in some Muslim countries – such as stoning, amputation of parts of the body, female genital mutilation, inequality of men and women in court, and others – are criticised by the UN, by Western countries and by non-governmental organisations as unacceptable in the context of international standards of human rights.

Conclusions

The extent and scope of this article do not allow for an exhaustive discussion of the complex problem of cultural determinants of the creation and observance of universal standards human rights, which undeniably deserve a thorough analysis.

The United Nations and the European systems of human rights protection will keep being confronted with culturally conditioned practices that will be at variance withuniversal human rights. We should expect that we still are dealing with two parallel processes. Culturally motivated infringements on human rights will surely persist, as a consequence of the power of traditions, religious laws, beliefs, prejudice, and often also their structural nature, which is difficult to overcome.[53] Where different values and principles collide, especially the religious ones, there will be a radicalisation of attitudes. On the other hand, education and promotion of the universal standards of human rights will contribute to the change of the dominant values, beliefs and cultural practices.

---

51 In the Islamic world, law is based on the Quran, the Prophet's tradition (*Sunnah*) and judgements made by doctors of Muslim law.

52 See especially: A. A. An-Na'im (ed.), *Human Rights in Cross-Cultural Perspectives: A Quest for Consensus*, Philadelphia 1991; A. A. An-Naim, *Islam and the Secular State. Negotiating the Future of Shari'a*, Cambridge, MA 2008; A. B. Sajoo, 'Islam and Human Rights: Congruence or Dichotomy', in A. S. Rosenbaum (ed.), *The Philosophy of Human Rights: International Perspectives*, Westport, CT 1980.

53 See e.g.: M. Koenig, P. Guchteneire, *Democracy and Human Rights in Multicultural Societies*, Ashgate 2006.

Grażyna Michałowska

Legal, Political and Cultural Determinants of Gender Policy

Key words: gender, culture, equality, sexual orientation, social roles

Abstract: This article analyses the terms 'gender', 'gender policy' and 'gender identity', their emergence in the context of combating stereotypes and the discrimination of women in social, economic and political life. It also discusses legal regulations as well as cultural and political barriers related to gender equality.

Basic concepts

One can define *gender* as a set of traits, attitudes, social roles, and behaviours considered appropriate for men or women by broadly understood culture.[1] In one's own cultural environment, internalisation of the expectations related to this starts at the moment of birth and is further confirmed by upbringing and education. The term was introduced into scientific literature in 1955 by John William Money, an American psychologist specialising in studies of gender identity and biology of the sexes.[2]

The categories of *sex* and *gender* are explained by the World Health Organisation, according to which '*sex* refers to the biological and physiological characteristics that define men and women', while '*gender* refers to the socially constructed roles, behaviours, activities, and attributes that a given society considers appropriate for men and women.' This is reflected by the divisions: male vs. female and masculine vs. feminine.[3]

The term *gender* is also used by the World Bank, which in 2011 launched the first of a cycle of publications titled *World Development Report 2012: Gender*

---

1 L. Marszałek, 'Kulturowe uwarunkowania roli kobiety we współczesnym społeczeństwie' (Cultural Determinants of the Role of Women in the Modern Society), *Seminare. Poszukiwania Naukowe*, TNFS, 2008, no. 25, p. 267.

2 J. Money, 'Hermaphroditism, Gender and Precocity in Hyperadrenocorticism: Psychologic Findings', *Bulletin of the Johns Hopkins Hospital*, no. 96, 1955, pp. 253–264; J. Money, A. A. Ehrhardt, *Man and Women, Boy and Girl: The Differentiation and Dimorphism of Gender Identity from Conception to Maturity*, Baltimore 1972.

3 WHO, *What do we mean by 'sex' and 'gender'?*, http://www.who.int/gender/whatisgender/en/index.html (accessed on 2 May 2013).

Equality and Development. It focuses on four areas with greatest inequalities between the genders: excessive women mortality and education gap; availability of economic activity and wage gap; significance of women's voice in the family and society; repeating gender inequality by subsequent generations.

The Council of Europe, in turn, describes this notion as 'the (re)organisation, improvement, development and evaluation of policy processes, so that a gender equality perspective is incorporated in all policies at all levels and at all stages, by the actors normally involved in policy-making.' Thus, it is not about some extraordinary privileges but a simple democracy of genders. This point of view is shared in Article 23 of the Charter of Fundamental Rights of the European Union: 'The principle of equality shall not prevent the maintenance or adoption of measures providing for specific advantages in favour of the under-represented sex.'

Gender mainstreaming is a notion related to the strategy of ensuring equal opportunities of women and men in institutions, organisations, politics, and to including the principle of gender equality in mainstream politics. It was officially formulated at a conference in Beijing in 1995 and has been reflected in the 13 anti-discrimination directives adopted by the EU so far and in Article 3(2) of the Treaty of Amsterdam.

Under the term gender policy we understand the action and inaction of the state, including the laws and institutions, serving to reduce and eliminate the different treatment of genders. Regardless of the state's intentions, this does not immediately imply actual equality, as factors such as history, tradition, and the local customs are more strongly set in people's consciousness than the fear of potential sanctions. The law orders social relations and even if it seems right from the point of view of civilisation processes but perceived as directed against the people, it is not observed and can be criminogenic. Francis Fukuyama aptly observed that 'Formal rules can be readily changed as a matter of public policy; cultural rules cannot, and while they change over time, it is much harder to direct their development.'[4]

Sources of the phenomenon

In human history, gender has determined the position of individuals throughout their entire lives. Essentially, regardless of the civilisation, there has been a very clear division between women and men, not only due to their biological traits. The notion of the weak or weaker sex has been integral to the expectations and roles

---

4 F. Fukuyama, *State-Building: Governance and World Order in the 21st century*, New York: Cornell University Press 2004, p. 29.

considered appropriate for men and women in culture, the society and family life (the so-called gender contract). The related stereotypes have showed women as frail, emotional, dependent, submissive, and naïve.[5] Women were categorised even when their tasks did not solely come down to giving birth to children, supervising the servants and accompanying men, but when they actually required initiative, intelligence, physical strength, and responsibility.

Support for the stereotypical perception of women iis found both in philosophy and in scientific or pseudoscientific publications. Ancient philosophers rarely appreciated women. Aristotle even wrote that the female was a defective male, a deviation from the norm. While he believed that women should be educated and in a marriage the wife and the husband should support each other, he also claimed that the man was to be the dominant one and that the husband was due more love from the wife than the wife from the husband.[6]

Early Christian thought made references to the Old Testament. Due to the actions of the biblical Eve, women were accused of all possible sins. Saint Thomas Aquinas believed that women were something misbegotten, a mistake made by nature and that they were meant to give birth to children, raise them and do housework. He also claimed that a male embryo becomes a human after 40 days, while a female embryo only after 80 days. Even the great mind of the Renaissance Erasmus of Rotterdam did not think much of women; however, that did not prevent him from suggesting that they should be educated.

The scholars of the late 19th and early 20th centuries were trying to prove that women were incapable of matching men because their brains are built differently. In 1911, the German physician Julius Bayerthal argued that women would never equal men in terms of intellect as they had a smaller skull circumference (no more than 52 cm) and their brains were smaller from male brains by 15 per cent on average. Consequently, he believed that brilliant women simply cannot exist.[7] Sometime earlier, a similar argument for lower intelligence of women was brought up by the French surgeon and neurologist Pierre-Paule Broca, and later by the American zoologist Leigh Van Valen.[8] Furthermore, the French physician, sociologist and social psychologist Gustave le Bon claimed that the brains of Parisian women were the same size as gorilla brains and that this proved their intellectual

5 L. Marszałek, *Kulturowe...*, p. 269.

6 Aristotle, *Nicomachean Ethics*, Books VIII–IX.

7 J. Bayerthal, *Erblichkeit und Erziehung in ihrer individuellen Bedeutung*, Wiesbaden 1911.

8 L. Van Valen, 'Brain Size and Intelligence in Man', *American Journal of Physical Anthropology*, no. 40, 1974, pp. 417–423.

deficiency, while Charles Darwin argued that women were less evolved than men. In time, it turned out that the actual differences in the construction of the brain[9] do not entail any other consequences than physiological ones.

Due to their predispositions, women were to integrate the family, solve conflicts within it, ensure that it would function in harmony, cultivate tradition, and consolidate models and values. They were the ones who were to deal with such activities as helping in other people's homes, nursing the sick, looking after children, or prostitution. Men had more ambitious and responsible roles in the social structure and these gave rise to different models of patriarchate in various cultures. As a result, it was the role of men to make history. As long as women were not rulers themselves, or wives or mistresses of rulers or otherwise well-known men, they were forgotten, ignored or their input was belittled.

Matriarchal structures probably appeared relatively rarely. Today an approximation of this family model can be found with the Tuareg people and with the ca. 30 thousand Na (Mosuo, Moso) people living in the Chinese province of Yunnan. The Tuaregs are nomadic Berber people living in West Sahara. They are called desert pirates, the Blue People, or the People of the Veil. In contrast to the Islamic countries, with the Tuaregs it is the men who hide their faces (probably due to practical reasons), while the women do not. They trace their lineage on the distaff side and they hold women in very high esteem. The woman's family is more important than the man's family. It is also women who make the most important decisions, including the ones on exclusion from the group. Nevertheless, it is the man who is considered head of the family.[10]

In the Mosuo tribe, in turn, in accordance with a tradition of 1600 years, men live with their mothers and only visit their wives from time to time. The notion of 'wife' is actually rather informal as the Mosuo do not care much for formal bonds. The notions of rape and jealousy are alien to them. The principal occupation of Mosuo men is looking after domesticated animals and slaughtering them. The women are the heads of households, performing the most important tasks, managing the family possessions, and making decisions in business matters. Children bear their mothers' surnames and are raised by them. Couples form according to their own preference, with no external pressure.[11] Women enjoy full sexual freedom. The tribe is often referred to as the 'kingdom of women.'

---

9 A. Moir, D. Jessel, *Brain Sex: The Real Difference between Men & Women*, New York: Carol Publishing Company 1991.

10 A. Rybiński, *Tuaregowie z Sahary* (*The Tuaregs of Sahara*), Warszawa 1999.

11 http://www.bezmapy.pl/przewodniki/swiat/chiny/jezioro-lug-lud-mosu-prowincjajunnan-ciekawemiejsce274.html (accessed on 2 May 2013).

But apart from that, the situation of women has almost always and almost everywhere been worse. In Classical Greece, regardless of their position, women were to look after the house. The husband, selected by the father, could have several mistresses, but a woman who committed marital infidelity could even be banished.[12] Exceptions from this were the hetaerae, who were usually rich, educated, independent women, and enjoyed a special social position.

In Ancient Rome, women were relatively emancipated, educated and had numerous rights, including property rights and the right to participate in social life. Matrons enjoyed a large dose of respect. They could not, however, hold offices and personally argue their cases in courts. They were considered less reliable.

Before the emergence of Islam, women living in the south of the Arabian Peninsula enjoyed a lot of freedom, including sexual freedom. They had premarital and extramarital affairs, and having children born out of wedlock was not considered a dishonour. Polyandry was practiced as well and women could have up to ten husbands.[13]

In Europe of the Late Middle Ages, the social status of men and women was relatively equal. Until the 14th century, there were only a few differences between the education of boys and girls. Education of children was mainly the domain of women. Girls reached formal adulthood at the age of 12. This entitled them to get married. Their independence in the marriage was guaranteed by their dowry. Their position was further strengthened by giving birth to children. Unmarried women and widows were free to make their own decisions, including financial ones, as well as concluding contracts and conducting trade. Only later, after the Aristotelian point of view was adopted, they were gradually pushed into the background. Religion contributed to these divisions as well. Both Christianity and the Islam, and to a certain extent Confucianism, were strengthening the patriarchal relations between the genders, in which women were limited to being good wives and wise mothers.[14]

In the context of this general perception of social roles, it is hard to treat the relations in the first kibbutzim in Israel as more than an interesting experiment. Under the policy of equality, the female characteristics were masked by wearing

---

12 B. Ramian, M. Robaszkiewicz, 'Aktywność filozoficzna kobiet w Grecji okresu klasycznego' (Philosophical Activity of Women in Classical Greece'), *Analiza i Egzystencja*, no. 2, 2005, p. 177.

13 E. Machut-Mendecka, 'Kobieta bez zasłony' (Women without Covers), in D. Chmielowska, B. Grabowska, E. Machut-Mendecka (eds.), *Być kobietą w Oriencie* (*To Be a Woman in the Orient*), Warszawa 2001, p. 19.

14 L. Edwards, *Gender, Politics, and Democracy: Women's Suffrage in China*, Stanford 2008, p. 185.

loose clothes, avoiding makeup, performing men's work. Pregnancy and labour were treated simply as biological phenomena. Children were not divided into sons and daughters and were brought up together. In time, however, these practices were abandoned.

Legal and political basis of gender equality

Discrimination on the grounds of gender is unequal treatment of women and men not justified by objective reasons. It does not only refer to the situations when women are discriminated against by men or vice versa but also when women discriminate against women or men discriminate against men on the grounds of gender.[15]

In international law, the prohibition of discrimination on the grounds of gender is a fairly recent occurrence. On the global scale, the issue is addressed,among others, in the Charter of the United Nations, the Universal Declaration of Human Rights, the International Covenants on Human Rights, conventions of the International Labour Organization, and the UNESCO Convention against Discrimination in Education of 1960. Documents solely dedicated to women include the Convention on the Elimination of All Forms of Discrimination against Women of 1979 and the Optional Protocol to it, the Convention on the Political Rights of Women, and the Convention on the Nationality of Married Women. On the regional scale, the problem is addressed in the forum of the Council of Europe, the European Union and the Organization of American States.

In the political perspective, the international conferences dedicated to women were of special importance to the change in the perception of women's social, legal and political situation. When analysing the documents adopted there, we can see that women were becoming 'mature' enough to take up the challenges posed by civilisational change. While evaluating the debate, we should take into account that the women involved in women's and emancipation movements who participated in these conferences were rather exceptional, but it is a fact that the growing aspirations articulated there, previously considered a feature exhibited only by women of the Western world, spread to other circles as well, resulting in extensive solidarity in the approach and attitude to various issues. This does not mean, however, that all women shared this opinion or even had awareness of it, and this is true of the peripheral, backward countries as well as the societies of highly developed countries.

The first conference was held in Mexico in 1975 and coincided with the celebrations of the International Women's Year. It focused on the promotion of equality

15 J. Tomaszewska, *Dyskryminacja ze względu na płeć i jej przeciwdziałanie* (*Preventing Discrimination on the Grounds of Sex*), Warszawa 2004.

of men and women and on women's contribution to building world peace. The conference in Copenhagen in 1980 expanded the debate to include issues related to women's employment, health and education. A new element, added to the debate in Nairobi, in 1985, were the demands for changes in legislation in order to take into account women's rights to a full and equal participation in all areas of social life.

The fourth conference was held in Beijing on 4–5 September 1995 and had 189 participating countries. It was not only a summary of the accomplishment of demands made earlier but several new demands were made there as well. It was there that The Platform for Action defined and adopted 12 areas which were considered of key importance for combating discrimination of women. It appealed to state governments to, among others: increase women's access to education, improve medical services for women, disseminate information on family planning methods and contraception, prevent social marginalisation of women and undertake actions aimed at elimination of violence against women.

Five years after the meeting in Beijing, in June 2000, the 23rd Special Session of the UN General Assembly was held under the title: 'Women 2000: Gender Equality, Development and Peace for the Twenty-First Century.' The aim of the conference was to assess the progress in the implementation of the Beijing Platform for Action. In the document adopted there, the international community for the first time expressed the need to officially ban honour killings and forced marriage. The participant countries declared that they would undertake more decisive action to combat rape in marriage and violence against women, especially violence on a racial basis.

In 1995, the UNDP allocated funds to the establishment of two new indexes: the Gender-related Development Index (GDI) and the Gender Empowerment Measure (GEM). The reports of the latter are based on three indicators: the percentage of women holding seats in parliaments, the percentage of women in the process of making economic decisions and wage gaps.

Signs of unequal treatment

Today, particular attention is paid to the barriers faced by women in the labour market. This aspect of unequal treatment is the lead topic in all the discussions on the discrimination of women. The reason behind this is the fact that inequality in this field affects the largest share of the population. We could say that it is 'the most popular' and best-publicised.

In professional relations, women are perceived as less creative, worse at decision-making, unable to lead large teams, and inflexible due to their parenting duties. This perception limits their employment and promotion opportunities.

Consequently, they also occupy less prestigious and lower-paid jobs. Thus, we can still observe the anachronistic thinking drawing on the already invalid model in which the husband and father was the sole breadwinner in the family and the only women to work were either single or completely dedicated to their occupation.

Nowadays, the situation is improving virtually every year. Even despite the persisting inequality in wages, the economic share of women in the social and political life is increasing. Studies conducted in the United States by Pew Research Center in Washington in the first half of 2012 show that more than 60 per cent of women consider a well-paid job their priority in life, compared to 58 per cent men. In education, this translates to a higher percentage of women studying at universities than men (44 and 38 per cent, respectively) and better results in learning. At the same time, the fact that they are career-oriented does not preclude them from participating in family life.[16] While we cannot infer from the American example that the phenomenon is universal, it seems to illustrate the observed tendencies quite accurately.

Far less attention is paid to women's political rights. Although in some countries women were granted these rights fairly late (e.g. in Liechtenstein in 1984 and in Kuwait in 2005), and in three (Saudi Arabia,[17] Brunei, United Arab Emirates) they still do not enjoy them, the reason for this is a vicious circle effect as in these states women do not actually show any greater interest in politics. Where there are considerable disproportions in the share of women in the public life, various quotas are introduced in order to lower the differences – interestingly, this is also true of less developed countries. 20 per cent of countries have prescribed female representation in companies, 30 per cent have prescribed female representation in politics.[18] Quotas are also included in the statutes of political parties.

In practice, there is no universal instrument for bringing more women into institutions traditionally reserved for men. It will probably be long before it is no longer determined by the asymmetrical pattern of relations between men and women conditioned by the lack of political will, religion, cultural tradition, (including the conviction held e.g. in China that women bring bad luck in politics), education and spare time balance. Nevertheless, the first women to become prime ministers were those in 1960 in Sri Lanka and in 1966 in India, that is in countries which even now, half a century later, still struggle with gender inequality.

---

16 C. Dougherty, 'Women Set New Goal for Careers and Lives', *The Wall Street Journal*, 19 April 2012.

17 Starting from 2015, they are to participate in local elections and they will also be allowed to become members of the Consultative Assembly, the monarch's advisory body.

18 Global Gender Gap Report 2011, *World Economic Forum*, 1 November 2011 (the index was introduced to the Forum in 2006).

An analysis of both the national and the international law reveals that the initial expectations of the suffragettes were, at least formally, largely fulfilled. According to the report of the World Economic Forum titled Global Gender Gap 2011, within the last six years, 85 per cent of the 135 countries examined have improved their gender equality indexes. The four parameters taken into account were: economic participation and political capabilities, education, health, and survival. These were evaluated compared to the ideal, i.e. 50/50. The countries to score highest in the ranking are, just as the year before, Island, Norway and Finland, while the ones to score the lowest are Yemen, Chad and Pakistan.[19]

Another publication, the UNDP report of 2011,which analyses various parameters of gender equality, places Sweden highest, right before the Netherlands and Denmark (Poland ranked 25th), and Yemen, Chad and Niger ranked the lowest.[20] What is interesting, in the United States (78th place in the ranking), where women constitute 51 per cent of the population, only 16.6 per cent of the Members of Congress are female, which is lower than the global average (19.3 per cent) and less than in countries such as Rwanda, Cambodia, or Costa Rica.[21]

The improved situation of women does not necessarily imply eliminating all cases of discrimination. Nevertheless, they are smaller in scale and do not affect entire populations but rather individuals, who in various cultural and economic circumstances are forced to struggle, often solitarily, for their own dignity.[22] The data collected by the World Bank shows that approximately 4 million women 'disappear' every year in developing countries. Furthermore, women account for 58 per cent of unpaid employees. Between 1980 and 2008, 552 million women were suffering unfree labour, approximately 40 per cent girls were never born due to the fact that boys were preferred, every sixth girl died in early childhood, and every third woman died in economically productive age.[23]

Moreover, problems such as trafficking in women, inequality in marriage and the limited right to education still remain valid, although in a modernised version, and they coincide with new problems, either previously ignored or left to be

---

19 *Ibid.*

20 *UNDP Human Development Report 2011*, Gender Inequality Index and related indicators, Statistical Tables, pp. 139–142.

21 *Women in the United States Congress: 1917–2012, CRS Report*, Report Number: RL 30261, 21 February 2012, Congressional Research Service.

22 Indexes proving an increasing improvement in the social status of women are taken into account by the report of the World Bank: *World Development Report 2012: Gender Equality and Development*.

23 *Ibid.*

solved in the privacy of homes or workplaces. They include issues such as family violence, stalking or mobbing. Generally, we can conclude that individual states and the international community are trying to solve the issues of gender inequality in the public sphere more quickly and more readily than in the private sphere, which is more difficult or even impossible to access.

Contemporary trafficking in women, which is a form of slavery, manifests itself primarily in treating them as goods to be traded in order to be used as workforce, to provide various services or to generate revenue from prostitution or pornography. These activities alone are admissible in many countries subject to certain conditions, usually regulated by internal law. Thus, what we mean here are situations in which the relation is involuntary, where there is physical or mental exploitation, a lack of remuneration, or punishment for disobedience. A ban of such practices is included in the *Convention for the Suppression of the Traffic in Persons and of the Exploitation of the Prostitution of Others*. Although it covers both sexes, in social practice, especially in its second part, it concerns mainly women.[24] The Convention has been signed by 82 countries and is complemented by the *Protocol to Prevent, Suppress and Punish Trafficking in Persons, Especially Women and Children, supplementing the United Nations Convention against Transnational Organised Crime*, adopted on 15 November 2000. In Europe, the issue is regulated by the Council of Europe Convention on Action against Trafficking in Human Beings, which, however, does not single out trafficking in women.[25]

Human trafficking, particularly in women, is difficult to uncover and it is difficult to provide precise statistics for it, even in Europe (due to shame, fear of revenge). However, it concerns not only the relations between the state and the individual but also horizontal relations, in which, according to international law, the state is obliged to prevent and criminalise such practices. They are the most pronounced in Asia, where women are subject to services-based trafficking, not only for housework and work in small workshops but also for prostitution. According to the US Department of State, approximately 3 in a 1000 inhabitants of this region are victims of human trafficking.[26] Such trafficking is generated equally by tradition of getting rid of women in the household and by poverty. In Manila or Bangkok, which foreign tourists tend to perceive as an exotic paradise, where a young woman can be 'bought' as easily as a pack of cigarettes, many girls

---

24 *Convention for the Suppression of the Traffic in Persons and of the Exploitation of the Prostitution of Others* of 2 December 1949, http://www.ohchr.org/EN/ProfessionalInterest/Pages/TrafficInPersons.aspx (accessed on 29 September 2013).

25 Council of Europe Treaty Series, no. 197.

26 *Trafficking in Persons Report 2011*, Department of State, 1 November 2011.

working in the sex industry come from the poorest regions of the country or from the slums of the capital, where it is a common practice that the prettiest daughter goes to work in 'the industry' to earn money for the entire family.

Cultural norms are another frequent barrier to the actual implementation of the equality rights in force. They have to confront the hard rules of patriarchal thinking, according to which women are but parts of the household. However, many countries treat the law they make with reserve because they consider the sex industry and sex tourism an important source of income.

In many Asian countries, female foetuses are more often aborted than male ones, girls are neglected during childhood, receive worse healthcare, are married young, they get kidnapped or even sold. In India, they are primarily subject to 'internal' trafficking. In Burma, more often than in other countries, it is the method of forcing them to marry. In Cambodia, virgins are considered especially valuable and can be sold for as much as 4000 US dollars.[27]

In Africa, trafficking in women is a phenomenon established in the colonial past and continued along the lines of a traditional reduction of people requiring support in the family or the community. Parents give women over to work in richer households, in the country or abroad, where in exchange for services they receive better living conditions, remuneration and access to education.

In Latin America, organised gangs are often involved in trafficking and kidnapping women. The main charge against these countries is that not only do they lack relevant legal regulations, but they also fail at explaining the risks sufficiently and their law enforcement is ineffective, which, in turn, results in low detectability of crime and low conviction rate.

In all these cases, the circumstances conducive to the enslavement of women are worse job opportunities, a weak social position and economic status (feminisation of poverty), urbanisation and migration, and often illiteracy. Sometimes this overlaps with simple human gullibility, the belief in promises of a better future and better opportunities of a wealthy life. On the state's part, it is usually weak political will, limited penalisation of misdeeds, as well as the lack of intensive action aimed at improving legal awareness and the rehabilitation of the victims.

In China, there are some interesting practices in certain provinces, where an old tradition of purchasing wives for relatives who are unable to find them on their own is still cultivated. Between 2009 and 2011, the police freed 3500 kidnapped

---

27 *Ibid.*

Chinese women and 206 foreign women.[28] In Kyrgyzstan, there is a custom of kidnapping women for matrimonial purposes. It is estimated that every year 14–25 thousand women are affected. Kidnapping eliminates the obligation to pay the compulsory fee for a bride. In defiance of the law, this custom is tolerated by the police and the prosecutors. In the worst case, a kidnapper can be sentenced to 3 years of imprisonment, while the penalty for theft would be 11 years.[29] Kidnapping of women is also a problem in Ingushetia.

The tradition of trading young women in some regions of Bulgaria has a cultural context as well. They are 'showed' on the market as if they were exhibits. They are subject to evaluation, and efforts and transactions are made by rich men looking for pretty wives. In exchange, the parents of such 'brides' receive between 7500 and 11,300 US dollars. The actual price depends on the girl's looks. Even despite the formal prohibition of such practices, the Bulgarian authorities do not intervene because the women consent to this and treat this as a kind of a fashion and beauty show where they make their best to beat the 'competition.' None of them report it as a crime because all of them are trying to find wealthy husbands.

In Europe, the risk of becoming involved in a slave relationship is related to the present wave of migration, in which there is a large share of women looking for work and expecting fair salaries (there is even talk of feminisation of migration). With their usual poor knowledge of the host country's language and their low professional qualifications, they are often employed to provide simple household services, where they are often exposed to unethical or brutal actions of their employers.

Since 2000, the US Department of State has been producing annual reports on trafficking in persons.[30] The 2010 report shows that all over the world, 12.3 million people were subject to trafficking in order to be used for unfree labour or forced prostitution.[31] Most countries were the supplier, the transit country and the destination at the same time. The countries which, according to the report, are the least diligent at observing the standards set by international law include: Burma, the Democratic Republic of the Congo, Cuba, the Dominican Republic, Equatorial

28 'Handel kobietami w Chinach' (Trafficking Women in China), 3 November 2011, http://wiadomosci.radiozet.pl/Swiat/Wiadomosci/Handel-kobietami-w-Chinach (accessed on 3 November 2012).

29 'Kirgiska branka' (Kyrgyz Captive), *Polityka*, no. 31, 1 August 2012.

30 Trafficking in persons should be understood as a term for all the actions consisting of recruiting, hiding, transporting, delivering, and purchasing people for unfree labour or commercial sexual abuse, using force, deception and coercion (see: *Trafficking in Persons Report 2012*, Department of State, 19 June 2012.

31 *Trafficking in Persons Report 2010*, Department of State, 14 June 2010.

Guinea, Eritrea, Iran, North Korea, Kuwait, Mauretania, Papua New Guinea, Sudan, Saudi Arabia, and Zimbabwe.[32] In 2012, the order changed slightly to: Burma, Libya, the Democratic Republic of the Congo, South Sudan, Somalia, Sudan, and Yemen.[33]

In April 2004, by resolution no. 2004/110, the Commission on Human Rights established the function of the Special Rapporteur on the Human Rights Aspects of the Victims of Trafficking in Persons, Especially Women and Children. The mandate taken over by the Human Rights Council includes forced marriage, unfree labour (including work in households, agriculture, manufacturing, and mining), prostitution and sexual abuse.

Violence against women

Although women are not the only victims of violence, according to global data they constitute a vast majority of 95 per cent of this group. In the opinion of the WHO, approx. 20 per cent of women suffer violence. The studies conducted by the Organization show that from 15 per cent women in Japan to 71 per cent women in Ethiopia and Peru experience physical and/or sexual violence from a close partner on at least one stage in their lives.[34]

There is no universal definition of violence against women as different cultural groups perceive the phenomenon in different ways. Some consider brutal treatment of women as pathological, while others consider it a normal behaviour or even a time-honoured custom. Article One of the UN Declaration on the Elimination of Violence Against Women of 1993 defines violence against women as 'any act of gender-based violence that results in, or is likely to result in, physical, sexual or psychological harm or suffering to women, including threats of such acts, coercion or arbitrary deprivation of liberty, whether occurring in public or in private life.'[35] In Lithuania, the National Strategy on Elimination of Violence Against Women, adopted in 2006, extends this list to include economic violence, which is the least visible to the outside world and which manifests itself in, for instance, forbidding women to pursue a career, controlling the family budget and refusing to support children.[36]

---

32 *Ibid.*

33 *Trafficking in Persons Report 2012…*

34 *Violence against Women*, WHO, Fact sheet 239, September 2011.

35 *Declaration on the Elimination of Violence against Women*, Resolution adopted by the UN General Assembly 48/104, 20 December 1993, A/RES/48/104.

36 *Domestic Violence against Women in Lithuania*, Kretinga Women Information and Training Centre, 2010, p. 4.

Violence against women is a common occurrence, which has 'always' been there in all parts of the world, all cultures and all societies. But today, it most often occurs in households where women have lower income than men and where they are economically dependent on their partners. It is usually justified by custom, culture, tradition, and religion. However, the phenomenon evokes an ever greater opposition, with both the victims and the entire international society. This opposition is most evident in the countries of the West, where violence or enslavement caused by the man's social, political or economic position is ever more frequently and strongly condemned. Silvio Berlusconi's infamous 'bunga bunga' sex parties, or the similar excesses of Dominique Strauss-Kahn or the ones of the MPs from the Polish 'Samoobrona' party evoke disgust, to say the least.

In Islam, certain aspects of such violence are considered a cultural norm, a time-honoured custom, which women should accept with humility, especially when they 'deserve' it due to their behaviour. However, in most interpretations of the *Quran*, this is not the religious norm.[37]

In India, 1/3 of women aged 15–49 have experienced violence. Only 1/4 of them sought any help, while the majority have not informed anyone about their ordeal. 51 per cent of men believe that women should accept violence when it is justified. Interestingly, this view is shared by a stunning 54 per cent of women.[38] The American psychologist Martin Seligman calls this learned helplessness, which explains depression.[39]

On 25 February 2008, the Secretary-General of the UN announced the launching of the campaign 'UNiTE To End Violence Against Women.' It is to last until 2015, so that its end coincides with the date of achieving the Millennium Development Goals. In the western hemisphere, the issue is regulated by the Inter-American Convention on the Prevention, Punishment and Eradication of Violence against Women,[40] adopted in 1994.

In many countries, even the economically underdeveloped and politically unstable ones, the law provides equal rights to men and women but does not equip women with appropriate implementation instruments to combat the degrading

---

37 P. K. Taylor, 'Domestic violence and Islam', *The Washington Post*, 27 February 2009. For interesting statistics on violence against women in Turkey, which has well-developed modern laws meant to prevent it, see: N. Kelek, *Bittersüsse Heimat. Bericht aus dem Inneren der Türkei*, Köln: Kiepenheuer & Witsch 2008.

38 *Gender Fact File – India*, Report 2009, South Asia regional campaign, http://wecanendvaw.org/gender-fact-file/india (accessed on 2 May 2013).

39 M. Seligman, *Helplessness: On Depression, Development and Death*, New York 1991.

40 3 IHRR 232 (1996).

customs. For some of them, taking any radical steps towards change would be too risky in relation to their own interests and not worth an open confrontation with the society. They seem powerless in the face of such practices, common in many cultures, such as: fattening women, female genital mutilation, forced early marriage, honour killing, and virginity tests.[41] Their desire to escape such threats by leaving the cultural environment often ends in the so-called honour-revenge, which takes the form of acid throwing,[42] face disfiguring or even honour killing.

In Chechnya, the situation of women in this respect is very complex. While the international agreements signed by Russia are in force there, there are still many local laws and customs which are at variance with these agreements and the policy of the current authorities of the republic is deeply set in Islam and clearly regressive compared to the previous system. President Ramzan Kadyrov strives after a 'spiritual revival' of the republic. He supports treating women as the husband's property and limiting their role to giving birth to children and considers killings motivated by the women's dissolute behaviour as justified. The security forces confiscate mobile phones from women, to prevent illegal contacts with men. They also apply the practice of paintball-marking women who move about public places without headscarves. The authorities use local television and the press to promote these norms of behaviour.[43]

In Europe, the idea of the Convention on preventing and combating violence against women and domestic violence (the Istanbul Convention)[44] emerged during the Warsaw Summit of the Council of Europe held on 16 and 17 May 2005. The draft Convention was adopted by the Committee of Ministers on 6 April 2011. The Convention was presented for signing on 7 May 2011 at the Istanbul Summit. Article 3 thereof defines gender-based violence against women as 'violence that is directed against a woman because she is a woman or that affects

---

41 The women undergoing hymen reconstruction surgery at the European Institute for Esthetic and Plastic Surgery – Institut Européen de Chirurgie Esthétique et Plastique, or IECEP, most often come from Tunisia, Lebanon, or Senegal (cf. *Rzeczpospolita*, 26 July 2012).

42 In 2005, 267 women in Bangladesh became victims of acid attacks; *Gender Fact File – Bangladesh*, Report 2009, South Asia regional campaign, http://wecanendvaw.org/genderfactfile/bangladesh (accessed on 2 May 2013).

43 Z. Magomadova, 'Unprotected', *Open Democracy*, 19 June 2012, http://www.opendemocracy.net/author/zalina-magomadova (accessed on 2 May 2013).

44 *Council of Europe Convention on preventing and combating violence against women and domestic violence*, Council of Europe, CM(2011) 49 final, 7 April 2011, https://wcd.coe.int/ViewDoc.jsp?id=1772191, http://www.conventions.coe.int/Treaty/EN/Treaties/Html/210.htm (accessed on 2 October 2013).

women disproportionately' and domestic violence as 'all acts of physical, sexual, psychological or economic violence that occur within the family or domestic unit or between former or current spouses or partners', including 'coercion or arbitrary deprivation of liberty, whether occurring in public or in private life.' The new element here is the fact that among other forms of violence, the Convention includes stalking (Article 34), female genital mutilation (Article 38), forced abortion and forced sterilisation (Article 39), sexual harassment (Article 40), and among the protective measures it includes emergency barring orders (Article 52).

The Convention defines gender as 'the socially constructed roles, behaviours, activities and attributes that a given society considers appropriate for women and men' and the category of woman 'includes girls under the age of 18.' The Convention also states that the implementation of its provisions is to be 'secured without discrimination on any ground', including religious and political views, social origin, sexual orientation, gender identity and other criteria. (Article 4, Point 3).

Furthermore, the convention obliges the parties to ensure that violence, including domestic violence, is punishable (Articles 45, 46). Depending on the degree of social harmfulness of the various offences, the sanctions should be either criminal or civil (e.g. compensation from the perpetrator, Article 30). In some cases, it is left to the states to select the regulation method most adequate for the given matter.

The Convention places several obligations on the signatories, including providing women with access to counselling, housing, healthcare, social services, education, trainings, employment assistance, as well as financial support and assistance to victims of rape and sexual violence and to children witnessing violence. The states are also to undertake actions 'to promote changes in the social and cultural patterns of behaviour of women and men with a view to eradicating prejudices, customs, traditions and all other practices which are based on the idea of the inferiority of women or on stereotyped roles for women and men' (Article 12, Point 1), including in the field of education (Article 14). Furthermore, they are to ensure that culture, custom, religion, tradition, or misunderstood 'honour' are not used as justification of violence. Finally, they are to 'take the necessary legislative or other measures to ensure that marriages concluded under force may be voidable, annulled or dissolved without undue financial or administrative burden placed on the victim' (Article 32).

Some of the discrimination practices are carried by the immigrants coming to Europe, forcing European countries to face very serious dilemmas. On the one hand, political correctness requires a large dose of tolerance regarding the preservation of cultural identity of separate ethnical groups and the respect for human rights prevents any deeper interference with family issues where home is treated as a sanctuary, but on the other hand, they cannot openly ignore reports of people breaking the law to satisfy time-honoured tradition. For example, in March 2012, results of a study conducted among Muslim immigrants already educated in British schools and concerning domestic violence was published in the United Kingdom. More than 2/3 of the respondents believed that all Muslim communities should live in accordance with the Islamic principle of 'izzat' (honour), and approx. 18 percent supported violence against women when they commit or want to commit a deed which would bring shame to them or their family. Women are punished for disobeying fathers and husbands, refusing to marry the man chosen by the family, wanting to file for divorce, and many other things.[45]

In Poland, a culture-based opinion on the Convention on preventing and combating violence against women was expressed publically by the Minister of Justice Jarosław Gowin. The Minister referred to Christian axiology, in which genders have clearly assigned tasks, and believed the Convention to be a manifestation of feminist ideology and its content radical and harmful to the traditional family model.[46] In other words, sharing the views of the Church, he believed that women should know their place and that suffering ennobles. Poland's signing of the Convention (with two reservations) on 18 December 2012 met with strong opposition of the Polish Episcopal Conference. The bishops were particularly alarmed by the obligation of the parties to the Convention to educate and promote 'non-stereotyped gender roles' and, as they claimed, joining the just principle of preventing violence with an attempted dangerous interference with the educational system and values upheld by millions of parents in Poland.[47] The opposition parties labelled the Convention a Trojan horse of feminist organisations.[48]

---

45 'Anglia: Co piąty młody muzułmanin uznaje przemoc wobec kobiet' (Every Fifth Muslim Accepts Violence against Women), Euroislam.pl, 11 April 2012, http://www.euroislam.pl/index.php/2012/04/anglia-co-piaty-mlody-muzulmanin-uznajeprzemoc-wobec-kobiet/ (accessed on 2 May 2013).

46 'Gowin: krytycznie oceniam konwencje RE o przemocy wobec kobiet' (Mr Gowin: I Am Critical Towards the Convention on Violence against Women), *Gazeta Wyborcza*, 12 April 2012.

47 'Episkopat Polski: konwencja wskazuje, że źródłem przemocy są religia, tradycja i kultura' (The Polish Episcopate: The Convention Implies that Religion, Tradition and Culture Are at the Source of Violence), Polish Press Agency, 18 December 2012, http://wiadomosci.wp.pl/kat,8311,title,Episkopat-Polski-konwencja-wskazujeze-zrodlem-przemocy-sa-religia-tradycja-i-kultura,wid,15189272,wiadomosc.html (accessed on 2 May 2013).

48 '"To koń trojański feministek." PIS i SP przeciwne konwencji w sprawie przemocy wobec kobiet' (The Convention is the Trojan Horse of the Feminists. PIS and SP Parties Oppose the Convention on Violence against Women), *Polska*, 18 December 2012.

The attitude of the Polish authorities to this issue is not at all irrelevant because police statistics show that in 2012 there were 76 993 victims of domestic violence, including 50 241 women, 7580 men, and 19 172 minors. This data represents only the cases in which the police and the judiciary intervened, while a large number of cases of domestic violence is never revealed, since the police is either not informed of them or chooses not to launch an inquiry.[49]

State practice. Cultural and religious barriers

Relatively few countries reject the general principles of equal treatment of both genders. In April 2012, the Convention to Eliminate All Forms of Discrimination Against Women[50] was adopted by 187 states, which proves that most countries accept these principles although they often do that with some reservations based on their national traditions, culture or religion.

These reservations concern diverse issues. Many Islamic countries reserved the right to refrain from applying these articles of the Convention which are at variance with the sharia. Algeria's reservation, for instance, conditioned the application of the Convention's individual articles on them not being at variance with the Algerian family code, e.g. regarding the issue of equal rights of both genders during marriage and after its dissolution. Bahrain declared it would apply the Convention only where it is consistent with the sharia (this concerns especially Article 16). Therefore, it does not apply the provisions concerning equal rights regarding citizenship of the children and the choice of place of stay or residence. Kuwait rejected Article 16(f) (concerning guardianship, wardship, trusteeship and adoption of children) as at variance with the sharia. The Maldives declared they would not apply the Convention to all matters related to marriage and family relations.

An interesting reservation was made by Malta, which reserved the right to prohibit or restrict women's employment in such fields or types of work that could involve a threat to their health and safety. New Zealand, in turn, does not apply these articles of the Convention which are inconsistent with the customs practiced on the Cook Islands. Niger reserved the right to refrain from complying with the Convention in the field of social and cultural models of male and

49 www.statystyka.policja.pl/st/wybrane-statystyki (accessed on 2 May 2013). According to the data of the World Bank, in Poland the 3 per cent ratio of violence against women translates to 1465 cases of such violence per day (see: *World Development Report 2012: Gender Equality and Development*).

50 http://www.ohchr.org/EN/ProfessionalInterest/Pages/CEDAW.aspx (accessed on 2 October 2013).

female behaviour, as well as regarding the choice of the place of residence only by unmarried women. Lesotho reserved the right to exclude women from succession to the throne and state leadership, and even Spain reserved the right to observe different regulations concerning the succession to the throne.

India's concerns were of a yet different nature. The country voiced an objection to Article 5(a) ('to modify the social and cultural patterns of conduct of men and women, with a view to achieving the elimination of prejudices and customary and all other practices which are based on the idea of the inferiority or the superiority of either of the sexes or on stereotyped roles for men and women') as contrary to the Hindi principle of non-interference with the private affairs of communities without their consent or initiative, as well as regarding Article 16.2, which concerns compulsory registration of marriages in an official registry, due to the size of India's territory, multitude of customs, religions and literacy level.

In India, culture-based discrimination is particularly pronounced and visible at the family level, community level and even state level. Families maintain hierarchical relations manifested in unequal division of labour and money. Communities accept male control of female sexuality, mobility and employment. The state fails to take any radical remedial measures, largely consents to the traditional practices and acknowledges its own ineffectiveness. It can do virtually nothing to limit the time-honoured custom of giving women a suitable dowry. A woman who has no such dowry is eliminated from the ranks of desirable potential life partners, which is a substantial economic burden for the family but also saves the woman from lifelong humiliation. Therefore, poor families consider the prospect of a girl being born a threat to their very existence and try to eliminate girls already at the prenatal stage. The act of 20 September 1994 which forbids the use of USG tests to inform pregnant women of the child's sex is commonly ignored and it is not the woman but her family who decides whether the pregnancy should be continued. On the other hand, abortion performed without the husband's approval is grounds for a divorce. Another common practice is passive female infanticide, resulting from neglect, undernourishment, and belated medical assistance. This is referred to as death for social reasons.[51]

One clear manifestation of inequality and discrimination is the different position of women and men in terms of the law and the judiciary. In the sharia, a woman's voice in court has half the value of that of a man's. There are also differences in inheritance law. In Egypt, for instance, the criminal code states that if a woman is beaten by her husband in good faith, proceedings are not instituted

51 S. Saravanan, *Violence Against Women in India. A Literature Review*, New Delhi 2000.

against him. A particularly absurd procedure concerns the establishing of guilt of men and women accused of adultery. For men, the testimony of four witnesses is needed, while for women, a pregnancy is considered a sufficient proof. In Saudi Arabia, a woman who has served her prison sentence can leave the jail only when a male guardian comes to collect her.

In the everyday sphere, discrimination of women is manifested in the form of mutilation, especially common in South and Central Africa. In May 2012, after the phenomenon was fought for several years by the previous Egyptian authorities, the Muslim Brotherhood offered women surgery for a small fee under social benefits.

Of course, in various Islamic countries the practice is different. In Morocco, due to the efforts of king Mohammed VI, in 2004 the parliament passed reforms which introduced several requirements for polygamy and making it effectively impossible; it raised the age when women can get married to 18, gave responsibility for the family to both spouses, established that a divorce has to be conducted by the court and is possible only without prejudice to all the rights of the spouse (before that, the man received all the rights to the children and could deprive the mother of any opportunity to see them). Men and women received equal rights in marriage and wives were no longer obliged to obey their husbands. In 2006, the first women were promoted to spiritual leaders, tasked with interpreting and promoting the Quran. Until then, no Muslim country allowed women to perform that function.

Discrimination in the access to education is clearly culturally determined. Although indexes describing the level of education are improving everywhere in the world, primarily due to the efforts of UNESCO and UNICEF, the societies of many less developed countries believe that educating girls is essentially pointless and if people have to choose whom to send to school, they usually choose boys over girls. This is, however, not only true of economically weak countries. In rich Saudi Arabia, where the political system ensures free education to all citizens and where there are seven universities, only a small percentage of women have any education at all and less than 1 per cent are university graduates.

Different treatment of women does not only come down to discrimination but also to restrictions and limitations, especially in the Islamic countries. Women usually treat them as natural but sometimes consider them a burden. Such restrictions include the requirement to dress 'appropriately', rigorously enforced in, for example, Iran, where since May 2012 the police are obliged to pursue and immediately arrest the so-called 'street models.' In Saudi Arabia, in turn, wearing unconventional clothing (mini, shorts) is an offence punishable by flogging.

In the European Union, states are required to either directly apply or implement anti-discrimination norms. However, gender perspective is discussed with increasing frequency not as a state expenditure but rather as an investment in the future which could yield a return in the form of economic growth (Gender Key Message). But even in Europe, although on a much smaller scale than elsewhere, there are differences resulting from the histories of individual states, dominance of a different branch of Christianity and the state's ties with the church.

Prospects

The terms 'gender', 'gender policy', 'gender identity' emerged in the context of combating stereotypes and discrimination of women in the social, economic and political life. This took place in the circumstances where the two sexes – female and male – were still clearly defined. The sexual revolution of the 1960s essentially shattered this order. Since then, manifesting one's sexuality has been treated as the right and choice of every human being.

The problems emerging in relation to this will surely continue growing with women's increasing self-confidence and emancipation, as well as with the ever more commonly observed non-standard attitudes to gender, homosexuals, transsexuals (people psychically non-accepting of the gender attributed to them at birth), and the so-called third sex (intersexuality, hermaphroditism[52]). In Western culture, the latter is usually corrected right after birth when the carers and physicians arbitrarily select the physical attributes of the child, sometimes contrary to the child's psychic and later gender self-identity. However, already Plato remarked that at first, there had been three sexes in humans, apart from the male and the female; there had also supposedly been a third sex which was a kind of amalgamation of the other two but now it is no more and only its name remains.[53]

Even though statistically, more children are born with an unspecified gender than children with the Down syndrome, in European culture they are nonetheless qualified as one of the traditional sexes and considered a taboo. In light of the WHO's International Statistical Classification of Diseases and Related Health

---

52 The name comes from a bisexual god in Greek mythology, a child of Hermes and Aphrodite.

53 'Trzecia płeć, czyli czym jest hermafrodytyzm' (The Third Sex – Explaining Hermaphroditism), *Zdrowie i Uroda*, 7 February 2011, http://urodaizdrowie.pl/trzecia-plec-czyli-czym-jest-hermafrodytyzm (accessed on 2 May 2013).

Problems (ICD-10), transgenderism is considered a mental disorder and a pathology that requires treatment.[54]

In other cultures, however, transgenderism is fully accepted. In the cultures of the South-East, including the Indian subcontinent, the so-called hijras are people born as biological men who do not identify themselves socially and psychically with this gender and the male roles in the society. Their number is estimated at approx. 5 million. Tradition has it that they have extraordinary powers of healing, as well as bringing wealth and prosperity. Therefore, even though hijras usually live at the edge of the society, they are commonly invited to weddings and after the birth of a child. Since 2000, they have been represented in the authorities, since 2005 the third sex has been registered in passports, and since 2011 it has been taken into account in the general census. Since autumn 2011, as part of the campaign to combat gender discrimination, in Australian passport applications people have the opportunity to mark their gender as 'indeterminate' (X). In January 2013, the category of the third sex was introduced into the legislation of Nepal. Faced with overt discrimination (such as refusal to accept a person to a school or hospital), in December 2009 the third sex has also been acknowledged by the Supreme Court of Pakistan. Furthermore, the Thai culture has a time-honoured place for the so-called ladyboys (kathoey). In the history of ancient Siam there were no strictly defined social roles ascribed to the sexes. Women and men exchanged duties freely and there was also the conviction, originating with Buddhism, that there are three sexes. In the future incarnations, a human being could be any of them.

In the opinion of Zbigniew Lew-Starowicz and Agnieszka Fijałkowska-Grabowiecka, until recently such people were incorrectly labelled as homosexuals, transvestites or transsexuals (gynemimesis and andromimesis),[55] while in fact they constitute an entirely different category of sexually non-heteronormative people. In a resolution of September 2011, the European Parliament addressed the WHO asking it to cease treating transgender people as mentally ill.[56] The policy of equality, tolerance and non-discrimination will surely remain the subject of political discourse, which will be affected by the results of psychological studies more and

---

54 WHO Geneva, *The ICD-10 Classification of Mental and Behavioural Disorders*, item F 64; in February 2010, as the first country in the world, France removed transgenderism from the list of mental disorders.

55 Z. Lew-Starowicz, A. Fijałkowska-Grabowiecka, *Seks kontrowersyjny* (*Controversial Sex*), Warszawa 2004. The authors cite the example of the Cheyenne people, who can freely change their gender identity and keep enjoying respect of the community.

56 Homosexuality was on the ICD list until 1990.

more frequently pointing to the existence of psychic androgyny of people able to adopt non-traditional social and cultural roles.[57]

Tadeusz Jasudowicz, who was been analysing the case law of the European Court of Human Rights related to complaints made by homosexual and transsexual people, points out the change in the approach to the problem of gender. He quotes justifications of rulings, in which there have been considerable changes since the adoption of the Convention for the Protection of Human Rights and Fundamental Freedoms. He notes that the Convention is a living document, which has to take into account the progress in science and medicine and adapt to the modern social circumstances.[58]

The analysis of the gender policy of states or – more broadly – cultures does not really yield any clear conclusions. While there are visible changes in all of them, even if not on the same scale, towards strengthening human dignity, the question whether dignity is an objective value remains open, since the interpretation of dignity is strongly culture-dependent. Sometimes, women's dignity is at variance with the dignity of men or a group and the government's compensating actions hit an insurmountable barrier or fall on a completely barren ground. It is so deeply rooted in the local tradition that even the threat of sanctions cannot change it, while any more radical actions involve the risk of causing a disintegration of social groups. The permanence of cultural differences remains so fundamental that, most probably, international standards will remain just an idea – as valuable as it is – for a long time to come.

The original version of this text was published in the academic journal "Społeczeństwo i Polityka", no. 4, 2012.

57 S. L. Bem, 'Psychological androgyny and sexual identity', in P. G. Zimbardo, F. L. Ruch (eds.), *Psychology and Life*, Glenville: Scott Foresman 1977.

58 T. Jasudowicz, 'Poskromienie złośnicy – Europejski Trybunał Praw Człowieka wobec zmiany okoliczności' (The Taming of the Shrew – the European Court of Human Rights in the Changing Circumstances), in C. Mik, K. Całka (eds.), *Między wykładnią a tworzeniem prawa* (*Between Interpreting and Making Law*), Toruń 2011, pp. 56, 58.

Janusz Symonides

Role and Importance of Cultural Rights in the Protection of Minorities and Indigenous Peoples

Key words: protection, cultural rights, cultural identity and diversity, vulnerable groups, United Nations and UNESCO

Abstract: The article presents the role of cultural rights as formulated by universal and regional instruments in the protection of vulnerable groups. The implementation of cultural rights of minorities and indigenous peoples is not a source of conflicts but rather an important factor for peace and stability. Without their recognition, democratic society cannot function properly.

Introduction

In the 21st century, despite the progress that can be observed in many areas, humanity is still facing conflicts, pathologies, the use of violence and military force. Extreme nationalism, xenophobia, racism, and religious fundamentalism cause tensions and conflicts on the local, national and regional level. Violence fuelled by hate propaganda and aimed at 'the others', 'the alien', 'the different' is becoming a serious threat to national and international security. At its core often lies the violation of cultural rights, both individual and collective. Refusal to accept the identity of other groups, especially minorities, indigenous peoples or nations with no representation and no country of their own, who are different from the majority, denying them the right to use their own language, as it is the case with the Kurds, for example, as well as attacks on the followers of different religions are very common in Africa, in the Middle East and in Asia. Denial of the right to cultural autonomy, to own cultural institutions, questioning the right to cultural self-determination is a frequent problem in many regions of the world. Even terrorism assumes a cultural aspect, when attacks are aimed against schools or against places of worship.

Why is the observance of the cultural rights of vulnerable groups, especially minorities and indigenous peoples so crucial? The reason is that it is the prerequisite for their survival and existence and for the preservation of their cultural identity. The fact that their cultural rights are questioned is a source of tensions and conflicts, as has become especially clear in the late 20th and early 21st century.

In the period when the United Nations were being established and when the United Nations Charter was being drafted, the significance of cultural rights, especially in the collective aspect, was underappreciated and disregarded. In the Universal Declaration of Human Rights, cultural rights are only mentioned as individual rights. Why were the rights of minorities forgotten, even though they had been considered by the League of Nations earlier?

The factors which contributed to this were many. The adoption of a liberal, individualist concept of human rights justified the thesis that the effective observance of individual rights and freedoms and elimination of all forms of discrimination against individuals will naturally lead to respect of the rights of minorities and indigenous peoples. In accordance with this thesis there is, therefore, no need to deal with the rights of vulnerable groups (in particular, the risk of discrimination) such as women, children, migrants, foreigners, or disabled persons. In the case of minorities, the opposition to acknowledging their rights was additionally a result of some states' fear that giving them cultural rights and especially recognising their cultural autonomy could lead to secession, thus becoming a serious threat to the territorial integrity and the political independence of these states.

In the period of Cold War, the notion of collective rights became the subject of ideological disputes between the East and the West. Democratic countries put an understandable emphasis on political rights but as a result, the importance of the entire category of economic, social and cultural rights was questioned. The East highlighted this category as extremely important, however, in the West, the concept of collective rights was seen as a threat to the rights of individuals, a tendency to limit their freedoms to promote the group or collective of which they are a part of.

Another important factor in the context of the discussion and a controversy concerning cultural rights is also the fact that this category of human rights refers to the notion of 'culture', which has for years been the subject of disputes regarding whether this term is to be understood and interpreted narrowly or broadly.[1] The solution to this issue has had considerable impact on the catalogue of cultural

---

1 For more on this subject see: J. Symonides, 'Prawa kulturalne – niedoceniana kategoria praw człowieka' (Cultural Rights – An Underestimated Category of Human Rights), in E. Mikos-Skuza, K. Myszona-Kostrzewa, J. Poczobut (eds.), *Prawo międzynarodowe – teraźniejszość, perspektywy, dylematy. Księga jubileuszowa Profesora Zdzisława Galickiego* (*International Law – the Present, Perspectives, Dilemmas. Liber amicorum Professor Zdzisław Galicki*), Warszawa: Lex, 2013, pp. 265–291; J. Symonides, 'The Implemetation of Cultural Rights by the International Community', *International Communication Gazette*, vol. 60, 1998, pp. 7–25.

rights. The broader understanding of cultural rights means that they also cover the right to education, participation in scientific progress and access information, as well as the right to gain benefits from them. The dispute between the narrow and the broad understanding of culture was decided in favour of adopting the broader definition. As the UNESCO Universal Declaration on Cultural Diversity of 2 November 2001 explains, 'culture [...] encompasses, in addition to art and literature, lifestyles, ways of living together, value systems, traditions and beliefs.[2]'

The end of the Cold War, the fall of communism and the resulting disappearance of the ideological disputes between the East and the West opened the way for a change in the approach to cultural rights, especially regarding their collective aspect. This new approach to cultural rights became apparent in the 1990s. At that time, their role in economic and human development has already been recognised, in particular by the 1995 World Summit for Social Development in Copenhagen, which deemed it the necessary condition for the development of the individual. It was established that without respecting the right to education, the right to participation in cultural life, without artistic and scientific freedom, development was not possible. Even earlier, the UN General Assembly had proclaimed 1988–1997 the World Decade for Cultural Development. Among the goals of the decade, three were directly related to the implementation of cultural rights: affirming and enriching cultural identities, broadening participation in culture and promoting international cultural co-operation.[3]

In 1992, in cooperation with the UN General Assembly, UNESCO established the World Commission on Culture and Development.[4] The Commission dedicated much of its attention to cultural rights. In a report published in 1995, among ten recommendations concerning cultural cooperation, the seventh was 'Protecting cultural rights as human rights'.[5] The notion of cultural rights, especially the right to participate in the cultural life, was also included in the works and action

---

2 This definition is in line with the conclusions of the World Conference on Cultural Policies (MONDIACULT, Mexico City, 1982), of the World Commission on Culture and Development (Our Creative Diversity, 1995), and of the Intergovernmental Conference on Cultural Policies for Development (Stockholm, 1998).

3 Out of 1200 programmes executed by 166 states and 23 international governmental organisations and 66 non-governmental organisations, most concerned various aspects of the implementation of cultural rights.

4 The Commission was established under Resolution 3.4 adopted in 1991 at the 26th Session of the General Assembly.

5 Report of the World Commission on Culture and Development, *Our Creative Diversity*, UNESCO 1996, pp. 281–283.

plan adopted by the international conference dedicated to cultural policies for development, held in Stockholm in 1998. The cultural rights of minorities were introduced to the UNESCO programme earlier in 1992.[6] Two years later, the UNESCO Executive Board was discussing protection and promotion of cultural rights of persons belonging to national minorities. There was considerable progress in the development and adoption of international instruments concerning cultural rights of persons belonging to minorities. In 1992, the UN General Assembly adopted a declaration concerning their rights and a number of instruments were adopted by European organisations, such as OSCE and the Council of Europe. A review of the international instruments devoted to cultural rights adopted in the second half of the 20th century and the first decade of the 21st century confirms the thesis that international community, the UN system and regional organisations have been paying growing attention to cultural rights – both individual and collective.

Cultural rights of persons belonging to minorities

The origins of international regulations concerning the protection of minorities lie in the 16th century. In 1555, the Augsburg Settlement established the protection of religious minorities for the first time. The Peace of Westphalia of 1648 as well as the Polish–Russian agreements of 1767 and 1775 guaranteed the rights of the dissidents, while the Treaty of Vienna of 1815 not only guaranteed the freedom of belief of religious minorities but also gave them certain civil rights. Relatively far-reaching commitments concerning the protection and equality of all citizens were also imposed on Turkey and the Balkan countries by the Treaty of Berlin of 1878.

The struggle of national minorities aiming at establishing independence in Central and Eastern Europe was an important factor during World War I. The treaties concluded after the war between the victorious and allied countries of Eastern Europe and the Balkans provided for the protection of educational, racial, linguistic and religious minorities in these states. The League of Nations was required to supervise the performance of these obligations and every breach was to be acted upon by the Organisation. Countries could report breaches of the treaty to the Council of the League of Nations, and in many cases the notifications were forwarded to the Permanent Court of International Justice. Furthermore, private individuals also had the right to file petitions. The new system was not equal and the obligations were only imposed on the newly established and defeated countries.

---

6 UNESCO, Approved Programme and Budget for 1992 – 1993, Paris, 1992, p. 176.

In 1947, United Nations Secretariat announced that the minority system of the League of Nations had ceased to exist in favour of a new, universal and individualist concept of human rights.

The UN Charter does not mention minorities. This can be explained by both the complex experience of Europe during World War II and the fact that the countries which were the destination of migration from Africa wanted to assimilate foreigners instead of protecting their rights. The Economic and Social Council authorised the International Law Commission to issue recommendations concerning this issue and approved the establishment of the Sub-Commission on Prevention of Discrimination and Protection of Minorities in 1947.

The notion of protecting persons belonging to minorities was included in the provisions of the International Covenant on Civil and Political Rights. Article 27 of the Covenant states that: 'In those States in which ethnic, religious or linguistic minorities exist, persons belonging to such minorities shall not be denied the right, in community with the other members of their group, to enjoy their own culture, to profess and practise their own religion, or to use their own language.'[7] Similarly, the UNESCO Convention against Discrimination in Education takes into account the rights of persons belonging to minorities: 'It is essential to recognise the right of members of national minorities to carry on their own educational activities, including the maintenance of schools and, depending on the educational policy of each State, the use or the teaching of their own language.'(Article 5.1c).[8]

Among UNESCO declarations, there are two that are particularly important for the recognition of the rights of minorities. These are: the Declaration on Race and Racial Prejudice of 1978, which states that 'all individuals and groups have the right to be different, to consider themselves as different and to be regarded as such' (Article 1.2), and the Declaration of the Principles of International Cultural Co-operation, stating that 'each culture has a dignity and value which must be respected and preserved', and that 'every people has the right and the duty to develop its culture' (Article 1.1 and 1.2).

On 18 December 1992, by Resolution 47/135 the United Nations General Assembly adopted the Declaration on the Rights of Persons Belonging to National or

---

7 International Covenant on Civil and Political Rights (ICCPR). Adopted and opened for signature, ratification and accession by General Assembly resolution 2200A (XXI) of 16 December 1966, entry into force 23 March 1976, UN Treaty Collection, https://treaties.un.org/Pages/ViewDetails.aspx?src=TREATY&mtdsg_no=IV-4&chapter=4&lang=en.

8 Cf.: J. Symonides, V. Volodin, *UNESCO and Human Rights, Standard-Setting Instruments, Major Meetings, Publications*, Paris: UNESCO, 1999, p. 48.

Ethnic, Religious and Linguistic Minorities.[9] Thus the work initiated in 1978 with the establishment of a working group by the UN Commission on Human Rights culminated in a success. The Declaration formulates the states' responsibility to protect the existence and identity of minorities in their territory. Among the rights of persons belonging to minorities the document lists the following: to enjoy their own culture, to profess and practice their own religion, to use their own language, to participate effectively in cultural, religious, social, economic and public life, to participate effectively in decisions concerning the minority to which they belong, to establish and maintain their own associations, to establish and maintain, without any discrimination, free and peaceful contacts with other members of their group and with persons belonging to other minorities as well as contacts across frontiers with citizens of other States to whom they are related by national or ethnic, religious or linguistic ties (Article 2). In order to avoid misinterpretation, the Declaration explicitly states that nothing in it may be interpreted as consent for any activity contrary to the provisions of the UN Charter, including sovereign equality, territorial integrity and political independence of states.

The Vienna Declaration and Programme of Action adopted by the World Conference on Human Rights on 25 June 1993, appealed to the UN Commission on Human Rights to analyse the means and measures of promotion and effective protection of the rights of persons belonging to minorities as specified by the Declaration on the Rights of Persons Belonging to National or Ethnic, Religious and Linguistic Minorities. These documents call upon states and the international society to promote and protect the rights of persons belonging to minorities. The measures to be taken should include 'facilitation of their full participation in all aspects of the political, economic, social, religious and cultural life of society and in the economic progress and development in their country.'[10]

Cultural rights in the European minority protection system

Council of Europe

Article 14 of the European Convention for the Protection of Human Rights and Fundamental Freedoms of 1950 contains only a general provision on non-discrimination stating that 'the enjoyment of the rights and freedoms set forth in

9 Declaration on the Rights of Persons Belonging to National or Ethnic, Religious and Linguistic Minorities, UN General Assembly, 3 February 1992, A/RES/47/135.

10 Vienna Declaration and Programme of Action, UN General Assembly, 12 July 1993, A/CONF.157/23.

this Convention shall be secured without discrimination on any ground such as [...] association with a national minority.'

In 1992, the Council of Europe adopted the European Charter for Regional or Minority Languages. The Charter is based on the assumption that 'the protection and promotion of regional or minority languages in the different countries and regions of Europe represent an important contribution to the building of a Europe based on the principles of democracy and cultural diversity within the framework of national sovereignty and territorial integrity.'

In 1994, the Ad Hoc Committee for the Protection of National Minorities – under the auspices of the Committee of Ministers of the Council of Europe – prepared the Framework Convention for the Protection of National Minorities, opened for signing on 1 February1995. The Convention imposes the obligation to observe a series of cultural rights of persons belonging to minorities, including: the right to retain the essential elements of their national cultural identity, the right to a free use of their language, the right to establish private educational institutions, the right to teach their own language, the right to establish and maintain contacts with other people of the same ethnic, cultural, linguistic or religious identity. The convention entered into force in 1998.

Although the chief principle of the protection of the cultural rights of persons belonging to minorities is its recognition in constitutions and in internal legislation, little efforts are made outside Europe to develop relevant instruments, create relevant legal norms and establish concrete regional procedures for protecting minorities, and particularly their cultural rights.

Organization for Security and Co-operation in Europe

The Final Act of the Conference on Security and Co-operation in Europe of 1975 stated, among others, that 'The participating States on whose territory national minorities exist will respect the right of persons belonging to such minorities to equality before the law, will afford them the full opportunity for the actual enjoyment of human rights and fundamental freedoms and will, in this manner, protect their legitimate interests in this sphere.'[11]

The Concluding Document of the meeting in Madrid in 1983 highlighted the importance of lasting progress in ensuring that the rights of persons belonging to minorities are respected. Another step forward was made in 1989, at the conference in Vienna. In the new international atmosphere, during the perestroika

11 Final Act of the Conference on Security and Co-operation in Europe, Helsinki, 1 August 1975.

and the end of the ideological confrontation between the East and the West, the document concluding the conference placed an obligation on all the participating states to create favourable conditions for the promotion of ethnic, cultural, linguistic, and religious identity of national minorities on their territory.

For many countries the Copenhagen Meeting of the Conference on the Human Dimension of the CSCE of 1990 was a convenient forum for expressing their positive approach to the protection of the rights of minorities. The Copenhagen Document[12] confirmed the principle of non-discrimination and equality and listed the characteristic cultural rights of persons belonging to national minorities, namely: to freely express, preserve and develop their ethnic, cultural, linguistic or religious identity, to use freely their mother tongue, to establish and maintain their own educational, cultural and religious institutions, organisations or associations, to establish and maintain unimpeded contacts across frontiers with citizens of other States with whom they share a common ethnic or national origin, cultural heritage or religious beliefs, to establish and maintain organisations or associations within their country and to participate in international non-governmental organisations.

The participating countries agreed to not only protect ethnic, cultural, linguistic and religious identity but also to create favourable conditions for this protection. Among the measures aimed at promoting identity the document listed: establishing local or autonomous administrations corresponding to the specific historical and territorial circumstances of minorities (Part IV/Paragraph 35), instruction of their mother tongue or in their mother tongue as well as, wherever possible and necessary, its use before public authorities, in conformity with applicable national legislation (Article/Paragraph 34).

The Paris Charter, adopted at the CSCE meeting on 21 November 1990, confirmed the resolutions of the earlier documents on ethnic, cultural, linguistic and religious identity of national minorities and on the need to create conditions for the promotion of their identity. These principles were repeated in many bilateral agreements concluded by the countries of Central and Eastern Europe.

In 1992, at the CSCE Helsinki Summit, the office of the High Commissioner on National Minorities was established. The competences of the High Commissioner do not involve adjudication (trials, judgements) but rather focus on 'early warning' and suitable 'early reactions' undertaken in the earliest stages of emerging tensions concerning minorities-related issues which could, in the Commissioner's opinion, turn into peace-threatening conflicts, stability and the relations between CSCE

12 Document of the Copenhagen Meeting of the Conference on the Human Dimension of the CSCE, Copenhagen, 29 June 1990.

countries. Therefore, the office of the High Commissioner should be perceived as an important institution for monitoring the situation of minorities in Europe.

Cultural rights of indigenous peoples

Conventions of the International Labour Organization

In 1957, the International Labour Organization adopted the Convention Concerning the Protection and Integration of Indigenous and Other Tribal and Semi-Tribal Populations in Independent Countries.[13] According to the definition contained in Article 1, indigenous populations are 'tribal or semi-tribal populations in independent countries which are regarded as indigenous on account of their descent from the populations which inhabited the country, or a geographical region to which the country belongs, at the time of conquest or colonisation [...] and which, irrespective of their legal status, live more in conformity with the social, economic and cultural institutions of that time than with the institutions of the nation to which they belong.' The historical approach, which disregards the characteristic traits of these groups of people resulting from differences in culture, tradition, religion and language, has become the subject of justified criticism and did not win any broader acclaim. Even the very title of the Convention was criticised as it did not yet fully take into account the new approach to decolonisation and only referred to 'independent countries', thus failing to address the situation of indigenous peoples in dependent territories and colonies. Furthermore, the Convention does not use the term 'peoples' but instead speaks of indigenous 'populations', and it also fails to formulate the rights of these populations, instead establishing protection and requiring actions towards their integration. As a result, the Convention was never broadly and universally ratified and it became obvious that it had to be replaced by a new international agreement, one that would take into account the development that was taking place in the United Nations after the adoption of the International Convention on the Elimination of All Forms of Racial Discrimination (1965) and the International Covenants on Human Rights (1966).

Almost a quarter century later, on 7 March 1989, the General Conference of the International Labour Organisation adopted the Convention Concerning Indigenous and Tribal Peoples in Independent Countries.[14] It contains a new definition

13 Convention C107, 327 UNTS 247.

14 Text of the Convention C169, http://www.ilo.org/dyn/normlex/en/f?p=NORMLEXPUB:12100:0::NO::P12100_ILO_CODE:C169.

of indigenous peoples. Under Article 1.1(b), they are 'peoples in independent countries who are regarded as indigenous on account of their descent from the populations which inhabited the country, or a geographical region to which the country belongs, at the time of conquest or colonisation or the establishment of present state boundaries and who, irrespective of their legal status, retain some or all of their own social, economic, cultural and political institutions.' Consequently, the new definition is not restricted to solely historical and descent-related aspects.

The Convention formulates a series of obligations of countries. They have the responsibility to protect the rights of indigenous peoples and to guarantee respect for their integrity. Moreover, it stated that indigenous and tribal peoples shall enjoy the full measure of human rights and fundamental freedoms without hindrance or discrimination, that the social, cultural, religious and spiritual values and practices of these peoples are to be recognised and protected, and that in applying the provisions of the Convention, governments should: '(a) consult the peoples concerned, through appropriate procedures and in particular through their representative institutions, whenever consideration is being given to legislative or administrative measures which may affect them directly; (b) establish means by which these peoples can freely participate, to at least the same extent as other sectors of the population, at all levels of decision-making in elective institutions and administrative and other bodies responsible for policies and programmes which concern them'. Furthermore, the peoples concerned have the right to decide their own priorities for the process of development as it affects their lives, beliefs, institutions and spiritual well-being; and the right to retain their own customs and institutions, where these are not incompatible with fundamental rights defined by the national legal system and with internationally recognised human rights. This is also tied with respecting the methods customarily practised by the peoples concerned for dealing with offences committed by their members.[15] The Convention also states that the right of indigenous peoples of ownership and possession over the lands which they traditionally occupy should be recognised, that they may not be removed from the lands which they occupy and that, where the relocation of these peoples is considered necessary as an exceptional measure, such relocation must take place only with their free and informed consent.[16]

---

15 The responsibilities of states are covered in Articles 2–12, Part I of the Convention, 'General Policy'.

16 The right to land is covered in Articles 13–19. The Convention formulates a series of rights concerning the recruitment and the working conditions of indigenous workers, their right to benefit from vocational training and 'the opportunity to acquire education at all levels on at least an equal footing with the rest of the national community' (Article

Although Convention No. 169 is undeniably a step forward as compared to Convention No. 107, it is also not universally accepted. By 2013, it has been ratified by only twenty two countries.[17] Representatives of indigenous peoples point out that the ILO prepared it without consulting them, which is to say that they had no influence on the process of its creation. Another criticised aspect of the Convention is that, just as the previous one, it applies only to 'independent countries' and thus its territorial scope does not include dependent territories. There is also opposition to the expression 'tribal peoples' as it is associated with backwardness in all the areas of life, and to the fact that 'tribal peoples' will not necessarily be considered 'indigenous peoples'. Although there is some progress in comparison to Convention No. 107, as there is now talk of 'indigenous peoples' instead of 'indigenous populations', which under the commonly accepted rule of international relations gives them the right to self-determination, which is not specifically mentioned in the Convention. Furthermore, instead of decidedly stressing the right of indigenous peoples to their own cultural identity, similarly to Convention No. 107, the aim of Convention No. 169 is rather to facilitate the assimilation of autochthonous peoples with the rest of the society and the 'dominant culture', preventing discrimination rather than ensuring their free development, separateness and the right to autonomy. All these reservations mean that the convention of 1989 cannot be considered completely satisfactory by the representatives of indigenous peoples, who were working to have the UN adopt an international instrument that would guarantee all their rights and meet their expectations.

Adoption of the United Nations Declaration on the Rights of Indigenous Peoples

The work on the Declaration on the Rights of Indigenous Peoples began in 1985, when a special working group started preparing a draft declaration that would take into account the positions of the representatives of indigenous peoples and state governments who participated in the sessions. At the eleventh session,

---

26). Furthermore, governments are required to 'take appropriate measures, including by means of international agreements, to facilitate contacts and co-operation between indigenous and tribal peoples across borders, including activities in the economic, social, cultural, spiritual and environmental fields' (Article 32).

17 The parties to the Convention are mainly, although not exclusively, South American countries, the full list being as follows: Argentina, Bolivia, Brazil, the Central African Republic, Chile, Columbia, Costa Rica, Denmark, Dominica, Ecuador, Fiji, Guatemala, Honduras, Mexico, Nepal, the Netherlands, Nicaragua, Norway, Paraguay, Peru, Spain, and Venezuela.

in July 1993, the working group agreed on the final text of the draft and passed it on to the Sub-Commission, which adopted it in 1994.[18] It was then sent to the United Nations Commission on Human Rights, which in turn adopted a resolution of 1995 establishing a working group to elaborate the draft of the Declaration on the Rights of Indigenous Peoples.[19]

The subsequent session showed, however, that there were significant differences of opinion between the participating states. These differences concerned particularly the right to self-determination. Australia, Canada, New Zealand, Russia, the UK, and the US pointed out that while establishing the right to self-determination it should be explicitly stated that this concerns internal self-determination. These countries stressed that the right to self-determination should not be construed as implying the right to secession. The final text, agreed upon at the eleventh session of the working group as a compromise, was passed to the Commission on Human Rights in 2006 and once the Commission was replaced with the Human Rights Council, the text was put on its agenda. Already at its first session, on 19 June 2006, the Council adopted the Declaration on the Rights of Indigenous Peoples. In the resolution,[20] the Council writes that it adopts the United Nations Declaration on the Rights of Indigenous Peoples as proposed by the Chairperson-Rapporteur of the working group of the Commission on Human Rights to elaborate a draft declaration. It also recommends to the General Assembly that it adopt a resolution expressing appreciation to the Council for the adoption of the United Nations Declaration on the Rights of Indigenous Peoples and subsequently adopt the Declaration itself.

---

18 Resolution 1994/45: Draft United Nations Declaration on the Rights of Indigenous Peoples, was adopted on 26 August 1994, at the 46 session of the Sub-Commission on Prevention of Discrimination and Protection of Minorities by acclamation, without voting.

19 Resolution 1995/32 was adopted on 3 March 1995. In an annex to the resolution, the Commission established a procedure for organisations of indigenous peoples to be accredited to participate in the Commission's drafting working group. They could send a request to the High Commissioner for Human Rights, who asked the interested states to submit comments. The request and comments were examined by the Committee on Non-Governmental Organisations of the Economic and Social Council. The Committee approved the participation of more than ninety organisations of indigenous peoples in the working group.

20 Human Rights Council, Resolution 2006/2. Working group of the Commission on Human Rights to elaborate a draft declaration in accordance with paragraph 5 of the GENERAL Assembly resolution 49/214 of 23 December 1994.

The Declaration on the Rights of Indigenous Peoples was finally adopted towards the end of the 61st session of the UN General Assembly on 13 September 2007. 143 states voted for it, 4 voted against[21] (Australia, Canada, New Zealand and the US) and 11 abstained (Azerbaijan, Bangladesh, Bhutan, Burundi, the Russian Federation, Georgia, Kenya, Columbia, Nigeria, Samoa, and Ukraine).

The adoption of the Declaration on the Rights of Indigenous Peoples[22] can be considered a very important step in the actions of the United Nations towards development and promotion of their rights and fundamental freedoms. The Declaration comprises a preamble and forty six articles. In its first passages, the Preamble affirms that 'indigenous peoples are equal to all other peoples' and expresses concern 'that indigenous peoples have suffered from historic injustices as a result of, inter alia, their colonisation and dispossession of their lands, territories and resources, thus preventing them from exercising, in particular, their right to development in accordance with their own needs and interests'. Furthermore, it recognises 'the urgent need to respect and promote the inherent rights of indigenous peoples which derive from their political, economic and social structures and from their cultures, spiritual traditions, histories and philosophies, especially their rights to their lands, territories and resources'.

The first part of the Declaration is devoted to fundamental rights.[23] According to its provisions, indigenous peoples have the right to the full enjoyment of all human rights and fundamental freedoms as recognised in the Charter of the United Nations, the Universal Declaration of Human Rights and international human rights law, are free and equal to all other peoples and individuals and have the right to be free from any kind of discrimination, have the right to self-determination and in exercising this right they have the right to autonomy or self-government in matters relating to their internal and local affairs, as well as ways and means for financing their autonomous functions. They also have the right to maintain and strengthen their distinct political, legal, economic, social and cultural institutions, while retaining their right to participate fully, if they so choose, in the political, economic, social and cultural life of the State and the right to a nationality.

21 Australia (in 2009), New Zealand, Canada and the US (2010) while voting against, declared that they would undertake the appropriate actions to fully support the Declaration.

22 Available at: http://www.un.org/esa/socdev/unpfii/documents/DRIPS_en.pdf (accessed on 15 May 2013).

23 Articles 1–6.

The next group of articles focuses on life and security.[24] They mention the collective right of indigenous peoples to live in freedom, peace and security and the right of indigenous individuals to life, physical and mental integrity, liberty and security of person. They also state that, indigenous peoples and individuals have the right not to be subjected to any act of genocide, any form of forced assimilation or integration by other cultures or lifestyle imposed on them by legislative, administrative and other means. They have the right to maintain and develop their separate identity and characteristic features, including the right to consider themselves indigenous and be considered as such. Also, indigenous peoples shall not be forcibly removed from their lands or territories and they have the right to special protection and security during armed conflicts.

Articles 11, 12 and 13 speak of culture, religion and language. Indigenous peoples have the right to practice and revitalise their cultural traditions, customs and ceremonies, as well as histories, languages, oral traditions, philosophies, writing systems and literatures, and to designate and retain their own names for communities, places and persons.

The following articles contain provisions concerning education, the media and employment.[25] Thereunder, indigenous children have the right to all levels and forms of education of the State and indigenous peoples have the right to their own educational systems and to establish their own media in their own languages. They also have the right to enjoy fully all rights established under applicable international and domestic labour law.

Among the remaining provisions of the Declaration, particularly noteworthy is the right of indigenous peoples to participate, through representatives chosen by themselves, in decision-making in matters which would affect their rights (Article 18), life and future, as well as to maintain and develop their political, economic and social systems (Article 20) and to exercise their right to development (Article 23). A very special right is the right to their traditional medicines and health practices (Article 24). It is also important that indigenous peoples have been granted the right to control and protect their cultural heritage and intellectual property.[26] (Article 31). In the changing environment, with pressures from states and large enterprises, it is increasingly harder for indigenous peoples to achieve full protection of their cultural identity.

---

24 Articles 7–10.

25 Articles 14–17.

26 Article 31.

Influence of cultural globalisation on individual and collective cultural rights

Globalisation can be perceived in several dimensions. Three of them are of particular importance: a) economic globalisation – in other words the establishment of the global market, liberalisation of trade and finance; b) globalisation of information and communication – connected with development and new possibilities in the area of information technology, mass media, transfer of knowledge and interpersonal relations; c) cultural globalisation – the consequence of development and the new mass culture, as well as of the universal values and changes in the model of human behaviour.

Economic globalisation is connected with liberalisation and intensification of trade, growth of investments and capital flows. However, rapid transformations, adjustment of economies and the introduction of neoliberal principles are often accompanied by poverty, unemployment and non-observance of human rights, particularly the economic, social and cultural ones.[27] The right to work and the right to just and favourable conditions of work is threatened where there is an excessive emphasis on competitiveness – it can be detrimental to the respect for the labour rights contained in the International Covenant on Economic, Social and Cultural Rights. The right to form and join trade unions and an exclusion of collective bargaining, including closing off the right to strike, may be threatened by restrictions claimed to be 'necessary' in a global economy. Regardless of its positive consequences, privatisation can weaken social security and the right to education as well as restrict the possibilities of participating in cultural life if scientific, cultural and artistic activity is governed only by the principles of the free market.[28]

New information technologies are the foundation of the globalisation of communication and have considerable influence on individuals, societies, states, and international organisations. These changes led to the emergence of a new term, 'global information society', which is a response to the fact that many areas of the economic, social, cultural, and political activity are influenced by new information technologies.

---

27 Declaration and Programme of Action of the World Summit for Social Development, United Nations, 1995, Paragraph 14.

28 *Statement on Globalization*, UN Committee on Economic, Social, and Cultural Rights, 11 May 1998, available at: http://migration.ucc.ie/www/globalisation/Globalization.htm_(accessed on 12 May 2013).

Furthermore, globalisation of communication has had a rather positive impact on the cultural rights of individuals and groups. Interactive education and distance learning can improve the enjoyment of the right to education and allow access to education services by people inhabiting isolated countries or regions, can improve the quality of education and create possibilities for lifelong learning for everyone, which was not possible in the past.

The right to participate in cultural life gets a new meaning in relation to the unprecedented opportunities to visit the most famous museums and exhibitions or to participate in prestigious cultural events. The right to benefit from scientific progress is strengthened by the possibility of quick access to recent research results, to libraries located in foreign countries and regions, to scientific publications and periodicals. However, information highways can yield positive results only when they are available. Bearing this in mind, we should identify a new type of exclusion and poverty – information poverty. Although the economic dimension of globalisation and, to a lesser extent, the dimension related to communication, seem the most visible, cultural globalisation – that is the international spreading of cultures – is no less important than the spreading of economic processes.[29] Through the mass media, international ideas and values have been mixed and imposed on national cultures. The homogenous global culture is constantly developing, which leads to announcing the emergence of a 'global village'. The progress of popular culture means that more and more often people all around the world dress in the same clothes, sing the same songs, watch the same TV series, and some cultural attitudes, opinions and choices are becoming global trends.

As has been previously noted, culture should be understood not only as the creative activity and intellectual achievements of individuals expressed in music, literature, art, science but more broadly as the sum of human activity, the sum of values, lifestyle requirements and the need for communication.[30] This means that in this broad understanding, culture is influenced by economic globalisation as well as globalisation of information and communication. The spread of the same goods: cars, computers, mobile phones, TVs, washing machines, etc., the development of networks of the same hotels or restaurants in all the parts of the world, the fact that people watch the same TV broadcasts, admire the same rock stars, sportsmen, Nobel Prize winners – all this has an undeniable impact on their behaviour, system of values and beliefs, or in other words, on their culture.

---

29 UNDP Human Development Report 1997, New York/Oxford 1997, p. 83.

30 J. Symonides, 'The Implementation of Cultural Rights by the International Community', *International Communication Gazette*, no. 60, 1998, pp. 8–24.

As a result, a question appears about the impact of cultural globalisation on human rights. The effect of cultural homogenisation and the gradual process of adopting common values and behavioural patterns strengthen the universality of human rights, create bonds between various parts of the world and help to eliminate certain traditional practices that are often discriminatory.

However, the negative aspects of cultural globalisation are related to its negative consequences for certain groups, such as minorities, indigenous peoples or migrant workers. It can also weaken the existing cultural identity, ethical norms, social cohesion, as well as the sense of belonging, thus contributing to the emergence of internal conflicts. The UNESCO Convention for the Safeguarding of the Intangible Cultural Heritage of 2003 justly points out the danger that globalisation carries by stating: 'the processes of globalisation and social transformation, alongside the conditions they create for renewed dialogue among communities, also give rise, as does the phenomenon of intolerance, to grave threats of deterioration, disappearance and destruction of the intangible cultural heritage, in particular owing to a lack of resources for safeguarding such heritage.' As stressed at the UNESCO General Conference: 'Just as the protection of biological diversity is indispensable to the physical health of humanity, so the safeguarding of cultural diversity – linguistic, ideological and artistic – is indispensable to its spiritual health.[31]'

The individual and collective right to cultural identity can be perceived as the articulation of the right enshrined in Article 1 of the UNESCO Declaration on Race and Racial Prejudice of 1978: 'All individuals and groups have the right to be different, to consider themselves as different and to be regarded as such.'[32]

At the World Conference on Cultural Policies held in Mexico City in 1982, the delegates emphasised the growing awareness of cultural identity, the pluralism resulting from it, the right to be different, the respect of one culture to another, including minorities. Presently, the right to cultural identity is recognised by instruments of human rights and national constitutions. Article 29 of the Convention on the Rights of the Child states that children's education should be directed

31 'UNESCO PRESS, 29th session of the General Conference, N 97219. In his closing speech the President of the General Conference formulated an opinion that cultural cleansing is maybe more dangerous than a biological one. Wherever it occurs, the thermometer of intellectual competition registers a drop in temperature'.

32 Cf.: J. Symonides, V. Volodin (eds.), *UNESCO and Human Rights, Standard-Setting Instruments*, 2nd ed., UNESCO, Paris 1999, p. 109.

to: 'the development of respect for the child's parents, his or her own cultural identity, language and values.'[33]

The right to enjoy respect for one's cultural identity means that everyone, individually or in a society, can freely choose their cultural identity in various aspects such as language, religion, heritage, traditions, etc. Everyone can have one or more cultural identities and can freely choose to identify with one or more cultural communities.

The threat that globalisation poses to the preservation of cultural identity has given rise to strong opposition in developing countries, where cultural globalisation is considered an attempt of the developed countries to impose foreign models. The Western popular culture has become one of the top subjects of cultural debates on globalisation. It should be also noted that in many European countries cultural globalisation is perceived as Americanisation of their cultures, which is primarily connected with the expansion of the English language and the influence of American culture, science and technology.

However, rejecting popular Western culture and defending the 'Islamic' or 'Asian' values[34] can also have a different dimension. The prohibition of access to Western information, movies, videos, or satellite television employed by some authoritarian Arab and Asian regimes is actually aimed at controlling behaviours and suppressing modernisation, liberalisation and democratisation of their political and social systems. Under the guise of protecting traditional values, they refuse to change the traditional role of women in the society or to allow a democratic participation in governance.

Despite cultural differences, no element of universal human rights should be rejected. What is more, these differences cannot serve as a justification of non-observance of such fundamental rights as equality of men and women. Traditional cultural practices violating the rights of women and children need to be changed. These traps, resulting from the persisting cultural differences, are definitely limited.

Acceptance of cultural diversity by the international community

In the 21st century, UNESCO proposes a new, alternative approach to cultural specificity, which essentially comes down to replacing 'cultural relativism' with

33 Text in *Human Rights, A Compilation of International Instruments*, vol. 1, *Universal Instruments*, United Nations, New York 1993, p. 186.

34 See: 'Introductory remarks', in J. Symonides (ed.), *Human Rights: New Dimensions and Challenges*, Aldershot 1999, pp. 27–28.

'cultural diversity'. The Declaration on Cultural Diversity,[35] adopted on 2 November 2001 at the 31st Session of the UNESCO General Conference, confirms that the General Conference 'is committed to the full implementation of the human rights and fundamental freedoms proclaimed in the Universal Declaration of Human Rights and other universally recognised legal instruments, such as the two International Covenants'. In the part devoted to cultural diversity and human rights, the Declaration stresses that 'the defence of cultural diversity is an ethical imperative, inseparable from respect for human dignity'. It imposes the obligation to respect 'human rights and fundamental freedoms, in particular the rights of persons belonging to minorities and those of indigenous peoples'. It explicitly states that 'no one may invoke cultural diversity to infringe upon human rights guaranteed by international law, nor to limit their scope'. The Declaration employs a broad understanding of culture, which is perceived as the set of distinctive features of society or a social group and eliminates the traps that a free interpretation of cultural diversity could pose to the implementation of human rights.

The ideas expressed in the Declaration are further elaborated in the Convention on the Protection and Promotion of the Diversity of Cultural Expressions.[36] It was adopted at the 33rd Session of the UNESCO General Conference on 20 October 2005 and is presently binding for 126 countries (including Poland). The Preamble of the Convention celebrates 'the importance of cultural diversity for the full realisation of human rights and fundamental freedoms proclaimed in the Universal Declaration of Human Rights and other universally recognised instruments'. Its objectives are, among others: to protect and promote the diversity of cultural expressions, to create the conditions for cultures to flourish, to encourage dialogue among cultures, to develop cultural interaction. Article 2 states that 'cultural diversity can be protected and promoted only if human rights and fundamental freedoms, such as freedom of expression, information and communication, as well as the ability of individuals to choose cultural expressions, are guaranteed' and that 'no one may invoke the provisions of this Convention in order to infringe human rights and fundamental freedoms as enshrined in the Universal Declaration of Human Rights or guaranteed by international law, or to limit the scope thereof'. Consequently, as compared to relativism, the concept of

---

35 UNESCO Universal Declaration on Cultural Diversity, UNESCO, 2 November 2001, available at: http://portal.unesco.org/en/ev.php-URL_ID=13179&URL_DO=DO_TOPIC&URL_SECTION=201.html (accessed on 10 January 2014).

36 UNESCO Convention on the Protection and Promotion of the Diversity of Cultural Expressions, available at: http://portal.unesco.org/en/ev.php-URL_ID=31038&URL_DO=DO_TOPIC&URL_SECTION=201.html (accessed on 10 January 2014).

cultural diversity represents the view that all cultures deserve respect. It recognises the positive values of diversity, stresses its importance for human rights and rejects invoking diversity to justify infringing or restricting human rights. The concept of cultural diversity has also been adopted in the Charter of Fundamental Rights of the European Union,[37] and specifically its Article 22: 'the Union shall respect cultural, religious and linguistic diversity'.

There is no doubt that acceptance of cultural diversity is essential for the consolidation of cultural rights. In a world where discrimination and violation of the cultural rights of minorities, indigenous peoples and immigrants are significant causes of conflicts, recognising cultural diversity becomes one of the most important factors in solving them. In this context, it is worth noting that the states party to the Convention on the Rights of the Child agreed that 'the education of the child shall be directed to [...] the development of respect for the child's parents, his or her own cultural identity, language and values, for the national values of the country in which the child is living, the country from which he or she may originate, and for civilizations different from his or her own'. The idea of respecting cultural diversity and pluralism very aptly was formulated.

Final remarks

An analysis of the international instruments dedicated to cultural rights, both individual and collective, shows that the last decade of the 20th century and the first decade of the 21st century have brought them gradual development and recognition. The experience of the recent years has proved the thesis that respecting the cultural rights of minorities and indigenous peoples and their identity does not in fact give rise to threats to the territorial integrity of states and does not lead to the emergence of divisions in the societies. On the contrary, it actually eliminates their sources. As stated in the UNESCO Universal Declaration on Cultural Diversity and the Convention on the Protection and Promotion of the Diversity of Cultural Expressions, acceptance of cultural diversity and observance of cultural rights is necessary, and is one of the best guarantees of peace and security on the local, national and international level. The exercise of these rights is the prerequisite to proper functioning and existence of any democratic society and the rule of law. Consolidation of cultural rights and their increasing importance is also a function of the consolidation of economic, social and cultural rights perceived as a whole. The Vienna Declaration and Programme of Action adopted by the World

37 Charter of Fundamental Rights of the European Union, OJ C 326, 26.10.2012, pp. 391–407.

Conference on Human Rights in 1993 stresses the need for a concerted effort to ensure recognition of economic, social and cultural rights at the national, regional and international levels.[38]

However, the state of realisation of cultural rights raises serious reservations, as proven by the considerable number of infringements upon them. While discussing what actions could be undertaken to change that, the World Commission on Culture and Development proposed a whole range of actions: from drawing up a list of cultural rights, preparing an international code of conduct and establishing the office of ombudsman for this category of rights, to establishing an international court which could deal with the complaints of individuals and groups concerning violations of their cultural rights. These proposals, however, have only a little chance of being implemented.[39]

Surely, it would be an important step to conclude the international agreements which would turn the declarations adopted by the General Assembly on the rights of minorities and indigenous peoples of 1992 and 2007 into hard law. As a matter of fact, this method has been frequently employed in international practice. It can be observed that the present universal instruments are in fact soft law, while in the European system of human rights protection, the standards concerning the rights of minorities take the form of commitments under international agreements, both bilateral and multilateral.[40]

---

38 *Vienna Declaration and Programme of Action*, Par. 98.

39 The idea to establish a court for cultural rights and, what is more, one with the possibility to file individual complaints has never had an actual chance to be realised, neither in the late 20th century, nor in the second decade of the 21st century. It is far more important to specify or explain the normative scope of individual cultural rights. For this reason, it is only prudent to emphasise the importance of the General Comments adopted by the Committee on Economic, Social and Cultural Rights concerning: No. 13 (1999) on the right to education (Article 13 of the Covenant), No. 17 (2005) on the right of everyone to benefit from the protection of the moral and material interests resulting from any scientific, literary or artistic production of which he or she is the author (Article 15(1) (c), of the Covenant), and No. 21 (2009) on the right of everyone to take part in cultural life (Article 15(1)(a), of the Covenant). These General Comments provide a functional interpretation of individual rights, thus indirectly contributing to expanding the list of cultural rights.

40 In the situation when a large number of international agreements, declarations and resolutions adopted by the UN, specialised organisations such as the UNESCO, as well as regional organisations mention various cultural rights, sometimes formulated in a different way, it is highly justified to create a list of all the cultural rights in a single normative instrument, that is, in other words, codifying this category of human rights.

The control procedures provided in the International Covenant on Economic, Social and Cultural Rights and functioning in the UNESCO are also of importance for the implementation of cultural rights. However, they are based primarily on reports presented to treaty committees and the Human Rights Council under a universal, periodical review, which means that there is a need to supplement them with the possibility of filing notifications (petitions) by individuals about violations of their cultural rights. Such a possibility exists under the Optional Protocol to the International Covenant on Economic, Social and Cultural Rights, which was adopted unanimously by the General Assembly on 10 December 2008.[41] It equips the Committee on Economic, Social and Cultural Rights with the competence to receive notifications of its decisions being breached.[42] The Protocol entered into force on 5 May 2013, once the required number of 10 ratifications had been achieved. The procedure of filing notifications of infringements on cultural rights established by the UNESCO and providing the possibility to present complains regarding the violation of cultural rights is not well known. As a result, its application is rather limited. Currently, there are proposals presented to add the notifications procedure to the European Framework Convention for the Protection of National Minorities. Strengthening and recognition of cultural rights requires that they are to be known and understood better, which can be achieved primarily through broadly understood education, formal and informal, as well as promotion by the mass media and by all civil society actors.

Such an instrument would be of key importance for their implementation, understanding and education. Unfortunately, this would be very hard to achieve.

41 General Assembly Resolution A/RES/63/117.

42 Notifications of infringement on cultural rights can be filed with other treaty committees but only within their competences. The Human Rights Committee has relatively the broadest competences in this regard, as it monitors the observance of the International Covenant on Civil and Political Rights, which provides for such a possibility in Article 27.

Hanna Schreiber

Cultural Genocide – Culturecide: An Unfinished or Rejected Project of International Law?

Key words: cultural genocide, Raphael Lemkin, indigenous peoples, human rights, culturecide

Abstract: The article analyses the evolution of the definition of 'cultural genocide' from the debates of the 1948 Genocide Convention to the 2007 U.N. Declaration on the Rights of Indigenous Peoples. It presents how Raphael Lemkin originally envisioned this notion. It discusses examples of culturecidal practices and possible developments of this concept in the future.

Introduction

> *New conceptions require new terms. By 'genocide' we mean the destruction of a nation or of an ethnic group. This new word, coined by the author to denote* ***an old practice***[1] *in its modern development, is made from the ancient Greek word genos (race, tribe) and the Latin cide (killing), thus corresponding in its formation to such words as tyrannicide, homocide, infanticide, etc. Generally speaking, genocide does not necessarily mean the immediate destruction of a nation, except when accomplished by mass killings of all members of a nation. It is intended rather to signify a coordinated plan of different actions aiming at the destruction of essential foundations of the life of national groups, with the aim of annihilating the groups themselves. The objectives of such a plan would be* ***disintegration of the political and social institutions, of culture, language, national feelings, religion****, and the economic existence of national groups, and the destruction of the personal security, liberty, health, dignity,* ***and even the lives of the individuals*** *belonging to such groups. Genocide is directed against the national group as an entity, and the actions involved are directed against individuals, not in their individual capacity but as members of the national group.*[2]

This passage opens the most important chapter of the ground breaking work written by Raphael Lemkin and published in the United States in 1944: *Axis Rule*

1 Unless otherwise noted, all highlights in the text by H. Schreiber.

2 R. Lemkin, 'Genocide', in R. Lemkin, *Axis Rule in Occupied Europe. Laws of Occupation, Analysis of Government, Proposals for Redress*, Carnegie Endowment for International Peace, Washington 1944. This is the most important work by Raphael Lemkin and it had an immense influence on later international law in terms of international criminal law and the criminalisation of the most serious crimes.

in Occupied Europe. Laws of Occupation, Analysis of Government, Proposals for Redress – the work that has given the world the name for what Winston Churchill referred to as 'a crime without a name'.[3]

The first aim of this article is to study how Raphael Lemkin originally envisioned the definition of 'genocide'. Then, I would like to show how this definition has evolved with regard to cultural and identity-related issues in the debates on the shape of the 1948 Convention on the Prevention and Punishment of the Crime of Genocide.[4] Finally, I will try to present the contemporary contexts (the U.N. Declaration on the Rights of Indigenous Peoples of 2007 – UNDRIP 2007) in which the term 'cultural genocide' – eventually excluded from the official definition of genocide – appears. In the contemporary context, I propose to use the term 'culturecide' instead. Where it appears in its original historical context – that is when I present Lemkin's idea and describe the debate during the drafting of the Convention of 1948 – I shall leave it as 'cultural genocide'. The study of the history of this concept in international law is expected to help answer the question posed in the title of this article: whether it is an unfinished project, one which could re-emerge in the future in the framework of international law, or rather a rejected one.

At the roots – culture as the key to the concept of genocide in the thought of Raphael Lemkin

Today, although the 'crime of crimes'[5] has had a name for more than six decades, the author of this name remains virtually anonymous in his own homeland (except for a narrow group of researchers, including lawyers and sociologists dealing with genocide-related issues[6]). For a long time, his works were essentially

---

3 In a radio speech of 24 August 1941. After: J. T. Fussel, *'A Crime Without a Name'. Winston Churchill, Raphael Lemkin and the World War II Origins of the Word 'Genocide*, available at: http://www.preventgenocide.org/genocide/crimewithoutaname.htm (accessed on 10 January 2013).

4 UN Convention on the Prevention and Punishment of the Crime of Genocide, 9 December 1948, ratified by Poland on 18 July 1950. Hereinafter: Convention of 1948.

5 This expression was coined by Lemkin himself and is used in his unpublished autobiography *Totally Unofficial Man*. Edited fragments have been published in S. Totten, S. L. Jacobs (eds.), *Pioneers of Genocide Studies: Confronting Mass Death in the Century of Genocide*, Westport 2002, p. 383. For more on this publication see Footnote 9.

6 Cf. selected recent Polish publications on this subject: L. M. Nijakowski, *Rozkosz zemsty. Socjologia historyczna mobilizacji ludobójczej* (*Historical Sociology of Genocidal Mobilisation*), Warszawa 2013; K. Wierczyńska, *Pojęcie ludobójstwa w kontekście orzecznictwa międzynarodowych trybunałów karnych ad hoc* (*The Concept of Genocide in*

not translated into Polish[7] and his presence in world literature is marked only by a handful of publications. A well-known researcher of Lemkin's ideas and the concept of genocide, Anthony Dirk Moses, wrote that despite some occasional undertakings, literature on Lemkin 'is still in its infancy'.[8] Ryszard Szawłowski confirms that it is also true for Poland.[9] Another reason for this is probably that his achievements in this field still have not been published, even in the form of post-mortem 'collected works', which is not an uncommon practice.[10] The subject of genocide has become popular as it is considered to be of great importance, and consequently, as it often happens with success, it has come to have many fathers – 'pioneers of genocide studies'.[11] In fact, however, Raphael Lemkin, a Polish lawyer

---

the Context of Judicature of Ad Hoc International Criminal Courts), Warszawa 2010; D. Dróżdż, *Zbrodnia ludobójstwa w międzynarodowym prawie karnym* (*The Crime of Genocide in International Criminal Law*), Warszawa 2010.

7 *Axis Rule in Occupied Europe* was translated and published only recently by Wydawnictwo Scholar: R. Lemkin, *Rządy państw osi w okupowanej Europie*, Warszawa 2013.

8 A. D. Moses, 'Raphael Lemkin, culture, and the concept of genocide', in D. Bloxham, A. D. Moses (eds.), *The Oxford Handbook of Genocide Studies*, Oxford–New York 2010, p. 20.

9 R. Szawłowski, 'Rafał Lemkin (1900–1959) – polski prawnik twórcą pojęcia ludobójstwo' (Rafał Lemkin (1900–1959) – A Polish Lawyer Who Coined the Term Genocide), in R. Ignatiew, A. Kura (eds.), *Zbrodnie przeszłości. Opracowania i materiały prokuratorów IPN* (*Crimes of the Past. Compilations and Materials of IPN Prosecutors*), vol. 2, Warszawa 2008. So far, in Poland, the fatherland of Lemkin, only one book entirely devoted to the broad influence of the thought and concepts of Lemkin has been published: A. Bieńczyk-Missala, S. Dębski (eds.), *Rafał Lemkin. A Hero of Humankind*, Warszawa 2010.

10 The entirety of Lemkin's work remains in the form of typescript and notes stored essentially in three institutions: 1) 7 boxes at the Jacob Rader Marcus Center of the American Jewish Archives (AJA), located at the Hebrew Union College in Cincinnati, Ohio. These are materials of 1942–1959, donated to this institution in two parts: by a cousin of Raphael Lemkin, Robert Lemkin, in April 1965, and complemented by the donation of Rabbi David Saperstein of the Union of American Hebrew Congregations in November 1983. The materials are not available online; 2) 12 boxes, donated in 1975 to the American Jewish Historical Society, mainly from 1944–1952 – moved in 2001, when the main seat of the AJHS moved from Massachusetts to New York. The greater share of the collection, including the fragments of the unpublished *The History of Genocide*, which is also cited in this text, is available online on the website of the AJHS; 3) 5 boxes of microfilmed materials from the years 1946–1959, donated by a friend of R. Lemkin, Alexander Gabriel, to the New York Public Library (hereinafter: NYPL), Archives and Manuscripts Division, in 1982. These materials are available online.

11 See: S. Totten, S. L. Jacobs (eds.), *Pioneers of Genocide Studies*… In the *Introduction* the authors describe how they started the work on the publication: 'Initially, we started by

of Jewish origin, was the only true pioneer and we owe it to him and his efforts that this crime – today considered the most serious type of crime that can be committed against a national, ethnic, racial or religious group, bearing the largest legal, political and moral weight – appeared in international law and in the awareness of the international community. This does not mean, of course, that the phenomenon itself appeared thanks to Lemkin; he himself describes it as 'an old practice in its modern development'.

The cultural aspect was at the centre of the concept of genocide created by Raphael Lemkin[12]. Despite being distinguished as a separate category, it is also present in the other aspects of genocide: political, social, religious, economic, and moral. However, it also shared the fate of most of these aspects by being excluded from the final definition that appeared in the 1948 Genocide Convention (only the religious aspect made it in).

Meanwhile, in his most important work (and the only one published) *Axis Rule in Occupied Europe* Lemkin elaborated on his vision of genocide as follows:

> Genocide has two phases: one, **destruction of the national pattern of the oppressed group**; the other, the imposition of the national pattern of the oppressor. This imposition, in turn, may be made upon the oppressed population which is allowed to remain or upon the territory alone, **after removal of the population and the colonization by the oppressor's own nationals.**[13]

It is important to note that this description does not include what is nowadays considered obvious and crucial in the discussion on genocide: physical extermination of the population. Instead, it speaks of national patterns, which refer us directly to the notion of culture. Lemkin distinguishes eight 'techniques of genocide in various fields', which were made into characteristics of groups subject to genocide during the work on the Convention of 1948: political, social, cultural, economic, biological, physical, religious and moral.

---

noting those individuals who wrote the earliest and most significant works on genocide theory, and among those individuals were Lemkin, Charny, Kuper, Fein, Horowitz, and Cohn'. Lemkin is among the 35 authors eventually considered 'pioneers', but it was only he whose unremitting work and involvement in the issue of punishing genocide brought about its criminalisation (the authors eventually admit this in the introduction to a fragment of his autobiography).

12 Already in 1933 Lemkin addressed International Conference for the Unification of the Criminal Law held in Madrid, with the report presenting his definitions of 'acts of vandalism' and 'acts of barbarity', which later evolved into cultural genocide concept.

13 Cf. Footnote 2. Unless otherwise noted, all other quotations are from Chapter 9 of *Axis Rule....*

Political

> In line with this policy of imposing the German national pattern, particularly in the incorporated territories, the occupant has organized **a system of colonization of these areas**. In western Poland, especially, this has been done on a large scale. The Polish population have been removed from their homes in order to make place for German settlers who were brought in from the Baltic States, the central and eastern districts of Poland, Bessarabia, and from the Reich itself. The properties and homes of the Poles are being allocated to German settlers; and to induce them to reside in these areas the settlers receive many privileges, especially in the way of tax exemptions.

The issue of colonisation and territorial occupation was extremely important to Lemkin and he was very familiar with it, since he was interested in the history of the colonisation of Hispanic America. He studied the writings of the most famous defender of Indians Bartolomé de Las Casas, as well as of Francisco de Vitoria. The former was even Lemkin's hero: 'his name has lived on through the centuries as one of the most admirable and courageous crusaders for humanity the world has ever known'.[14] Lemkin's knowledge and in-depth studies of the colonisation period surely influenced the concept of genocide, the fundamental elements of which were territorial conquest and occupation in the form of colonisation.[15] The title of his book, *Axis Rule in Occupied Europe*, also points to the issue of territorial occupation as being crucial to his concept of genocide. An inseparable element of this concept was the change of the demographic structure, although not necessarily through mass killings but also, for example, through deportation of the native population and the settling of new people from the oppressor nation, which Lemkin explicitly

---

14 R. Lemkin, 'Spain Colonial Genocide', AJHS, P-154, box 8, folder 12. After: A. D. Moses, 'Raphael Lemkin, culture…, p. 26.

15 At the same time, we should take notice of – as historians studying the age of colonisation and the knowledge about its true face in the Europe of that time do – that Lemkin's views in this respect did not completely stray from the views common in his time. He was not an opponent of colonisation as such but he condemned its brutal form. In peaceful colonisation ha saw the chance for improving civilisational progress of indigenous peoples. He was indignant at the Belgian genocide practices in Congo, which were a hot topic in Europe owing to E. Morel and R. Casement, he condemned genocide committed by Germans on the Herero in 1904–1908 but he also believed that King Leopold II of Belgium had the good will to stop the massacres and make the natives happy. In this sense, notwithstanding his undeniable greatness, Lemkin was also a child of his century. Cf.: D. J. Schaller, 'Raphael Lemkin's view on European colonial rule in Africa: between condemnation and admiration', *Journal of Genocide Research*, vol. 7, no. 4, 2005, pp. 531–538.

called 'colonisation'. It is not a coincidence that this term appears in this context; it is obvious that it was used on purpose, given the studies conducted by Lemkin, also while working on *The History of Genocide*. Genocide is a 'technique' of occupation and comes down to colonisation and conquest, which has been, since World War II, 'an old practice in its modern development' in Europe:

> The enemy nation within the control of Germany must be destroyed, disintegrated, or weakened in different degrees for decades to come. Thus the German people in the post-war period will be in a position to deal with other European peoples from the vantage point of biological superiority. Because the imposition of this policy of genocide is more destructive for a people than injuries suffered in the actual fighting, the German people will be stronger than the subjugated peoples after the war even if the German army is defeated. **In this respect genocide is a new technique of occupation aimed at winning the peace even though the war itself is lost.**

The other techniques of genocide also essentially refer to the notion of culture and its intangible, spiritual values, enshrined however to the specific, elite social group – intelligentsia.

Social

> The social structure of a nation being vital to its **national development**, the occupant also endeavours to bring about such changes as may weaken the **national, spiritual resources**. The focal point of this attack has been the intelligentsia because this group largely provides the national leadership and organizes resistance against Nazification.

It is important that Lemkin presents a very particular vision of culture, manifested exactly in passages such as this one. For him, culture is first of all what we would call high culture, the product of intelligence, the depository of 'national, spiritual resources'. This is further confirmed by another fragment of Lemkin's works:

> All our cultural heritage is a product of the contribution of all nations. We can best understand this when we realize how impoverished our culture would be if the people doomed by Germany such as the Jews had not been permitted to create the Bible or give birth to an Einstein, a Spinoza; if the Poles had not had the opportunity to give the world a Copernicus, a Chopin, a Curie; the Greeks a Plato and a Socrates, the English a Shakespeare, the Russians a Tolstoy and a Shostakovich, the Americans an Emerson and a Jefferson, the Frenchmen a Renan and a Rodin.[16]

---

16 'Memorandum from Raphael Lemkin to R. Kempner', 5 VI 1946, United States Holocaust Memorial Museum, R. Kempner Papers (RS 71.001); quoted after: A. D. Moses, 'Raphael Lemkin, culture…, p. 29.

The same is confirmed by the description of the cultural techniques of genocide presented in *Axis Rule…* as it points almost exclusively to high culture, manifested in cultural activity, literary works or monuments:

Cultural

> In the incorporated areas the local population **is forbidden to use its own language** in schools and in printing. […] Moreover, in the Polish areas Polish youths **were excluded from the benefit of liberal arts studies** and were channelled predominantly into the trade schools. The occupant apparently believes that the study of the liberal arts may develop independent national Polish thinking, and therefore he tends to prepare Polish youths for the role of skilled labour, to be employed in German industries.
>
> In order to prevent the expression of the national spirit through artistic media, **a rigid control of all cultural activities has been introduced**. All persons engaged in painting, drawing, sculpture, music, literature, and the theatre are required to obtain a license for the continuation of their activities. Control in these fields is exercised through German authorities. […] especially in Poland, were **national monuments destroyed and libraries, archives, museums, and galleries of art carried away**. In 1939 the Germans burned the great library of the Jewish Theological Seminary at Lublin, Poland. This was reported by the Germans as follows:
>
> 'For us it was a matter of special pride to destroy the Talmudic Academy which was known as the greatest in Poland. … We threw out of the building the great Talmudic library, and carted it to market. There we set fire to the books. The fire lasted for twenty hours. The Jews of Lublin were assembled around and cried bitterly. Their cried almost silenced us. Then we summoned the military band and the joyful shouts of the soldiers silenced the sound of the Jewish cries.'

Universities, museums, libraries, galleries of art mentioned by Lemkin in this passage belong to a vision of culture, which is created, encoded and made available only to the society's elites.

However, the central significance of culture for the techniques of genocide transpires also in other areas. Destruction of culture is the first step towards the destruction of a nation as a whole, even though the methods applied can manifest themselves in the spheres of economy, religion or morality, by preventing people from sustaining their culture and fulfilling other (spiritual, religious, intellectual, etc.) than very basic needs or 'basic instincts' (food, shelter, simple survival):

Economic

> The destruction of the foundations of the economic existence of a national group necessarily brings about a crippling of its development, even a retrogression. **The lowering of**

> **the standards of living creates difficulties in fulfilling cultural-spiritual requirements.** Furthermore, a daily fight literally for bread and for physical survival may **handicap thinking in both general and national terms.**

Religious

> In Luxemburg, where the population is predominantly Catholic and religion plays an important role in national life, especially in the field of education, **the occupant has tried to disrupt these national and religious influences**. Children over fourteen years of age were permitted by legislation to renounce their religious affiliations, for the occupant was eager to enroll such children exclusively in pro-Nazi youth organizations. [...] Likewise in Poland, **through the systematic pillage and destruction of church property and persecution of the clergy, the German occupying authorities have sought to destroy the religious leadership of the Polish nation.**

Moral

> In order to weaken the spiritual resistance of the national group, the occupant attempts to create an atmosphere of moral debasement within this group. According to this plan, the **mental energy of the group should be concentrated upon base instincts and should be diverted from moral and national thinking**. It is important for the realisation of such a plan that the desire for cheap individual pleasure be substituted for the desire for collective feelings and ideals based upon a higher morality.

Except for the physical and biological aspects of genocide, in all the others it is the culture that is usually attacked, as the carrier of identity and cohesion of the group concerned, of its 'national thinking', language, religion, values, and morality. However, out of the eight techniques of genocide listed by Lemkin, it is exactly these two – the physical and the biological – that have dominated our present-day understanding of this concept and had shaped the debate on the final definition of genocide in the Convention of 1948.

Another interesting source on the basis of which we can reconstruct Lemkin's views on the concept of genocide, is a fragment of his notes titled *The Concept of Genocide in Anthropology*.[17] In the section 'The Significance of Cultural Genocide', Lemkin writes:

17 I would like to sincerely thank Dirk Moses for providing me with a scan of this document, which is stored in NYPL archives and is inaccessible online. R. Lemkin, 'The Concept of Genocide in Anthropology', NYPL, box 2, folder 2. This fragment was written in the period 1946–1959.

> In our definition of genocide we have included cultural genocide. The question might arise whether we are justified in including the attack upon a culture per se in the definition of a concept which is primarily concerned with the destruction of a social group. [...] If the culture of a group is violently undermined, the group itself disintegrates and its members must either become absorbed in other cultures which is a wasteful and painful process or succumb to personal disorganisation and, perhaps, physical destruction. [...] **According to this view it is clear that the destruction of cultural symbols is genocide** because it implies the destruction of their function and thus **menaces the existence of the social group which exists by virtue of its common culture.**[18]

Lemkin owes this approach to the notion of culture to the influence of another great Pole whose works he studied – Bronisław Malinowski, who was making a staggering career in Anglo-Saxon science at that time.[19] His innovative (for those times) method of participant observation, which required staying among the studied group for a long time, as well as the conclusions concerning the need for a functional and comprehensive treatment of all manifestations of culture are both reflected in Lemkin's text, which occasionally even directly quotes Malinowski.[20]

While elaborating on the notion of cultural genocide, Lemkin clearly differentiated it from cultural changes taking place in normal circumstances, in particular including cultural diffusion, to which he dedicated a separate section of his text.

> Cultural genocide is a more or less abrupt process, that is **it must not be confused with the gradual changes a culture may undergo**. Such gradual changes occur by means of the continuous and slow adaptation of the culture to new situations. The new situations arise from physical changes, creative energies within the culture and the impact of outside influences. Without them the culture becomes static [...].[21]

Consequently, what constitutes the difference between diffusion and cultural genocide is the manner and time in which these processes take place. In Lemkin's thought diffusion is essentially a long-term and rather spontaneous process of adopting foreign cultural elements, whereas cultural genocide does not necessarily need to imply the presence of new elements in the given culture. It can, however, mean the weakening of the group so that it is ultimately helpless when faced with the physical extermination that awaits it.

---

18 R. Lemkin, *The Concept of Genocide...*, p. 2.

19 This concerns primarily the work *A Scientific Theory of Culture*, published post-mortem in 1944.

20 R. Lemkin, *The Concept of Genocide...*.

21 *Ibid.*, p. 3.

> Where cultural genocide appears to be merely a step towards physical extermination, there will certainly be no difficulty in distinguishing it from diffusion[22]

This fragment very clearly shows the broad concept of genocide, entailing the destruction of culture, as an introduction to or a stage preceding a **possible** physical elimination of the group. As a matter of fact, this fragment is not the only one that confirms this vision – the initial paragraph of Chapter 9 of *Axis Rule…*, quoted at the beginning of this article, seems to confirm it too.[23] The analysis of the 'techniques' of genocide characterized by Lemkin himself allows us to conclude that cultural aspects (referred to as spiritual, religious, national requirements, resources or identity) have always been in the centre of Lemkin's vision of the nature of genocide.

Cultural genocide in the debate on the Convention of 1948

Lemkin played a significant role in the creation of 1948 Convention, although he acted as a 'totally unofficial man'[24]. On 11 December 1946 – with the unanimous adoption of Resolution no. 96/I by the UN General Assembly, proposed by Lemkin – the two-year work on the Convention officially started. The first words of the Resolution, penned by Raphael Lemkin himself, read as follows:

> Genocide is a denial of the right of existence of entire human groups, as homicide is the denial of the right to live of individual human beings; such denial of the right of existence shocks the conscience of mankind, **results in great losses to humanity in the form of cultural and other contributions represented by these human groups**, and is contrary to moral law and to the spirit and aims of the United Nations.

William Schabas points out that this first sentence of the Resolution has in fact possibly affected the future understanding of genocide: as compared to homicide but one conducted on a massive scale on a group, which placed the

---

22 *Ibid.*, p. 4.

23 Lemkin's approach to the notion of culture is also shown in the broad studies he conducted in preparation for *The History of* Genocide, which might have been his other *opus magnum*. Yet, although the draft of the book was presented several times to a number of publishers, it has never been published. It presents genocide in the historical context: from the Antiquity, through the Middle Ages, to the contemporary age, and many passages thereof show what great importance Lemkin ascribed to cultural genocide.

24 This is how Lemkin was described in the introductory article to the Sunday issue of the *New York Times* of 20 October 1957, titled 'The Crime of Genocide'. Lemkin later gave the same title to his unpublished – until recently – autobiography (see: R. Lemkin, *Totally Unofficial: The Autobiography of Raphael Lemkin*, Donna-Lee Frieze (ed.), Yale University Press, 2013).

focus on the physical dimension.[25] Thus, the following passage about the loss of a group's cultural contribution appears in the context of physical genocide – as its consequence – and does not suggest the possibility that certain actions aimed solely against the culture of the group may have a genocidal aspect.[26] This is the direction taken by the debate on cultural genocide in the main text of the Convention, even though the documents from the preparatory works for the Convention clearly show that Lemkin fought long to have the concept of cultural genocide included. He even wrote in the Memorandum on the Genocide Convention: 'Cultural Genocide is the most important part of the Convention.'[27] Consequently, it is only his determination that allowed cultural genocide to return in the second draft.

In the first draft, prepared by the UN Secretariat in June 1947 (the Secretariat Draft), the proposed definition of genocide was as follows:

Article I: Definitions

I. [Protected groups] The purpose of this Convention is to prevent destruction of racial, national, **linguistic**, religious or **political** groups of human beings.

II. [Acts qualified as Genocide] In this Convention, the word 'genocide' means a criminal act directed against any one of the aforesaid groups of human beings, with the purpose of destroying it in whole or in part or of preventing its preservation or development.

Such acts consist of:

1. [Physical genocide] Causing the death of members of a group or injuring their health or physical integrity by:
   (a) group massacres or individual executions; or
   (b) subjection to conditions of life which, by lack of proper housing, clothing, food, hygiene and medical care, or excessive work or physical exertion are likely to result in the debilitation or death of the individuals; or
   (c) mutilations and biological experiments imposed for other than curative purposes; or
   (d) deprivation of all means of livelihood, by confiscation of property, looting, curtailment of work, denial of housing and of supplies otherwise available to the other inhabitants of the territory concerned.

25 W. A. Schabas, *Genocide in International Law. The Crime of Crimes*, Cambridge 2000, p. 152.

26 *Ibid.*

27 Quoted after: A. D. Moses, 'Raphael Lemkin, culture..., p. 37.

2. [Biological genocide] Restricting births by:
   (a) sterilization and/or compulsory abortion; or
   (b) segregation of the sexes; or
   (c) obstacles to marriage.
3. [**Cultural genocide**] Destroying the specific characteristics of the group by:
   (a) **forcible transfer of children to another human group**; or
   (b) forced and systematic exile of individuals representing the culture of a group; or
   (c) prohibition of the use of the national language even in private intercourse; or
   (d) systematic destruction of books printed in the national language or of religious works or prohibition of new publications; or
   (e) systematic destruction of historical or religious monuments or their diversion to alien uses, destruction or dispersion of documents and objects of historical, artistic, or religious value and of objects used in religious worship."[28]

The second draft, still discussed as late as in April 1948 (the *Ad Hoc* Committee Draft), stated as follows:

"Article I: [Genocide: a crime under international law]

Genocide is a crime under international law whether committed in time of peace or in time of war.

Article II: ['Physical and biological' genocide]

In this Convention genocide means any of the following deliberate acts committed with the intent to destroy a national, racial, religious or **political** group, on grounds of the national or racial origin, religious belief, or political opinion of its members:

1. Killing members of the group;
2. Impairing the physical integrity of members of the group;
3. Inflicting on members of the group measures or conditions of life aimed at causing their deaths;
4. Imposing measures intended to prevent births within the group.

---

28 UN Secretariat, *Secretariat Draft. First Draft of the Genocide Convention*, V 1947, UN Doc. E/447.

Article III [**'Cultural' genocide**]

In this Convention genocide also means any deliberate act committed with the intent to destroy the language, religion, or culture of a national, racial or religious group on grounds of the national or racial origin or the religious belief of its members such as:

1. Prohibiting the use of the language of the group in daily intercourse or in schools, or the printing and circulation of publications in the language of the group.
2. Destroying or preventing the use of libraries, museums, schools, historical monuments, places of worship or other cultural institutions and objects of the group.[29]

However, also during the *Ad Hoc* Committee debates, the question of leaving or deleting 'cultural genocide' has been a matter of great concern[30]. In the final version of the Convention, adopted on 9 December 1948, the scope of the definition contained in Article 2 was considerably limited:

Article II: In the present Convention, genocide means any of the following acts committed with intent to destroy, in whole or in part, a national, ethnical, racial or religious group, as such:

(a) Killing members of the group;

(b) Causing serious bodily or mental harm to members of the group;

(c) Deliberately inflicting on the group conditions of life calculated to bring about its physical destruction in whole or in part;

(d) Imposing measures intended to prevent births within the group;

(e) **Forcibly transferring children of the group to another group**.

Why is it that cultural genocide disappeared from the draft of the Convention? A detailed history of the debate on the definition of genocide has been reconstructed from official UN documents by, for example, William Schabas. With regard to the notion of cultural genocide, it should be stressed that it had been a subject of controversy from the very beginning of the debate. What is more, the official main task of some delegations, for example the delegation of Canada, was to make every effort not to allow cultural genocide to make it to the final text of the Convention;

29 *Ad Hoc Committee Draft, Second Draft of the Genocide Convention Prepared by the Ad Hoc Committee of the Economic and Social Council (ECOSOC), meeting between April 5, 1948 and May 10, 1948*, UN Doc. E/AC.25/SR.1 to 28.

30 *Report of the Committee and Draft Convention and Draft Convention Drawn Up by the Committee*, E/794, 24 May 1948, p. 17–20.

some countries went as far as to order their delegations to vote against the adoption of the Convention as a whole should their request not be granted.[31]

From the very beginning, the idea of cultural genocide was also opposed by the United States and France (later joined by most other countries, its proponents being only Poland, the USSR, Venezuela, Siam, China, and Lebanon), who stressed that it should be moved to the debate on human rights and the protection of minorities.[32] As a result of this, a proposal was subsequently made to include this idea in the Universal Declaration of Human Rights instead, because it was being developed at the same time as the Convention and adopted only a day after it, on 10 December 1948. However, this proposal has not been realised either.[33] The main argument was that an excessively broad definition would threaten the will to adopt the document and would decrease the largest possible number of countries ready to ratify the Convention. Furthermore, the opinion of the Danish delegate, biased and superficial, essentially coming down to the statement that focusing on mass killings and on the closing of libraries in the same convention proves lack of logic and proportion became widespread.[34]

While some arguments for rejecting cultural genocide seem reasonable, those raised by other countries – especially considering the practices they employed towards the indigenous peoples – already heralded the problems the international community still has with this politically explosive issue even today.[35] Sweden admitted outright to its concerns that the Christianisation of Laplanders could result in future cultural genocide accusations against it. Brazil cautioned that some minorities might use this argument when opposing 'perfectly normal assimilation'. New Zealand, in turn, pointed out that if the concept of cultural genocide had been indeed included in the Convention, accusations of genocide could have been brought up even against the UN Trusteeship Council, which had stated: 'the now

31 W. A. Schabas, *Genocide...*, p. 184.

32 *Ibid.*, pp. 180–181.

33 *Ibid.*, pp. 180 and 183. This story is presented in detail in J. Morsink, 'Cultural Genocide, the Universal Declaration, and Minority Rights', *Human Rights Quarterly*, vol. 21, no. 4, 1999.

34 Cf.: M. Lippman, 'The Drafting of the 1948 Convention on the Prevention and Punishment of the Crime of Genocide', *Boston University International Law Journal*, no. 3, p. 45, 1985.

35 These problems were so great that the next international act, and what is more, one belonging to soft law – the Declaration on the Rights of Indigenous Peoples – was adopted only after almost 30 years of debates on whether it should be passed at all. For more see: H. Schreiber, 'Międzynarodowa ochrona kultury i dziedzictwa kulturowego ludów tubylczych' (International Protection of Culture and Cultural Heritage of Indigenous Peoples), *Stosunki Międzynarodowe – International Relations*, vol. 35, no. 1–2, 2007.

existing tribal structure was an obstacle to the political and social advancement of the indigenous inhabitants.' South Africa agreed with New Zealand's argumentation and noted the danger posed by Article 3 in a situation if it was applied to 'primitive or backward groups'.[36] From today's perspective, after we have experienced the attempts to settle the accounts of the colonial past, we can say that they were indeed right. Those 'prophetic' forecasts are now returning with increased intensity and are voiced by 'naturally assimilated' groups of 'barbarians'.[37]

Thus, the only shred of evidence left in the Convention of 1948, pointing to the long debate on whether cultural genocide was to be included or not, is the fragment of the definition of genocide in Article 2(e): 'forcibly transferring children of the group to another group'. Schabas remarks that this point 'was added to the Convention almost as an afterthought, with little substantive debate or consideration',[38] which justifies the opinion that it has been included in the main definition of genocide sort of 'by accident'.[39] This point appeared, upon the motion of Greece, only at the final stage of the work on the Convention, already after the decision to exclude cultural genocide from the definition. The delegation of Greece justified its motion by saying that while many states opposed the idea of including cultural genocide in the Convention, they 'did not necessarily oppose "forced transfer"'.[40] Another confirmation is the particularly unanimous opinion on this particular matter of the three experts who were consulted on the advisability of including cultural genocide in the main text (while two spoke against cultural genocide, they all agreed on the inclusion of forced transfer of children).[41] Consequently, while Point (e) remains a reminiscence of cultural genocide, which was eventually excluded, it is in fact considered an element of biological genocide – e.g. by the International Law Commission.[42]

---

36 After: W. A. Schabas, *Genocide...*, p. 184.

37 See below: section 'Culturecidal practices – selected forms and examples'.

38 W. A. Schabas, *Genocide...*, p. 175.

39 This is also shown by the result of the vote on this point of the definition: 20 votes 'for', 13 'against' and as many as 13 'abstained' (*ibid.*).

40 *Ibid.*

41 *Ibid.*

42 This point was opposed, for example, by the Polish lawyer Manfred Lachs: 'the word "transfer" could also be applied to the evacuation of children from a theatre of war' (*ibid.*). Platon Morozov, in turn, said that 'no one had been able to quote any historical case of the destruction of a group through the transfer of children' (*ibid.*). As a matter of fact, the latter argument was never very apt, even in the debate on the Convention. The concerns and opposition of states employing the practice of forced transfer of children from indigenous peoples in Canada, Australia or New Zealand in the context

It should be emphasised, however, that forced transfer of children from one group to another has not only a biological aspect – by physically depriving a group of the chances for survival (when, for example, further births within the group are prevented or when parents are murdered) – but also a cultural one – in the form of forced assimilation to the customs, values and language used by the dominant group.[43] Although this issue concerns especially children from indigenous peoples living in colonised regions, we should remember that a plan of forced transfer of children was also implemented by Nazi Germany on Polish territories, as part of the Master Plan East (*Generalplan Ost*). On the basis of numerous sources, it is estimated that, in total, approximately 200,000 children were removed from Poland; they were deemed 'racially valuable' and worth of being submitted to Germanisation, frequently after their parents had been murdered. After the war, only approximately 30,000 of these children have been recovered.[44]

Culturecide in the U.N. Declaration on the Rights of Indigenous Peoples (art. 7–9)

Although the concept of cultural genocide was excluded from the legal definition of genocide in 1948, it very often appears in contemporary debates on the role of culture in the preservation of identity of groups and, consequently, their survival. In order to avoid confusion with the definition of genocide established in the Convention of 1948 (which emphasises the physical aspects of destroying a group for national, ethnic, racial, or religious reasons), in the context of the ongoing political debate I propose using the term 'culturecide', which directly points to the possibility of 'killing a culture', without the necessity to physically exterminate its depositaries. The principal connotation of the term 'cultural genocide' suggests that members of a group are killed due to cultural reasons. However, while such physical extermination may accompany culturecide, it does not necessarily have

---

of the interpretation of cultural genocide only confirm the opposite. For more on this, see further parts of this article.

43 D. Nersessian, 'Rethinking Cultural Genocide Under International Law', *Human Rights Dialogue*, Spring 2005.

44 Cf.: R. Z. Hrabar, *Hitlerowski rabunek dzieci polskich. Uprowadzanie i germanizowanie dzieci polskich w latach 1939–1945* (*Forced Transfer of Polish Children by Nazis. Abduction and Germanisation of Polish Children 1939–1945*), Katowice 1960; R. Z. Hrabar, *Na rozkaz i bez rozkazu. Sto i jeden wybranych dowodów hitlerowskiego ludobójstwa na dzieciach* (*Upon Orders and Without Orders. 101 Selected Proofs of Nazi Genocide Against Children*), Katowice 1968. The same issue was analysed in the RuSHA Trial (*United States of America v. Greifelt et al.*).

to be the goal – as proven by historical examples. On the contrary, preserving the lives of a 'lower race' to use them as slaves or quasi-slaves can actually be in the interest of the dominant group, which will, at the same time, try to eliminate all manifestations of cultural identity of the subdued group as they represent its self-awareness and ties existing within the group. In other words, a group deprived of its own culture, its integrating element, is easier to subdue, degrade and force into a subservient role to the ruling group (not necessarily dominant in numbers). While agreeing to the rejection of Lemkin's broad definition of genocide in the international legislative act such as the Convention of 1948, we cannot ignore the dramatic cases of struggling with culturecidal practices or their consequences, which last at least a lifetime of the people who experienced them.

The physical survival of a group does not guarantee its existence if its members cannot develop their own culture. Consequently, this notion in its original form of cultural genocide once again tried to 'enter' the legal language and appeared in the draft Declaration on the Rights of Indigenous Peoples of 1994.[45]

Article 7 of this draft[46] illustrates the interdependence of the right to life and the right to maintain one's own culture. The concept of cultural genocide is presented as equal to ethnocide:

> Indigenous peoples have the collective and individual right not to be subjected to **ethnocide and cultural genocide**, including prevention of and redress for:
>
> (a) Any action which has the aim or effect of depriving them of their integrity as distinct peoples, or of their cultural values or ethnic identities;
>
> (b) Any action which has the aim or effect of dispossessing them of their lands, territories or resources;
>
> (c) Any form of population transfer which has the aim or effect of violating or undermining any of their rights;
>
> (d) Any form of assimilation or integration by other cultures or ways of life imposed on them by legislative, administrative or other measures;
>
> (e) Any form of propaganda directed against them.[47]

In the final version of the Declaration, adopted by a resolution of the UN General Assembly on 13 September 2007, Article 7 took the following wording:

---

45 It appeared, however, during these five decades under other names in other legal acts – see: 'Conclusion'.

46 http://daccess-dds-ny.un.org/doc/UNDOC/GEN/G94/145/56/PDF/G9414556.pdf?OpenElement, p. 107.

47 UN Doc. E/CN.4/Sub.2/1994/56.

1. Indigenous individuals have the rights to life, physical and mental integrity, liberty and security of person.
2. Indigenous peoples have the collective right to live in freedom, peace and security as distinct peoples and shall not be subjected **to any act of genocide or any other act of violence, including forcibly removing children of the group to another group.**[48]

It should be stressed that the final version of the Declaration no longer includes notions of ethnocide and cultural genocide. The list of practices is the same but the terms that gave rise to concerns and objections of some states were abandoned. Ethnocide and cultural genocide were replaced with forced assimilation and destruction of culture. In the end, the definitions appear in unchanged form (except for their names) in Article 8, which begins as follows:

1. Indigenous peoples and individuals have the right not to be subjected to **forced assimilation or destruction of their culture**.
2. States shall provide effective mechanisms for prevention of, and redress for:
   (a) Any action which has the aim or effect of depriving them of their integrity as distinct peoples, or of their cultural values or ethnic identities;
   (b) Any action which has the aim or effect of dispossessing them of their lands, territories or resources;
   (c) Any form of forced population transfer which has the aim or effect of violating or undermining any of their rights;
   (d) Any form of forced assimilation or integration;
   (e) Any form of propaganda designed to promote or incite racial or ethnic discrimination directed against them.

Additionally, the following passage was added to the Preamble of the Declaration:

> [...] all doctrines, policies and practices based on or advocating superiority of peoples or individuals on the basis of national origin or racial, religious, ethnic or cultural differences are racist, scientifically false, legally invalid, morally condemnable and socially unjust.

The possible actions presented in Article 8 refer to complex and diverse behaviours, not necessarily related to the official state policy that can lead to the destruction of cultural identity and the resulting destruction of a group as such. This destruction takes place through de-ethnicisation, deculturalisation and disintegration

48 UN Declaration on the Rights of Indigenous Peoples, Resolution 61/295, adopted at the 107th plenary meeting of the UN General Assembly on 13 September 2007.

of the social structure[49] According to Aleksander Posern-Zieliński, the practical actions leading to ethnocide usually take three primary forms, regarding: 1) the cultural aspect in the strict sense (planned elimination of indigenous values and imposition the values of the dominant culture, interruption of the intergenerational transmission of traditions, discrediting authorities); 2) the territorial aspect (translocation, territorial marginalisation, ecological degradation of land); 3) the socioeconomic aspect (social marginalisation due to the group's dependence on the economic system of the dominant society, combined with the phenomena of social pathology).[50]

This definition is in agreement with Raphael Lemkin's vision. In the first footnote to Chapter 9, in which he comments on the introduction of the word genocide, he writes:

> Another term could be used for the same idea, namely, *ethnocide*, consisting of the Greek word 'ethnos' – nation – and the Latin word 'cide'.[51]

Usually, these actions (de-ethnicisation, deculturalisation and disintegration of the social structure) are accompanied by depopulation planned and aimed at eradication of cultural identity, which bears the hallmarks of classic genocide. However, the fundamental issue here is acting with intent to physically destroy and kill, which undermines the recognition of the practices used against indigenous peoples as genocide as they were primarily focused on forced and brutal – but 'only' assimilation. The best-known and best documented examples concern the Aborigine tribes of Australia, the Inuits of Canada, the Native American tribes of the United States, and the Sami people of Norway, but these are not the only ones. The fact that the intent to destroy these groups is almost impossible to prove (despite the perfectly documented practices fulfilling the requirements of Point (e) of the definition laid down in the Convention of 1948: 'forcibly transferring children of the group to another group', including the fiasco to use the argument of intentional acting in the famous Australian report *Bringing Them Home*[52]) is the

---

49 Cf.: A. Posern-Zieliński, 'Etnocyd' (Ethnocide), in Z. Staszczak (ed.), *Słownik etnologiczny – terminy ogólne* (*Ethnological Dictionary – General Terms*), Warszawa–Poznań 1987, p. 87.

50 *Ibid.*, p. 88.

51 Cf.: Footnote 2.

52 Cf.: R. Van Krieken, 'Cultural Genocide Reconsidered', *Australian Indigenous Law Review*, vol. 12, 2008, special edition, pp. 76–81. R. Gaita, 'Genocide: the Holocaust and the Aborigines', *Quadrant*, vol. 4, 1997, pp. 17–22.

reason why, nowadays, these peoples are much more eager to invoke the notion of culturecide – which constitutes a 'weaker version' of genocide.

Culturecidal practices – selected forms and examples

A well-known example of culturecidal practices[53] was the case of forcibly taking children away from Aborigine mothers under the pretext of creating opportunities for development, which was to hide the true intention of depriving them of their native culture ('biological absorption', practiced until 1970). These children were called the 'Stolen Generation',[54] and even though the Aborigine culture has not been completely destroyed, almost 200 years of culturecidal practices (going far beyond the aforementioned policy of forced assimilation of children) led to depopulation and far-reaching disintegration of Aborigine tribes. In 1988, when Australia celebrated '200 Years of Australia' (counted from the beginnings of British settlement in 1788), Aborigines spoke of 200 years of slavery.[55] It was only on 13 February 2008 that a historic gesture was made – the new Prime Minister Kevin Rudd said what hundreds of thousands of Aborigines have been waiting to hear for so long: 'we say sorry'.[56]

A similar gesture was made half a year later in June, in Canada, where the government was using very similar practices – it had forcibly removed children from Inuit families (their number is estimated at more than 100,000) and placed

---

53 The film *Rabbit-Proof Fence*, directed by Philip Noyce and made popular in 2002, told the story of these events.

54 According to estimates of the Australian Bureau of Statistics (ABS) of 1994, 1 in 10 Aborigine children were forcibly transferred this way. However, this issue became a topic of public interest only in 1992, after the judgement in the case concerning the land of the Melanesian Mabo (public address of Prime Minister Keating, in which he apologised for the ignorance and prejudice which had led to children being taken away from their families). In 1995, the Attorney-General of Australia started the National Inquiry into the Separation of Aboriginal and Torres Strait Islander Children from Their Families, which was concluded in 1997 with the report *Bringing Them Home – Report of the National Inquiry*.

55 26 January, officially the 'Australia Day', is called 'Invasion Day', 'Day of Mourning' or 'Survival Day' by the Aborigines. After: *Australia Day – Invasion Day*, available at: http://www.creativespirits.info/aboriginalculture/history/australia-day-invasion-day#toc1 (accessed on 10 May 2013).

56 For more see: H. Schreiber, 'Pojednanie międzykulturowe w Australii?' (Intercultural Reconciliation in Australia?), available at: http://www.stosunkimiedzynarodowe.info/artykul,65,Pojednanie_miedzykulturowe_w_Australii.html (accessed on 12 January 2013).

them in special residential schools managed by the Protestant Church, where the children had been subjected to forced acculturation (referred to as resocialisation of children of Native American descent) for almost 200 years (from around 1800 until 1980).[57] On 23 May 2005, an agreement was reached concerning the payment of compensations for the victims of this system and the Indian Residential Schools Truth and Reconciliation Commission was established to monitor the actions and document the events in this respect. It was finally approved by the government on 10 May 2006. The Commission was based on similar commissions already functioning in Africa (Sierra Leone, South Africa).

The experience related to such practices resulted in adding the following passage to the Preamble of the Declaration:

> Recognising [...] the right of indigenous families and communities to retain shared responsibility for the upbringing, training, education and well-being of their children, consistent with the rights of the child.

A different example (in the institutional sense) of solving the tensions between the state and the native people is Norway. In 1997, at an official opening of the Sámediggi (the parliament of the Sami people), King Harald V said:

> The state of Norway was founded on the territory of two peoples – the Sámi people and the Norwegians. Sámi history is closely intertwined with Norwegian history. Today, we express our regret on behalf of the state for the **injustice committed against the Sámi people through its harsh policy of Norwegianization**.[58]

Norway's policy towards the Sami (who also inhabit some areas of Finland, Sweden and Russia) has been gradually changing since the 1950s.[59] It was also in

57 J. J. Llewellyn, 'Dealing with the Legacy of Native Residential School Abuse in Canada: Litigation, ADR, and Restorative Justice', *University of Toronto Law Journal*, vol. 52, no. 3, 2002. Native American children were sexually abused in schools on a mass scale, and due to the lack of adequate funding for the schools they were also subjected to forced hard physical labour. There was also virtually no true education in these schools, as it mainly came down to depriving the children of their native language, culture, customs, and spirituality. In some of these schools the mortality rate of children was as high as 50 percent; cf.: http://www.cbc.ca/news/politics/story/2013/04/26/truth-and-reconciliation-saganash-paul-martin.html (accessed on 26 April 2013).

58 Quotation after: the official website of the Embassy of Norway in Poland: http://www.amb-norwegia.pl/AboutN, orway/policy/Ludno/population/sami/policy/ (accessed on 10 March 2013).

59 In 1956, the Minister of Culture and Church Affairs established a commission to deal with the problems of the Sami. A report issued by the commission in 1959 proposed a new political line which completely departed from the policy of Norwegianisation and

Norway that education had once been used to systemically eliminate the Sami culture. In 1974 the Sami Development Fund was established, and two years later the Reindeer Husbandry Agreement was adopted. In the 1980s, the Sami Rights Committee and the Sami Culture Committee were established. This resulted in the adoption of an act establishing the Sámediggi and an act regulating the legal status of the Sami. The first elections to the Sámediggi were held together with the elections to the Norwegian parliament in September 1989 and the first session was officially opened by King Olaf on 7 October 1989.

In 2000, the Norwegian parliament established a fund for the Sami that is managed by the Sámediggi. The money from the fund is used for actions aimed at supporting the development of the language, culture and lifestyle of the Sami and is meant as a collective compensation for the damage and injustice suffered by the Sami due to Norway's actions.

We could say that the establishment of mechanisms to deal with the past in all the countries in which the indigenous peoples are finally starting to participate in the public debate is simply a necessity. The motto 'never again' has become central to the settlement of the dramatic past not only in the countries which are rising from military dictatorships (Latin America) or communist regimes (East-Central Europe) but also in those which saw a fundamental change in the perception of the rights of people (minorities or indigenous peoples) which used to live on the margins of the official social life.

The concept of the right to the truth emerged as a new component of human rights, based upon the existing norms, such as the requirement to ensure freedom of speech and the civil right to seek information, the requirement to make information available and to convene proceedings in cases concerning the violation of human rights.[60] In the light of this right, apology and compensation for culturecidal practices committed against indigenous peoples in the past are a prerequisite for the implementation of the idea of 'cultural justice' and the foundation of the process of cultural reconciliation. One of the means of ensuring

assimilation practiced at that time. On the basis of recommendations in 1962–1963 the Ministry presented a report to the Storting which became the foundation for the first comprehensive parliamentary debate on the principles which were to underlie the Norway's policy towards the Sami people. After: http://www.amb-norwegia.pl/facts/sami/sami/sami.htm (accessed on 20 January 2007).

60 G. Skąpska, 'Law, rights and democracy after totalitarianism', in A. Soeteman (ed.), *Pluralism and Law*, Dordrecht–Boston 2001, p. 155 ff; see also: J. E. Mendez, *An Emerging Right to Truth: Latin America Experiences*, Oñati 1999.

restorative justice for the victims of culturecidal practices can be the truth and reconciliation commissions.[61]

Culture and cultural life fifty years after Lemkin

In the part of the chapter of *Axis Rule…* devoted to genocide, titled 'Recommendations for the Future', Lemkin formulated important objectives which allow us to narrow down his vision of culture:

> The world represents only so much culture and intellectual vigour as are created by its component national groups. […]The destruction of a nation, therefore, results in the loss of its future contributions to the world. […]Among the basic features which have marked progress in civilization are the **respect for and appreciation of the national characteristics and qualities contributed to world culture by the different nations** – characteristics and qualities which, as illustrated in the contributions made by nations weak in defence and poor in economic resources, are not to be measured in terms of national power and wealth.[62]

Lemkin's devotion to the idea of cultural diversity and his vision of multicultural states, respecting the minorities living within their borders, was deeply rooted in his identity of a patriotic Pole and a Jew by descent. Anthony Dirk Moses sums it up very aptly:

> Lemkin's was an ecumenical cosmopolitanism. Being a Polish patriot and advocate for all cultures never entailed renouncing his Jewish heritage or cultural rooting. His Jewish identity was not structured like a zero sum game. He always mentioned the genocidal persecution of the Jews by the Nazis in the same breath as the mass murder of Polish Christians, Roma, and other victims. Central was his attachment to the notion of 'spiritual nationality', a concept that most likely can be traced to Jewish sources as well as to Herder.[63]

Although cultural genocide is not a separate category recognised by international law, its partial inclusion in the definition of genocide in Point (e) of the

---

61 Such a commission was also established in Australia by the parliament act of 1991 (the Council for Aboriginal Reconciliation). Its mandate was not limited to the issues of the Stolen Generation; it concerned the entire process of reconciliation between the indigenous peoples of Australia and the white settlers. Its mandate expired in 2000 with the presentation of the Australian Declaration Towards Reconciliation and the Roadmap for Reconciliation to the government and with the establishment of the non-governmental organisation Reconciliation Australia in its stead (http://www.reconciliation.org.au/).

62 Cf.: Footnote 2.

63 A. D. Moses, 'Raphael Lemkin, culture…, p. 24.

Convention of 1948 is an important proof that at least some of its forms are considered unacceptable. The same concerns the U.N. Declaration on the Rights of Indigenous Peoples, which while including the description of culturecidal practices in points (a)–(e) of Article 8, despite eventually not referring to them with the collective term culturecide or ethnocide, points to the fact that culturecide is actually criminalised in this form under the category of forceful assimilation and destruction of culture.

Although the other binding instruments in the area of human rights seemingly do not address culturecide and focus on fundamental rights, such as the right to life, the right to a fair trial or the prohibition of torture, there is also Article 27 of the International Covenant on Civil and Political Rights, which since 1966 has been setting the standard of state responsibilities in the field of guaranteeing the right to cultural life, and Article 15 of the International Covenant on Economic, Social and Cultural Rights, of 1966:

Article 27 ICCPR

In those States in which ethnic, religious or linguistic minorities exist, persons belonging to such minorities **shall not be denied the right**, in community with the other members of their group, **to enjoy their own culture**, to profess and practise their own religion, or to use their own language.

Article 15 ICESCR

1. The States Parties to the present Covenant recognize the right of everyone:
   (a) **To take part in cultural life**;
   (b) To enjoy the benefits of scientific progress and its applications;
   (c) To benefit from the protection of the moral and material interests resulting from any scientific, literary or artistic production of which he is the author.
2. The steps to be taken by the States Parties to the present Covenant to achieve the full realisation of this right shall **include those necessary for the conservation, the development and the diffusion of science and culture**.
3. The States Parties to the present Covenant undertake to respect the freedom indispensable for scientific research and creative activity.
4. The States Parties to the present Covenant recognize the benefits to be derived from the encouragement and development of international contacts and **co-operation in the scientific and cultural fields**.

In preparing to draw up its General Comment to Article 15, on the basis of Rule 65 of the Rules of Procedure, the Committee on Economic, Social and Cultural Rights (henceforth: CESCR) held two debates – one in 1992 and another in 2008

– dedicated solely to the issue of the right to take part in cultural life with the participation of representatives of international non-governmental and governmental organisations as well as academic institutions. Already in 1992 it was decided that the concept of 'cultural life' should be given a much broader meaning, taking into account both the individual and the collective aspect and reflecting the understanding of culture as 'a way of being and feeling, in short, the community's way of life and thought'[64]. In 2008, the CESCR ordered 17 background papers[65] for the debate on the contemporary understanding of the right to take part in cultural life. It must be stressed that the initial understanding of the notion of 'cultural life' by the drafters of the Covenant – as reflected by the *travaux préparatoires*[66] – was restricted to the participation of the masses in the sphere of cultural practice created by an elite, that is in 'high' culture. Nowadays, both the national reports and the guidelines of the Committee itself address such 'new' notions (compared to the international reality of the 1960s and 1970s) as multiculturalism, cultural identity or cultural pluralism. Many states now refer to the promotion of intercultural dialogue, cultural education, and the protection of the culture of minorities and indigenous peoples, including the protection of minority languages[67]. The need to adopt a broad, anthropological definition of culture, reflecting actual practice, is considered essential in all the positions submitted to the CESCR.

In various forms, the protection of the right to live in one's own culture under the notion of the right to take part in cultural life is also included in the provisions of other instruments of international law, specially human rights, for example the International Convention on the Elimination of All Forms of Racial Discrimination (Article 1), the Framework Convention for the Protection of National Minorities (Article 5), the European Charter for Regional or Minority Languages, as well as in several declarations, such as the Declaration on the Rights of Persons Belonging to National or Ethnic, Religious and Linguistic Minorities, adopted by

64 S. R. Konaté, *Implementation of Cultural Rights. Analytical Study of Article 15 of the ICESCR*, 1992, E/C.12.1992/WP.4.

65 Committee on Economic, Social and Cultural Rights, *Background Papers*, 2008, E/C.12/40/3 ff.

66 *Annotation of the Text of the Draft International Covenants on Human Rights*, 1955, UN Doc. A/2929.

67 Y. Donders, *Cultural Life in the Context of Human Rights. Background Paper*, 2008, E/C.12/40/13, p. 5.

the UN General Assembly in 1992. Furthermore, it also appears in the judgements of international criminal courts.[68]

In this new line of interpreting 'cultural life' culture comprises all aspects of life, and in that way is in accordance with the Lemkins' definition of culture and his vision of its crucial role for sustaining also other aspects of life: social, political, moral, biological, physical, religious or economic.

Conclusions and final considerations

Many grave human rights violations, as mentioned in the examples of Aboriginal tribes, Sami or Inuits, imply a real danger of cultural genocide. The World Commission on Culture and Development noted on this threat for indigenous peoples:

> Quite frequently, ... their disappearance as identifiable communities is not simply a regrettable by-product of development but results from a stated or implicit policy. This process has been called cultural genocide or ethnocide. ... **Cultural genocide is the process whereby a culturally distinct people loses its identity** as its lands and resource base is eroded, and as the use of its language and social and political institutions, as well as its traditions, art forms, religious practices and cultural values is restricted. This may be the result of systematic government policy; but even when due to the impersonal forces of economic development, it is still ethnocidal in its effects.[69]

This situation points out to the fact that the distinction between biological and cultural aspects is still by no means clear. The word 'culturecide' might allow us to better grasp the disputed understanding of what it means to 'destroy' a human group: whether it is necessary to physically kill them, or whether they can be 'killed' in more subtle and apparently 'civilised' ways.[70] Lately, this concept appeared again, describing the wanton destruction of cultural heritage sites as visible evidence of cultural identity and diversity in Mali, Syria and Iraq, raising great international concerns and inspiring actions to prevent these atrocities, including first UN Security Council Resolution devoted exlusively to unlawful destruction of cultural

---

68 Cf. e.g. the separate opinion of judge Mohamad Shahabuddeen in 2004 in the Krstić case (Case No. IT-98-33-T), tried before the International Criminal Tribunal for the former Yugoslavia; see also: Prosecutor v. Blaškić, Appeals Chamber, Case IT-95-14-T (2004) (Judgment); Prosecutor v. Jakić, Case IT-01-42/I-S, Trial Chamber, 51 (2004) (Judgment).

69 *Our Creative Diversity, Report of the World Commission on Culture and Development*, UNESCO Publishing, Paris 1996, pp. 69–70.

70 R. Krieken, 'Rethinking cultural genocide: Aboriginal child removal and settler-colonial state formation', *Oceania*, vol. 75, Issue 2, December 2004, pp. 125–151.

heritage in the context of armed conflicts and terrorist attacks (Resolution 2347, adopted on 24 March 2017) and following this Resolution Joint Declaration of the Ministers of Culture of G7, expressing 'deep concern about the destruction of cultural heritage sites, as such actions obliterate irreplaceable patrimony, extinguish the identity of targeted communities and erase any evidence of past diversity or religious pluralism'[71]. In this context a new term has been used by the Director General of UNESCO Irina Bokova: 'cultural cleansing'.[72]

> The *modus operandi* consists of an extremely coherent and violent attempt to «cleanse» the society from any form of diversity, as well as and from all its places and vectors of cultural practice and free thinking. This includes deliberate attacks on places of worship and memory, as well as the killing of journalists and teachers, and the revision of education curricula to foster hatred against the other.[73]

Therefore, the concept of banning cultural genocide in international law has not really been 'rejected'; it is in fact 'silently present'. Its presence in international law is silent because it is hidden under different names (e.g. forced assimilation or forcible transfer of children)[74] and fragmented in diverse international law instruments: human rights law, international humanitarian law, international criminal law and international cultural heritage law[75].

Although it seems quite unlikely for the very notion of 'cultural genocide' to be included in the catalogue of international crimes, in the political and international sphere it definitely manifests itself quite 'loudly'. It is directly articulated by the

---

71 The First G7 Ministerial Meeting on Culture, *Joint Declaration of the Ministers of Culture of G7 o the Occasion of the Meeting "Culture as an Instrument for Dialogue Among Peoples"*, Florence, 30 March 2017.

72 http://en.unesco.org/news/director-general-irina-bokova-firmly-condemns-destruction-palmyra-s-ancient-temple-baalshamin, accessed on June 2016.

73 *The Protection of Heritage and Cultural Diversity: A Humanitarian and Security Imperative in the Conflicts of the 21st century. Background note to the International Conference "Heritage and Cultural Diversity at Risk in Iraq and Syria"*, UNESCO Headquarters, Paris, 3 December 2014, p. 6.

74 As a result of which some researchers speak of a solely rhetorical power of the argument of cultural genocide (cf.: A. Xanthaki, *Indigenous Rights and United Nations Standards: Self-Determination, Culture and Land*, Cambridge 2007, p. 114; and: A. D. Moses, 'Raphael Lemkin, culture..., p. 39). According to Moses, unfortunately today everything that does not meet the requirements of the conventional narrow definition of genocide 'falls beneath the radar of international public opinion' (*ibid.*, p. 41).

75 Y. Donders, 'Old Cultures Never Die? Cultural Genocide in International Law', in I. Boerefijnetal (ed.), *Human Rights: Pre-Conflict, In Conflict, and Post-Conflict,* Intersentia 2012.

descendants of culturally uprooted indigenous peoples. Culturecide thus has a central place in the debate on settling the accounts of the colonial past in the territories of former colonial empires. This 'unfinished' project of international law, started by Raphael Lemkin in 1940s, is finding its continuation in the modern public debate and political argumentation today, going far beyond the colonial discourse. It will surely not disappear from international relations, and its continued presence in the legal and political discourse for more than 70 years can also mean that it will be given a proper separate form and name in international law in the future. Paul Martin, former Prime Minister of Canada (2003–2006), said at a hearing before the Canadian Truth and Reconciliation Commission in April 2013: 'Let us understand that what happened at the residential schools was **the use of education for cultural genocide**, and that the fact of the matter is — yes it was. Call a spade a spade.'[76] Calling these kinds of practices simply "destruction of culture", "loss of cultural heritage" or "forced assimilation" in the context of dramatic suffering of thousands of people seems no longer enough today: not in the political sense, and neither in the moral or legal one.

76 CBC News, 'Paul Martin Accuses Residential Schools of "Cultural Genocide"', available at: http://www.cbc.ca/news/politics/story/2013/04/26/truth-and-reconciliation-saganash-paul-martin.html (accessed on 26 April 2013). One of the witnesses at these hearings, Romeo Saganash, who had been removed from his family of the Cree people, said: 'I can never be normal. And none, none of those kids who were sent to residential schools can claim to be normal today. It's impossible' (*ibid.*).

Patrycja Grzebyk

Culture and Prosecution of International Crimes

Key words: international crimes, legal culture, genocide, international criminal tribunals, international criminal procedure

Abstract: The article focuses on the impact of culture on the prosecution of international crimes. It describes in what way states, influenced by their legal order, shape the international criminal law and what types of difficulties resulting from the cultural context can be encountered during proceedings concerning individual criminal responsibility for international crimes.

Without the knowledge of law, one cannot understand how culture works and what it consists of. On the other hand, however, in order to understand law, one needs to remember that it is a part of culture.[1] In other words, law is a reflection of culture and, at the same time, law shapes culture.[2]

The law is built on certain values which it is supposed to implement and protect.[3] These values make up the legal culture of a country, which additionally includes the opinions and expectations of the society with regard to the functioning of the legal system (that is the set of binding laws), guidelines concerning

1 In this context, it is worth citing a broader fragment of Lawrence Rosen's statement: 'Law is one of these cultural domains. Like the marketplace or the house of worship, the arrangement of space or the designation of familial roles, law may possess a distinctive history, terminology, and personnel. But even where specialisation is intense, law does not exist in isolation. To understand how culture is put together and operates, therefore, one cannot fail to consider law; to consider law, one cannot fail to see it as part of culture.' (L. Rosen, *Law as Culture. An Invitation*, Princeton 2006, p. 4–5).

2 B. Banaszak *et al.* (eds.), *Główne kultury prawne współczesnego świata* (*Main Legal Cultures of Contemporary World*), Warszawa 1995, p. 200; see also: A. Kojder, 'Kultura prawna: problem demarkacji i użyteczności pojęcia' (Legal culture: the problem of demarcation and usefulness of the term), in *Kultura prawna i dysfunkcjonalności prawa* (*Legal Culture and Dysfunctionality of Law*), joint publication, Warszawa 1988, p. 19.

3 T. Stawecki, P. Winczorek, *Wstęp do prawoznawstwa* (*Introduction to law*), 4th ed., Warszawa 2003, p. 25; see also: B. Banaszak *et al.* (eds.), *Główne kultury prawne...*, p. 18; and A. Kojder, *Kultura prawna...*, p. 14.

conduct, behaviour and attitude towards the legal system, knowledge of legal rules and their interpretation, as well as the methods of legal thinking.[4]

Every country participating in the creation of international law tries to sway the other entities in favour of supporting its own vision of law and its interpretation. It attempts to introduce the legal institutions which it knows well into international law and to remodel the ones which are alien to its culture, so that they resemble the familiar models. This is also the reason why any negotiations of multilateral international treaties concerning legal issues are so difficult and lengthy and why their final outcome is so often incoherent and full of repetitions.

It is worth noting that the diversity of legal systems (and, indirectly, legal cultures)[5] is treated as a value, as confirmed by the provisions of the statute of the International Criminal Court (ICC), under which 'The States Parties shall, in the selection of judges, take into account the need, within the membership of the Court, for: (i) The representation of the principal legal systems of the world',[6] and the statute of the International Court of Justice (ICJ), which stresses that in the elected body of judges 'the representation of the main forms of civilization and of the principal legal systems of the world should be assured'.[7] Academic literature usually differentiates between the following main legal systems in the world: civil law (also called Romano-Germanic law or continental law), common law, Far Eastern law, Islamic law, Hindu law, African law, and sometimes even Nordic

4 T. Stawecki, P. Winczorek, *Wstęp...*, p. 37, A. Kojder, *Kultura prawna...*, p. 29, T. Stawecki, 'Konwergencja i dywergencja porządków prawnych w sferze tworzenia prawa' (Convergence and divergence of legal orders in the sphere of creating law), in O. Nawrot, S. Sykuna, J. Zajadło (eds.), *Konwergencja czy dywergencja kultur i systemów prawnych?* (*Convergence or Divergence of Legal Cultures?*), Warszawa 2012, p. 27.

5 Although the term 'legal system' is defined in academic literature as a set of binding rules applicable in a country or territorial international community in a given period (T. Stawecki, *Konwergencja...*, p. 27), hence it does not include legal culture, we cannot fail to notice that the system is created under the influence of legal culture, it stems from it and, at the same time, shapes it.

6 Rome Statute of the International Criminal Court of 17 July 1998, UNTS, vol. 2187, pp. 3 ff, Article 36 (8)(a).

7 *Statute of the International Court Of Justice*, Article 9, UNTS vol. 1, pp. XVI ff; see also: Article 8 of the Statute of the International Law Commission, adopted by the United Nations General Assembly by resolution 174 (II) of 21 November 1947, as amended by resolutions 485 (V) of 12 December 1950, 984 (X) of 3 December 1955, 985 (X) of 3 December 1955 and 36/39 of 18 November 1981.

law.[8] Representatives of the common law system usually prefer to speak of legal traditions rather than main legal systems, thus stressing their historical roots, and they usually extend the above list by adding the local or indigenous legal tradition, the Talmudic legal tradition, and the Socialist legal tradition.[9]

The entirety of the legal order of a state (which includes legal culture, the legal system and concrete actions of the addressees of laws in relation to these laws)[10] translates into their approach to the prosecution of international crimes. Therefore, the first aim of the present article is to show, basing on an analysis of documents and statements made by legal theorists, how states influenced by their legal order attempt to shape the provisions of international law that concern the criminalisation of various crimes; the second aim is to identify the influence of the legal system of states on the adoption of specific models of prosecuting international crimes; the third goal is to show what types of difficulties resulting from the cultural context can be encountered during proceedings against individuals charged with committing international crimes and what solutions should be adopted in order for justice to be served.

Criminalisation of international crimes

Since the beginning of the development of international criminal law, it has been clear that individual states had an immense influence on the extent of criminalisation of various acts. These countries, bearing in mind their own experiences, have been trying to convince the international community to forbid some types of action or nonfeasance to protect the values they hold close.[11] For example,

---

8 L. Morawski, *Wstęp do prawoznawstwa* (*Introduction to jurisprudence*), 14th ed., Toruń 2012, p. 67; see also: R. David, G. Grasmann, *Einführung in die grossen Rechtsysteme der Gegenwart*, München 1988.

9 Patrick Glenn stressed that in the epistemological sense, the term 'legal tradition' is better than the term 'legal culture', as in contrast to the latter it does not refer solely to the current forms of human activity and, consequently, it does not disregard the normative forms that originate in the past (H. P. Glenn, *Legal Traditions of the World*, 4th ed., Oxford 2010, pp. xxiv–xxv; also see: M. Joutsen, 'Legal traditions', in M. Natarajan, *International Crime and Justice*, Cambridge 2011, p. 67; R. Tokarczyk, *Współczesne kultury prawne* (*Contemporary Legal Cultures*), 9th ed., Warszawa 2012, p. 92 ff).

10 T. Stawecki, *Konwergencja...*, p. 27.

11 For instance, one of the first treaties to define international crime was the Convention of 16 November 1937 for the Prevention and Punishment of Terrorism (the same day the Convention for the Creation of an International Criminal Court was adopted), the adoption of which was spurred by the assassination of Alexander I, King of Yugoslavia,

during the debate on the definition of genocide under the Convention on the Prevention and Punishment of the Crime of Genocide of 10 December 1948,[12] scepticism about including 'forcibly transferring children of the group to another group' [current Article 2 (e)] was overcome by Greece who pointed out that its citizens were falling victim to such actions and that the Ottomans were taking away Christian boys to convert them to Islam.[13] In turn, the delegate from Poland, Manfred Lachs, drew the delegates' attention to the need of extending the definition of genocide to include 'deliberately inflicting on the group conditions of life calculated to bring about its physical destruction in whole or in part' [current Article 2 (c)], as he was painfully aware of how the Polish society was starved during World War II through reductions of food rations.[14] Furthermore, as shown by the negotiations regarding the list of serious infringements of the Geneva Conventions for the Protection of War Victims of 12 August 1949 (GC I–IV)[15] and the additional Protocol of 8 June 1977 relating to the Protection of Victims of International Armed Conflicts (P I),[16] the existence of specific national regulations which penalise the actions in question was also a very important argument for the adoption of relevant prohibitions on the international level.[17]

---

and Jean Louis Barthou, Prime Minister of France (for details of the discussion on the said Conventions see: B. B. Ferencz, *An International Criminal Court. A Step Toward World Peace – A Documentary History and Analysis*, vol. 1: *Half a Century of Hope*, London 1980, p. 269 ff).

12 Adopted by United Nations General Assembly Resolution 260 (III) A.

13 H. Abtahi, P. Webb, *The Genocide Convention. The Travaux Préparatoires*, vol. 2, Leiden 2008, p. 1495; also see: W. A. Schabas, *Genocide in International Law: The Crime of Crimes*, Cambridge 2009, p. 202; also see the article concerning abduction of Greek children during the civil war in Greece in 1948–1949: T. Vervenioti, 'The children of the Greek civil war. Saved or kidnapped?', *Acta Universitatis Carolinae, Studia Territoralia* 2010, suppl. 1, p. 117 ff.

14 H. Abtahi, P. Webb, *The Genocide…*, p. 1450; see also: M. Lachs, *War Crimes: An Attempt to Define the Issues*, London 1945, p. 21.

15 See: Article 50 GC I, Article 51 GC II, Article 130 GC III, Article 147 GC IV, UNTS vol. 1975, pp. 31 ff.

16 Protocol Additional to the Geneva Conventions of 12 August 1949, and relating to the Protection of Victims of International Armed Conflicts, UNTS vol. 1125, p. 3 ff.

17 See e.g.: J. de Preux, *The Geneva Conventions of 12 August 1949. Commentary. III Geneva Convention Relative to the Treatment of Prisoners of War*, International Committee of the Red Cross, Geneva 1960, p. 628; O. M. Uhler, H. Coursier, *The Geneva Conventions of 12 August 1949. Commentary. IV Geneva Convention Relative to the Protection of Civilian Persons in Time of War*, International Committee of the Red Cross, Geneva 1958, p. 600.

However, calling only upon one's own unique experiences can sometimes prove a 'kiss of death' for a given idea. When the examples cited by a state were considered atypical and too specific, the others would often not be swayed in favour of adopting the relevant provisions. This was the case with the Polish proposal to penalise preparations for genocide. Many countries believed that it would be very hard to prove that given actions constitute preparations for this crime and the example cited by Lachs of two German factories near Gdańsk that (as proven by experts) were dedicated solely to the manufacture of soap from human corpses was deemed an individual, unique case.[18] China also failed to convince the other countries that the expression 'causing serious [...] mental harm to members of the group' included in the final definition of genocide [current Article 2 (b)] should be associated with the practice of making people addicted to drugs. It seems that the Chinese representatives focused too much on condemning the policy of Japan which, in their opinion, being unable to eradicate the Chinese nation by traditional means, tried to make it addicted to drugs, and for this purpose built a factory in Mukden producing drugs on a mass scale.[19] Nonetheless, the Chinese proposal has not been entirely forgotten, and it has influenced the interpretation of the Convention by legal theorists[20] and its content has been the aim of reservations and interpretative declarations made by various countries in relation to the Convention of 1948.[21]

A particularly strong commitment of a country or a group of countries to the criminalisation of specific actions can sometimes, at least in the short term, make

---

18 H. Abtahi, P. Webb, *The Genocide...*, p. 1564. Convention on the Prevention and Punishment of the Crime of Genocide of 1948 prohibits 'conspiracy to commit genocide' [Article 3 (b)], while Article 118(3) of the Polish Penal Code of 1997 (Polish Journal of Laws of 1997, no. 88, item 553) penalises the undertaking of any and all preparations for genocide; see also: M. Flemming, J. Wojciechowska, *Zbrodnie wojenne. Przestępstwa przeciwko pokojowi, państwu i obronności. Rozdział XVI, XVII, XVIII Kodeksu karnego. Komentarz* (*War crimes. Crimes against peace, state and security. Chapters XVI, XVII, XVIII of the [Polish] Penal Code. A commentary*), Warszawa 1999, pp. 48–49.

19 H. Abtahi, P. Webb, *The Genocide...*, pp. 1103 and 1226; see also: W. Schabas, *Genocide...*, p. 181.

20 See: N. Robinson, *The Genocide Convention. A Commentary*, New York 1960, p. ix.

21 In the *U.S. reservations, declarations, and understandings, International Convention on the Prevention and Punishment of the Crime of Genocide*, the United States stresses that 'the term "mental harm" [...] means permanent impairment of mental faculties through drugs, torture or similar techniques'. The United States ratified the convention on 25 November 1988. The text of aforementioned document is available at: http://treaties.un.org.

other states perceive the given problem as purely regional and consequently, prevent them from accepting the need to introduce the relevant definitions into their legal systems, even those adopted at the international arena. A good example of this phenomenon is the approach exhibited by many states towards the adoption of the International Convention for the Protection of All Persons from Enforced Disappearance of 2006,[22] which was particularly strongly promoted by states, non-governmental organisations and associations of families of missing persons from Latin America. The Convention has been adopted, eventually, but many countries seem to be strongly convinced that the practice of enforced disappearances is either history or is territorially limited to the Americas and, consequently, it does not require criminalisation in national law, and the existing provisions are a sufficient protection from such practices.[23] It is all the more surprising that among the 41 states, which were parties to the Convention (state as of 31 December 2013), one third were from South and Central America.

The convictions of states not only lead to the inclusion of new acts in the list of international crimes but can also be the reason for fervent opposition against including certain acts in a given category of crime. For instance, Israel stated that one of the reasons for its refusal to ratify the Statute of the International Criminal Court was that its definition of war crime covered: 'transfer, directly or indirectly, by the Occupying Power of parts of its own civilian population into the territory it occupies, or the deportation or transfer of all or parts of the population of the occupied territory within or outside this territory.'[24] Their opposition was only natural because criminalisation of the said act would effectively condemn Israel's settlement practice and possibly imply criminal responsibility of Israeli citizens, while Israel itself believes such practice to fall under the sovereign prerogatives of the state.[25] Also, in the case of negotiations concerning the definition of aggression (both as an act of a state and a crime of an individual), the United States exhibited considerable determination to have the definition exclude military operations undertaken due to humanitarian reasons or constituting incidental

---

22 The said convention was adopted by the General Assembly in resolution 61/177 on 20 December 2006.

23 A. Szpak, *Wymuszone zaginięcia. Wybrane zagadnienia* (*Forced Disappearances. Selected problems*), Toruń 2009, p. 27.

24 Article 8(2) (b)(viii), Rome Statute of the International Criminal Court.

25 W. A. Schabas, *An Introduction to the International Criminal Court*, 2nd ed., Cambridge 2004, p. 61; see also: L/ROM/22, 17 July 1998. In this context, it is worth noting that Article 120 of the Rome Statute of the ICC prohibits any reservations made to the Statute.

infringement of territorial integrity.[26] Of course, it is no secret that the United States has on several occasions taken such actions as part of the War on Terror and has considered them legal.[27]

It can be argued that there exists a hard core of the catalogue of international crimes, and that the penalisation of each of these crimes is in the interest of all countries as they have, eventually, decided to adopt a list – however short – of international crimes in the Statute of the ICC. From the point of view of the general prohibition of war crimes, crimes against humanity and genocide,[28] we can even put forward a thesis that there exists an international legal culture that protects supranational values.[29] However, the boundaries of the definitions of said crimes are debatable and no definition is treated as a dogma. Patricia Wald, a former judge of the International Criminal Tribunal for the Former Yugoslavia, stresses that each new international court has introduced new elements to the definition of crime against humanity and war crime.[30] Even with regard to the definition of genocide, which was copied in an unchanged form to the statutes of several courts, there were attempts to extend protection to include, for example, social or political groups.[31] Therefore, it seems that instead of a proof of the existence

26 See, for instance, the amendments proposed by the United States at the review conference in Kampala in June 2010, which are cited in J. Trahan, 'The Rome Statute's amendments on the crime of aggression: Negotiations at the Kampala Review Conference', *International Criminal Law Review*, vol. 11, 2011, pp. 73–74.

27 See: M. Sapiro, *Iraq: The Shifting Sands of Pre-emptive Self-Defense*, AJIL 2003, vol. 97, p. 599 ff.

28 I intentionally omit the crime of aggression mentioned in the Statute of the ICC, as despite the relevant amendments of the definition of the crime of aggression and the conditions for the Court's jurisdiction in this respect on 11 June 2010 (RC/Res.6), it is still uncertain whether the Court will in fact exercise jurisdiction over this crime (see: P. Grzebyk, 'Definicja zbrodni agresji [po konferencji przeglądowej MTK]' ('Definition of the Crime of Aggression [after the ICC review conference]'), *Państwo i Prawo* 2011, no. 1[779], p. 45 ff).

29 The scholars who claim this include Roman A. Tokarczyk; see: B. Banaszak et al. (eds.), *Główne kultury prawne...*, p. 200.

30 P.M. Wald, 'Reflections on judging: At home and abroad', *University of Pennsylvania Journal of Constitutional Law*, vol. 7, 2004, pp. 219 and 235.

31 Such attempts were made by Cambodia while devising an agreement concerning the establishment of Extraordinary Chambers in the Courts of Cambodia; see: P. Grzebyk, 'Kambodżańska droga ku sprawiedliwości' ('Cambodia's Road towards Justice'), in J. Nakonieczna, J. Zajączkowski (eds.), *Azja Wschodnia i Azja Południowa w stosunkach międzynarodowych. Bezpieczeństwo – Gospodarka – Cywilizacja* (*East Asia and South Asia in International Relations. Security-Economy-Civilisation*), Warszawa 2011, p. 212.

of a universal legal culture, there is more proof of the existence of a multitude of cultures, which are sometimes subject to convergence.[32]

But it is not only the definitions of crimes that can be controversial. The fundamental principles of criminal responsibility can be questioned as well. For example, every country has different rules and age of criminal responsibility. International courts such as The International Criminal Court, The International Criminal Tribunal for the former Yugoslavia (ICTY) or The International Criminal Tribunal for Rwanda (ICTR), prosecute only those people who have committed crimes at the age of at least 18.[33] However, a problem arose when there was a need to establish an international court to prosecute the crimes committed in Sierra Leone as the age of criminal responsibility in that country was ten,[34] and the authorities feared that if people below 18 were excluded from prosecution, local communities might start meting out justice on their own.[35] If one of the functions of assigning criminal responsibility is payback for the committed evil, how does one explain to the local people that a given person will not be held responsible because the international community considers that person a child,

---

32 For more see: O. Nawrot, S. Sykuna, J. Zajadło, *Konwergencja…*, passim.

33 Article 26 of the Statute of the ICC clearly states: 'The Court shall have no jurisdiction over any person who was under the age of 18 at the time of the alleged commission of a crime'. The statutes of the ICTY (UN Security Council resolution 808 of 22 February 1993, as amended) and ICTR (UN Security Council resolution 955 of 8 November 1994, as amended), just as earlier the Charter of the IMT (United Nations, *Agreement for the prosecution and punishment of the major war criminals of the European Axis*, 8 August 1945, 82 UNTS vol. 280, p. 82 ff) or the IMTFE (General Order No. 20, General Headquarters Supreme Commander for the Allied Powers, 26 March 1946, U.S. Department of State Publications 2675, pp. 11–16), do not specify the age of persons subject to the courts' jurisdiction. However, the practice of these courts shows that the age of 18 is – as Joanna Nowakowska-Małusecka notes – the assumed threshold below which no person will have to answer for crimes before the courts (J. Nowakowska-Małusecka, *Sytuacja dziecka w konflikcie zbrojnym. Studium prawnomiędzynarodowe* (*Situation of Children in Armed Conflicts. An International Law Study*), Bydgoszcz–Katowice 2012, p. 322 ff).

34 For more on legislation in Sierra Leone concerning the age of criminal responsibility see: A. Skelton, Ch. Badenhorst, *The Criminal Capacity of Children in South Africa. International Developments & Considerations for a Review. A Research Report*, Cape Town 2011, p. 12.

35 J. Nowakowska-Małusecka, *Sytuacja dziecka…*, p. 326; A. McDonald, 'Sierra Leone's shoestring Special Court', *International Review of the Red Cross*, vol. 84, no. 845, 2002, p. 135.

while the same person is considered an adult by the local community?[36] Despite the above arguments, under an agreement between the United Nations and Sierra Leone, it has been established that the Special Court for Sierra Leone would have jurisdiction over people who were alleged to have committed crimes listed in the statute while being 15 or older.[37] This age limit was not accidental because in accordance with other provisions of the statute, the Court would also penalise recruiting children below the age of 15.[38] In the end, however, the Court did not prosecute persons below the age of 18 and, as a result, it effectively complied with the international standard.

Each state has different regulations regarding the responsibility for various forms of crime, the problem of guilt or the circumstances relieving a person of responsibility.[39] Consequently, it comes as no surprise that the statutes of international courts are sometimes grossly inconsistent and often contain repetitions.[40] For example, the list of circumstances relieving a defendant of criminal responsibility in ICC proceedings includes acting pursuant to an order of a superior,[41] even though the statutes of all the previous international courts excluded this as a circumstance relieving of criminal responsibility and considered it only a mitigating circumstance which could lower the sentence.[42] If we take a closer

---

36 It should be noted, however, that in accordance with the definition contained in Article 1 of the Convention on the Rights of the Child of 20 November 1989 (adopted by General Assembly resolution 44/25 of 20 November 1989, UNTS vol. 1577, p. 3 ff), 'a child means every human being below the age of eighteen years [...]'. Sierra Leone did not present any reservations to this article, even though other countries exercised this right.

37 Article 7 of the Statute of the SCSL of 16 January 2002, UN Security Council, available at: http://www.sc-sl.org/LinkClick.aspx?fileticket=uClnd1MJeEw%3D& (accessed on 20 November 2013); see also: B. Krzan, 'Trybunał Specjalny dla Sierra Leone' (Special Court for Sierra Leone), *Nowa Kodyfikacja Prawa Karnego*, vol. 20, 2006, p. 173; for more on additional process guarantees for children, see: J. Nowakowska-Małusecka, *Sytuacja dziecka...*, p. 325.

38 Article 4.

39 M. Królikowski, P. Wiliński, J. Izydorczyk, *Podstawy prawa karnego międzynarodowego* (*Basics of International Criminal Law*), Warszawa 2008, p. 183 ff.

40 See: M. Scallotti, 'Defences before the International Criminal Court: Substantive grounds for excluding criminal responsibility', part 2, *International Criminal Law Review*, vol. 2, 2002, pp. 36 and 45; K. Ambos, 'General principles of criminal law in the Rome Statute', *Criminal Law Forum*, vol. 10, 1999, p. 21.

41 Article 33, Statute of the ICC.

42 See e.g.: Article 8, Charter of the International Military Tribunal; Article 7(4), Statute of the ICT Y; Article 6(4), Statute of the ICTR.

look at the construction of the superior order adopted in the ICC statute, we can see that it actually describes a special case of a mistake of fact or mistake of law.[43] The construction of the mistake of fact or mistake of law requires, according to the said statute, that lack of awareness of certain circumstances or law must be proven,[44] and this fact, in turn, excludes responsibility on the basis of lack of intent.[45] Consequently, in the opinion of many legal theoreticians, the construction of mistake in the ICC statute constitutes an obvious *superfluum*.[46] Another proof of an unsuccessful attempt to combine different visions of law is the approach to the issue of voluntary intoxication in the ICC statute.[47] The Arab states were stressing that it should be considered an aggravating circumstance, while common law states consider such a situation a mitigating circumstance.[48] In the end, voluntary intoxication has been included in the ICC statute but with some serious restrictions.

Another controversial issue in international criminal law is the system of punishments, especially the regulations concerning the death penalty. For instance, the fact that the International Criminal Tribunal for Rwanda was unable to declare a death penalty was one of the reasons why Rwanda voted against the UN Security Council's resolution establishing this court because Rwanda's law at that time included the death penalty. On the other hand, when the statute of the Iraqi Special Tribunal allowed the death penalty in accordance with Iraqi law, a large part of the international community considered this to be an infringement on international standards, which precluded any cooperation or participation of the international community in the proceedings before this court.[49] Leaving

---

43 See: A. Van Verseveld, *Mistake of Law: Excusing Perpetrators of International Crimes*, The Hague 2012, p. 91; Y. Dinsten, *The Defence of 'Obedience to Superior Orders' in International Law*, Oxford 2012, p. xx ff, p. 49 ff.

44 Article 32, Statute of the ICC.

45 Article 30, Statute of the ICC.

46 A. Eser, 'Individual criminal responsibility. Mental elements – mistake of fact and mistake of law', in A. Cassese (ed.), *The Rome Statute of the International Criminal Court: A Commentary*, Oxford 2002, p. 934; see also: M. Płachta, *Międzynarodowy Trybunał Karny (International Criminal Court)*, vol. 1, Zakamycze 2004, p. 599.

47 Article 31 (1) (b), Statute of the ICC.

48 M. Scallotti, *Defences…*, p. 36.

49 Kofi Annan (former UN Secretary-General) stressed in the context of possible cooperation between the UN and the IST that the UN would not support courts which have the possibility of passing a death sentence (*New York Times*, 14 November 2004; see also: P. M. Wald, 'Iraq, Cambodia, and international justice', *American University International Law Review*, vol. 21, 2006, p. 545).

the controversial issue of the acceptability of death penalty aside, we cannot fail to notice that there are huge differences between the systems of punishment in different countries – even in those that share the same legal tradition – and each of them can influence the way a punishment is executed. As far as international courts such as the ICC, ICTY or ICTR are concerned, even if they sentence a defendant to a punishment declared in their statutes and the relevant regulations,[50] the punishment must still be adjusted to the legal system of the country in which the sentenced person will be serving their sentence, and the person will be able to use all the opportunities given by this system, including a request for pardon or early release.[51]

Procedures before the organs prosecuting international crimes

An analysis of the work on the establishment of relevant judicial institutions and the adoption of the procedures to be applied before them (especially in the case of internationalised courts) shows that there is no universal model for prosecuting international crimes and every country is attached to their own solutions

---

50 Pursuant to Article 77 of the Statute of the ICC, the Court may impose one of the following penalties: a) imprisonment for a specified number of years, which may not exceed a maximum of 30 years; or b) a term of life imprisonment. In addition to imprisonment, the Court may order: a) a fine; b) a forfeiture of proceeds, property and assets derived directly or indirectly from that crime, without prejudice to the rights of bona fide third parties. However, the fact that this list does not include capital punishment does not imply that there is either general consensus or an *opinio juris* to abolish capital punishment (see: E. Myjer, 'Uniform justice and the death penalty', in J. Doria, H.-P. Gasser, M.Ch. Bassiouni (eds.), *The Legal Regime of the International Criminal Court. Essays in Honour of Professor Igor Blishchenko*, Leiden 2009, p. 928).

51 See: Article 3 of the Agreement between the Government of the Republic of Poland and the United Nations on the Enforcement of Sentences of the International Criminal Tribunal for the Former Yugoslavia of 18 September 2008, available at: http://www.icty.org/x/file/Legal%20Library/Member_States_Cooperation/enforcement_agreement_poland_18_09_08_en.pdf (accessed on 20 November 2013). There are, however, considerable restrictions under which, if the sentence served in Poland is shorter than the one passed by the Tribunal, the Minister of Justice shall notify the Registrar of the ICTY of the fact and the Tribunal may move the person serving the sentence to a different country where further serving of the sentence is possible. The Tribunal must also be notified in the event where the person serving the sentence is eligible for early release or pardon, whereupon the President and the judges decide whether in the given situation the person may indeed use the said rights.

and attempts to implant them in the principles of an institution when it is established. This trend can be seen everywhere from the discussion on the Charter of the International Military Tribunal to the debate on the specific provisions of the International Criminal Court or the internationalised courts. Sometimes, countries introduce entirely original modes of prosecution, as it has been the case with Rwanda and the *gacaca* system.[52] The main battle, however, is usually fought over the dilemma whether the procedure should be adversarial (as in the common law system), where judges are only observers of the proceedings and all evidence is presented by the prosecution and defence, or rather inquisitorial (which is characteristic of the continental system, especially of France), where judges play an active role in the proceedings, can ask additional questions and request the presentation of additional evidence.[53]

As for internationalised courts, they have usually applied the mode of procedure most familiar to the country in which they functioned. Therefore, the procedure before the Special Court for Sierra Leone is essentially adversarial, while the procedure in the Extraordinary Chambers in the Courts of Cambodia resembles the inquisitorial system, including the adaptation of the function of investigating magistrates, whose role is primarily to gather evidence in a case before the commencement of the court proceedings. Of course, it is of no small significance that Sierra Leone used to be a British colony and Cambodia used to be a French colony. In the case of the Iraqi Special Tribunal, which was theoretically established as a national body but actually was heavily influenced by the United States in terms of the rules of functioning, it was necessary to make an attempt to combine the basic principles of the inquisitorial system, adopted by Iraq through Egypt (which in facthad drawn on the French model[54]), and of the adversarial system used by the US and consequently, was much more familiar and comprehensible to Americans.[55] As a result, the competences of

52 P. Ch. Bornkamm, *Rwandas Gacaca Courts. Between Retribution and Reparation*, Oxford 2012; see also: K. Bieniek, D. Heidrich, 'Pojednanie w Rwandzie – zwycięstwo sprawiedliwości czy sprawiedliwość zwycięzców' (Reconciliation in Rwanda – A Victory of Justice or the Victors' Justice?), *Stosunki Międzynarodowe*, 2007, no. 3–4, p. 199 ff.

53 C. Kress, 'The Procedural Law of the International Criminal Court in Outline: Anatomy of a Unique Compromise', *Journal of International Criminal Justice,* vol. 1, 2003, pp. 604–605; M. Joutsen, *Legal traditions…*, p. 68 ff.

54 R. Swift, 'Occupational jurisdiction: A critical analysis of the Iraqi special tribunal', *New York International Review* vol. 19, 2006, p. 123.

55 In this context, it is worth noting that even among the representatives of the common law doctrine, there are opinions that while common law is typical of democratic

investigative judges and prosecutors effectively overlapped, thus lengthening the entire procedure.[56]

During the trials before the International Military Tribunal, the United States were complaining that the procedures were incomprehensible for them and they stated that one of the reasons for their lack of involvement in the organisation of further trials before the next international military courts was the desire to conduct proceedings in accordance with the adversarial system, typical of common law countries.[57] However, imposing models unfamiliar to the society concerned must result in ineffective participation in the proceedings and in disturbances in the communication between those who testify or provide explanations and the court officials.[58] For instance, ad hoc courts initially applied procedures typical of common law, including the practice of subjecting witnesses to cross-examination.[59] The problem, however was that such procedures were often considered degrading or humiliating, especially by the witnesses, which naturally affected their will to cooperate and the manner in which they delivered their testimonies.[60] In time, however, the procedures evolved towards the inquisitorial mode, which was surely a consequence of the participation of lawyers from the continental system in the proceedings and the need for a greater involvement of the judges in order to establish the truth and balancingout the chances of the defence, which

countries, civil law is typical of authoritarian systems (see: R. C. Caenegem, *Judges, Legislators and Professors: Chapters in European Legal History*, Cambridge 1987, p. 73; see also: L. Rosen, *Law as Culture...*, p. 140).

56 S. Zappalà, 'The Iraqi Special tribunal's draft rules of procedure and evidence', *Journal of International Criminal Justice*, vol. 2, 2004, pp. 862–863.

57 *Final Report to the Secretary of the Army on the Nuernberg War Crimes Trials Under Control Council Law No. 10 by Telford Taylor, Brigadier General, U.S.A. Chief of Counsel for War Crimes*, Washington DC, 15 August 1949, pp. 26, 27, 282.

58 J. Almqvist, 'The impact of cultural diversity on international criminal proceedings', *Journal of International Criminal Justice*, vol. 4, 2006, p. 747; P. M. Wald, 'The International Criminal Tribunal for the Former Yugoslavia comes of age: Some observations on day-to-day dilemma of an international court', *Washington University Journal of Law & Policy*, vol. 5, 2001, p. 117. Tim Kelsall claims that it was the fact of imposing a culturally foreign model of international crime prosecution that was the reason for the lack of reaction to the sentence of the International Military Tribunal for the Far East (T. Kelsall, *Culture under Cross-Examination. International Justice and the Special Court for Sierra Leone*, Cambridge 2009, s. 11).

59 P. Robinson, 'So you want to be an international criminal lawyer? Getting and defending a case at the International Criminal Tribunal for Rwanda', *New England Journal of International & Comparative Law*, vol. 14, 2007–2008, p. 288.

60 J. Almqvist, *The impact...*, p. 750.

did not have such capabilities as the prosecution.[61] For example, it was a shock to lawyers coming from common law countries that witnesses testifying under oath could lie,[62] while it does not surprise lawyers from the continental system.

Regarding the Statute of the ICC, Claus Kress stresses that the mode of procedure before the ICC is not hybrid but rather unique.[63] It seems, however, that it would be more adequate to describe it simply as a *patchwork*, as essentially we are dealing with a *sui generis* procedure which combines elements of both common law and civil law.[64] The ICC procedure is thus an excellent material to show how the legal culture of the various states has influenced the adoption of specific solutions. While terms specific to only some cultures (e.g. investigative judges) have been avoided, countries have attempted to smuggle in solutions familiar to them under different names. The very structure of the Pre-Trial Chamber alludes to the institution of the investigative judges (*juge d'instruction*), and the confirmation of charges to the French *chambre d'accusation*.[65] Although the possibility of conducting proceedings *in absentia*,[66] present in French law, has been rejected (it should be noted, however, that Martin Bormann was, in fact, tried in absentia by the IMT), the possibility of confirming the prosecution's charges before the trial and in the absence of the defendant, i.e. *in absentia*, has been admitted.[67] As far as the submission of evidence is concerned, in accordance with the ICC statute: 'The parties may submit evidence relevant to the case [...]. The Court shall have the authority to request the submission of all evidence that it considers necessary for the determination of the truth'.[68] This means that depending on the attitude of the judges, the trial could more closely follow the adversarial mode or the inquisitorial mode, and this would undoubtedly be influenced by the procedure to which the judges are more accustomed. We should also remember that cultural differences can result in some judges requesting evidence which would be considered

---

61 R. Heinsch, 'How to achieve fair and expeditious trial proceedings before the ICC: Is it time for a more judge dominated approach?', in C. Stahn, G. Sluiter (ed.), *The Emerging Practice of the International Criminal Court*, Leiden 2009, p. 488.

62 P. Robinson, *So you want...*, p. 286.

63 C. Kress, *The procedural law...*, p. 605; see also: G. Kirk McDonald, 'Trial procedures and practice', in G. Kirk McDonald, O. Swaak-Goldman (ed.), *Substantive and Procedural Aspects of International Criminal Law: The Experience of International and National Courts. Commentary*, vol. 1, The Hague 2000, p. 556.

64 R. Heinsch, *How to achieve...*, p. 487.

65 C. Kress, *The procedural law...*, p. 608.

66 M. Płachta, *Międzynarodowy...*, pp. 135–136.

67 Article 61(2), Statute of the ICC; see also: C. Kress, *The procedural law...*, pp. 610–611.

68 Article 69(3), Statute of the ICC.

completely irrelevant by others.[69] A good example of these cultural differences is the entirely different approach to the assessment of witness' credibility or even the defendants' guilt presented by the judges from the countries of Islamic law and those from continental and common law countries. What is of key importance for the former is the background of the given person, its social relations and family background, while the latter do not believe that background itself is sufficient to determine a person's credibility.[70]

Procedural difficulties

In the common law culture, there is a notion of cultural defence, whereas the continental law culture recognises cultural offences. Cultural defence occurs where the body applying the law takes into account certain cultural norms present in the given social group which differ considerably from the standards accepted in the society as a whole, consequently, treating them as mitigating circumstances or even as grounds for excluding criminal responsibility.[71] The problem of cultural defence returns also in the proceedings concerning international crime as a type of mistake of fact or law, or simply a certain circumstance relieving of responsibility. It is a dubious issue why a citizen of Sierra Leone is to be punished for 'conscripting or enlisting children under the age of 15 years into armed forces or groups or using them to participate actively in hostilities,'[72] if according to the rules of his

69 This is related to the existence of many modes of thought; see: W. Fikentscher, *Modes of Thought. A Study in the Anthropology of Law and Religion*, Tübingen 1995, p. 3 ff.

70 Lawrence Rosen cites the following statement made by a Saudi high court judge: 'I can always tell if a man is lying once I know his background and relationships' (L. Rosen, *Law as Culture...*, p. 138).

71 J. Van Broeck, 'Cultural Defence and Culturally Motivated Crimes (Cultural Offences)', *European Journal of Crime, Criminal Law and Criminal Justice*, vol. 9, 2001, p. 1 ff; A.D. Runteln, *The Cultural Defense*, Oxford 2004, passim; S. Sykuna, J. Zajadło, 'Kontrowersje wokół tzw. obrony przez kulturę – okoliczność wyłączająca winę, okoliczność łagodząca czy nadużycie prawa do obrony?' (Controversy Surrounding Cultural Defence – Circumstances Relieving the Defendant of Responsibility or an Abuse of the Defence Rights?), *Przegląd Sądowy*, June 2007, p. 27; see also: E. Snajdr, *Culture and Crime*, in M. Natarajan, *International...*, p. 57 ff; A. Kleczkowska, 'Rola "cultural defence" w wymiarze sprawiedliwości karnej' (The Role of "Cultural Defence" in Criminal Justice), *Ruch Prawniczy, Ekonomiczny i Społeczny*, no. 2, 2012, p. 72; Ch. M. Wong, 'Good Intentions, Troublesome Applications: The cultural Defence and Other Uses of Cultural Evidence in Canada', *Criminal Law Quarterly*, vol. 42, 1999, p. 367 ff.

72 Article 4 point (c), Statute of the SCSL, available at: http://www.sc-sl.org/LinkClick.aspx?fileticket=uClnd1MJeEw%3D& (accessed on 20 November 2013).

community a teenager can be considered an adult pursuant to other determinants of maturity than age.[73] Another example is treating rape on a woman as a crime only if the victim was a virgin (in some countries, as for example Sierra Leone).[74] Tim Kelsall argues that we cannot disregard the fact that a person did not consider what they were doing evil.[75]

Cultural defence is, however, controversial because it essentially implies the recognition and acknowledgement of cultural relativism, to which weaker people, such as women and children, usually fall victim.[76] This situation provokes the question whether the main aim of the proceedings should be to protect the culprit or the victim. Richard Goldstone stressed that calling upon cultural relativism represents a dangerous trend, which should have no place, particularly in proceedings concerning international crimes.[77] Essentially, we should agree with that statement. Calling on cultural issues to justify crimes such as genocide, crimes against humanity or war crimes should not influence the need to assign and bear responsibility. However, in order to properly assess the facts and apportion guilt, it is necessary to include certain cultural circumstances and to show some cultural sensitivity.[78] Was a judge to disregard the cultural context, this could lead to utter alienation of the proceedings, not only to the defendant but also to the victims and the entire society interested in the prosecution of the crime, as the trial would be

---

73 P. Knowles, 'The Power to Prosecute: The Special Court for Sierra Leone from a Defence Perspective', *International Criminal Law Review*, vol. 6, 2006, p. 409.

74 C. Damgaard, 'The Special Court for Sierra Leone: Challenging the Tradition of Impunity for Gender-Based Crimes?', *Nordic Journal of International Law*, vol. 73, 2004, pp. 502–503.

75 T. Kelsall, *Culture...*, p. 158.

76 See: A. Kleczkowska, 'Rola "cultural defence"'..., p. 82.

77 R. Goldstone, 'Symposium: Prosecuting International Crimes: An Inside View', *Transnational Law and Contemporary Problems*, vol. 7, 1997, p. 11.

78 See: Rule 18 (d) of the ICC Rules of Procedure and Evidence (*Official Records of the Assembly of States Parties to the Rome Statute of the International Criminal Court, First session, New York, 3–10 September 2002,* ICC-ASP/1/3 and Corr.1, part. II-A; see also: J. Almqvist, *The Impact...*, p. 756. Regarding the problems of cultural deference, Agata Kleczkowska mentioned evidence-related issues such as using an unusual alphabet, spelling, imprecise specification of dates due to the use of a different calendar, the use of different terminology for describing kinship, culturally specific classification of disease (see: A. Kleczkowska, 'Rola "cultural defence"..., p. 73). It seems, however, that we should differentiate between the problem of defence based on culture as a mitigating circumstance or a circumstance relieving of responsibility from full cultural awareness, which is necessary for proper evaluation of the actual state of affairs.

incomprehensible for them and would seem unfair, and moreover the sentence would be inadequate to the guilt and consequently, considered too harsh or too lenient. This, in turn, would prevent the trial from fulfilling the principal objectives of international crime prosecution, such as for instance, the preventive effect, which is so often questioned.[79]

Problems concerning the proper assessment of the witnesses' testimony resulting from cultural differences arose in the proceedings of the International Criminal Tribunal for Rwanda, which pointed out in its judicature that citizens of Rwanda would often fail to see the difference between describing events which they witnessed and reporting what they heard from somebody else.[80] The defence was stressing that in the local culture, there was a tradition according to which 'the perceived knowledge of one becomes the knowledge of all'.[81] Of course, skilled questioning helps separate the facts witnessed by the person questioned from the ones that the person only heard about,[82] but testimony based on second-hand knowledge must not necessarily be discarded outright – it should be evaluated in the context of its credibility and adequacy.[83]

The evaluation of witnesses' credibility requires that the cultural factor is taken into account, if only because in the Western culture a person who avoids eye contact and gives evasive replies will be considered untrustworthy,[84] while in Rwandan culture giving indirect answers to questions concerning sensitive issues is only natural,[85] and it is considered unacceptable to point the finger at anyone.[86] The victims would often admit to having been raped only during second or third

---

79 I. Tallgren, 'The Sensibility and Sense of International Criminal Law', *European Journal of International Law*, vol. 13, 2002, p. 583.

80 ICTR, judgement (Trial Chamber), *The Prosecutor v. Jean Paul Akayesu*, 2 September 1998 (ICTR-96-4-T), para. 155.

81 ICTR, judgement (Trial Chamber), *The Prosecutor v. Alfred Musema*, 27 January 2000 (ICTR-96-13-A), para. 103.

82 This is why the ICTY introduced the following formula to the witnesses' testimonies: 'I understand that I am requested to describe things I know because I observed them and I will clearly indicate in my statement facts I learned from others' (cited after: N. A. Combs, *Fact-Finding Without Facts. The Uncertain Evidentiary Foundations of International Criminal Convictions*, Cambridge 2010, p. 97).

83 ICTR, judgement (Trial Chamber), *The Prosecutor v. Alfred Musema...*, para. 103.

84 N.A. Combs, *Fact-Finding...*, p. 79.

85 *Ibid.*; see also: ICTR, judgement (Trial Chamber), *The Prosecutor v. Alfred Musema...*, para. 103; ICTR, judgement (Trial Chamber), *The Prosecutor v. Jean Paul Akayesu...*, para. 156.

86 N.A. Combs, *Fact-Finding...*, p. 92.

questioning.[87] It is therefore necessary to try to decode,[88] that is, take into consideration certain social and cultural circumstances.[89]

The ICTR also noted that while evaluating the testimonies of witnesses, it should be taken into account that they can struggle with specifying time and space properly and that they are not accustomed to using maps, films, photographs, etc., which, however, should not entirely discredit them.[90] One cannot expect that every person will correctly identify a location shown on an aerial photograph shown by the prosecutor if the person is seeing this type of material for the first time.[91]

Determining the significance of certain behaviours also requires a certain amount of knowledge about the given culture. An exchange of cows that seems a simple transaction can in fact be a sign of intimacy or even love.[92] In one culture lying is a natural thing (Sierra Leone),[93] while in another eavesdropping on somebody's conversation is unacceptable (Rwanda).[94] During the proceedings concerning the Duch case, the Extraordinary Chambers in the Courts of Cambodia emphasised that for a Cambodian it was particularly humiliating and causing a great mental distress to be forced to pay homage to images of a dog with the head of Ho Chi Minh or Lyndon B. Johnson.[95] The judges of the Special Court for Sierra Leone, in turn, had to take into consideration that raping a nursing mother, a woman after menopause, a virgin, and an incestuous rape constitute a violation of the taboo in Sierra Leone and should be considered an aggravating

87 *Ibid.*, pp. 86–87.

88 ICTR, judgement (Trial Chamber), *The Prosecutor v. Jean Paul Akayesu...*, para. 156.

89 ICTR, judgement (Trial Chamber), *The Prosecutor v. André Rwamakuba*, 20 September 2006 (ICTR-98-44C-T), para. 40.

90 ICTR, judgement (Trial Chamber), *The Prosecutor v. Alfred Musema...*, para. 104; ICTR, judgement (Trial Chamber), *The Prosecutor v. Jean Paul Akayesu...*, para. 156. Combs cites the example of a witness who testified that she had been raped for 4 hours. When the judge expressed doubts about the length of the rape, the witness responded that she did not know whether it was four hours or a year but it had hurt very much (N. A. Combs, *Fact-Finding...*, p. 82).

91 ICTR, judgement (Trial Chamber), *The Prosecutor v. Alfred Musema...*, para. 104.

92 ICTR, judgement (Trial Chamber), *The Prosecutor v. Vincent Rutaganira*, 14 March 2005 (ICTR-95-1C-T), para. 123.

93 T. Kelsall, *Culture...*, s. 232.

94 ICTR, judgement (Trial Chamber), *The Prosecutor v. Léonidas Nshogoza*, 7 VII 2009 (ICTR-07-91-T), para. 91.

95 ECCC, judgement, *Case 001*, 26 July 2010, para. 243.

circumstance.[96] Various cultures can define kinship differently,[97] which in turn can be of key importance for the assessment whether a given person is impartial or directly aggrieved.[98]

Another problem which always appears in relation to international and internationalised courts is the quality of translation. The ICTR encountered considerable difficulties with the interpretation from Kinyarwanda into French and English as there were no direct equivalents for many words (including 'rape') used by the witnesses.[99]

In the end, it is worth noting that a restrictive application of the principle of *in dubio pro reo* in connection with cultural problems in the submission of evidence can serve only the culprits, because it is hard to obtain convincing testimony confirming the guilt of a defendant originating from a society that maintains a culture of secrecy or even a prohibition of speaking about the dead (Sierra Leone, East Timor),[100] if it is impossible to conduct an exhumation of the victims' bodies since the local Sharia law forbids this. Therefore, it is advisable for the judges, being aware of all these cultural restrictions, to be open to evidence different from the ones they are used to. Otherwise, culture will protect primarily the culprits.

Concluding remarks

Legal systems leave a visible mark on the international criminal law and the procedure of prosecuting international crimes. The involvement of various states convinced that certain values should be protected or just the opposite, that certain values do not merit protection, influences the extent of criminalisation of various actions and the responsibility for them. Although there is convergence between some legal systems, we are still often dealing with patchworks. Some consider this the charm of international criminal law, other believe it to be a sign of its weakness and incoherence.

Rarely do we deal with an ideal situation, where the local society is involved in prosecution of crimes committed by their members in accordance with the

96 C. Damgaard, *The special court...*, pp. 486–487.

97 ECCC, judgement, *Case 001...*, para. 643; ECCC, judgement (appeal), *Case 001*, 3 February 2012, paras. 449, 560.

98 N.A. Combs, *Fact-Finding...*, p. 86; E. Snajdr, *Culture...*, p. 59.

99 ICTR, judgement (Trial Chamber), *The Prosecutor v. Jean Paul Akayesu...*, paras. 145 ff; see also: N. A. Combs, *Fact-Finding...*, p. 76 ff; and: M. A. Drumbl, *Atrocity, Punishment and International Law*, Cambridge 2007, p. 189.

100 T. Kelsall, *Culture...*, p. 172.

universal standards of international crimes and with a full adoption of generally recognised international regulations. Either the local society is not objective or simply the legal order is at such a low level that there is a need for the involvement of the international community. In this case, however, it is necessary for the procedure to be understandable, first of all to the people directly involved – the victims, the culprits, the witnesses – and it should not be selected on the basis of the judges' preferences. What is more, the judges need to be culturally sensitive in order to properly assess the severity of the deeds and the guilt of the culprits, in order to establish contact with the witnesses and properly read their testimonies. However, the judges should not use culture to justify their surrender in the struggle for uncovering the truth and to defend the culprits' actions.

To sum up, although the aim of this article was to prove that the legal cultures of states influence the development of international criminal law, we need to remember that we are in fact dealing with a positive feedback between the two, that is, that the legal solutions adopted in the international arena directly affect the legal systems of individual countries. Because countries adjust their national laws to comply with the international regulations which they are a part of or which could directly affect their citizens.

The original version of this text was published in the academic journal "Społeczeństwo i Polityka", no. 4, of 2012.

Index of Names

T

www.ingramcontent.com/pod-product-compliance
Ingram Content Group UK Ltd.
Pitfield, Milton Keynes, MK11 3LW, UK
UKHW041825100926
8556IPUK00002B/20

9 783631 679029